Endorsement Statement from Pearson

In order to ensure that this resource offers high-quality support for the associated Pearson qualification, it has been through a review process by the awarding body. This process confirms that this resource fully covers the teaching and learning content of the specification or part of a specification at which it is aimed. It also confirms that it demonstrates an appropriate balance between the development of subject skills, knowledge and understanding, in addition to preparation for assessment.

Endorsement does not cover any guidance on assessment activities or processes (e.g. practice questions or advice on how to answer assessment questions), included in the resource nor does it prescribe any particular approach to the teaching or delivery of a related course.

While the publishers have made every attempt to ensure that advice on the qualification and its assessment is accurate, the official specification and associated assessment guidance materials are the only authoritative source of information and should always be referred to for definitive guidance.

Pearson examiners have not contributed to any sections in this resource relevant to examination papers for which they have responsibility.

Examiners will not use endorsed resources as a source of material for any assessment set by Pearson.

Endorsement of a resource does not mean that the resource is required to achieve this Pearson qualification, nor does it mean that it is the only suitable material available to support the qualification, and any resource lists produced by the awarding body shall include this and other appropriate resources.

ESSENTIALS OF US POLITICS AND GOVERNMENT

PEARSON EDEXCEL A-LEVEL

Andrew Colclough

BLOOMSBURY ACADEMIC
LONDON • NEW YORK • OXFORD • NEW DELHI • SYDNEY

BLOOMSBURY ACADEMIC
Bloomsbury Publishing Plc
50 Bedford Square, London, WC1B 3DP, UK
1385 Broadway, New York, NY 10018, USA
29 Earlsfort Terrace, Dublin 2, Ireland

BLOOMSBURY, BLOOMSBURY ACADEMIC and the Diana logo
are trademarks of Bloomsbury Publishing Plc

First published in Great Britain 2024

Cover design: Eleanor Rose
Cover image: Sky © Alamy; Washington skyline © Getty Images

A catalogue record for this book is available from the British Library.

ISBN: HB: 978-1-3503-3772-5
PB: 978-1-3503-3771-8
ePDF: 978-1-3503-3769-5
eBook: 978-1-3503-3770-1

Typeset by Integra Software Services Pvt. Ltd.
Printed and bound in Great Britain by Bell and Bain Ltd, Glasgow

To find out more about our authors and books
visit www.bloomsbury.com and sign up for our newsletters.

Brief Contents

Contents

Specification Table

Component III: United States and Comparative Politics	
4. US Supreme Court and civil rights	
4.1 The nature and role of the Supreme Court	Chapter 5 pages 122–124
4.2 The appointment process	Chapter 5 pages 124–130
4.3 The Supreme Court and public policy	Chapter 5 pages 132–138
4.4 The protection of civil liberties	Chapter 5 pages 138–143
4.5 Race and rights	Chapter 5 pages 149–156
4.6 Interpretations and debates	
Political versus judicial	Chapter 5 pages 143–145
Living constitution and originalism	Chapter 5 pages 145–148
Civil and constitutional rights	Chapter 5 pages 138–143
Extent of powers and effectiveness of checks and balances	Chapter 5 pages 129–132
The success and failures of measure to promote racial equality	Chapter 5 pages 149–156
Immigration reform	Chapter 4 page 106 Case Study 4.1 Chapter 5 pages 156–157
5. Democracy and participation	
5.1 Electoral Systems	Chapter 6 pages 162–185
5.1.1 Presidential elections	Chapter 6 pages 162–185
5.1.2 Campaign finance	Chapter 6 pages 186–189
5.2 The key ideas and principles of the Democratic and Republican parties	Chapter 7 pages 134–210
5.3 Interest groups in the USA	Chapter 7 pages 211–218
5.4 Interpretations and debates	
Advantages and disadvantages of the Electoral College	Chapter 6 pages 175–180
The role of campaign finance	Chapter 6 pages 186–189
The role of incumbency	Chapter 6 pages 183–185
Interest groups influence on government	Chapter 7 pages 219–222
Interest groups and democracy	Chapter 7 pages 214–217
Interest groups, PACS and SuperPACs	Chapter 7 pages 218–222
6. Comparative approaches	
6.1 Theoretical approaches	Chapter 8 page 226
6.2.1 Comparing constitutions	Chapter 8 pages 227–231
6.2.2 Rational, structural and cultural approaches	Chapter 8 page 232
6.2.3 Comparing legislative branches	Chapter 8 pages 233–237
6.2.4 Rational, structural and cultural approaches	Chapter 8 pages 237–238
6.2.5 Comparing executive branches	Chapter 8 pages 238–240
6.2.6 Rational, structural and cultural approaches	Chapter 8 page 241
6.2.7 Comparing Supreme Courts and civil rights	Chapter 8 pages 241–244
6.2.8 Rational, structural and cultural approaches	Chapter 8 pages 244–245
6.2.9 Comparing US and UK democracy	Chapter 8 pages 245–250
6.2.10 Rational, structural and cultural approaches	Chapter 8 pages 250–251

Illustrations

Figures

Photos

Maps

Tables

Key Topic Debates

Case Studies

About the Author

ANDREW COLCLOUGH is the Head of Politics and the Head of Humanities at d'Overbroeck's, Oxford as well as the Deputy Head (Academic) for the Sixth Form. With over thirty years' experience as an A-Level Politics teacher, Andrew has served as a long-standing examiner, acting as an A-Level Senior Examiner for a large examination board. He has a particular interest in US Politics, and is also a contributing author, writing the US chapters, of *Edexcel AS and A-Level Politics* (Pearson, 2017). He is a regular contributor to Hodder Education events, offering training for A-Level Politics teachers, as well as speaking at revision conferences to students around the country.

Tour of the Book

Chapter Previews
These offer a broad outline of what each chapter will cover. Each uses a UK reference point that you can use as a comparison to something that you are likely to have studied.

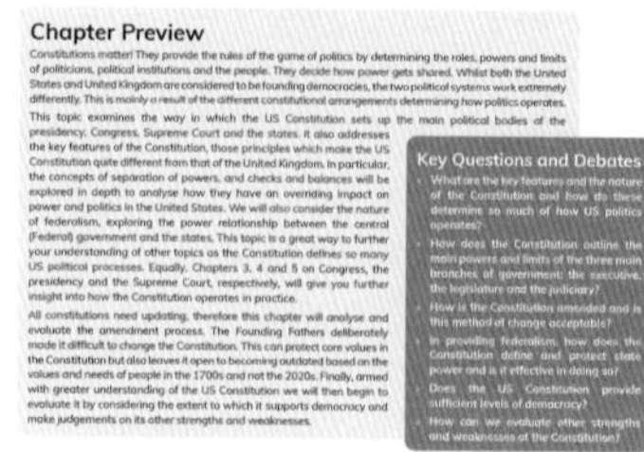

Key Questions and Debates
A list of the key questions and debates addressed by the chapter.

Specification Checklists
A useful checklist of the points from the Edexcel specification that will be covered by each chapter.

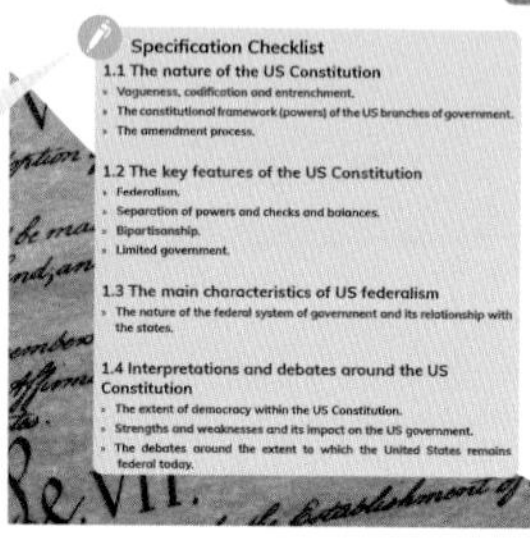

Definitions
A definition of political terms that are essential to a good understanding of US politics.

Exam Tips
Key advice on how to do well in specific aspects of your exam.

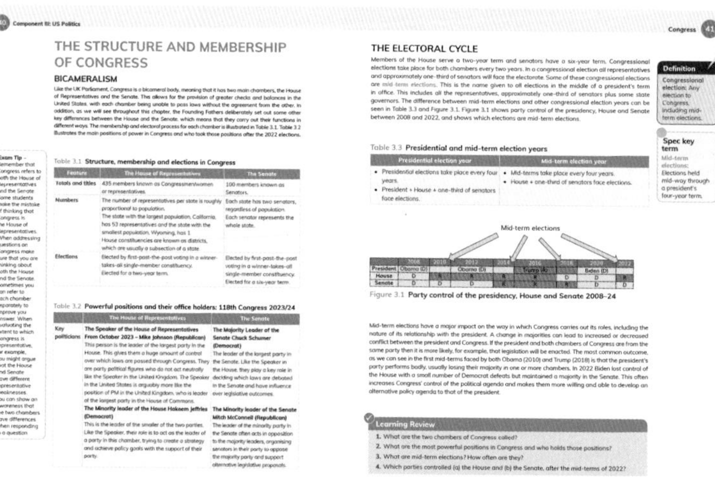

Spec Key Terms
A definition of the key terms named in the Pearson Edexcel specification. It is important to know what they are because they can be used in exam questions.

Case Studies
Relevant case studies to illustrate key issues in US politics and enhance your understanding of them.

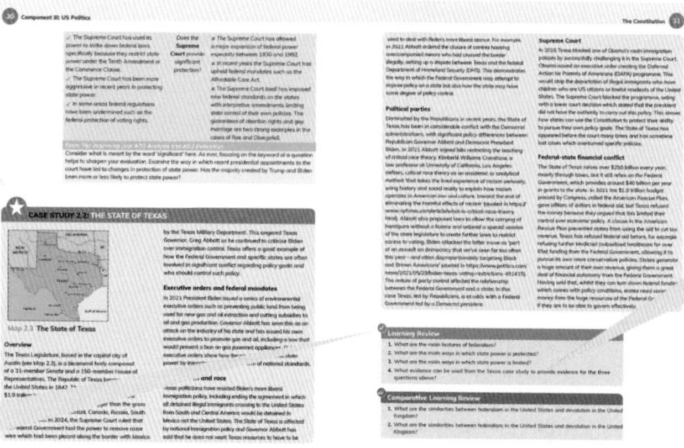

Comparative Knowledge Checks
These occur whenever a topic is relevant to the A-Level specification requirement to compare with the United Kingdom. There is a whole chapter (Chapter 8) on comparative politics, but these checkpoints will refresh your recall of UK politics and sharpen your analysis when making comparisons.

Knowledge Checks
These short quizzes appear at regular intervals and give you an opportunity to check your understanding and factual recall.

Exam Focus Chapter
A whole chapter devoted to exam skills, with detailed instructions on how to structure your essays and meet key A-Level requirements.

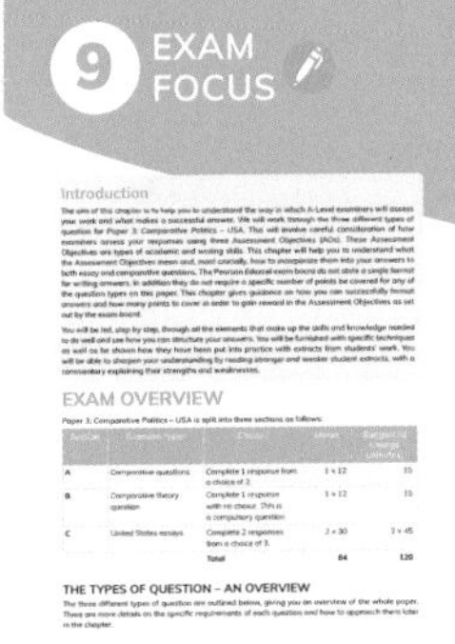

Key Topic Debates
A great deal of this book is organised around these key debates in US politics. Debates typically include three areas of focus, with for and against points given for each. This design will help you to structure your essays.

Key Debate Summaries
These summaries of each side of the debate can be used to gain a quick overview or to revise from.

Key Topic Debate Summary: Is the president significantly restricted in foreign policy?

FOR	KEY CRITERIA	AGAINST
✓ Congress can continue to place restraints in foreign policy using the power to declare war, budgetary power and the Senate ratification of treaties. ✓ A great deal of foreign policy does not require unilateral presidential action. There are no practical reasons why Congress cannot be involved in foreign policy decisions on climate change or trade agreements.	Does the nature of **modern foreign policy** allow Congress to restrict the president?	✗ Modern military policy is much faster and more deadly, which means that the president must be free to act without always consulting Congress. ✗ The increased complexity and secrecy requited means that the president, with access to superior sources of information such as the NSC, is better placed to make decisions.
✓ Congress has specific foreign policy powers such as the power to declare war and the power to accept or reject requests from the president to attack other countries as stated in the War Powers Act. ✓ The Senate has the power to reject presidential treaties and therefore thwart some of the president's key policy goals.	Does **the Constitution** give Congress sufficient power to restrict the president's foreign policy agenda?	✗ As commander in chief, the president can order military action and argue that he or she has the right to act unilaterally. ✗ Presidents have ignored the War Powers Act, rejecting the right of Congress to assert control over the initiation of military action. ✗ Finally, the president can use executive agreements to make deals with other countries and bypass the need for Senate ratification of treaties.
✓ Individual members of Congress can claim a mandate and will want to represent the views of their constituents on foreign policy issues. ✓ Ultimately Congress can claim a stronger mandate than the president after a mid-term election, especially where the president's party loses a majority.	Does Congress have **political advantages** that allow it to restrict the president in the area of foreign policy?	✗ As the nationally elected head of government, the president can avoid foreign policy restraint and use the authority of their national mandate to determine US-wide policy. ✗ Members of Congress only possess a local mandate and have less authority to speak on international issues.

Exam Tip: Improve your AO2 analysis and AO3 advanced evaluation
Don't make assumptions about words that seem to have an obvious meaning. The concept of 'foreign policy' is a great case in point. There is a major difference between a short-term military raid, a long-term invasion of a country, negotiating a budget deal with neighbouring countries or securing an environmental treaty. The president will have more or less control in each of these scenarios and you could bring this in to add to your analysis and evaluation.

Evaluative view: Do presidents dominate foreign policy?
On balance, the president is given greater constitutional power than Congress, which allows him or her to be the dominant force in foreign policy. Most importantly, in the modern era, the power of the president in this area has evolved as military policy has become fast moving and more deadly. This has led to a significant imbalance of power in which the president is able to dominate. Whilst Congress has attempted to limit the president, it has often failed to do so. Much of the evidence that is used to demonstrate congressional control ends with presidents prevailing in the end. Even though the Constitution aims to create many checks and balances in the area of foreign policy, contemporary evidence strongly supports the view that the president dominates foreign policy.

Consider the key topic debate and debate summary as well as any new evidence you can find. Do you agree or disagree with this evaluative view?

Exam Tips: Improve you AO2 analysis and AO3 Evaluation
Found at the end of every Key Topic Debate Summary, this feature gives tips on how to improve your analysis and evaluation for this particular debate.

Evaluative Views
These model the kind of language you will use when you evaluate the arguments in a debate. They demonstrate how to move beyond just learning the arguments, additionally allowing you to see how to make evaluative judgements about a debate. They could also be the starting point for a debate.

Chapter Summaries
Bullet lists summarising the key points covered by the chapter, reminding you of what you have read.

Chapter Summary

- ✓ The president is given several specific powers and roles by the Constitution including head of state, commander in chief and head of the executive branch.
- ✓ The president has a number of informal sources of power including their mandate as well as the resources provided to them by the cabinet and the Executive Office of the President.
- ✓ The separation of powers and checks and balances should mean that there are significant restrictions on the president in both domestic and foreign policy.
- ✓ The imperial presidency suggests that the president is extremely powerful and can overcome constitutional limitations.
- ✓ Checks and balances also operate between the president and Supreme Court.
- ✓ The power of the president can vary both within and between presidencies.

Exam Style Questions

- **Evaluate the view that the presidents' constitutional roles give them major political power. (30 marks)**
- **Evaluate the view that the cabinet and the Executive Office of the President play a significant role in influencing the policy and actions of the president. (30 marks)**
- **Evaluate the view that presidents are more powerful in foreign policy than domestic policy. (30 marks)**
- **Evaluate the view that the president can dominate the Supreme Court. (30 marks)**
- **Evaluate the view that mid-term elections are the most important factor that causes changes to presidential power. (30 marks)**

Exam Style Questions
These questions are in the same style as the ones you will respond to on your exams. You can use them to practise your question interpretation and planning skills, as well as to practise drafting full answers.

Further Resources
A list of books, articles, websites and films that will help you to explore further.

Further Resources

Greenberg, M. and Tait, D. (2020) *Obama: The Historic Presidency of Barack Obama – Updated Edition* (New York: Sterling).
Wolf, M. (2021) *The Final Days of The Trump Presidency* (New York: The Bridge Street Press).
Woodward, B. (2019) *Fear: Trump in the White House* (New York: Schuster).
The official White House website has an overview of all the EXOP offices and personnel as well as the latest news from the presidential office. Available at https://www.whitehouse.gov/ (accessed 23 July 2023).
A brilliant insight into decision-making and conflict within the Biden administration on the issue of immigration is Zolan Kanno-Youngs, Michael D. Shear and Eileen Sullivan, 'How Infighting over the Border Divided the Biden White House', *The New York Times*, 9 April 2022. Available at https://www.nytimes.com/2022/04/09/us/politics/biden-border-immigration.html (accessed 23 July 2023).

Visit https://bloomsbury.pub/colclough-essentials-us to access additional materials to support teaching and learning.

Digital Resources

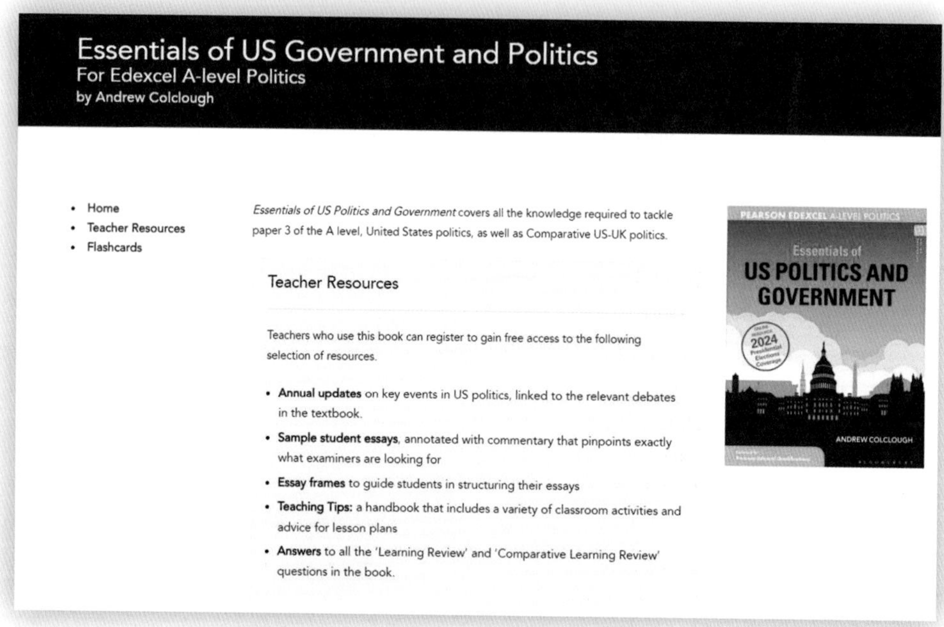

Teachers who use this book gain access to a password-protected selection of resources to support teaching and learning. Visit **https://bloomsbury.pub/colclough-essentials-us** to find:

- **Yearly updates** providing information and analysis on key developments in US Politics. These updates will be linked to the relevant key debates in the textbook so you know how they can be applied. In addition, they will give you up-to-date examples to use in your essays.
- **Interactive flashcards** so you can check your understanding of all the key terms found in your book.
- **Sample student essays** highlighting the common strengths and weaknesses found in student answers. These are annotated with author commentary that explains what examiners are looking for and how they apply assessment objectives. These samples will help you to write strong answers that meet the requirement of the examination board.
- **Essay frames** to guide you in planning and structuring your essays.
- **Teaching tips:** a handbook for teachers to help them get the most out of using this textbook. It includes a variety of classroom activities designed to enhance student knowledge, understanding and skill, helping teachers to develop effective lesson plans.
- **Answers to all the 'Learning Review' and 'Comparative Learning Review' questions** found in the book.

How to Use the Book

Welcome to *Essentials of US Politics and Government*, which has been designed to cover **every aspect of the 2017 Edexcel Pearson Specification for Paper 3A Politics of the USA.** In addition, there is huge array of advice and support on the skills you will develop to be successful in this A-Level.

A tour of the book on pages xviii-xix explains all of the key features of the book, which have been carefully designed to help you maximise your knowledge, understanding and skill. Please take the time to read this as it will help you to use this book as effectively as possible.

Each chapter is arranged around a series of 'Key Topic Debates'. These typically cover three arguments on each side of a debate, giving you both arguments and evidence to help you tackle A-Level questions and understand how to use content in an essay. The arguments in these 'Key Topic Debates' are then placed in a 'Key Topic Debate Summary'. This should make it easier for you to manage all the information and to revise the main arguments you will need to learn and apply in your exam.

As well as the 'Key Topic Debates', there is a whole chapter devoted to developing the key skills necessary to be successful in A-Level Politics. Chapter 9, 'Exam Focus', guides you through what the exam looks like and what examiners are looking for. You will be led, step by step, through all the elements that make up the skills and knowledge needed to do well. It includes detailed guidance on how you can structure your answer and shows you techniques to improve your writing. You will also read student extracts, with a commentary explaining their strengths and weaknesses. You may want to explore this chapter at an early stage of studying A-Level Politics so that you know what you are working towards.

Please remember that the study of A-Level Politics requires you to understand the US political system as it operates in a contemporary setting. As such, this book makes use of recent political examples and case studies. We will occasionally delve into the history of the United States but only where it helps us to make sense of the present. Knowing what is happening today is a major advantage to the successful study of A-Level Politics. Even though this book is packed with examples and case studies, you are strongly encouraged to maintain an awareness of the latest political developments via the media.

Finally, Table 0.1 gives you an outline of the chapters, covering the United Kingdom equivalent for the US topics. This should give you an overview of what you will study as well as an indication of how you can use your knowledge of UK politics as a departure point. Chapter 8 covers the comparative element of the specification and shows you exactly what needs to be compared between the United States and United Kingdom.

Table 0.1 **Chapters covering US topics and how they connect to UK topics**

CHAPTER	UNITED STATES	UNITED KINGDOM EQUIVALENT
2	The Constitution	The Constitution
3	Congress	Parliament
4	Presidency	Prime Minister (the executive branch)
5	Supreme Court	Supreme Court
6	Elections	Elections
7	Parties and Interest Groups	Parties and Pressure Groups
8	Comparative United States and United Kingdom	

I have thoroughly enjoyed the challenge of trying to put my experience (as an A-Level teacher of over thirty years, an A-Level Politics examiner and an A-Level Politics author) to good use in producing this book. I sincerely hope it will provide the ideal guide to US politics for your A-Level Politics studies and that you enjoy this wonderful opportunity to explore the political processes of such a fascinating and important country.

Acknowledgements

Author's Acknowledgements

I would like to thank the many people at Bloomsbury who have contributed to this book. This includes Milly Weaver as the commissioning editor and Emily Lovelock who helped me through the early and challenging stages of starting out with the process. Particular acknowledgement goes to Lauren Zimmerman whose positivity and patience helped make it all far more enjoyable. Her edits, suggestions and contributions played a major role in the shaping of this book for the better.

Several anonymous reviewers also helped to shape the book – thank you, whoever you are! Also, thank you to Kathy Schindler for helping me to get the textbook rolling with the publishers. I am thrilled that, as well giving permission to use their logo, the Native American Rights Fund took the time to make improvements to my text, in order to represent themselves more accurately. Finally, a massive thank you to my wonderful family, Caroline, Finn and Benji, who have done so much to help me write this book.

Publisher's Acknowledgements

The publisher and author also wish to thank the organisations listed below for permission to reproduce material from their publications.

- DISA Global Solutions, Inc. for Map 2.2: Marijuana regulations in US states
- The Native American Rights Fund for the use their logo in Figure 5.3: Three racial rights groups in the United States
- OpenSecrets for Figure 6.8: Campaign expenditure in presidential elections 1999-2016 and Table 7.2: Highest spending super PACS in 2020.

1 GETTING STARTED ON US POLITICS

Introduction

Welcome to the captivating world of US politics where you will be able to explore major contemporary issues in the context of the particular, and some would say peculiar, setting of the US political system. This book, and the A-Level, will allow you to gain an insight into a country that has had a profound impact – culturally, economically, militarily and politically – on the world as we know it.

US politics never stands still. Over the past thirty years, I have taught US politics through history in the making. This has included the events of 9/11 and the US response, the invasions of Afghanistan (2001) and Iraq (2003), as well as the election of the first Black president of the United States, Barack Obama in 2008. I have taught and learnt about US politics during the impeachments of both President Bill Clinton in 1998 and President Trump in 2019 and 2021, as well as the threats to the status of the United States as a democracy that have emerged in recent years. A-Level Politics, and therefore also this book, will allow you to explore major events such as these as a means to understand how the US political system works. Chances are that there will be many more major political developments as you study.

The book contains many examples and case studies covering recent US events and explains how they shed light on the politics of the United States. You will study the big issues that matter enormously to our everyday lives: the devastating impact of global warming; the social and economic crises caused by COVID-19; moral issues such as gay and transgender rights; other rights issues such as guns, race and immigration; and US involvement in military conflicts around the world. As you become more familiar with the workings of US politics, you will be able to make better sense of the developments you see in the media.

Essentially, all politics is about people. It is about the processes that have a profound impact on the way in which individuals and groups live their lives. This book will allow you to understand how these political processes operate in the United States today and how they shape the lives of the people who live there. Not only is it a joy to understand the politics of a new country but it also helps to sharpen your understanding of your own country as you make comparisons with your own experience. You will also be able to make more sense of just how different the United States is, both culturally and politically, from other countries.

The rest of this chapter highlights some of the most important themes in US politics today. This will give you an understanding of the current context in which the US political system is operating; what are the big political issues of today? The chapter then moves on to cover four enduring features of the US political system, which you will see addressed throughout this book.

US POLITICS TODAY

So, what are these themes and developments that will help you to unlock a deeper understanding of US politics? We will begin with the concept of culture wars.

CULTURE WARS

Culture wars exist in the United States today between those with liberal and conservative viewpoints. In the United States, there is significant conflict over issues such as race, gender, sexuality, abortion, guns and immigration. These areas are often referred to as social or moral policies.

The more liberal group of people in the United States advocate for greater respect for and protection of women, gay and transgender individuals, and racial minorities. This includes raising consciousness about the inequality and discrimination that these groups have faced and continue to face in the United States. Opposing this is a more conservative group who can be seen as reacting against this liberal movement, viewing it as a threat to their traditional views and way of life. Such conservatives may reject the desirability of providing protections for these social groups and individuals. They may also argue that the liberal view of inequality is excessive or unfounded. Conservatives are much more likely to focus on support for gun rights, opposing abortion and challenging immigration.

In the United States, not only are there *major differences* in values within society but also there is a *major clash* between people who hold these values. A central feature of the culture wars is that each side is struggling for cultural dominance, attempting to establish their worldview as the one that should be accepted by all. This is partly because each side sees the other side as a threat to their lifestyle and their worldview. It is in this sense that there is a war between these two ideological groups. This war is fought out in many different places, including the media. Throughout this book, you will see this war being fought, using political processes to establish cultural dominance.

These culture wars are not inevitable or natural. In some countries, there is a much higher level of consensus on these matters and a lack of conflict. In the United Kingdom, there is a much lower level of disagreement amongst the public and politicians on issues of abortion, guns, gay marriage and race. In the United States, however, this culture war has intensified in recent decades.

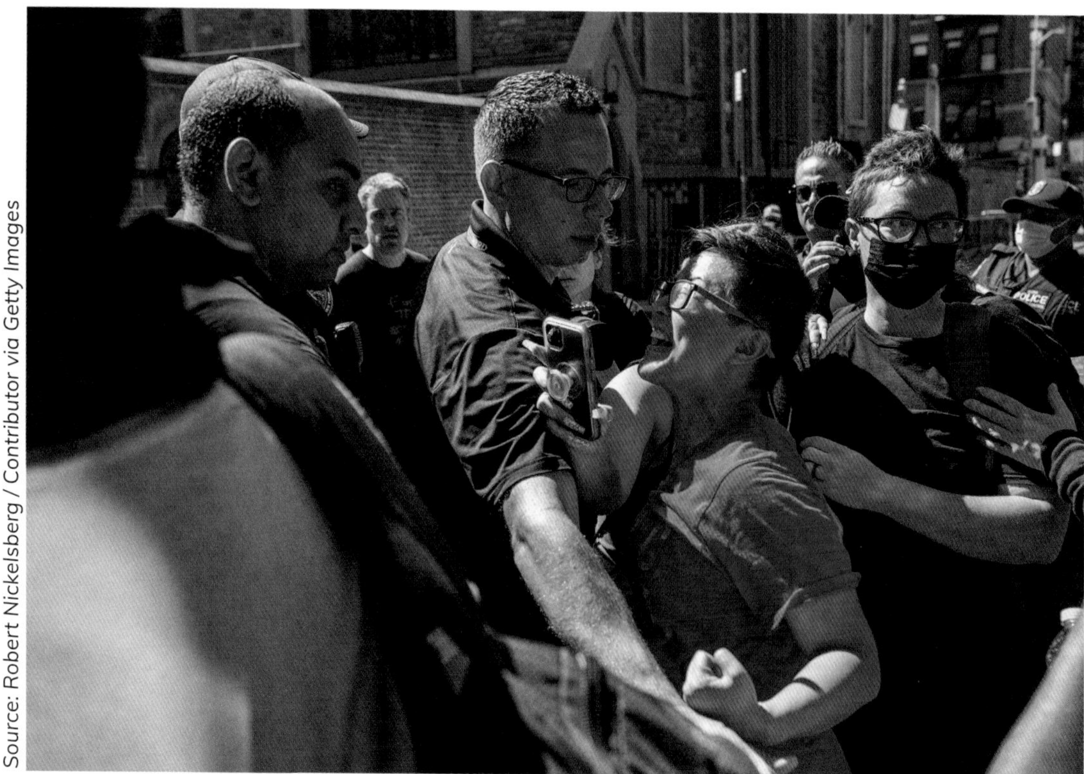

Source: Robert Nickelsberg / Contributor via Getty Images

Photo 1.1 **Pro-choice and anti-abortion protesters clash at a demonstration outside a Catholic church in New York, 2022**

One example can be seen in the ongoing battle over race and racism in the United States. Liberals will emphasise the existence of historical and ongoing inequality, racial discrimination and incidents of major injustice. They try to raise awareness of concerns as well as to make changes to the law to overcome inequality and discrimination. Conservatives are more likely to reject this view of US society or to focus on other issues. They might argue that a law or practice is not discriminatory and may also be necessary for other, non-racial purposes. For example, in recent years many states have imposed restrictive election laws that make it harder for people to vote. Research by the Brennan Center for Justice showed that in the first six months of 2021 alone, forty-three states introduced more than 250 such laws. Liberals will point out that such laws, for instance photo ID requirements for voters, have a particularly negative effect on racial minority voter turnout and that this huge array of bills marks a systematic attempt to restrict members of racial minority groups from voting. Conservatives reject this, arguing that no one is banned from obtaining photo ID and these rules are needed to prevent voter fraud.

A Florida proposal called 'Individual Freedom' became state law in 2022 and provides a case study of the culture wars in the United States. The law, proposed by Governor Ron DeSantis and pushed by conservatives, stops the teaching of material that causes people to feel discomfort or any other form of psychological distress on account of their race. This bill is similar to others recently introduced in over thirty states, with DeSantis adding further laws in Florida in 2023. Liberals say that such bills are an attempt to stop educational institutions highlighting historical or ongoing discrimination against racial minorities and that these bills will restrict educational institutions from exploring racial issues for fear of litigation. On signing the bill, DeSantis said that it would reduce conflict between racial groups in Florida. This is part of a long line of actions on this issue. In 2020, President Trump attacked the teaching of classes that highlight racial discrimination saying there were too many lies in schools. He announced the creation of the 1776 Commission to promote 'patriotic education'. On gaining office, President Biden disbanded the commission. In addition, he advocated a new law, the For the People Act, which attempted to regulate voting and protect people's access to the ballot. This law failed to gain enough support in Congress. Each side in the culture wars is engaged in constant efforts to find new ways to establish their values and worldview as the dominant one.

ENVIRONMENTAL AND SOCIO-ECONOMIC POLICY

Focus on culture wars arguably comes at the expense of other critical policy areas in the United States. Environmental and socio-economic policy are two areas that have, and will continue to have, a massive impact on the lifestyles and life chances of people in the United States.

The United States, alongside the rest of the world, is facing an enormous crisis as a result of global warming. Back in 2018, The UN Secretary-General António Guterres described this as an existential threat to humanity. The United States is facing several different crises linked to global warming, including water shortages and wildfires. For example, 40 million people depend on the Colorado River for drinking water, and the river has experienced dramatic falls in water volume as a result of global warming. The river is also used to generate electricity and water crops, which are now threatened by a shortage of supply. President Biden has proposed a number of measures to address climate change such as much greater investment in renewable energy sources. Many argue, however, that the US political process is not responding with enough speed or solutions (or even that the system is so flawed that it cannot respond) to prevent more major disasters as well as further threats to human life and well-being.

A further example of a key policy can be found in regard to healthcare. At the time of Congress passing the Affordable Care Act 2010, the government estimated that 48 million Americans did not have health insurance and therefore might lack access to healthcare. The Act, the centrepiece of President Obama's election campaign in 2008, ensured that all Americans would then have health insurance. His proposals were fought over by politicians in Congress for more than a year, with heavy changes being made to the bill en route to becoming law. Democrats largely supported the bill whereas all Republicans voted against it. This law is still a source of conflict between the two parties today, with many Republicans attempting to amend or repeal the Act. Economic and welfare policy determine how much support, if any, an individual can get from the government to meet their needs such as food, housing, education and health. They therefore influence how much money individuals have, what they can or cannot buy, and their chances of living in poverty.

PARTISANSHIP AND POLARISATION

Partisanship involves politicians being strongly dedicated and loyal to their own political party and being highly likely to oppose the policies of the other main party. Partisanship tells us that the Democratic Party (the party on the left of US politics) is internally united, as is the Republican Party (the party of the right). Both Democrats and Republicans show very few signs of being willing to compromise with each other.

There has been a major rise in partisanship in the United States since the 1990s. This has led to much greater confrontation between the two parties and a lack of willingness to work together. In some ways, this reflects the culture wars discussed above in which liberals or Democrats strongly oppose conservatives or Republicans, and vice versa. The rising partisanship has often made it much harder to govern, especially if the president faces a Congress in which the opposing party has a majority.

Added to this is the process of polarisation. This refers to a process in which the two main parties are moving ideologically further apart. The Democrats have moved further to the left, whereas the Republicans have moved further to the right. This has led to even less scope for consensus and compromise within the US political system. Partisanship and polarisation can be seen in the Republican responses both to President Obama's Affordable Care Act and to President Biden's For the People Act. In both cases, all Republicans voted against the bills in Congress. There is a sense in which partisanship has started to exist for its own sake, with both parties, for example, deliberately voting against a bill regardless of its merits, simply because it was proposed by the opposing party.

Throughout this book, you will see examples of how the political process addresses (or fails to address) issues such as these, gaining a much greater insight into the complex processes of power and decision-making.

KEY FEATURES OF THE US POLITICAL SYSTEM

We will turn now to the key features of the US political system. An explanation of these features will help you to understand each topic in this book and help you to make connections between them.

SEPARATION OF POWERS

The separation of powers is a very simple concept but one that has a major effect on the way in which US politics operates. The separation of powers affects the roles, powers and limits of the president, Congress and the Supreme Court. As such, you can expect to see discussion of this concept in many chapters in this book.

The separation of powers states that there are three branches of government. These can be seen in Table 1.1.

Table 1.1 The three branches of government in the United States

Branch of government	US name	Main role
Legislature	Congress	• To legislate (make laws). • Congress is elected, with each member representing their area when making decisions (for example on new laws).
Executive	Presidency including president, vice president and cabinet	• The president is nationally elected and provides leadership by proposing new policies for Congress to consider. • The president plays a central role in foreign policy and particularly military matters.
Judiciary	The Supreme Court	• To decide whether other political institutions have broken constitutional rules. • They can overturn even the most powerful institutions such as the president and Congress if either of these two branches break the US Constitution.

The principle of the separation of powers also states that no one person can be a member of more than one branch at the same time. It is not, for example, possible to be part of the executive branch whilst also being a member of the legislative branch. This constitutional principle requires that the president and Congress are elected separately; US citizens get to vote for both the executive and legislature. In contrast, in parliamentary systems, such as the United Kingdom, there is only one election for both the legislature (known as Parliament) and the executive (known as the government). UK citizens only vote for Parliament, and the government is then drawn from the majority party in Parliament.

It is common to view the US President as a hugely powerful figure on the international stage. Within the United States, however, the president is relatively weak, finding it difficult to achieve policy goals. The separation of powers allows for extensive checks and balances between the three main institutions of government in the United States. In other words, each branch can restrict the other two. In turn, this requires the president, Congress and the Supreme Court to *share* power. For example, separate elections make it possible for the president to be from one party while the opposing party holds a majority in Congress. The president then faces a hostile Congress that is likely to oppose many of his or her goals. Also, the president cannot use the ongoing possibility of hiring or firing members of Congress to and from their cabinet as a way of pushing members of Congress to vote a certain way. In contrast, you will have seen how, in the United Kingdom, the government can dominate Parliament, as the prime minister holds a majority in the legislative branch. In addition, prime ministers can use their power of patronage (hire and fire) over Members of Parliament (MPs) from their own party to ensure high levels of support from those MPs when proposing legislation in Parliament.

A SOVEREIGN AND CODIFIED CONSTITUTION

Unlike the United Kingdom, the United States has a codified constitution that places all its rules for the political game into a single document. Of greater significance than this codification is the sovereign nature of the US Constitution. This means that the US Constitution is above all other institutions including president and Congress. This gives considerable power to the Supreme Court as the body that determines whether the Constitution has been broken. The Supreme Court can even overturn Acts of Congress and actions of the president if they judge that constitutional rules have been broken.

Given this, as well as the existence of many civil rights in the Constitution, the Supreme Court is a powerful force in the game of US politics. The ability of the nine unelected Justices of the court to have a huge political impact will be seen in several chapters across this book. For example, in 2010, the Supreme Court made a ruling that influenced the level of protection for freedom of speech and election laws. The court reviewed the Bipartisan Campaign Reform Act 2002, a law passed by Congress that limited the use of money in US elections. By ruling against this act, the majority opinion of the Supreme Court argued that it was protecting the First Amendment constitutional right to freedom of expression. At the same time, this ruling (known as *Citizens United v FEC*) allowed wealthy donors to have a bigger influence on election campaigns. In the United Kingdom, the Supreme Court does not possess the power to overturn an Act of Parliament. There is no codified constitution and Parliament is sovereign, which means that Parliament, and not courts, always has the final say.

REPRESENTATIVE DEMOCRACY

When writing the American constitution in 1787, the fifty-five Founding Fathers (the people who wrote the Constitution) wanted to establish a form of popular government, that is, a government based on the will of the people. As such, they set up a democratic republic in which some institutions of government would be accountable to the public. This reflected the dominant desire amongst the Founding Fathers to have the people's input into the government and to reject monarchies such as those practised in Britain. They created an elected lower chamber of Congress (the House of Representatives) and created a method for popular participation in the selection of the president. At the same time, many of the Founding Fathers had reservations about democracy, including the ability of the general public to make effective decisions about government. This is why, for example, the upper chamber of Congress (the Senate) was initially appointed by state governments and not elected by the people. Nonetheless, the principles of representative government were established in the Constitution from its very origins.

Arguably, a higher principle than representative government for the Founding Fathers was to ensure that no one group or institution could dominate political decision-making. They did not want democracy to be used to allow a dominant interest in society to oppress the interests of other, less dominant groups. To guard against this, extensive checks and balances were created to ensure that government was based on a consideration of different interests within society. Rather than having a purely majoritarian democracy, in which the majority gets what they want, the Constitution promotes consideration of the will of the people through regular elections and forces compromise between different views and interests. By separating out the executive, legislature and judiciary, the Constitution also forces compromise and cooperation between different branches and often, therefore, compromise between different interests, if policies and laws are to be put into practice.

In recent years, the existence of democracy has come under threat in the United States. President Trump rejected the result of the 2020 election, claiming that voter fraud meant that the election result was not a true reflection of the wishes of voters. Trump lost the election by more than 7 million votes, so his claim was quickly rejected by courts and even other Republicans, with other claims having no factual evidence to back them up. Some Republicans, however, continued to work with Trump to stop Biden from becoming president. This culminated in the events of 6 January 2021, in which 2,000 people stormed the Congressional building in an attempt to prevent Biden from becoming president on that day (Photo 1.2). Trump encouraged protests giving a speech on 6 January that ended with the words 'We fight. We fight like hell and if you don't fight like hell, you're not going to have a country anymore.' A gallows was erected outside the Capitol, and some protesters shouted 'Hang Mike Pence' after the vice president rejected claims made by Trump that the vice president could overturn the election results. Five police officers died while trying to prevent the attack and a further four were involved in suicide within a year of the riots. Arguably, the levels of partisanship and the intensity of the culture wars have become so strong that many conservatives could not accept the victory of Joe Biden in 2020.

Trump has generally held that the election was fixed but has sometimes also made comments that were critical of democracy itself, suggesting he would prefer to remove it. It has started to become a feature of the culture wars that some conservatives, including senior Republicans, are questioning the idea that the United States should be a democracy. In 2020, Republican Senator Mike Lee repeatedly questioned the desirability of democracy. He stated that 'democracy isn't the objective; liberty, peace, and prosperity are'. Lee continued to point out that the word democracy is not in the Constitution, and argued there was never any intention for the United States to be a democracy. He won re-election to the Senate in 2022.

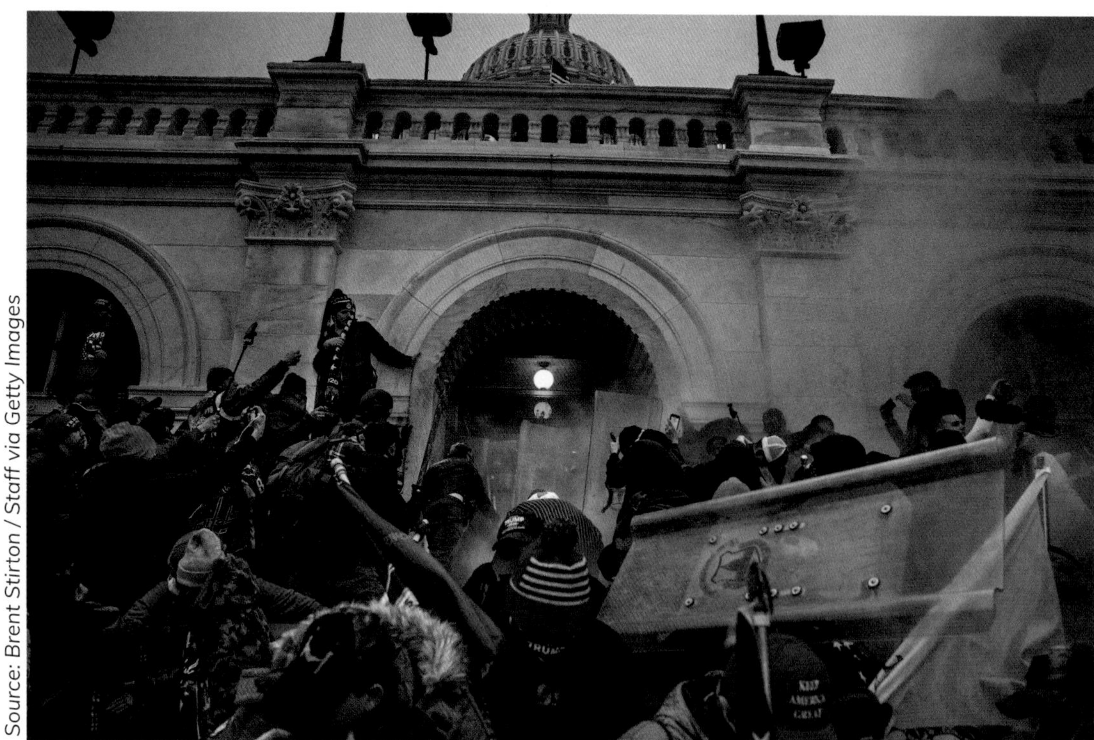

Source: Brent Stirton / Staff via Getty Images

Photo 1.2 **Trump supporters attempt to storm the Capitol building and prevent Biden being confirmed as president during the 'Stop the Steal' rally on 6 January 2021**

FEDERALISM

Another enduring feature of US politics is federalism. Federalism in the United States is a system in which power is shared between a central government (known as the Federal Government run by the president and Congress) and by the regional governments of the fifty states. Every American is subject to two different governments, the Federal Government and the government of their state. One question we will address throughout the book is 'who decides what'? In practice, states have significant control over many policy areas such as health, education and criminal law. For example, in some states it is legal to buy and sell marijuana, and in other states it is not. Or, to take another example, we have already seen evidence of conflict between the Federal Government and the State of Florida with Florida Governor Ron DeSantis and President Joe Biden in a dispute on the issue of race in education. Florida has different educational practices to other states such as New York or New Jersey.

In a federal system, such as the United States, regions have law-making power that is protected by the Constitution. In other words, the Federal Government cannot reduce or remove the power of states. Having said that, the US Constitution is vague, so the division of power between state governments and the Federal Government is often unclear. This leads to clashes between the two levels of government about who has the rightful power to make important decisions for citizens. Federalism also sets up potential conflict when the Federal Government has a different set of priorities than an individual state. There are regular power struggles in which the two levels of government use all their available powers to achieve their policy goals.

These features and developments should give you a great starting point as you begin to explore each chapter and the key topics of this subject. I wish you the best of luck as you study towards your A-Level in Politics and hope that you enjoy this opportunity to explore the captivating matter of US politics.

Further Resources

Critchlow, Donald (2015) *American Political History: A Very Short Introduction* (New York: Oxford University Press).

Klein, Ezra (2021) *Why We're Polarized* (London: Profile Books).

Levitsky, Steven and Ziblatt, Daniel (2018) *How Democracies Die* (New York: Penguin).

Valelly, Richard (2013) *American Politics: A Very Short Introduction* (New York: Oxford University Press).

Harvard EdX has an excellent online US government course. The first unit 'American Government: Constitutional Foundations' provides an extensive introduction to all that is covered in the A-Level. Available at www.edx.org/xseries/harvardx-us-government (accessed 20 July 2023).

Visit https://bloomsbury.pub/colclough-essentials-us to access additional materials to support teaching and learning.

2 THE CONSTITUTION

Chapter Preview

Constitutions matter! They provide the rules of the game of politics by determining the roles, powers and limits of politicians, political institutions and the people. They decide how power gets shared. Whilst both the United States and United Kingdom are considered to be founding democracies, the two political systems work extremely differently. This is mainly a result of the different constitutional arrangements determining how politics operates.

This topic examines the way in which the US Constitution sets up the main political bodies of the presidency, Congress, Supreme Court and the states. It also addresses the key features of the Constitution, those principles which make the US Constitution quite different from that of the United Kingdom. In particular, the concepts of separation of powers, and checks and balances will be explored in depth to analyse how they have an overriding impact on power and politics in the United States. We will also consider the nature of federalism, exploring the power relationship between the central (Federal) government and the states. This topic is a great way to further your understanding of other topics as the Constitution defines so many US political processes. Equally, Chapters 3, 4 and 5 on Congress, the presidency and the Supreme Court, respectively, will give you further insight into how the Constitution operates in practice.

All constitutions need updating, therefore this chapter will analyse and evaluate the amendment process. The Founding Fathers deliberately made it difficult to change the Constitution. This can protect core values in the Constitution but also leaves it open to becoming outdated based on the values and needs of people in the 1700s and not the 2020s. Finally, armed with greater understanding of the US Constitution we will then begin to evaluate it by considering the extent to which it supports democracy and make judgements on its other strengths and weaknesses.

Key Questions and Debates

- What are the key features and the nature of the Constitution and how do these determine so much of how US politics operates?
- How does the Constitution outline the main powers and limits of the three main branches of government: the executive, the legislature and the judiciary?
- How is the Constitution amended and is this method of change acceptable?
- In providing federalism, how does the Constitution define and protect state power and is it effective in doing so?
- Does the US Constitution provide sufficient levels of democracy?
- How can we evaluate other strengths and weaknesses of the Constitution?

Specification Checklist

1.1 The nature of the US Constitution

- Vagueness, codification and entrenchment.
- The constitutional framework (powers) of the US branches of government.
- The amendment process.

1.2 The key features of the US Constitution

- Federalism.
- Separation of powers and checks and balances.
- Bipartisanship.
- Limited government.

1.3 The main characteristics of US federalism

- The nature of the federal system of government and its relationship with the states.

1.4 Interpretations and debates around the US Constitution

- The extent of democracy within the US Constitution.
- Strengths and weaknesses and its impact on the US government.
- The debates around the extent to which the United States remains federal today.

Source: istock.com/Koele

THE HISTORY OF THE US CONSTITUTION

All constitutions are a product of their time, often reacting against the previous regime and reflecting the hopes and principles of the people who write it. The US Constitution was written in 1787 by the fifty-five **Founding Fathers**, the people responsible for the Constitution, and was largely a rejection of the powerful monarchies and political systems at the time, such as that of the United Kingdom. To fully understand the Constitution today we will first examine some of the ideals of the Founding Fathers as well as the issues they were reacting to at the time of writing.

Definition

Founding Fathers: The name given to the fifty-five men, acting as delegates from the colonies, who met to write the US Constitution in 1787.

Source: MPI / Stringer via Getty Images

Photo 2.1 **The signing of the US Constitution in 1787**

It was the Constitution which established the United States of America in 1789. Within a few hundred years of Columbus' arrival in the Americas from Europe in 1492, almost the entire continent had been taken from the people who had lived there for thousands of years. European countries sliced up the continent and assumed control, often killing Native Americans or forcing people off their land. On the eastern side of what we now call the United States of America, thirteen colonies developed, with different national and religious origins (see Map 2.1). Many had developed from people escaping religious and political persecution in Europe, who travelled to the New World to be free from tyrannical government.

Britain eventually claimed control of all colonies, which increasingly resisted British rule. These colonies declared their independence from Britain on 4 July 1776. The British were not willing to give up such important territory, leading to the American Revolutionary War (1775–83) between the two sides. The colonies gained independence from the British in 1783, leaving them with the critical decision of the extent to which they should remain as thirteen separate countries. Many of the colonists were keen to stay separate from each other and feared a large powerful government that might create a new tyranny and ignore their specific interests. On the other hand, there were forces which pulled the colonies together:

- Collective security from Native Americans who resisted colonisation
- Collective security from European forces, especially the British.
- Trade between colonies requiring cooperation on currency, weights and measures.

These push and pull factors resulted in **The Constitutional Convention** in 1787, at which the Founding Fathers argued over competing priorities and political visions for the future.

Definition

The Constitutional Convention: The meeting of the fifty-five Founding Fathers in Philadelphia, in which political and constitutional issues were debated and the current US Constitution was written.

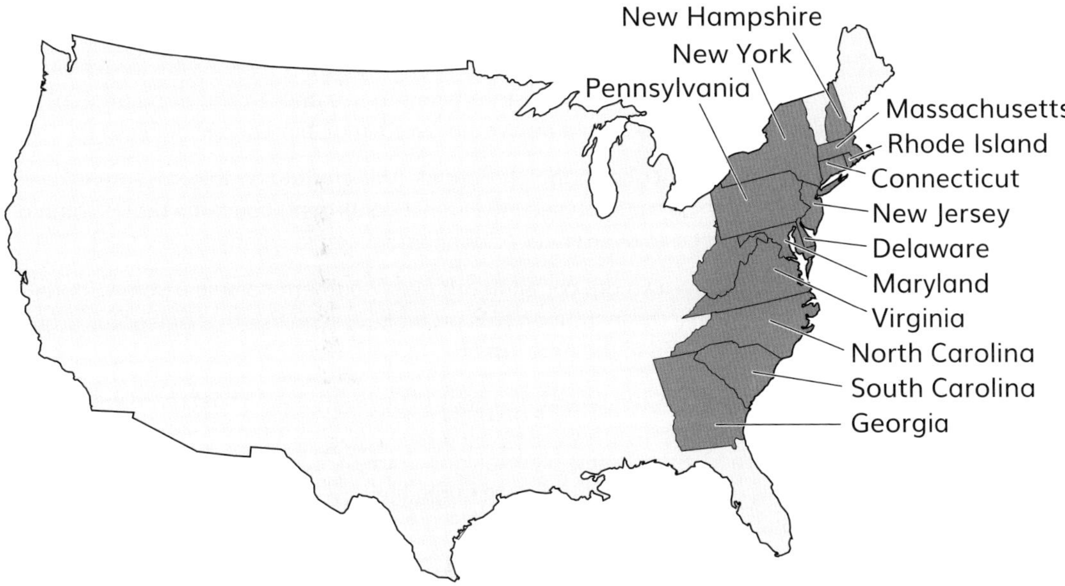

Map 2.1 **The original thirteen colonies of the United States**

Article 1	Congress	These are the original sections of the US Constitution written in 1787.
Article 2	Presidency	
Article 3	Supreme Court	
Article 4	States and federalism	
Article 5	Amendment process	
Article 6	The supremacy of the Constitution	
Article 7	The ratification of the Constitution	
Amendment 1	Freedom of speech and freedom of religion	Amendments 1–10 were all passed at the same time in 1791 and are collectively known as the Bill of Rights.
Amendment 2	The right to bear arms	
Amendment 5	The right to a fair trial	
Amendment 8	Freedom from cruel and unusual punishment	
Amendment 10	Reserved powers of the States	
Amendment 14	Equal treatment, preventing racial discrimination	Since 1791 there have only been a further seventeen amendments added. The latest, Amendment 27 was ratified by Congress in 1992, limiting pay rises for members of Congress.
Amendment 19	The right of women to vote	
Amendment 22	Term limits for presidents	
Amendment 25	Temporary succession of the vice president to the presidency	

Figure 2.1 **The articles of the US Constitution and selective amendments**

Some issues and conflicts at the Constitutional Convention included:

- Large versus small states. A major debate raged over representation, with larger states demanding that the number of politicians per state was proportional to the population of the state. Smaller states feared that they would be overpowered in a union of all colonies.
- Threats to security from Native Americans and Europeans. This created a major incentive for the colonies to work together for their common security, whilst generating concerns that a common army of all colonies could be used to overpower or dominate a single colony.
- The existence of slavery, which was more common amongst southern colonies. Some Southern colonies refused to join the union if the institution was prohibited, even as other delegates argued forcefully for slavery to be outlawed in the new nation.
- The power of states/colonies versus the power of a central government. Whilst there were many factors such as inter-colony trade and threats to security which encouraged cooperation, colonies generally remained concerned that a new central government could lead to an excessively powerful government. This new central government might limit the freedoms of colonies and the rights of individuals within them.
- Relationships between colonies including trade. This made a common system of weights and measures, as well as currency more desirable, requiring a centralised institution to oversee this and regulate relationships between states. Again, this created concerns about protection of colony interest.

So, what did the ensuing constitution look like? The Founding Fathers developed seven articles (the seven sections of the original constitution) and over time twenty-seven amendments have been added. You can see an outline of this in Figure 2.1.

THE NATURE OF THE US CONSTITUTION

Whilst there is a separate chapter covering comparative US and UK politics, it is useful, at this stage, to be aware of a few key features of the US Constitution and how this makes US politics work differently from the United Kingdom. Table 2.1 gives you an overview. These features will be explored in more detail both throughout this chapter and the book as a whole, and you will develop more complexity of understanding as we go.

VAGUENESS, CODIFICATION AND ENTRENCHMENT

The US Constitution has a number of notable features, these three – vagueness, codification and entrenchment – will help us to understand how the Constitution operates in practice today.

Vagueness

Despite being written and codified, the US Constitution is much shorter than those of other countries making the meaning of the Constitution vague. If the rules of a game are unclear, then this can easily lead to clashes over what is and what is not permissible according to those rules. The outcome of these clashes can have a major impact in determining who gets power. There are some aspects of the Constitution which are well defined and not subject to significant dispute, but even these are sometimes contested. This lack of clarity has three important outcomes:

- Dispute over the meaning of the Constitution with clashes over which institutions have which roles or powers.
- The possibility of flexibility by interpreting and applying the rules to meet the needs of the day without having to change the Constitution formally.
- The Supreme Court becomes even more powerful because it has a great deal of flexibility in how it interprets the Constitution.

Table 2.1 **Key differences between UK and US constitutions and their significance**

UK	USA	Significance
Part written, uncodified constitution (meaning one that is drawn from several sources)	Written, codified constitution (meaning one that is contained within a single written document)	Arguably constitutional rules are clearer in the United States. The written constitution is also a symbol of America and an authoritative document which people generally respect.
Parliamentary sovereignty	Constitutional sovereignty	Constitutional sovereignty gives major power to the courts over the president and Congress. In the United States the Supreme Court can strike down an Act of Congress but the UK Supreme Court cannot overturn an Act of Parliament. Courts are much more powerful in the United States.
Easily-changed constitution	Entrenched constitution – protected from easy change	This gives additional power to the US Supreme Court because it is virtually impossible to overturn a court ruling as it would require a change to the US Constitution. In the United Kingdom, Parliament can easily pass new laws which can undermine any court ruling they do not like.
Parliamentary System in which people vote for Parliament, not government, and government is drawn from Parliament.	Presidential System and separation of powers. People vote for the president and Congress separately. There is also a separation of personnel. It is not possible to be in Congress and work for the president at the same time.	This has a massive impact on the relationship between the executive and legislature. In the United Kingdom the government tends to dominate Parliament. It has a majority in Parliament. The PM can hire and fire people from Parliament to and from their cabinet. This system of patronage keeps MPs loyal to their party leader. In the United States, no such ongoing patronage exists. Members of Congress tend not to be looking for a position in the executive branch. Additionally, the presidency and Congress may be controlled by different parties, making it very hard for the president to control policy. The president is much weaker than the prime minister within their own country.

Some ambiguities in the US Constitution are:

- The president is commander in chief and Congress has the power to declare war. In practice, presidents often initiate military action without asking Congress. It is unclear what the Constitution allows in cases of war.
- Which powers or policies belong to the states and which belong to the Federal Government? The Constitution is particularly brief and therefore vague in this area. In practice the power of the **Federal Government** over the states has grown enormously over time without any changes to the Constitution.
- The Second Amendment: the right to bear arms protects gun rights, but it is unclear whether this relates to the right of an individual to own a gun or the right of a state to set up a state militia.

Definition

Federal Government: The national government of the United States which includes the president and Congress.

Spec key term

Codification: The process of placing all constitutional rules into a single document.

Entrenchment: The process of making a constitution difficult to change, for example by requiring a super-majority rather than just 50% plus to agree to a change to the rules.

Codification

The US Constitution is codified, meaning that all major constitutional rules are placed in a single document. This has the potential benefit of helping to give the rules a greater level of authority by placing key constitutional principles into a well-recognised single document. In addition, **codification** can allow for greater clarity of rules. If there is a dispute about whether, for example, the president has the right to carry out a certain action then the codified constitution can be consulted. As we have already seen, however, despite its codified nature the Constitution remains vague.

Entrenchment

The process of **entrenchment** makes it difficult to alter the US Constitution. The Founding Fathers created significant barriers to changing constitutional rules. The process requires support from different institutions as well as requiring super-majorities that would prevent constitutional change without cross-party support. The process for updating the Constitution and an evaluation of that process is addressed in the amendment section below.

THE CONSTITUTIONAL POWERS OF THE US BRANCHES OF GOVERNMENT

The Founding Fathers created three main institutions of the Federal Government known as the three branches of government. Figure 2.2 below shows these three branches and how they were created in the US.

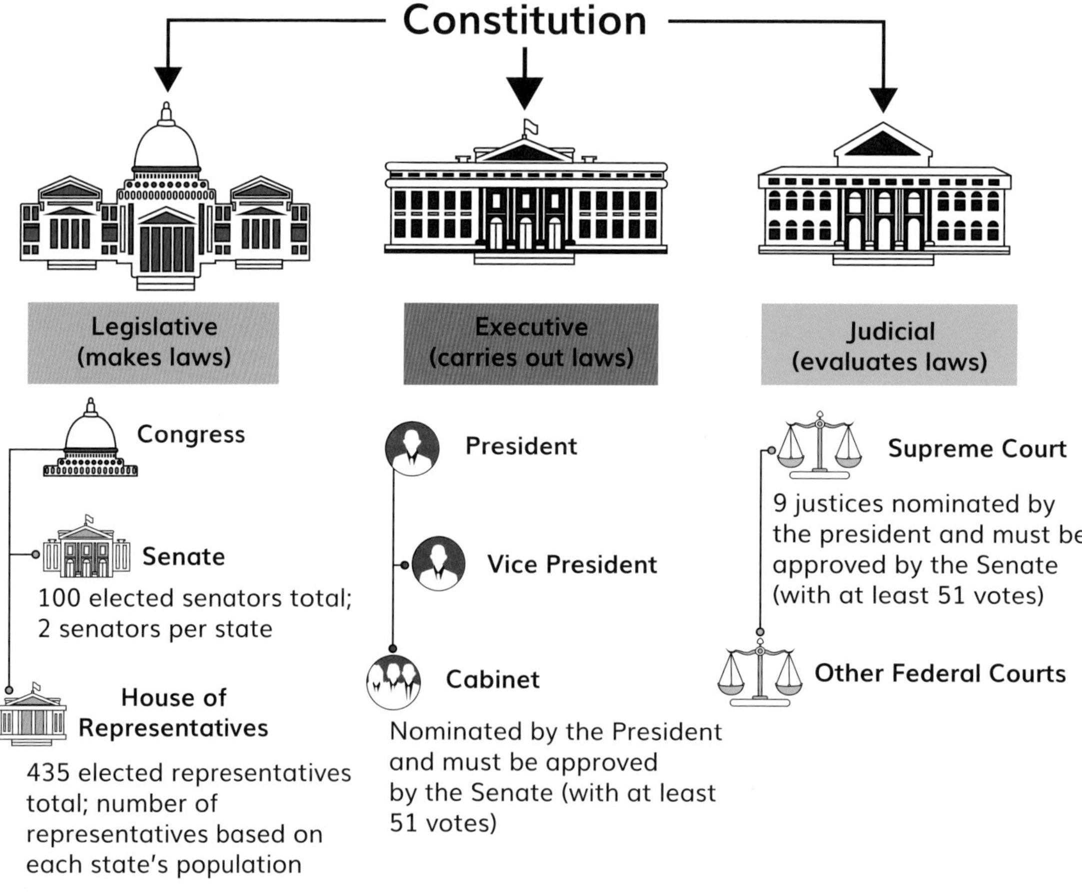

Figure 2.2 **The three branches of US government**

Instead of having an all-powerful executive, as was the case in the United Kingdom at the time, the Founding Fathers intended Congress to have significant powers in leading the country, outlining its role and powers in Article 1. Congress was created as a bicameral (two chamber) legislature with the House of Representatives and the Senate having equal legislative power. The president's role and powers is outlined in a much shorter Article 2 making him the Commander in Chief of the Armed Services, allowing him to propose measures to Congress and to veto bills. The power of the judiciary is outlined in the even shorter Article 3. Whilst Article 3, section 2 states that 'The judicial Power shall extend to all Cases, in Law and Equity, arising under this Constitution, the Laws of the United States, and Treaties made.' There is little clarity on the exact level of power that the court should possess.

ENUMERATED AND IMPLIED POWERS

The constitution awards specific powers to each branch, known as their enumerated powers. In addition, given the vagueness of the Constitution there are several powers which could be assumed from that wording. These are known as **implied powers.** These enumerated and implied powers are laid out in Table 2.2. The following three areas are particularly contested parts of the Constitution.

Spec key term

Enumerated Powers: Powers explicitly stated in the Constitution which are awarded to a specific institution.

Definition

Implied powers: Powers which are suggested by interpretation of the Constitution without being clearly stated.

Table 2.2 **Enumerated and implied powers in the US Constitution**

	Congress	President	Supreme Court
Enumerated	• Legislative power – the power to make laws • Amend the Constitution (with state agreement) • Declare War • Collection of taxes and borrowing money • Regulation of international and inter-state commerce • Other enumerated powers given to one chamber only. See Chapter 3, pages 42–44 for these exclusive powers.	• Head of the executive branch • Propose measures to Congress • Veto legislation • Grant pardons • Commander in chief.	• Rule on all cases arising under the Constitution, the laws of the United States and treaties.
Implied	• The necessary and proper clause • The use made of the commerce clause.	• The use of executive orders • The use of the commander in chief clause.	• The power of judicial review in having the ability to overturn other bodies including the president and Congress.

Commander in Chief

The power of commander in chief is a good example of the relationship between enumerated and implied powers. The Constitution explicitly says in Article 2, Section 2 that 'the President shall be Commander in Chief of the Army and Navy of the United States, and of the Militia of the several States, *when called into the actual Service of the United States*' (my emphasis). It also states that Congress has the power to declare war. Whilst it is explicit (or enumerated) that the president is commander in chief, it is not at all explicit what this means. The wording of the Constitution suggests that the president can act as the commander in chief (the person who directs the military) only when Congress calls the military into action through a declaration of war. Yet presidents have continually claimed the constitutional authority to initiate military action.

The necessary and proper clause

Article One of the constitution allows Congress to pass any law that is 'necessary and proper' in carrying out their enumerated powers. The clause states that Congress can pass any law in relation to powers that are explicitly given to them by the constitution. This includes the power to collect taxes, declare war and maintain a navy. The necessary and proper clause can be seen as excessively vague because it allows Congress to pass laws that have only limited connections to their actual enumerated powers. Congress has successfully used this clause to justify considerable law-making power, for example, by establishing several economic and criminal laws by linking them to the enumerated powers. The test case for this was *McCulloch v Maryland* (1819) in which Congress successfully argued that it had the constitutional right to establish a national bank. The opinion of the court justified this ruling based on the specifically enumerated powers of Congress to lay and collect taxes, to borrow money and to regulate commerce.

The commerce clause

The commerce clause gives Congress the power to 'regulate Commerce with foreign Nations, and among the several States, and with the Indian Tribes'. This has been used to justify widespread congressional laws regulating business and employment practices despite opposition from states who claim that no such regulations can be enforced on practices in their state. During certain periods of US history, especially the **New Deal** of the 1930s, it was used to expand federal power over the states. Again, whilst the Constitution explicitly states that Congress can 'regulate commerce ... among the several states', the extent to which this has been used by Congress arguably stretched beyond what is enumerated. The commerce clause is further discussed with evidence on on pages 25-30 in the 'Federalism' section.

Definition

The New Deal: A broad set of government-directed projects introduced by President Franklin Delano Roosevelt (FDR) to overcome the economic crisis of the Great Depression in the 1930s. It included economic and welfare policies that marked a major expansion in the role of the Federal Government over the states and citizens.

Learning Review

1. What is the difference between articles and amendments in the US Constitution?
2. What are the main amendments outlined so far and what is their general meaning?
3. What is meant by vagueness, codification and entrenchment?
4. What are three vague or contested parts of the US Constitution?
5. What is the difference between an enumerated and an implied power?

Comparative Learning Review

1. What are the main differences between the US and UK constitutions?
2. How do these differences have an impact on US and UK political processes?
3. How do checks and balances operate differently in the two political systems?

THE AMENDMENT PROCESS

The amendment process is outlined in Article 5 of the US Constitution. The entrenchment of the US Constitution, making it particularly difficult to change, has contributed to preventing a huge range of proposed amendments. It has limited the total number of amendments to just twenty-seven in over 230 years.

To amend the US Constitution both Congress and the states need to agree. Two-thirds of the House and two-thirds of the Senate can decide on the wording of a constitutional amendment and then pass this on to the states for consideration. A proposed amendment must then be ratified by the legislatures of three-quarters of the states. It is also possible for two-thirds of the state legislatures to ask Congress to convene a Constitutional Convention to propose an amendment. This proposal would require the support of three-quarters of the states. This process can be seen in Figure 2.3. In practice, all successful amendments to date have been initiated by Congress.

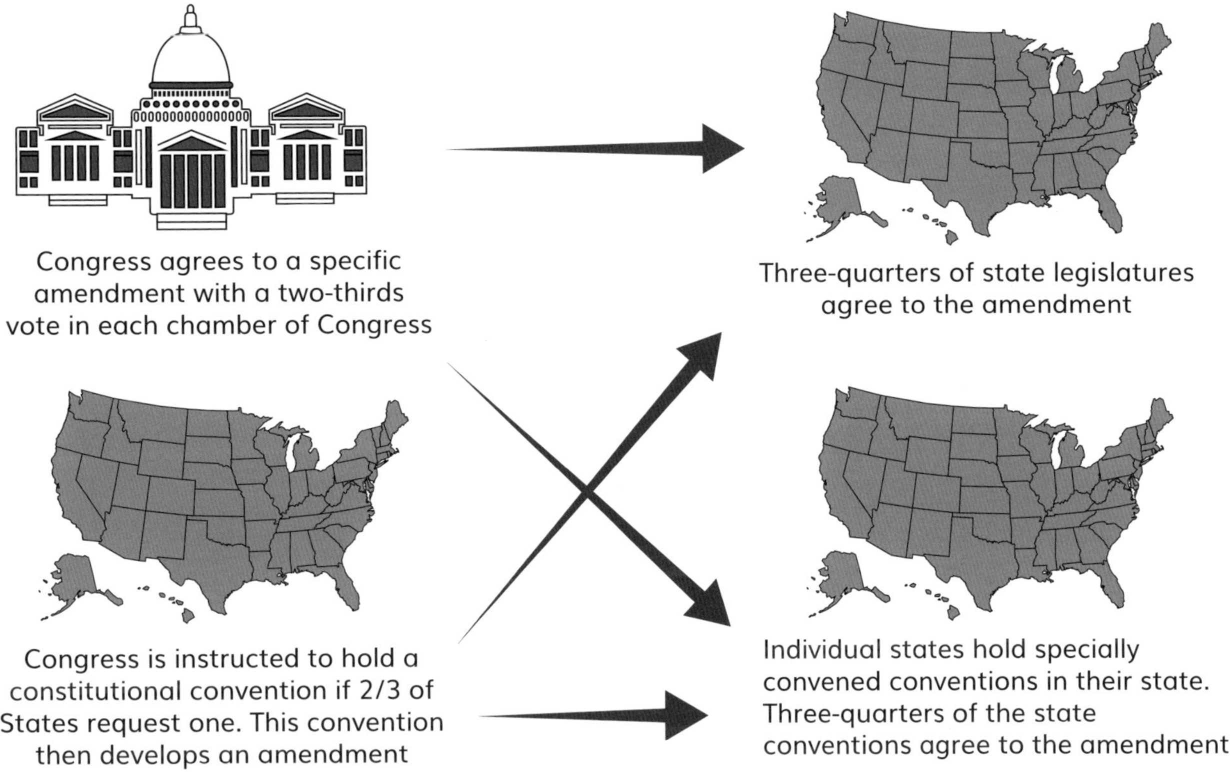

Figure 2.3 **The constitutional amendment process**

Breaking the process down into its component parts, we can see several different barriers to amending the Constitution. Collectively, they work together to ensure that there are very limited chances of success for proposed amendments. These barriers are:

- The requirement for both House and Senate support. The Constitution requires two-thirds of each chamber to accept an amendment. Both the House and Senate may have different priorities, for example due to their two- and six-year terms and the extent to which they are influenced by populist sentiment.
- The requirement for both Federal Government (in this case Congress) and the states to agree. The fact that states must always ratify changes means that the Federal Government cannot impose new practices on the states. This is a major element of a federalist system where regional power is constitutionally protected.
- The particularly high threshold required. The Founding Fathers created a constitution that is highly entrenched, requiring 66.6% plus and 75% plus votes as opposed to 50%.
- Whilst the role of parties is not outlined by the Constitution, the thresholds required for change mean that bipartisan support is almost certainly needed. If there is not some cross-party consensus the Constitution is not going to be changed.

CASE STUDY 2.1: DISTRICT OF COLUMBIA VOTING RIGHTS AMENDMENT

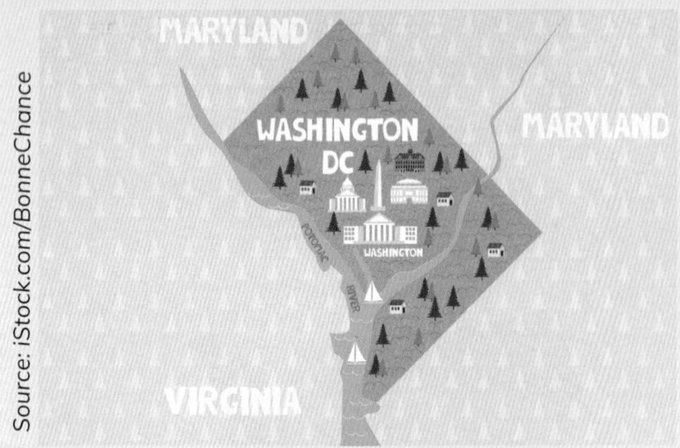

Source: iStock.com/BonneChance

Photo 2.2 **Washington DC map**

Overview

Washington DC, as the capital of the United States, was placed outside the jurisdiction of any single state to prevent giving that state special status. This created a problem; not being a state, the population of DC did not have any opportunity to vote for the president, House or Senate. This was partly overcome by the Twenty-third Amendment, which gave DC three Electoral College votes and the right to participate in presidential elections. There is still no right to vote for congressional candidates, despite having a population of over 700,000 people. This has led many to campaign for a constitutional amendment to give full voting rights to DC. In 2024 the battle for voting rights in DC continues. The latest attempt to make DC into a state was by proposing an Act of Congress not amending the US Constitution itself. This proposed Act of Congress failed to gain enough support in a congressional vote in 2021.

Congress

Democrats in Congress proposed the DC Statehood Act. This would create a new smaller area, the seat of government, containing only government buildings such as the Capitol and the White House. The remainder of the area, where almost all of the 700,000 live, would then become a state. The bill was proposed when the Democrats had a majority in both the House and Senate, but having passed the House, it did not get enough votes to pass the Senate. The two chambers have equal legislative power, and both must agree for a new law to be passed.

The Constitution

Amending the Constitution requires a two-thirds vote in each chamber and therefore a great deal of cross-party support. For this reason, the Democrats attempted to make the change not through a constitutional amendment but through an Act of Congress instead, which requires only a 50% plus vote in each chamber. Some members of Congress, including Democratic Senator Joe Manchin, argued that Congress does not have the authority to make this change through an Act of Congress. If Congress should be successful in passing such an Act, then, the issue might be taken to the Supreme Court. Many commentators feel that the current conservative court is likely to rule that the Constitution does not allow Congress to make such changes via an Act of Congress.

Democracy and parties

The issue of DC statehood may seem like a simple question of democracy. Making this change would allow 700,000 people to vote and create political equality with people across the whole of the United States. The proposal is a highly partisan one, however; Democrats strongly support the plan and Republicans (for example in 2021, unanimously) oppose it. This is because DC is a strong Democrat area. In the 2020 presidential elections Joe Biden received 92% of the vote to President Trump's 5%. Making DC into a state would give Democrats two more Senators and an additional member of the House, increasing their chances of winning elections. As such, Republicans strongly oppose the bill. This suggests that partisan alignment is more important than democratic principle for many members of Congress.

Race and interest groups

DC has one of the highest percentages of racial minority members in general and Black residents in particular of any area of the United States. As such, the lack of voting rights for DC residents is a racial issue. It is unsurprising that the National Association for the Advancement of Colored People (NAACP) and Black Lives Matter (BLM) see the lack of willingness to support statehood for DC as a form of deliberate racial discrimination. Both groups have supported the movement to give voting rights to DC, and BLM, for example, has a section on their website urging voters from across the country to contact their local member of Congress to lobby them on this issue. Both groups see this as an ongoing part of a long history of minority suppression in the area and part of a suppression of minority voting across the United States today. When Black people were given the right to vote in the United States, for example, the area of DC replaced elected officials with three people appointed by the president, thus holding back racial minority representation.

The Senate and Senators

Both chambers must agree to a bill for it to become law. Whilst we can see high levels of partisanship on this issue, Democratic Senator Joe Manchin stands with Republicans in opposition to the plan which is supported by all other Democrats in the Senate. Democratic leaders, including President Joe Biden, do not have sufficient power to pressurise Manchin into accepting this policy. Arguably Manchin is acting more in line with the constituents in his state of West Virginia than acting to support his party. West Virginia is a conservative state and Senator Manchin, in order to maintain his popularity there and retain his seat, often supports conservative or Republican causes.

KEY TOPIC DEBATE: IS THE CURRENT AMENDMENT PROCESS SUITABLE FOR THE UNITED STATES?

There are many arguments in favour of the amendment process:

✓ It prevents abuse of power

The requirement for support from the House, Senate and states, and in particular, the high threshold requiring bipartisan support, prevents one institution or party from changing constitutional rules for their own personal or political interest. This applies to the game of politics where Democrats or Republicans might change the rules to favour their own party, without the requirement for bipartisan support. This can be seen in the United Kingdom where there is no entrenched constitution and domestic law such as tax rates or education policy are changed in the same way as making changes to constitutional principles.

» In 2022 Parliament passed the Elections Act, requiring photo ID when voting. The measure has a disproportionate effect in reducing turnout amongst younger, lower income and racial minority groups who are less likely to have the required ID. These are groups who are significantly less likely to vote Conservative, leading to accusations that the Conservative Party is using its majority in Parliament to fix the electoral process to increase their chances of winning. If registration rules were placed in an entrenched constitution then this move would not be possible without cross-party support.

✓ It protects key principles of US society and the Constitution

Related to the abuse of power, the amendment process can protect important principles, such as state power, representative democracy and the First Amendment right to freedom of speech. By requiring the two-thirds vote, liberal and conservative politicians both need to see the necessity for change. Otherwise, these 'higher' principles should remain intact.

» After the Supreme Court overturned the Flag Protection Act in 1990 there were several attempts in Congress to pass a constitutional amendment to protect the flag. Whilst this passed the two-thirds threshold in the House, it always fell short of the two-thirds needed in the Senate. It appears that the more populist House, with its shorter terms, is more likely to respond to public opinion, whereas the Senate is keener to protect key principles. Whatever the motivation, the principle of free speech was protected in this case.

✓ It creates stability

Frequent constitutional change can lead to uncertainty about the required rules of the political process. If rules continuously change, not only can this cause a lack of awareness of *constitutional* rules, but it can also undermine people's faith in the Constitution. People and politicians may challenge these changes as arbitrary and want to return to previous rules. In addition, if the constitutional amendments are passed with the support of only one party, say the Republicans, then Democrat politicians and their supporters may find it much harder to accept those changes.

» Several attempts have been made to change the Electoral College, including the Every Vote Counts Amendment introduced in Congress in both 2005 and 2009. This amendment would remove state-based voting and the Electoral College and ensure that the winner of the popular vote would always become the president. It failed to get out of committee stage in Congress with no votes being held. Whilst there may be problems with the Electoral College in the United States, maintaining it creates stability and upholds a recognised tradition of the United States.

Here are some of the main criticisms of the amendment process:

! **Exam Tip** – Don't get confused between acts of Congress and amendments to the Constitution. The court can overturn acts of Congress but cannot overturn the Constitution or amendments to it. Most congressional acts are not constitutional in content; they change domestic law such as tax rates, healthcare reform or environmental protection. It is significantly harder to amend the Constitution than to pass a law through Congress.

It is undemocratic

The amendment process is undemocratic as a minority of people are capable of stopping an amendment. Only thirteen states have to be in opposition to block an amendment that may otherwise have overwhelming support. A majority are denied a change they would like to see in their society, thus challenging a fundamental principle of democracy. In addition, entrenchment protects undemocratic elements of the Constitution written in 1787 at a time when modern representative democracy was in its infancy and the public were not always entrusted to make decisions themselves.

» The Flag Protection Amendment was supported by a significant majority of elected politicians in Congress yet failed to pass because it did not reach the threshold requirement. In 2006, it had the support of 286 representatives (previous votes had been above 300) with 130 voting against, clearing the two-thirds requirement, whereas in the Senate the vote was 66–34, falling just one vote short. With over 70% of politicians calling for change the minority view held out and the amendment failed, ignoring the will of a clear majority.

Excessive power of unelected justices

The high bar required to change the US Constitution, along with the vagueness of the document, gives enormous power to the Supreme Court justices who uphold it. They have the scope to interpret the Constitution according to their own views and values often in a way that is criticised as going beyond the meaning of the text. Once the justices have made such decisions then it is virtually impossible for elected politicians to overturn that decision through a constitutional amendment.

» The protection of the right to choose to have an abortion was granted by the Supreme Court in *Roe v Wade* (1973) and then taken away again by *Dobbs v Jackson* (2022) when the Supreme Court overturned the Roe ruling. In both cases Supreme Court justices were accused of delivering rulings based on their own views and not basing their decision on the Constitution. Once justices issue an opinion, it is virtually impossible for elected politicians to overturn the court ruling with a constitutional amendment. The last amendment to overturn a Supreme Court decision was the Twenty-sixth Amendment in 1971, which overturned *Oregon v Mitchell* (1970). Congressional legislation required that all states adopt a voting age of 18 for state and federal elections. Some states, aiming to retain a voting age of 21, challenged this as unconstitutional federal overreach. In *Oregon v Mitchell*, the court had ruled that states were allowed to set voting ages for state and local elections, but this ruling was overturned in by the Twenty-sixth Amendment, which set the voting age at 18 for all elections.

> **Exam Tip** – Remember to apply evidence to a question. Evidence does not speak for itself so you will need to explain what it tells us about a certain question. In this section the Electoral College has been used as evidence on both sides of the debate about the amendment process. This can be a useful technique and shows how the same evidence can be applied to competing arguments. The consideration of one piece of evidence from different perspectives can improve the sophistication of your analysis and evaluation.

An out-of-date constitution

This has two aspects. Firstly, it can be difficult to remove outmoded aspects of the Constitution. Written in 1787, the US Constitution has survived enormous social, economic, cultural and political change with very little alteration of its wording. It is unsurprising therefore that some elements may be seen as inappropriate for a modern society. Many of the values of the Founding Fathers reflected in the Constitution are either impractical or unacceptable today. Secondly as new ideas have developed, especially in terms of civil rights expectations, the Constitution has struggled to keep up.

» The inability to remove the Electoral College has been previously cited as evidence in favour of the amendment process, providing stability and authority to the Constitution and society. The Electoral College, however, can also be seen as an anachronism; an outdated concept that has no place in a modern democracy. The Founding Fathers did not fully trust the public, instead opting to allow voters to choose an Electoral College. This college of 538 people can use their own judgement when selecting the president of the United States. In addition, it might be considered fair to award electoral college votes to a state according to population. The Founding Fathers decided to over-represent small population states when awarding Electoral College votes. These aspects of presidential elections are undemocratic and should not exist today but cannot be removed because the smaller states will not vote to amend this part of the Constitution. In addition, attempts to include the Equal Rights Amendment and gay rights have both failed. Despite its basis in liberal democracy, the United States has still not granted equal legal rights to women in its constitution with an Equal Rights Amendment failing in the 1970s and 1980s.

Source: Tasos Katopodis / Stringer via Getty Images

Photo 2.3 **Former House Speaker Nancy Pelosi speaks at a congressional event to campaign for the Equal Rights Amendment in 2020**

Key Topic Debate Summary: Is the current amendment process suitable for the United States?

FOR	KEY CRITERIA	AGAINST
✓ The amendment process protects key principles of the Constitution. ✓ It ensures that amendments have widespread support and acceptance rather than being based on the views of one group in society. ✓ It is possible to amend the constitution when needed; it is flexible. In addition, the Supreme Court can update it through their interpretations.	Does it have the right balance of ensuring **continuity** but also allowing much-needed **change**?	✗ Entrenchment protects outdated parts of the Constitution, written in 1787, which are undesirable or unacceptable today. ✗ Barriers to changing the Constitution prevent new wording from being added to reflect new needs or values.
✓ The process protects democracy because it entrenches democratic processes such as elections and rights protection, preventing their easy removal. ✓ The requirement for cross-party support promotes democratic outcomes by preventing one party from abusing power and changing the game of politics in their favour.	Does the process provide sufficient **levels of democracy**?	✗ The process is highly undemocratic because proposals with overwhelming support can still fail. ✗ The entrenched nature of the Constitution is protecting undemocratic principles and practices already in the Constitution.
✓ Judges must have the final say to provide enforcement; otherwise politicians would not be restricted by constitutional rules. ✓ Judges have significant power but can ultimately be overturned by politicians with constitutional amendments.	**Politicians versus Judges** – who should decide?	✗ Politicians must have the final say as they are elected. This is a fundamental aspect of representative democracy. ✗ Justices are not neutral and will abuse their power to achieve their own personal ideological goals.

Exam Tip: Improving your AO2 Analysis and AO3 Evaluation

Consider the idea of rights protection and weigh up competing views. Would rights in the United States be better protected with or without an entrenched constitution?

Learning Review

1. How can the US Constitution be amended?
2. What are the different barriers which make it difficult to change the US Constitution?
3. What are the main arguments for the amendment process?
4. What are the main arguments against the amendment process?

KEY FEATURES OF THE US CONSTITUTION

The key features of the US constitution refers to the most important processes or regulations it creates. They are listed in the Edexcel/Pearson specification as:

- Separation of powers
- Checks and balances
- Bipartisanship
- Limited government
- Federalism.

We will deal with the first four features in this section, then address federalism and the wider debate about state protection. These key features, including federalism, can also be used to evaluate the impact of the constitution on US government. These are the features which shape the way in which the US government works or fails to work.

SEPARATION OF POWERS

This principle is deceptively simple but should be seen as one of the most important features of the US Constitution because it affects so much of the workings of US politics.

- The separation of powers might better be described as a separation of personnel between the three main branches of government: the executive, legislature and judiciary. It means that there is no overlap, with people only allowed to operate in one branch at any one time.
- The president cannot be a member of Congress whilst working in the executive branch. The separation of powers means that they are elected separately and that the president cannot exercise patronage power over members of Congress on a regular basis, bringing them in and out of the executive.
- The separation of powers prevents the sort of executive domination of the legislature that occurs in the United Kingdom where no such separation exists (the executive branch is drawn from Parliament and sits in Parliament). This is explored in more detail in Chapter 4, 'The Presidency'.

» Even though Biden was elected president in 2020, he has continued to find it difficult to pass legislation through Congress despite it having a majority of Democrats. President Biden has limited patronage power over the likes of Democrat Senator Joe Manchin, who often votes against Biden priorities, reflecting the wishes of the conservative state of West Virginia, which he represents. In 2012, President Obama was elected to the presidency for a second time, but in the congressional elections of the same day, voters returned a majority of Republicans to the House of Representatives. This could not happen in a parliamentary system where the prime minister is guaranteed a majority of some kind in Parliament.

Spec key term

Checks and balances: A system in which different institutions are set up (such as the president, Congress and Courts) with each having powers to check or restrain the other two. This creates a balance in which all power does not reside with one person or institution.

CHECKS AND BALANCES

Checks and balances are a system in which power is divided between different institutions, each having the ability to provide checks or restraints on each other. What then follows is a balance of power between these institutions in which no one should be excessively dominant.

- It is the separation of powers which allows checks and balances to be effective in the United States. By separating personnel and holding separate elections for president and Congress, the Founding Fathers were then able to award each of the three branches of government specific powers to check the other branches (see Figure 2.4). The result is that it is very difficult for one branch to act independently of another.

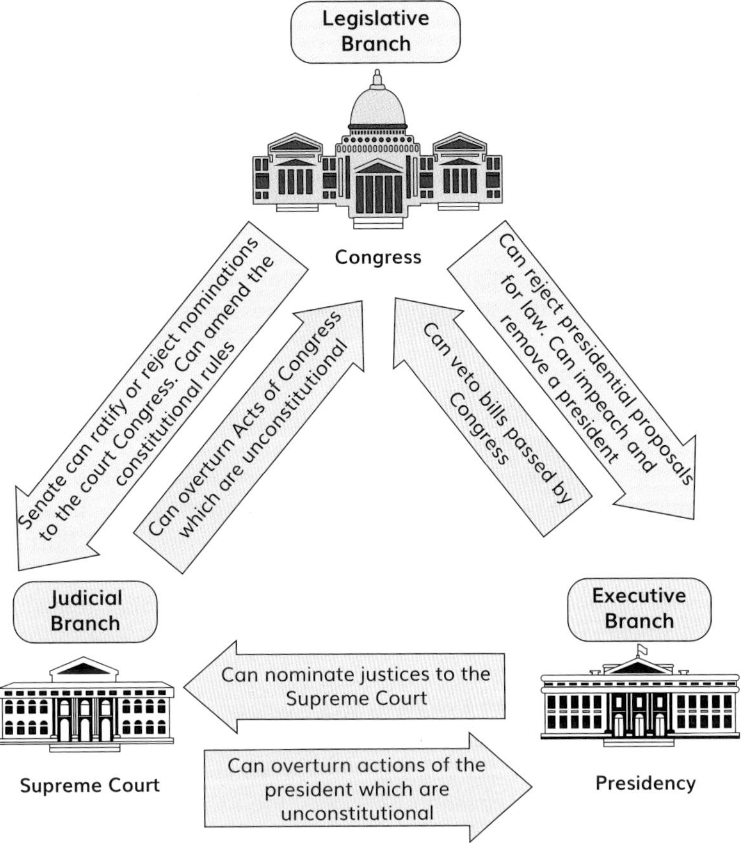

Figure 2.4 **Checks and balances of the US constitution**

- A central concern of the Founding Fathers was to prevent a powerful executive, rejecting the constitutional monarchy of the United Kingdom, where power is centralised in one person.
- Each branch has powers that the other does not possess, ultimately causing power to be shared.

» The separation of powers and checks and balances can be seen in action through the creation of healthcare policy in the United States in recent years. President Obama's healthcare reforms had a stormy passage through Congress. Obama was elected in 2008 on the basis of his proposed healthcare reform, and he had a Democrat majority in both chambers. Despite this, checks from the legislative branch meant that it took over a year to pass the bill and also that Obama was forced to compromise heavily on some of its key principles. Once the bill was enacted, the judicial branch enacted further checks. Although the Supreme Court upheld the main principle of the bill, it removed certain provisions such as the extension of the Medicaid programme. Once Obama lost his majority in both chambers, Republicans in Congress voted to repeal the Act (a check from the legislative branch), a measure which President Obama vetoed (a check from the executive branch in which the president can block a bill passed by Congress).

LIMITED GOVERNMENT

Limited government can be seen as the opposite to a dictatorship. It is one in which the government has restricted power, usually through checks and balances placed on it.

- This is a central principle of liberalism in which government is seen as a major threat to liberty and therefore needs to be curtailed.
- By placing such high levels of checks, especially on the president, the Constitution limits the government's ability to act and potentially limits the freedom of the people. Many of the Founding Fathers saw this as the most important aspect of writing a new constitution, after what they saw as the unjust rule of a powerful British monarch.
- As well as the checks and balances outlined above, limited government is achieved through constitutional rights such as the Bill of Rights and the Fourteenth Amendment. Amendments such as the First Amendment create limited government by ensuring that individuals have freedom from government control of their views and their religion.

Spec key term

Limited government: A government which is restricted in its ability to act as a result of significant constitutional limits to its power.

Bipartisanship: Agreement between the two main parties, for example on a legislative proposal.

Spec key term

Partisanship: This term describes high levels of unity within a political party. It can also describe the way in which politicians in one party consistently disagree with the policy goals of another party.

Exam Tip – It is important to plan your essay before writing. Keep your plan brief, as you will want to maximise time spent writing the essay itself. A brief three- or four-point plan, identifying the three or four mini-debate areas is a useful approach. For many (but not all) essays on the Constitution, three of the **key features** can be used as a three-point plan. If you are asked to evaluate the extent to which the US Constitution is fit for purpose or the extent to which it is democratic, you could take three or four of these key features and evaluate them in turn. There is usually more than one good plan for a question. In this case you could select other aspects of the US Constitution such as entrenchment or the Electoral College to replace some of the ones above.

BIPARTISANSHIP

Although parties are not mentioned in the Constitution there are many constitutional arrangements which strongly encourage and will sometimes even require the two main parties to work together to achieve policy goals. This **bipartisanship** can be seen in the following ways:

- In the constitutional amendment process, which requires two-thirds of each chamber of Congress having to agree to an amendment to the Constitution. Neither party is likely to have such a high majority in Congress.
- The separate elections for president, House and Senate, which mean that divided government is common. In this case, legislative success will require cross-party support. Recent presidents – Biden, Trump, Obama, Bush and Clinton – have all faced a majority from the opposing party in at least one chamber of Congress.

During the Trump presidency, Democrats holding a majority in the House of Representatives after the 2018 mid-term elections consistently prevented the president from achieving his policy goals such as building the border wall between the United States and Mexico. **Partisanship** (or, to put it another way, lack of bipartisanship) prevented Trump from passing the policy; he was unable to gain support from Democrats to achieve a 50% plus vote in the House to pass a bill. Parties have failed to compromise in recent years, leading to a lack of agreement in determining the annual budget for the United States. This has led to federal shutdown in which there is no funding, requiring many federal offices to be closed until the budget is settled. In 2018–19 there was a 35-day shutdown costing the Federal Government an estimated $5 billion.

A full understanding of how checks and balances work will be gained from exploring the three branches of US government (the legislature, the executive and the judiciary) in more detail. You will be able to make an informed evaluation of this key topic debate when you have read more about these three branches in Chapters 3, 4 and 5 covering Congress, the Presidency and the Supreme Court. Across these chapters, you will find lots of different arguments and evidence that suggest that checks and balances are functioning or are not functioning. Here is a useful summary of this key topic debate to help you manage the information you need for this debate.

Key Topic Debate Summary: Are checks and balances in the US Constitution functioning well?

FOR	KEY CRITERIA	AGAINST
✓ Checks between Congress and the president prevent one body from being dominant. Power is shared with presidents being restricted in their legislative agendas. ✓ Policymaking is based on compromise between different institutions and parties. ✓ The president is limited in his or her ability to control international policy given congressional control of military funding, the power to declare war and the Senate power to ratify treaties.	Are checks between the **president and Congress** functioning well?	✗ The imperial presidency theory suggests that checks are ineffective with a largely unrestrained presidency. This is explored in detail in Chapter 4. ✗ Presidents can issue executive orders or executive agreements to achieve legislative goals without the need for congressional approval. ✗ Presidents use their position as commander in chief to determine military action, bypassing Congress altogether.
✓ The Supreme Court, in upholding constitutional rules, effectively checks the president and Congress. ✓ The Supreme Court's power of judicial review allows it to overturn presidential and congressional actions. ✓ The entrenched constitution ensures that politicians cannot easily overturn and therefore ignore checks from the courts.	Does the **Supreme Court** provide the right level of checks and balances?	✗ The Supreme Court fails to provide sufficient levels of checks on the president, especially on foreign policy. ✗ The Supreme Court has become too powerful meaning that checks are excessive. The Supreme Court has become an imperial judiciary which has been willing to stretch the meaning of the Constitution in any way they see fit.

✓ Checks are at the right level, with presidents being forced to compromise but still able to provide leadership. ✓ President, House and Senate can and do agree, allowing much-needed policies to pass into law. ✓ High levels of checks are, in any case, desirable producing limited government as intended by the Founding Fathers.	Do the checks lead to **effective government**	✗ The Founding Fathers created so many checks that government in the United States is ineffective. Presidents are impaired, finding it virtually impossible to carry out policy promises. ✗ These checks come from the House and Senate in particular and have led to gridlock and federal shutdown. ✗ The checks now go beyond the level intended by the Founding Fathers as a result of partisanship in which the Democrats and Republicans refuse to compromise.

Exam Tip: Improving your AO2 Analysis and AO3 Evaluation

To make a strong judgement it is important for you to decide what is the right level of checks and balances. Do you favour a strong government in which elected politicians are largely free to act or do you think that potentially powerful politicians should have lots of restraints placed on them? What should those restraints be?

FEDERALISM

Federalism is a constitutional principle in which power is shared between a central government and regional governments. In the United States the central government is referred to as the Federal Government and the regional governments are known as states. This allows the states to take a great deal of control over affairs, making laws in a wide range of policy areas.

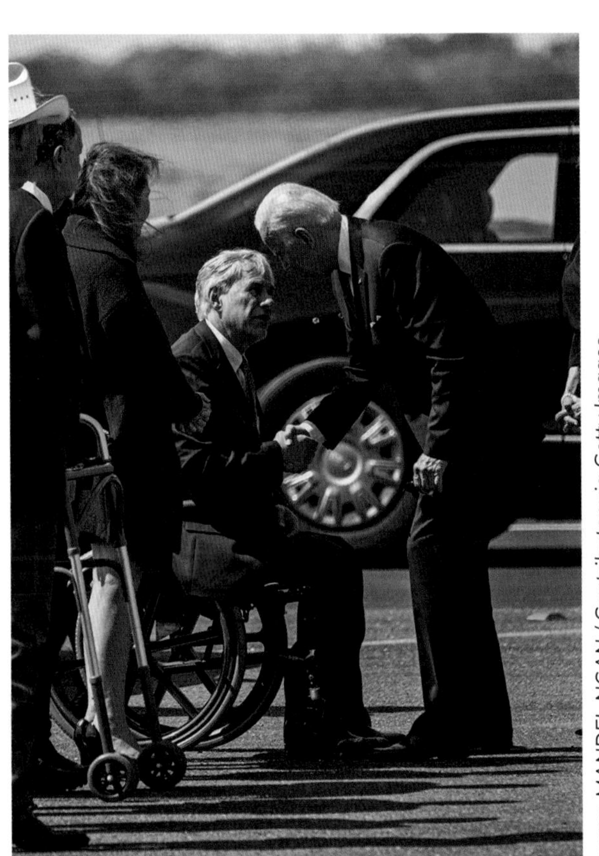

Source: MANDEL NGAN / Contributor via Getty Images

Photo 2.4 **President Biden shakes hands with Texas Governor Greg Abbott in 2022**

Within the federal system each state has its own political system with an executive, legislature and judiciary to propose, make and interpret the laws of each state. Most states have a political arrangement similar to that of the US national system of government, so you can think of each state as being a smaller version of the US system as a whole. Instead of a president, states have an elected governor as well as a state legislature and state Supreme Court. Some laws are made by the Federal Government for the whole United States and some are made by state government including a great deal of education policy, healthcare and criminal laws. In the United States, the states have huge power to make their own policies and laws. For example, each state has its own laws on drugs, traffic regulations and marriage, and states even set their own tax rates, including income tax.

Federalism can be better understood by comparing and contrasting it with devolution, which is practised in the United Kingdom (see Table 2.3).

Table 2.3 Similarities and differences between federalism and devolution

Similarities	
Power is shared between central and regional governments. Regional governments can have extensive law-making power, allowing them to take control of policy.	
Differences	
Federalism	**Devolution**
Regional power is guaranteed by the Constitution. The Federal Government cannot reduce the power of states without their support. In this sense sovereignty is shared between central and regional government.	Regional power is given by the central government. The central government can use legal powers to reduce or remove power of regions whenever they wish to. In the United Kingdom, parliamentary sovereignty means Parliament alone can determine regional power levels.
All regions are given the same level of law-making power. For example, either they can all set income tax rates or none of them can.	Regions can have different levels of power. In the United Kingdom, Scotland has more power than Wales, and England has no devolution and therefore no control over its own affairs.

The nature of the federal system and its relationship with the states

Spec key term

Federalism: The sharing of power between a central government and regional governments in which regions have their power guaranteed by the Constitution.

Federalism is one of the most important aspects of the US Constitution and shapes political activity and the daily life of US citizens today. As we saw at the start of the chapter, the United States originated with thirteen colonies with varied languages, cultures, identities and other interests, fearing an over-powerful government. Given this, it might be surprising that they agreed to join a single union and give up the autonomy they held as colonies. It is federalism, as the protector of state power, which encouraged them to take the advantages of a union whilst balancing this with the desire for self-determination.

Federalism has evolved enormously throughout the course of US history. Initially states had far more control over policymaking than the Federal Government. Over time, with the growth of transport systems, developments in media and the establishment of stronger national and international trade, the Federal Government has taken on more responsibilities and replaced the states as the dominant force in the everyday life of its citizens. All this change has taken place with virtually no relevant changes to the US Constitution. The vagueness of the Constitution has been used (or abused depending on your viewpoint) to allow the Federal Government to assume more power.

As a result of this growth there has been an ongoing debate about the legitimate role of the Federal Government, with many critics arguing that it has become excessively powerful. Supporters of the extended role of the Federal Government will argue that it has become essential to have greater federal controls given the creation of a national economy and that the Federal Government provides much-needed programmes and regulations.

Does the United States remain federal today?

The rest of this section examines the constitutional protections held by states, how Federal Government dominates the states and the level of power that states have today.

KEY TOPIC DEBATE: DOES THE US CONSTITUTION PROVIDE SIGNIFICANT PROTECTION OF STATE POWER?

How state power is protected

There are a number of key constitutional provisions that allow states to hold on to high levels of power.

Article 1 and Article 4

The Constitution gives states power to make and carry out their own laws according to Article 4. In addition, state power is protected through the idea of denied powers. Congress is only given the power to carry out the duties listed in Article 1. This creates the assumption that states will typically control policy areas such as health, education, and law and order policy.

» This can be seen in the major differences in state law regarding marijuana. In some states it is illegal to use marijuana under any circumstances whereas in other states it has become decriminalised, with some state allowing it to be sold publicly by licensed sellers. The diversity of state policy can be seen in Map 2.2. In 2021, Connecticut, Mississippi, New Mexico and New York were added to the list of states that legalised the use of recreational cannabis.

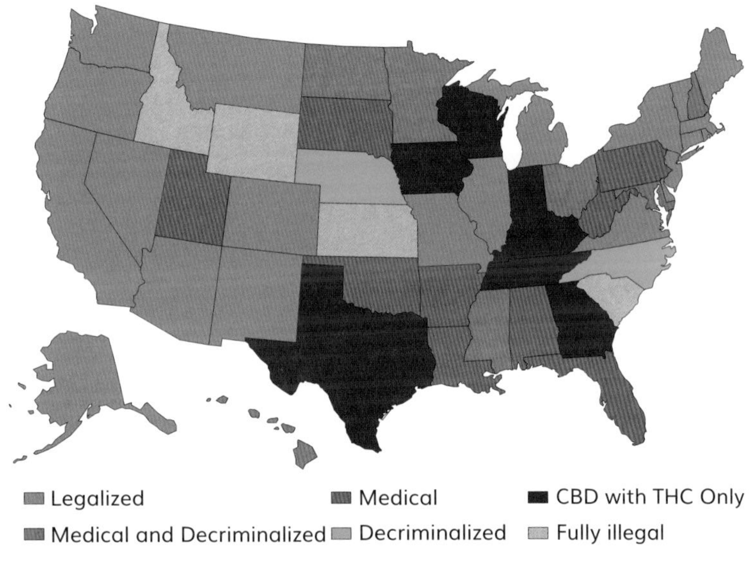

Map 2.2 **Marijuana regulations in US states**

Source: https://disa.com.

Tenth Amendment (reserved powers amendment)

The Tenth Amendment, or the **reserved powers amendment**, awards all powers that are not assigned to the Federal Government to the states. This therefore limits the powers of the Federal Government (as it only possesses powers delegated to it by the states or the people) while providing the states with tremendous scope to run their own affairs. Most importantly it has been used by states to protect themselves against new policies imposed on the states by the Federal Government, especially via congressional laws. States are sensitive to having power imposed upon them and often challenge the Federal Government in the Supreme Court, which can act to limit federal power.

» A notable example of this is the federal gun regulation created by the Brady Act of 1993. The Act required all states to perform background checks on anyone purchasing a gun. The Supreme Court, in a 5–4 decision, rejected the Federal Government's argument that this was a federal power under the necessary and proper clause and instead ruled that the Act violated the Tenth Amendment, reserved powers of the states.

> **Definition**
>
> **Reserved powers amendment:** The reserved powers amendment (the Tenth Amendment) states that any power not enumerated in the Constitution as a federal power should be assumed to be a state power.

The Commerce Clause (Article I, Section 8)

This permits the Federal Government to regulate commerce between states and with other countries. This means that the power of states to regulate business and trade *within* each state (intra-state commerce) is protected from federal intervention. As such, states have diverse business policies, including taxation, where states can set their own income tax (federal income tax also exists) and sales tax (a tax paid when purchasing goods). Whilst several states such as Alaska and Washington impose no state income tax, California typically has the highest figure, with high-income earners paying more than 12% on top of their federal income tax.

» A turning point for state protection came in 1995 in the case of *US v Lopez*. After years of rulings that favoured the Federal Government, this one overturned a national law, the Gun Free School Zones Act, which banned the possession of guns within 1,000 feet of a school premises. The Federal Government argued that this was justifiable under the commerce clause by stating that guns interfered with educational standards and therefore had an impact on qualifications for the workplace, in turn affecting inter-state commerce. This was seen by many as another example of the strained justification of the extension of federal power. The majority on the court agreed, stating that gun possession near schools was not about commercial relationships.

✓ **Amendment process**

The Constitution can only be amended with the agreement of three-quarters of the states ensuring that the powers granted to them by the Constitution are guaranteed. The fact that a super-majority is required makes this protection particularly strong, allowing states to feel confident that the Federal Government cannot remove key state powers. The super-majority acts as a deterrent and means that the Federal Government is unlikely to even propose amendments that restrict state control.

» As we saw earlier in the chapter attempts to reform the Electoral College have failed partly because the current system for electing the president over-represents small states, therefore working to their benefit.

How state power is restricted

✗ **Federal mandates**

A federal mandate is a law issued by the Federal Government that compels the states to act in a certain way. They restrict the states' ability to make their own laws creating a federal standard. There has been a major increase in both the number and scope of federal mandates since Roosevelt's New Deal. They form part of the notion of coercive federalism, which holds that the Federal Government has increased its power and has gained a far greater share of power in relation to the states. Whilst they can be challenged by states in the Supreme Court, the Federal Government has survived legal action in many cases, meaning that state control is significantly more limited today than it was one hundred years ago.

Spec key term

Federal mandates: Laws passed by the Federal Government, usually in the form of congressional acts, which impose a policy requirement on states.

» Historically, there have been a number of major federal mandates, such as the Civil Rights Act 1964, which, in seeking to remove racist practices, imposed on states a wide range of requirements in housing, business, education and voting. All states are required to comply with all aspect of this Act in policymaking in these areas. President Obama's Affordable Care Act 2009 is another example of a federal mandate, imposing healthcare policy on states and restricting their ability to adopt their own approaches.

» In 2021 President Biden delivered an executive order to stop the issuing of permits for gas and coal extraction on any public land. This restricted the ability of states to pursue their own energy policy, with fourteen states threatening to challenge this in the courts.

✗ **Fiscal control**

The Federal Government can constrain the states through financial means. The Federal Government now has enormous economic power and provides ample funding for states, which they have come to rely on. The Federal Government can issue grants to the states with certain conditions attached. Equally, funding can be withheld if states do not meet the set conditions.

» In 2021 the $1.9 trillion budget passed by Congress, the American Rescue Plan, directed funding to the employment of frontline health workers, the delivery of vaccines and other COVID-19 relief work. Twenty-one states have complained that this restricts their ability to control their own tax policy because of a clause which states that this money cannot be used to directly or indirectly reduce the tax revenue of a state. States such as Arkansas and Wyoming have argued that taking the much-needed money would limit their control over their own economic policy. Obama employed a similar method; he pursued his policy of enforcing transgender bathrooms in schools by threatening to withhold education funding for any state which did not comply.

The Supreme Court

The Supreme Court, through its interpretation of the ambiguous Constitution, is in a strong position to determine the levels of protection of state power. It can use judicial review either to protect or to undermine the states. Since the 1930s and the New Deal, justices have tended to side with the Federal Government. The Commerce Clause in particular has become a successful route for the Federal Government to justify major expansion of its power in business and trade. States lost every single Commerce Clause case from 1937 to the Lopez case in 1995, marking a major expansion of federal power during this period.

- In *Wickard v Filburn* (1947) the Supreme Court upheld Congress' power to impose a wheat production quota, limiting how much wheat a farmer could produce. The Supreme Court asserted that the collective impact of individual farming practices could affect the national price of wheat, therefore federal regulation was allowed under the Commerce Clause. This clause has also been successfully used by the Federal Government to ban homegrown cannabis used for medical purposes even when states want to allow this. Using similar arguments to the Wickard case, the federal government defended their policy in *Gonzales v Raich* (2002). They were able to convince the court that this law could affect the national trade in cannabis even though it is largely illegal and thus affected the US economy as a whole.
- Since the 1995 Lopez case, the court has been more willing to restrain the Federal Government. It did this, for example, in the *Shelby v Holder* case, which undermined central provisions of the Voting Rights Act of 1965. The impact of this ruling has been to give states much greater control over voting, including voter registration rules. For example, in 2021, Texas used this additional control to impose rules that restrict the hours of voting and also ban extending voting hours if there are queues of people still waiting to vote. You can see more details in the Texas case study. These more recent rulings, however, do not offset the major expansion of federal power since the 1930s, and many of these mandates remain in place.

Key Topic Debate Summary: Does the US constitution provide significant protection of state power?

FOR	KEY CRITERIA	AGAINST
✓ The Tenth Amendment and the Article 1 protect state power and forbid Congress from going beyond its enumerated powers. ✓ The amendment process is the ultimate protection ensuring that state power cannot be unilaterally reduced by the Federal Government. ✓ The Commerce Clause limits the power of the Federal Government as it can only regulate inter-state commerce.	Can the US Constitution protect states against **federal mandates?**	✗ Federal mandates have developed extensively giving the Federal Government significant control of policy. ✗ Any reversals in federal mandates in recent years have been limited and do not offset the major gains in federal power since the 1930s. ✗ The Commerce Clause and necessary and proper clauses are particularly vague and have allowed an expansion of federal control of business and economic matters.
✓ States raise the majority of their own revenue and have a great deal of control over how they spend their own money. ✓ States can and have refused federal funding, especially when this funding comes with policy conditions imposed by the Federal Government.	Can the US Constitution protect states against the **financial power of the Federal Government?**	✗ The Federal Government is in a superior economic position and can use this to provide aid in which states then carry out federal policy priorities. ✗ The Federal Government can impose conditions of aid and threaten the withdrawal of funds if states do not comply with federal demands.

✓ The Supreme Court has used its power to strike down federal laws specifically because they restrict state power under the Tenth Amendment or the Commerce Clause. ✓ The Supreme Court has been more aggressive in recent years in protecting state power. ✓ In some areas federal regulations have been undermined such as the federal protection of voting rights.	Does the **Supreme Court** provide significant protection?	✗ The Supreme Court has allowed a major expansion of federal power especially between 1930 and 1992. ✗ In recent years the Supreme Court has upheld federal mandates such as the Affordable Care Act. ✗ The Supreme Court itself has imposed new federal standards on the states with interpretive amendments limiting state control of their own policies. The guarantees of abortion rights and gay marriage are two strong examples in the cases of Roe and Obergefell.

Exam Tip: Improving your AO2 Analysis and AO3 Evaluation

Consider what is meant by the word 'significant' here. As ever, focusing on the keyword of a question helps to sharpen your evaluation. Examine the way in which recent presidential appointments to the court have led to changes in protection of state power. Has the majority created by Trump and Biden been more or less likely to protect state power?

CASE STUDY 2.2: THE STATE OF TEXAS

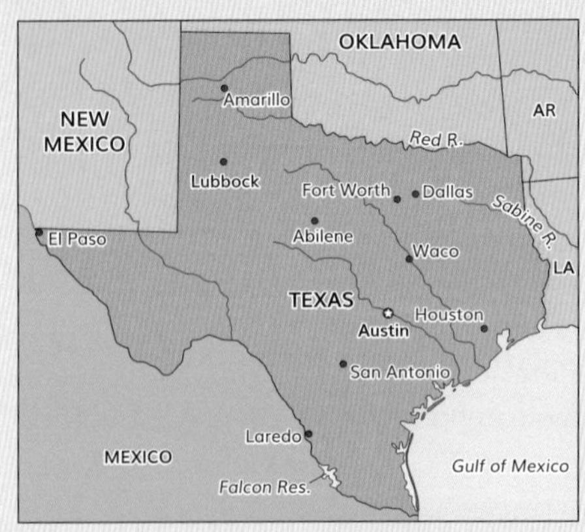

Map 2.3 **The State of Texas**

Overview

The Texas Legislature, based in the capital city of Austin (see Map 2.3), is a bicameral body composed of a 31-member Senate and a 150-member House of Representatives. The Republic of Texas became part of the United States in 1842. The gross state product was $1.9 trillion in recent years, the second highest in the United States, making its economy bigger than the gross domestic product (GDP) of Brazil, Canada, Russia, South Korea and Spain. In 2024, the Supreme Court ruled that the Federal Government had the power to remove razor wire which had been placed along the border with Mexico by the Texas Military Department. This angered Texas Governor, Greg Abbott as he continued to criticise Biden over immigration control. Texas offers a good example of how the Federal Government and specific states are often involved in significant conflict regarding policy goals and who should control such policy.

Executive orders and federal mandates

In 2021 President Biden issued a series of environmental executive orders such as preventing public land from being used for new gas and oil extraction and cutting subsidies to oil and gas production. Governor Abbott has seen this as an attack on the industry of his state and has issued his own executive orders to promote gas and oil, including a law that would prevent a ban on gas powered appliances. Biden's executive orders show how the president can limit state power by imposing policies in the form of national standards.

Immigration and race

Texas politicians have resisted Biden's more liberal immigration policy, including ending the agreement in which all detained illegal immigrants crossing to the United States from South and Central America would be detained in Mexico not the United States. The State of Texas is affected by national immigration policy and Governor Abbott has said that he does not want Texas resources to have to be used to deal with Biden's more liberal stance. For example, in 2021 Abbott ordered the closure of centres housing unaccompanied minors who had crossed the border illegally, setting up a dispute between Texas and the federal Department of Homeland Security (DHS). This demonstrates the way in which the Federal Government may attempt to impose policy on a state but also how the state may have some degree of policy control.

Political parties

Dominated by the Republicans in recent years, the State of Texas has been in considerable conflict with the Democrat administrations, with significant policy differences between Republican Governor Abbott and Democrat President Biden. In 2021 Abbott signed bills restricting the teaching of critical race theory. Kimberlé Williams Crenshaw, a law professor at University of California, Los Angeles defines, critical race theory as an academic or analytical method 'that takes the lived experience of racism seriously, using history and social reality to explain how racism operates in American law and culture, toward the end of eliminating the harmful effects of racism' (quoted in https://www.nytimes.com/article/what-is-critical-race-theory.html). Abbott also proposed laws to allow the carrying of handguns without a licence and ordered a special session of the state legislature to create further laws to restrict access to voting. Biden attacked the latter move as 'part of an assault on democracy that we've seen far too often this year – and often disproportionately targeting Black and Brown Americans' (quoted in https://www.politico.com/news/2021/05/29/biden-texas-voting-restrictions-491415). The nature of party control affected the relationship between the Federal Government and a state; in this case Texas, led by Republicans, is at odds with a Federal Government led by a Democrat president.

Supreme Court

In 2016 Texas blocked one of Obama's main immigration policies by successfully challenging it in the Supreme Court. Obama issued an executive order creating the Deferred Action for Parents of Americans (DAPA) programme. This would stop the deportation of illegal immigrants who have children who are US citizens or lawful residents of the United States. The Supreme Court blocked the programme, siding with a lower court decision which stated that the president did not have the authority to carry out this policy. This shows how states can use the Constitution to protect their ability to pursue their own policy goals. The State of Texas has appeared before the court many times and has sometime lost cases which overturned specific policies.

Federal–state financial conflict

The State of Texas raises over $250 billion every year, mainly through taxes, but it still relies on the Federal Government, which provides around $40 billion per year in grants to the state. In 2021 the $1.9 trillion budget passed by Congress, called the American Rescue Plan, gave billions of dollars in federal aid, but Texas refused the money because they argued that this limited their control over economic policy. A clause in the American Rescue Plan prevented states from using the aid to cut tax revenue. Texas has refused federal aid before, for example refusing further Medicaid (subsidised healthcare for over 65s) funding from the Federal Government, allowing it to pursue its own more conservative policies. States generate a huge amount of their own revenue, giving them a great deal of financial autonomy from the Federal Government. Having said that, whilst they can turn down federal funding which comes with policy conditions, states need some money from the huge resources of the Federal Government if they are to be able to govern effectively.

Learning Review

1. What are the main features of federalism?
2. What are the main ways in which state power is protected?
3. What are the main ways in which state power is limited?
4. What evidence can be used from the Texas case study to provide evidence for the three questions above?

Comparative Learning Review

1. What are the similarities between federalism in the United States and devolution in the United Kingdom?
2. What are the similarities between federalism in the United States and devolution in the United Kingdom?

THE US CONSTITUTION AND DEMOCRACY

Source: GREGG NEWTON / Contributor via Getty Images

Photo 2.5 **People queue to vote in the 2022 mid-term elections in Florida**

Whilst we might judge the US Constitution based on the extent to which it promotes democracy, we must remember that this was not the prime motivation of the authors of the Constitution. Many of the Founding Fathers were not only suspicious of giving too much power to the general public but also more preoccupied with creating checks and balances to prevent any one person, group or interest from becoming dominant. Whilst checks and balances may prevent tyranny, which is antithetical to democracy, it does not necessarily guarantee democracy. The US Constitution has been particularly criticised for its lack of democracy in the following areas:

- The Electoral College, especially its ability to allow a candidate to win the election without securing the most popular votes
- The Senate with two senators per state, over-representing small states
- The amendment process which prevents the majority from achieving reforms they feel strongly about
- The power of the Supreme Court, an unelected body that uses considerable bias, often overturning the policies of elected politicians
- In addition, the Constitution can be criticised for what is fails to tackle, such as the influence of corporations and money over elections and politicians, as well as allowing partisan gerrymandering for House elections.

KEY TOPIC DEBATE: DOES THE US CONSTITUTION PROMOTE DEMOCRACY?

Provision of elections

✓ The US Constitution creates representative democracy through frequent elections. In addition, there are three federal institutions that are each elected separately. Arguably this provides very high levels of representation as voters have significant choice. The short, two-year term limit of the House makes members of the lower chamber particularly sensitive to public opinion. Furthermore, the separation of powers means that elected members of Congress are not beholden to the president who has a separate mandate and limited patronage power. Members of Congress are more sensitive to public opinion than they are to the wishes of the president.

» The mid-term elections of 2022 allowed voters to choose new members of Congress and ensure that politicians responded to public opinion. Republicans took control of the House gaining a small majority. Democrat members such as Representative Alexandria Ocasio Cortez have been able to respond to constituency views regardless of the wishes of President Biden. Cortez has sometimes voted against Biden's measures on health and the environment because, she argues, they do not go far enough in protecting the interests of her constituents.

✖ On the other hand, the Electoral College, established by the Constitution, is democratically flawed. Not only is it based on a reluctance to create democracy, creating a College to decide who the president will be, it can create results where the winning candidate takes their place in the White House whilst receiving fewer votes than their opponent. The process for electing senators can also be seen as undemocratic with each state having two senators regardless of population. There are also major concerns about the use of first past the post for congressional elections given the issues created with safe seats and lack of voter choice. The Constitution does not impose this voting method but does allow states to choose whichever election process they wish.

» In both 2000 and 2016, George W. Bush and Donald Trump, respectively, achieved fewer votes from the public than their main rival for the presidency; Hillary Clinton received 2.8 million votes more than President Trump.

Rights protection

✔ The US Constitution places a high premium on the protection of rights. This can be seen as a central tenet of the establishment of a liberal democracy based on limited government. Rights are fundamental freedoms that give power to the people and prevent the government from removing this power. The First Amendment, freedom of expression, is critical to a free society where people can exercise control and challenge government policy. In addition, other rights such as the Fourteenth Amendment prevent the government from discriminating against people, treating all people equally regardless of race.

» A huge number of court cases have protected rights, including *Brown v Board of Education* (1953) (protecting racial equality by declaring separate facilities unconstitutional) and *Eichmann v United States* (1990) (which upheld freedom of expression, overturning a law protecting the US flag from defacement).

✖ Arguably, the Constitution has a poor track record when it comes to protecting rights. Despite the Fourteenth Amendment and voting rights, there are major concerns about the ability of people to vote in the United States, with many states creating laws that limit access to voting and have a disproportionately negative effect on racial minorities. In addition, the Constitution has failed to prevent undemocratic or less democratic practices. It is silent on the voting method each state should use to elect member of the House or to award Electoral College seats, yet all states use a winner-takes-all system, which creates safe seats and restricts voter choice to the two main parties. It has also failed to prevent partisan gerrymandering in which the party which dominates state elections can fix electoral boundaries to their advantage.

» According to the Sentencing Project, African Americans are 3.7 times more likely to be disenfranchised by felony voting restrictions than non-African Americans. Over 6.2% of the adult African American population is disenfranchised compared to 1.7% of the non-African American population.

Checks and balances

✔ A major aspect of the US Constitution is the provision of checks and balances. These checks can be helpful to democracy by preventing the concentration and abuse of power. A democracy provides government for the people, and checks can prevent leaders from working in their own interests rather than that of the public.

Checks and balances are also useful in allowing the consideration of different interests. In this sense, the US Constitution will encourage pluralist democracy rather than majoritarian democracy. Decisions must be made based on compromise rather than simply reflecting the will of the majority.

» In 2022 President Biden was forced to accept different viewpoints in US society regarding COVID-19 and individual freedoms. The National Defense Authorisation Act reflected a compromise of different perspectives, arguably maximising representation. It included a provision, demanded by many Republicans, to remove a mandate that required members of the armed forces to be vaccinated against COVID-19. An amendment to reinstate those who have been removed from the armed forces as a result of failure to have a vaccine, however, failed to pass.

✖ On the other hand, checks and balances can be seen as detrimental to democracy because they can prevent elected politicians from delivering their policy promises. An elected president is often thwarted by opposition in Congress. Whilst it is not the Constitution that is directly to blame, the rise in partisanship has made the United States less able to promote representative democracy in which politicians carry out the will of the people. The high level of checks makes it relatively easy for one party to block the policy goals of another. As such the Constitution is set up to create limited government more than allowing people to get what they have voted for.

» President Biden was elected in part because of the failure of President Trump to tackle the COVID-19 crisis. Opinion polls strongly suggest that Biden was seen as much stronger on this issue with a strong desire to have more government involvement. Despite this apparent mandate, in 2022 Republicans used their power in the Senate to add amendments to the National Defense Authorisation Act that undermined his COVID-19 regulations in relation to military personnel in 2022.

Key Topic Debate Summary: Does the US constitution promote democracy?

FOR	KEY CRITERIA	AGAINST
✓ The Constitution creates representative democracy through frequent elections. ✓ Three federal institutions are each elected separately providing voters with significant choice. ✓ The separation of powers means that elected members of Congress are more sensitive to public opinion than they are to the wishes of the president.	Does the US constitution **promote free and fair elections?**	✗ The Electoral College removes direct control from voters and can create results where the candidate with most public votes does not become president. ✗ Each state has two senators regardless of population. ✗ The use of first-past-the-post voting for congressional elections given the issues created with safe seats and lack of voter choice.
✓ The Constitution places a high premium on the protection of rights. ✓ The First Amendment, freedom of expression, is critical to a free society where people can exercise control and challenge government policy. ✓ Other rights such as the Fourteenth Amendment prevent the government from discriminating against people, treating all people equally regardless of race.	Does the US constitution **promote human rights?**	✗ The Constitution has a poor track record when it comes to protecting rights. ✗ Despite the Fourteenth Amendment and voting rights, there are major concerns about the ability of people to vote in the United States. ✗ The Constitution has failed to prevent undemocratic or less democratic practices. It has failed to prevent partisan gerrymandering in which the party which dominates state elections can fix electoral boundaries to their advantage.

✓ For	Debate	✗ Against
✓ Checks and balances preventing the concentration and abuse of power. ✓ Checks can prevent leaders from working in their own interests rather than that of the public. ✓ Checks and balances are also useful in allowing the consideration of different interests. Decisions must be made on the basis of compromise.	Does the US Constitution provide **democratic checks and balances?**	✗ Checks and balances can be seen as detrimental to democracy because they can prevent elected politicians from delivering their policy promises. ✗ The rise in partisanship has made the Constitution less able to promote representative democracy in which politicians carry out the will of the people. ✗ The Constitution is set up to create limited government more than allowing people to get what they have voted for.

Exam Tip: Improving your AO2 Analysis and AO3 Evaluation

Consider what is meant by the word 'democracy'. It is important that you apply the meaning of the word democracy to the theory and evidence you put forward. How does your theory or evidence show *how the power of the people is being increased or decreased* by the US Constitution? There are different types of democracy – how might your evaluation change if we consider this from the perspective of both pluralist and majoritarian democracy?

Evaluative view:

The US Constitution undoubtedly promotes a great deal of democracy but overall this level is not sufficiently acceptable. If we value a majoritarian democracy in which the majority gets what they want, then the US Constitution does not appear to be particularly effective at promoting democracy. The US Constitution is more focused on the provision of checks and balances and rights protection – protecting the individual from powerful government – than allowing the public to elect a government and see it deliver its mandate. US democracy is characterised by limited government but is insufficient in allowing voters to choose the policy and politicians they want to see in office and having those politicians successfully deliver the policy wishes of the people. The inability of recent presidents such as Trump and Obama to carry out their main electoral policy promises shows that US democracy is flawed.

Consider the key topic debate and debate summary as well as any new evidence you can find. Do you agree or disagree with this evaluative view?

STRENGTHS AND WEAKNESSES

As we reach the end of this chapter considering the strengths and weaknesses of the US Constitution is a useful way of reflecting on the chapter as a whole.

Considering strengths and weaknesses to evaluate a constitution is a difficult task. The first step must be to develop an evaluative framework: what criteria should we use to judge the suitability of a constitution? One way of dealing with this is to consider the intentions of the Founding Fathers. What were they trying to achieve and does this reflect constitutional practice today? Some may reject this approach because it is based on the outdated values of the Founding Fathers. Instead, we could examine the strengths by asking what purpose we think a constitution should have. A constitution should obviously set out guidelines for political practice and create procedures to ensure that its rules are followed. We might expect a modern constitution to promote democracy, for example, as discussed above.

Whatever our approach, it must take into account the realities of the United States today. As such we can use a mixture of our own ideal theory as well as considering the specific requirement of the United States. Here is a potential checklist which you could use to create an evaluative framework:

REPRESENTATION

We considered the extent to which the US Constitution promotes representation in the 'Democracy' section above.

CHECKS AND BALANCES AND EFFECTIVE GOVERNMENT

The Founding Fathers valued checks and balances but did they get the balance right between such checks and effective government? This was reviewed in the 'Checks and balances' section above on page 35. The Congress chapter also deals with this when it examines legislative gridlock and federal shutdown.

STATE RIGHTS

We cannot deny the history and importance of federalism in the United States, and we examined the extent of state protection in the 'Federalism' section above. Has the US Constitution created a desirable power split between the two levels of government?

HUMAN RIGHTS

The bill of rights and Fourteenth Amendment as well as the sovereign entrenched Constitution do a great deal to ensure that rights are well protected. Does the Constitution do enough to protect rights in the United States? This is addressed further in Chapter 5, 'The Supreme Court and Civil Rights'.

Learning Review

1. What are the main ways in which the US Constitution promotes democracy?
2. What are the ways in which the US Constitution undermines democracy?
3. What are the main strengths of the US Constitution?
4. What are the main weaknesses of the US Constitution?

Chapter Summary

- ✓ The US Constitution contains seven original articles and only twenty-seven amendments.
- ✓ Despite being codified the short length of the US Constitution means that its meaning is often vague.
- ✓ The US Constitution sets out three main branches of government – the executive, legislature and judiciary – and one of the main aims of the Founding Father was to create extensive checks and balances among them.
- ✓ The US Constitution is entrenched with the requirement for amendments to have the support of two-thirds of each chamber of Congress plus three-quarter of the states, making it virtually impossible to amend.
- ✓ As well as checks and balances other key features are the separation of powers, limited government and bipartisanship. The separation of powers is critical to the working of the US Constitution, with the separation of personnel in the executive, legislature and judiciary.
- ✓ The US constitution is also based on federalism in which power is shared between federal and state government with regional power being constitutionally protected.
- ✓ The US Constitution was not primarily intended to generate democracy but has a number of democratic strengths and weaknesses.

Exam Style Questions

- **Evaluate the view that it should be made significantly easier to amend the US Constitution. (30 marks)**
- **Evaluate the view that the US Constitution ensures that no one branch of government can dominate US politics. (30 marks)**
- **Evaluate the view that the US Constitution does not effectively protect state power. (30 marks)**
- **Evaluate the view that the US Constitution fails to provide sufficient levels of democracy. (30 marks)**
- **Evaluate the view that the main features of the US Constitution are no longer desirable in the modern United States. (30 marks)**

Further Resources

Bodenhamer, David J. (2018) *The U.S. Constitution: A Very Short Introduction* (Oxford: Oxford University Press).

Drakeman, Donald (2021) *The Hollow Core of Constitutional Theory* (Cambridge: Cambridge University Press).

You can find a copy of the full text of the United States Constitution at the National Constitution Center. Available at https://constitutioncenter.org/interactive-constitution/full-text (accessed 22 July 2023).

The Constitution Center website will allow you to explore different aspect of the US Constitution in more detail. Available at https://constitutioncenter.org/ (accessed 22 July 2023).

The Atlantic presents a useful critique of the US Constitution today. Sanford Levinson, 'The Constitution Is the Crisis', 1 October 2019. Available at https://www.theatlantic.com/ideas/archive/2019/10/the-constitution-is-the-crisis/598435/ (accessed 22 July 2023).

Visit https://bloomsbury.pub/colclough-essentials-us to access additional materials to support teaching and learning.

3 CONGRESS

Chapter Preview

Congress is the legislative branch of the US, the equivalent of Parliament in the United Kingdom. It has similar roles to Parliament including the power to legislate (to pass laws), to represent the American public and to provide checks on the executive branch.

A major part of this topic requires you to understand and evaluate these three roles. You will also need to understand what the US Constitution says about the role of Congress. As well as examining Congress as a whole, you will explore the structure of Congress to see where power lies within it. The most obvious aspect of this is that Congress is divided into two branches, The House of Representatives and the Senate.

Congress can be considered the most powerful institution in the United States and significantly more powerful than the UK legislative branch, Parliament. Key to understanding Congress is to appreciate the concept of the separation of powers and how this affects its role and political impact. In the United Kingdom the fusion of powers between executive (government) and legislature (Parliament) tends to mean that a government can dominate Parliament using its majority of seats and prime ministerial patronage over MPs. In the United States, separation of powers and separate elections for the president and Congress restricts the ability of the president to dominate Congress. Congress tends not to be a submissive or reactive body but is a powerful driving force in American politics and the daily lives of Americans. Presidents often find themselves thwarted by its considerable power.

Key Questions and Debates

- What are the main roles of Congress and how well does it perform them?
- What are the main differences between the House and the Senate?
- What are the constitutional roles and powers of Congress?
- How is Congress organised and where does power lie within Congress?
- How effectively does Congress restrict the president?
- How do parties influence the role of Congress?

Specification Checklist

3.1 The structure of Congress

- **Bicameral nature, the membership of Congress and the election cycle.**
- **The distribution of powers within Congress and its constitutional powers including the powers of each chamber.**

3.2 The functions of Congress

- **Representation: congressional elections and the significance of incumbency and factors that affect voting within Congress, including parties and caucuses, constituency, pressure groups and lobbyists.**
- **Legislation: the strengths and weaknesses of the legislative process, difference between chambers and the policy significance.**
- **Oversight and the relationship between Congress and the presidency. Factors affecting president–Congress relations and check on other branches.**

3.3 Interpretations and debates around Congress

- **Changing roles and powers of Congress.**
- **Changing significance of parties in Congress.**
- **Significance and effectiveness of the powers outlined in the US Constitution.**

Source: istock.com/Toshe_O

THE STRUCTURE AND MEMBERSHIP OF CONGRESS

BICAMERALISM

Like the UK Parliament, Congress is a bicameral body, meaning that it has two main chambers, the House of Representatives and the Senate. This allows for the provision of greater checks and balances in the United States, with each chamber being unable to pass laws without the agreement from the other. In addition, as we will see throughout this chapter, the Founding Fathers deliberately set out some other key differences between the House and the Senate, which means that they carry out their functions in different ways. The membership and electoral process for each chamber is illustrated in Table 3.1. Table 3.2 illustrates the main positions of power in Congress and who took those positions after the 2022 elections.

Exam Tip – Remember that Congress refers to both the House of Representatives and the Senate. Some students make the mistake of thinking that Congress is the House of Representatives. When addressing questions on Congress make sure that you are thinking about both the House and the Senate. Sometimes you can refer to each chamber separately to improve you answer. When evaluating the extent to which Congress is representative, for example, you might argue that the House and Senate have different representative weaknesses. You can show an awareness that the two chambers have differences when responding to a question.

Table 3.1 Structure, membership and elections in Congress

Feature	The House of Representatives	The Senate
Totals and titles	435 members known as Congressmen/women or representatives.	100 members known as Senators.
Numbers	The number of representatives per state is roughly proportional to population. The state with the largest population, California, has 53 representatives and the state with the smallest population, Wyoming, has 1. House constituencies are known as districts, which are usually a subsection of a state.	Each state has two senators, regardless of population. Each senator represents the whole state.
Elections	Elected by first-past-the-post voting in a winner-takes-all single-member constituency. Elected for a two-year term.	Elected by first-past-the-post voting in a winner-takes-all single-member constituency. Elected for a six-year term.

Table 3.2 Powerful positions and their office holders: 118th Congress 2023/24

	The House of Representatives	The Senate
Key politicians	**The Speaker of the House of Representatives From October 2023 – Mike Johnson (Republican)** This person is the leader of the largest party in the House. This gives them a huge amount of control over which laws are passed through Congress. They are party political figures who do not act neutrally like the Speaker in the United Kingdom. The Speaker in the United States is arguably more like the position of PM in the United Kingdom, who is leader of the largest party in the House of Commons. **The Minority leader of the House Hakeem Jeffries (Democrat)** This is the leader of the smaller of the two parties. Like the Speaker, their role is to act as the leader of a party in this chamber, trying to create a strategy and achieve policy goals with the support of their party.	**The Majority Leader of the Senate Chuck Schumer (Democrat)** The leader of the largest party in the Senate. Like the Speaker in the House, they play a key role in deciding which laws are debated in the Senate and have influence over legislative outcomes. **The Minority leader of the Senate Mitch McConnell (Republican)** The leader of the minority party in the Senate often acts in opposition to the majority leaders, organising senators in their party to oppose the majority party and support alternative legislative proposals.

THE ELECTORAL CYCLE

Members of the House serve a two-year term and senators have a six-year term. **Congressional elections** take place for both chambers every two years. In a congressional election *all* representatives and approximately one-third of senators will face the electorate. Some of these congressional elections are **mid-term elections**. This is the name given to all elections in the middle of a president's term in office. This includes all the representatives, approximately one-third of senators plus some state governors. The difference between mid-term elections and other congressional election years can be seen in Table 3.3 and Figure 3.1. Figure 3.1 shows party control of the presidency, House and Senate between 2008 and 2022, and shows which elections are mid-term elections.

Definition

Congressional election: Any election to Congress, including mid-term elections.

Spec key term

Mid-term elections: Elections held mid-way through a president's four-year term.

Table 3.3 **Presidential and mid-term election years**

Presidential election year	Mid-term election year
• Presidential elections take place every four years. • President + House + one-third of senators face elections.	• Mid-terms take place every four years. • House + one-third of senators face elections.

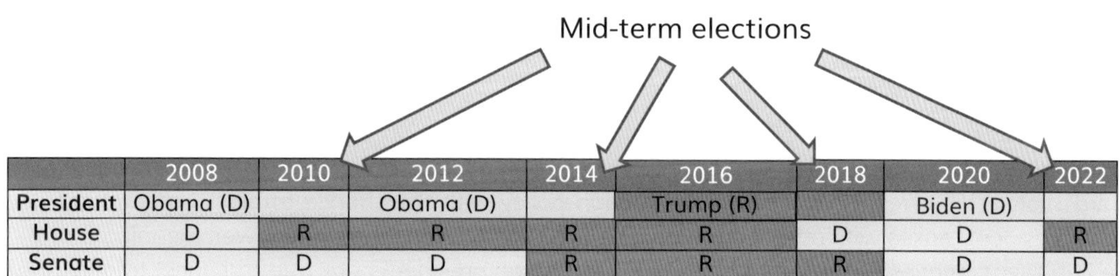

	2008	2010	2012	2014	2016	2018	2020	2022
President	Obama (D)		Obama (D)		Trump (R)		Biden (D)	
House	D	R	R	R	R	D	D	R
Senate	D	D	D	R	R	R	D	D

Figure 3.1 **Party control of the presidency, House and Senate 2008–24**

Mid-term elections have a major impact on the way in which Congress carries out its roles, including the nature of its relationship with the president. A change in majorities can lead to increased or decreased conflict between the president and Congress. If the president and both chambers of Congress are from the same party then it is more likely, for example, that legislation will be enacted. The most common outcome, as we can see in the first mid-terms faced by both Obama (2010) and Trump (2018) is that the president's party performs badly, usually losing their majority in one or more chambers. In 2022 Biden lost control of the House with a small number of Democrat defeats but maintained a majority in the Senate. This often increases Congress' control of the political agenda and makes them more willing and able to develop an alternative policy agenda to that of the president.

Learning Review

1. What are the two chambers of Congress called?
2. What are the most powerful positions in Congress and who holds those positions?
3. What are mid-term elections? How often are they?
4. Which parties controlled (a) the House and (b) the Senate, after the mid-terms of 2022?

THE DISTRIBUTION OF POWER WITHIN CONGRESS

It would be a mistake to assume that the Senate is more powerful than the House of Representatives. *Individual senators* enjoy greater recognition and often greater authority than their counterparts in the House. Politicians would typically prefer to be a member of the Senate than the House, as often illustrated by attempts to move from the lower to the upper chamber but not the other way around. And it is the case that individual senators generally have more power than individual House members. The smaller numbers in the Senate mean that a vote in the Senate has more weight than it does in the House. As a whole institution, however, there is a great deal of evidence suggesting that the two bodies have equal power.

The US Constitution outlines a number of **concurrent** and **exclusive powers** for the House and the Senate. Concurrent powers are those which are held by both the House and Senate. A concurrent power requires the House and Senate to operate separately but also to agree with each other for changes to take place. In addition, the Constitution awards the House and the Senate exclusive powers, those held by one chamber only.

Definition

Concurrent powers: Powers held by both the House and Senate.

Exclusive powers: Powers held by *either* the House or Senate, but not both.

KEY TOPIC DEBATE: IS THE SENATE MORE POWERFUL THAN THE HOUSE?

Exclusive powers of the Senate

Ratify treaties

The upper chamber has the ability to accept or reject treaties negotiated by the president with a two-thirds vote. This gives it a critical role in foreign policy with the chance to block some of the key deals the president makes with other countries. This is a reactive constitutional power, meaning that the Senate can reject treaties but not make them. Furthermore, presidents are free to cancel treaties that have already been ratified whenever they wish.

» The Senate has voted against twenty-two treaties put forward by the president. The last rejected treaty was one supported by Obama to protect the rights of people with disabilities in 2013. There are limits to this power and its ability to limit a president. President Trump proposed few treaties on relatively narrow issues but also withdrew the United States from several key treaties signed by Obama, such as the Paris Agreement on global warming. Obama was able to bypass the need for a two-thirds vote in the Senate by stating that it was not a treaty and would not be submitted to the Senate for approval. The power of the president to sign executive agreements with other countries avoiding the requirement of a Senate vote is discussed in more detail in 'The imperial presidency' section in Chapter 4, 'The Presisidency', starting on page 102.

Ratify presidential appointments

The Senate can reject presidential nominations to the federal judiciary, including the Supreme Court, as well as senior executive branch positions. These ratifications require a 50% plus vote. In practice rejections of nominations are rare, though some nominees have been withdrawn during the process. The Supreme Court vote is seen as particularly significant because a new nomination can shape the ideological outlook of the court for years to come. In rare cases the Senate has refused to conduct a vote on a presidential nomination, which has in effect blocked the president from making an appointment.

» The last time the Senate voted to reject a presidential nomination was Bush senior's nomination of John Tower to Defense Secretary in 1989.

» In 2015, the Republican majority refused to hold hearings and a vote on Obama's pick of liberal nominee Merrick Garland to replace conservative Scalia. The Senate did not hold a vote until after the 2016 presidential election, allowing newly elected President Trump to nominate a conservative justice, Neil Gorsuch, instead. This had a massive impact because it meant that a conservative rather than a liberal justice was placed on the Supreme Court.

Removal from office after impeachment

While the House has responsibility for impeaching an official (see 'Impeachment', below), the Senate then votes on whether to convict them. Note that impeachment does *not* mean that an official is removed. To be removed from office, the Senate must convict the official with a two-thirds vote. No president has been removed from office so far. The details of recent impeachments can be seen in Table 3.4.

Table 3.4 Recent presidential impeachments

President Party Year	Reason for impeachment	House vote (50% need to impeach)	Senate vote (two-thirds needed to convict and remove)
Clinton (Democrat) 1998	The Monica Lewinsky Affair. It was not the affair, sometimes conducted in the White House, that was an impeachable offence but the fact that Clinton lied under oath famously claiming, 'I did not have sexual relations with that woman.'	President impeached; 228 for, 206 against; five Democrats voted to impeach.	President not convicted; 45 for, 55 against; ten Republicans and all Democrats opposed conviction.
Trump (Republican) 2020	The president attempted to interfere in the 2020 US presidential election to help his re-election bid, abusing his power in office to do so. Trump withheld military aid from Ukrainian president Zelensky to pressurise the Ukrainian leader to investigate Joe Biden and Biden's connection with Ukraine. Trump also wanted Ukraine to promote a conspiracy theory that Ukraine, not Russia, was behind interference in the 2016 presidential election. He obstructed the inquiry itself by telling his administration officials to ignore subpoenas.	President impeached; 230 for, 196 against; all Republicans voted against the impeachment.	President not convicted; 48 for, 52 against; one Republican, Senator Mitt Romney, voted to convict.
Trump (Republican) 2021	The House contended that Trump had incited the 6 January 2021 attack on the US Capitol on the day that Congress was to confirm Biden as the next president. More than 2,000 rioters entered the building and some assaulted police officers. A gallows was erected in the west of the Capitol, and some rioters chanted 'Hang Mike Pence' after he refused to try to overturn the election result. After the election, Trump made several attempts to overturn the result. He encouraged people to attend the demonstrations, for example, with a Tweet that said 'Be there. Will be wild.' In a speech made hours into the event, Trump told the rioters 'We love you. You're very special.'	Trump impeached after he left office; 232 for, 197 against; ten Republicans voted to impeach the president.	President not convicted; 57 for, 43 against; seven Republicans voted to convict.

Exclusive powers of the House of Representatives

> **Definition**
>
> **Impeachment:** A process in which the House of Representatives initiates charges of misconduct against a federal official and then determines whether or not they are guilty of such misconduct.

Impeachment

The House has responsibility for initiating the **impeachment** process. It can bring charges against a federal official, including the president, on the grounds of committing treason, a high crime or misdemeanour. This allows the house to determine articles of impeachment – the specific reasons for accusing a federal official of wrongdoing.

The House then conducts hearings and votes on these articles with a 50% plus vote required to impeach. If a president is impeached this means that the House has determined that there is enough evidence for the Senate then to conduct a trial.

» Both President Clinton (1998) and President Trump (2020 and 2021) were impeached, but neither were removed from office by the Senate. You can see details of these impeachments in Table 3.4.

Revenue raising

Article 1, section 7 of the US Constitution gives the House the authority to initiate all 'bills for raising revenue'. This means that the House must vote first on any bill which raises revenue for the Federal Government, for example through taxation. The issue of taxation is particularly sensitive in the United States, and it was determined that the more representative of the two chambers should have greater control.

Presidential selection

In the event that no candidate obtains over 50% of the Electoral College vote, the House has the ability to select the president. All congresspeople from one state get a single collective vote, choosing one person they want to nominate to the presidency. This power has only been used twice (in 1800 and 1824).

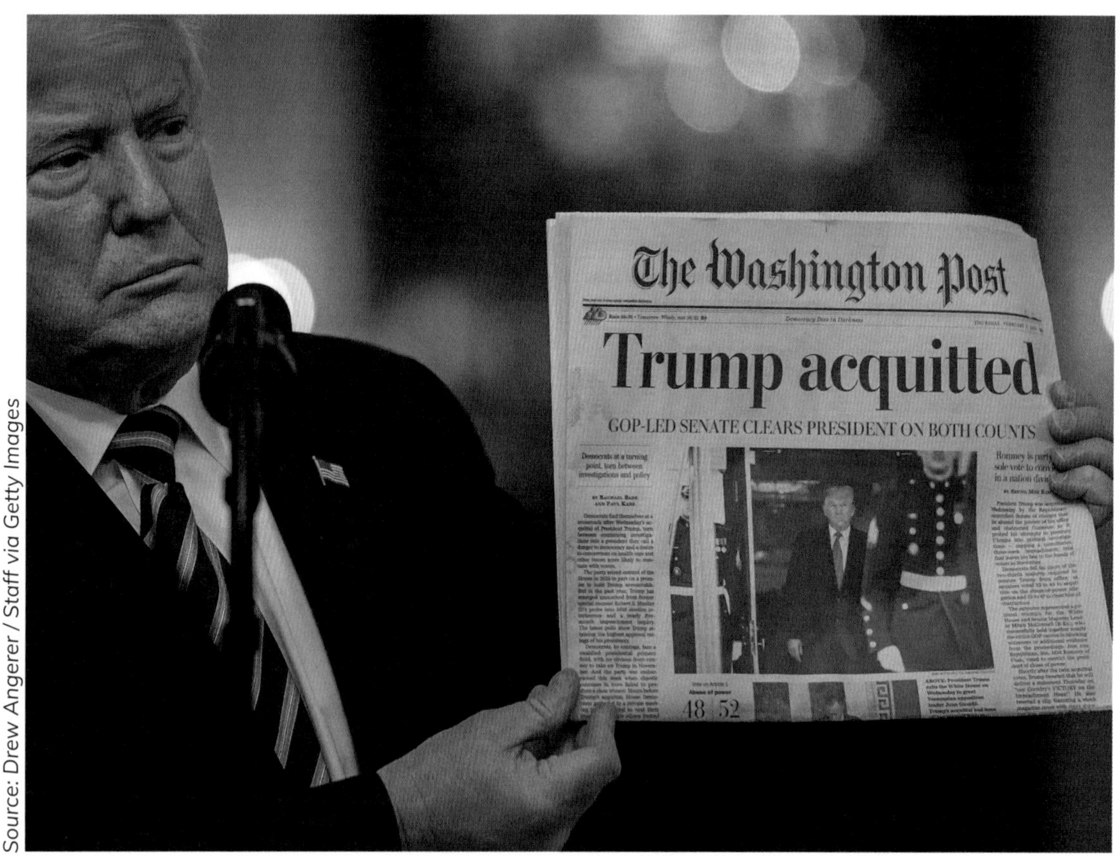

Source: Drew Angerer / Staff via Getty Images

Photo 3.1 **President Trump is acquitted by the Senate in 2020 after his first impeachment by the House of Representatives**

Concurrent powers

The US Constitution outlines several powers held by both the House and Senate. These powers can be used to argue that the two chambers have equal power rather than arguing that the Senate is actually more powerful than the House.

✖ To legislate

Article 1, section 1 states that 'all legislative Powers herein granted shall be vested in a Congress of the United States, which shall consist of a Senate and House of Representatives'. This gives Congress the sole right to initiate legislation, amend bills and vote to determine which proposals become law. Overturning a presidential veto requires a two-thirds vote in each chamber of Congress.

» In 2024, the House and Senate voted in favour of protecting domestic US manufacturing by requiring that electric vehicle charge stations purchased by the US federal government had to be mainly produced in the US. This came after President Biden tried to waiver this requirement in order to provide a short term acceleration of his bid to reduce CO_2 emissions.

✖ Declare war

Whilst the president is commander in chief when the armed forces are called into service, it is Congress that is granted the power to initiate war through a 50% plus vote in each chamber. In practice, presidents often initiate military action without seeking congressional approval. Similar to the Senate ratification of treaties, presidents often argue that the Constitution covers war but that some military action should not be classified as a war. Whilst there have not been recent declarations of war, Congress has voted on presidential requests to commit military action and has sometimes rejected it (see 'The Role and Power of the Presidency' section of Chapter 4 starting on page 111).

» In 2011 Obama ordered the bombing of Libya after calls for greater democracy in the country led to civil war. This contributed to the downfall of Libyan leader Muammar Gaddafi. Obama bypassed Congress altogether, facing considerable criticism. Both chambers were equally weak here as they were bypassed by Obama. It was this criticism and fear of losing a vote in Congress that may have led Obama to back down over his planned attack of President Assad's Syrian regime, which used chemical weapons and ethnic cleansing in its own civil war. The House and Senate each had the same power to block the president's military policy if a vote was held in Congress.

✖ Amend the Constitution

As we saw in Chapter 1, the House and Senate are given coequal power to amend the Constitution, with any changes requiring a two-thirds vote in each chamber. This has helped to limit the total number of amendments with very few proposals achieving the required support in ether chamber.

Learning Review

1. What is the difference between exclusive powers and concurrent powers?
2. What are the exclusive powers of the Senate?
3. What are the exclusive powers of the House?
4. What are the concurrent powers of the House and Senate?

Comparative Learning Review

1. What are the main arguments that suggest the US Congress is more powerful than the UK Parliament?
2. How does the different location of sovereignty in the two countries affect the power of Parliament and Congress?
3. In what ways do the House of Commons and the House of Representatives have similar levels of power to each other? In what way are they different?
4. In what ways do the House of Lords and the Senate have similar levels of power to each other? In what way are they different?
5. In what ways do the House of Commons and the House of Representatives fulfil their main roles to good effect? What are the problems with each chamber?
6. In what ways do the Lords and the Senate fulfil their main roles to good effect? What are the problems with each chamber?

Key Topic Debate Summary: Is the Senate more powerful than the House?

FOR	KEY CRITERIA	AGAINST
✓ The Senate retains power over the budget as it can still vote against budgetary decisions made by the House.	Does the Senate have greater control than the House over **domestic policy?**	✗ The House has the exclusive power to consider revenue raising bills before the Senate. ✗ Both chambers are equal as they both have to agree to legislative proposals.
✓ The Senate has the exclusive power to ratify treaties negotiated by the president.	Does the Senate have greater control than the House over **foreign policy?**	✗ The power to ratify treaties is limited by the president's ability to use executive agreements. This limits the Senate's advantage over the House. ✗ There are other more significant foreign policy powers that are concurrent. The House and Senate determine defence budgets and have the concurrent power to declare war.
FOR	**KEY CRITERIA**	**AGAINST**
✓ The Senate has the power to ratify presidential appointments to the judiciary and senior executive posts. ✓ The Senate decides whether to convict after an impeachment. House impeachment has very little impact if there is no Senate removal.	Can the Senate impose stronger **checks on the executive** than the House?	✗ The House can determine who the president will be if no candidate receives over 50% of the Electoral College vote. ✗ The House can impeach a president and the Senate cannot remove him or her unless the House impeaches. ✗ Both chambers would have to agree to any constitutional change that would reduce presidential power – as such they are equal in power.

Exam Tip: Improving your AO2 Analysis and AO3 Evaluation

If you are trying to determine which chamber is more powerful, remember to cover both the exclusive powers of the House and Senate as well as considering the concurrent powers. Instead of arguing one is more powerful than the other, consider arguing that they are equally powerful.

REPRESENTATION

We will now move on to discuss the first key function of Congress: representing the wishes and interests of the people. Representation refers to the idea of an individual or group working on behalf of others. Politically speaking, it involves political actors such as politicians promoting the wishes and interests of the public. We will consider just how successful Congress is at this essential function.

Congressional elections

Elections for the House and Senate, like those for the UK Parliament, use a **first-past-the-post** (FPTP) voting system. Single-member constituencies require the winner to gain a simple majority of the vote to gain the seat, and candidates or parties coming second gain nothing. Elections will be discussed in more detail in Chapter 6. In this chapter we will focus on the connection between those elections and representation.

Definition

First Past the Post: A voting system that elects one person per constituency in which the candidate with the most votes is elected.

Incumbency

Congress has a very high **incumbency** re-election rate, which means that the person in office has a very high chance of getting back into office at the next election. This can be seen in Table 3.5.

Table 3.5 Congressional incumbency re-election rates

	2016 (%)	2018 (%)	2020 (%)	2022 (%)
House	96.7	91	96.1	94.5
Senate	93.1	84.4	83.9	100

Spec key term

Incumbency: The process of being the current holder of a political office or the period during which someone holds a particular official position.

The causes of high incumbency re-election rates include:

- ***Incumbency advantage.*** The person in office has advantages such as name recognition and having an established campaign machine. Incumbents typically outspend their rivals significantly, giving them a major advantage in an uneven contest. See Table 3.6 for details of House and Senate election funding for the 2022 election.
- ***Safe seats.*** The use of FPTP voting means that, in some areas, one particular party is highly likely to win. In other words, there is a non-competitive election and no threat of removal.
- ***Gerrymandering.*** The existence of safe seats has been made worse by partisan ***gerrymandering*** in which the party in control of the states redraws district boundaries to give their party an advantage. This helps to explain why the incumbency re-election rates are higher in the House than the Senate.
- ***Voter satisfaction.*** The high re-election rate may have a more positive cause, reflecting a group of constituents who are satisfied with their politician and willing to return them to office.

Definition

Gerrymandering: The process of drawing up constituency (district) boundaries to influence the outcome of the election, for example by favouring one party or group.

Table 3.6 Funding for incumbents and challengers in congressional elections, 2022

	House		Senate	
	Incumbents	Challengers	Incumbents	Challengers
Total raised ($ million)	1,151.3	376.2	797.3	375.5
Average raised by each candidate ($ million)	2.8	0.3	28.5	2.1

High levels of incumbency re-election have been criticised as they suggest low levels of representation in Congress. The causes of incumbency, such as gerrymandering, FPTP voting and incumbency advantage, are not positive reasons for high re-election rates and all undermine fair competition. Some states have considered imposing term limits on their members of Congress, but this has not been accepted by the Supreme Court.

KEY TOPIC DEBATE: IS CONGRESS SUFFICIENTLY REPRESENTATIVE?

Strengths

Separation of powers

Separate elections for the president and Congress mean that members of Congress are highly sensitive to the views of their constituents. Members of Congress are not voted in to help choose who will form government in the way that MPs typically are in the United Kingdom. Rather, they can be chosen purely on the basis of how well they respond to constituency views. The voting record of a member of Congress therefore matters a great deal. In addition, the president, as head of the executive, has very limited powers of patronage over their own party members in Congress. This means that members of Congress are more accountable to their constituents than their party leader or president. As such the separation of powers is arguably the central representative strength of the US constitutional system.

» High levels of representation can be seen in the response of Republican Senator Susan Collins (Maine) to President Biden's agenda. She was one of nineteen Republican senators to support his $1 trillion Infrastructure Act and one of only three Republican senators to vote for his nomination of Brown Jackson to the Supreme Court in 2023. Collins also resisted many of President Trump's proposals, for example voting against attempts to repeal Obamacare. The Senator represents a moderate Democrat leaning state (Biden won the state in the 2020 presidential election).

Exam Tip – It is important that your answer to a question is closely connected to the key term(s) of a question. It will help if you have a good understanding of what, exactly, that key term means. In this case, having a clear definition of the concept of representation and an understanding of some of the complexity of the concept will help your AO2 analysis and AO3 evaluation. Make sure that you focus on the extent to which Congress responds to the wishes and interests of the public.

Two elected chambers

Congress has been designed to provide complementary or alternative forms of representation. Politicians who tend to respond directly to the wishes of the people are often referred to as delegates and those who use their own judgement to decide what is in the best interests of the voters can be referred to as trustees. House members represent relatively small constituencies (districts rather than whole state) and have very short terms of only two years. This means that they are highly sensitive to the wishes of the public because they must constantly battle for re-election. The Senate, on the other hand, with its larger constituencies and longer terms, can take a more considered view of what is in the (longer-term) interests of the public. Combining both types of representation, rather than taking one approach only, maximises representation.

» This has been reflected in the different responses of the House and the Senate to the proposal to protect the American flag with a constitutional amendment. In the 1990s the House repeatedly followed the patriotism of the public view and voted in favour of these measures. The Senate arguably took a more rational view in protecting minority views and First Amendment rights. The measure failed to achieve the required votes in the chamber with a six-year term.

Frequency of elections

Short House terms of only two years maximise the extent to which members of Congress will respond to the public view. In addition, the electoral cycle ensures that Senate elections occur every two years. Even though a Senator serves a six-year term, the elections are staggered with one-third facing re-election every two years. This means that the majority in the House *and* the Senate can change at once, reflecting shifts in public opinion. Also, Congress makes use of primary elections in which candidates from the same party compete to decide which one will stand to represent the party for a House or Senate seat. This increases voter choice and also means that there is competition during elections, even in safe seats.

» Alexandria Ocasio Cortez successfully defeated a well-established Democrat, Joe Crowley, in a primary challenge in 2018 as a younger, more progressive Democrat. Cortez' desire to promote the wishes and interests of her constituents can be seen in her response to the coronavirus legislation in April 2020: 'On behalf of my constituents in The Bronx and Queen's ... It is a joke when Republicans say that they have urgency around this bill. The only folks that they have urgency around are folks like [large corporations] Ruth's Chris Steak House and Shake Shack. Those are the people getting assistance in this bill. You are not trying to fix things for Moms and Pops.' Ocasio Cortez was the only Democrat in the House who voted against a COVID-19 relief plan, saying that it did not go far enough.

Source: Scott Heins / Stringer via Getty Images

Photo 3.2 **Alexandria Ocasio Cortez after beating Joe Crowley in a Democrat primary in 2018**

Weaknesses

First Past The Post (FPTP)

The use of single member or winner-takes-all constituencies causes significant problems for representation. In particular, it leads to safe seats in which elections are non-competitive and supporters of the minority party have no chance of gaining representation. This majoritarian approach can leave voters feeling frustrated that they do not have a politician who reflects their particular views. In some cases there is so little chance of losing that a seat is not contested by the opposing party. The voting system also makes it hard for third parties to compete, effectively forcing voters to choose from the narrow selection of Democrat or Republican parties. It can also produce results in which the party that gains a majority of the popular vote does not gain a majority of seats.

» This last occurred in 2012 when House Democrats secured in excess of a million votes more than the Republicans only to find that they remained as the minority party.

Gerrymandering

Gerrymandering, the process of drawing up constituency boundaries to favour one group, such as a racial group or specific party, is common practice in US House elections. In most states, the House district boundaries are drawn up by the party that wins state elections. It has become a highly political process which affects electoral outcomes. Gerrymandering was common along racial lines in the United States in the 1950s and 1960s but has largely been restricted by congressional acts or Supreme Court cases. Gerrymandering along party lines, helping one party win an election, has not been overturned by the Supreme Court. You can see how gerrymandering can be used to favour a party in Figure 3.2.

» Whilst gerrymandering continues on an almost annual basis, there was a particular push to change constituency boundaries by Republican-controlled states during the Obama presidency. Obama won the State of Pennsylvania in both 2008 and 2012. In the same time span, Democrats went from winning twelve House seats in 2008 to just five in 2012. After 2008 the Republican state governor of Pennsylvania signed into law new gerrymandered districts which allowed the Republicans to win more seats even though support for the Democrats was roughly the same in both elections. For Democrats 51% of the votes gave them just 28% of the House seats for that state. Such gerrymandering was challenged in the Supreme Court but in *Rucho v Common Cause* (2019) the court delivered a 5–4 ruling which declared that the Constitution did not forbid states from drawing up such partisan boundaries.

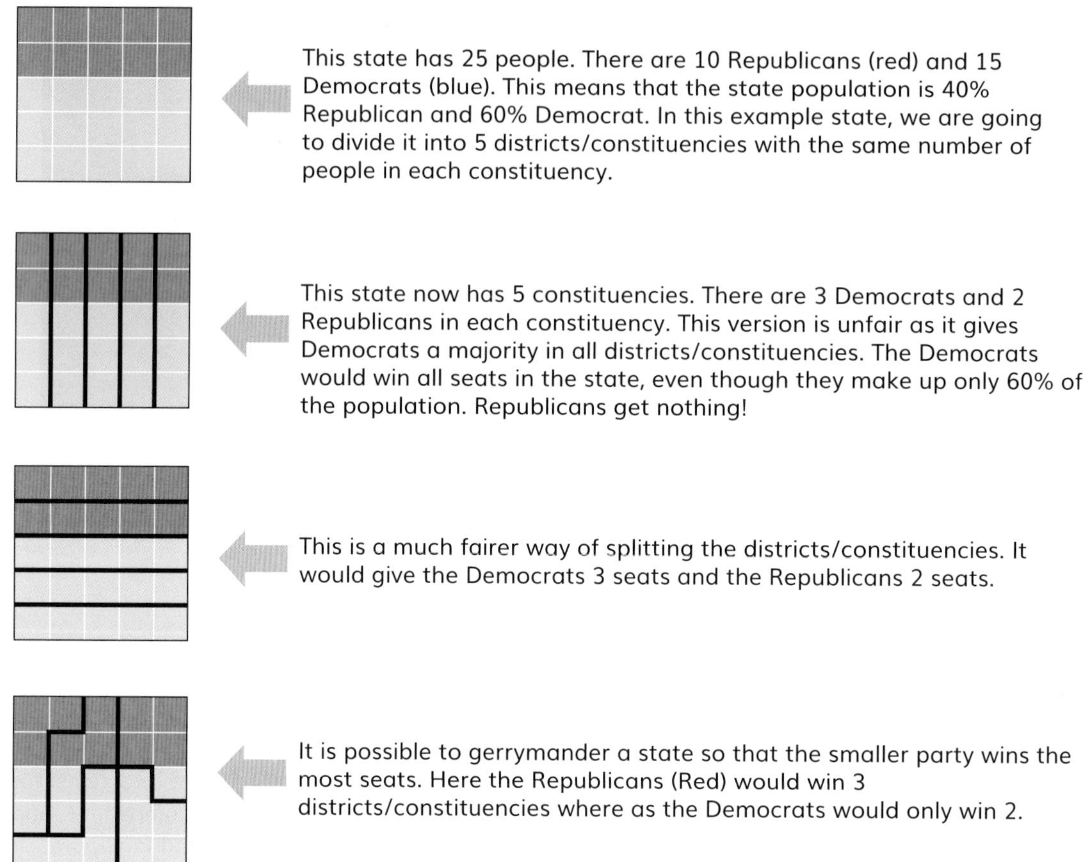

Figure 3.2 **How gerrymandering works**

Lack of social representation

As shown in Table 3.7, Congress does not reflect the gender, race or class make-up of the US population. Women, racial minorities and working-class members are all underrepresented in Congress. Whilst Pew Research reports that 14.3% identify as black, representation in the House is 12.8% and only 3% in the Senate. Nineteen per cent identify as Hispanic yet only make up 10.6% (House) and 6% (Senate). This causes two representative problems. Firstly, legislative outcomes may not reflect the interests of underrepresented groups. Congress may play a positive role in promoting the interests of specific groups in society but cannot claim to provide pluralist representation. Secondly, this provides a symbolic message for Americans. Regardless of the reality, women, racial minority members and the working classes may look at Congress and feel that it is not a place that they should be aspiring to get elected to or will serve their interests.

» Between 2019 and 2022 the 70%-plus male Congress repeatedly failed to reauthorise the Violence Against Women Act, eventually passing in March 2022. This measure partly stalled because the Democrats added new clauses to protect Native American women, which lacked sufficient support in Congress. In 2021 the Democrats prioritised the We the People Act, which attempted to prevent state laws that would reduce voter turnout amongst racial minority groups. Arguably the lack of diversity in social representation in Congress was the cause of these bills failing to pass, meaning that women and racial minorities are not achieving the legislative outcomes that are in their interests.

Table 3.7 **Social composition of Congress 2023/24**

Social group	House (%)	Senate (%)	% of total population
Women	29.0	25.0	50.0
Hispanic	10.6	6.0	18.0
Native American	0.9	1.0	1.0
Asian	3.2	2.0	6.0
Black	12.8	3.0	12.0
LGB	2.5	2.0	7.7

Source: US Census Bureau

Minority representation is stronger in the House partly because of the existence of high concentrations of minority members in the population of some House districts. The existence of majority-minority districts is likely to be a factor in increasing the number of racial minority candidates who run for office. In Senate elections all constituencies (states) have a majority white population.

Definition

Majority-minority districts: A constituency for the House of Representatives in which a racial majority group has the largest population in that area.

✖ Partisanship and gridlock

The coequal legislative power of the House and Senate, the need for presidential approval of bills and the increase in partisanship have often led to gridlock in which Congress is unable to secure enough agreement to pass a bill (these concepts are dealt with in further detail in the 'Legislation' section later in this chapter).

» This has led to some extreme cases where legislation has failed, such as the 35-day Federal Government shutdown in 2018–19. Such gridlocks fail to promote the interests of the US public or, even worse, does severe damage, for example by causing major falls in the stock market or increases in unemployment.

Key Topic Debate Summary: Is Congress sufficiently representative?

FOR	KEY CRITERIA	AGAINST
✓ Two elected chambers give voters high levels of choice. ✓ Provides complementary representation giving US citizens both delegates and trustees. ✓ Frequency of congressional elections allows congressional majorities in each chamber to reflect shifting public views.	Is Congress **nationally** representative? Does it reflect the wishes and interests of the country as a whole?	✖ Two elected chambers contribute to congressional gridlock in which Congress cannot pass legislation. ✖ The Senate is not representative. There are two senators per state regardless of population.
✓ Separation of powers makes members of the House and Senate highly sensitive to public opinion. ✓ House members are particularly responsive to voters as a result of their short terms.	Is Congress **locally** representative? Do constituents in districts and states get what they voted for?	✖ FPTP elections lead to limited voter choice or safe seats. ✖ Gerrymandering produces unfair elections in which one party has an advantage.
✓ Congress is increasingly diverse in gender and race terms. ✓ Primaries allow for greater choice and competition, preventing a top-down process in which party leaders impose a candidate on a constituency.	Does Congress provide **social** representation? Is Congress able to reflect a diversity of interests?	✖ Legislative outcomes do not reflect the wishes of all groups and lead to a sense of underrepresentation. ✖ Pressure groups, rather than promoting pluralist representation, directly attack it. Wealthy, elite interests dominate Congress in practice.

Exam Tip: Improving AO2 Analysis and AO3 Evaluation

Incumbency re-election rates are high. Do you see this as a negative (because it leads to a lack of competitive elections and lack of voter choice) or positive (because it suggests strong support for a successful member of Congress)? A delegate model of representation requires that a politician will respond to the public view acting on behalf of their expressed wishes. A trustee model suggests that it is better to make decisions based on their view of what is in the interests of the public. Are members of Congress more likely to act as delegates or trustees? How does your answer to these two questions affect your final conclusion?

Evaluative view: Is Congress sufficiently representative?

Congress provides sufficient levels of representation for the United States. It has a number of characteristics that make it very sensitive to the wishes of the public and is quick to respond to them. The separation of powers, short House election terms and complementary House and Senate representation, provides a solid basis for high levels of representation, which is not destroyed by first past the post or gerrymandering. It is fair to say that there are some important concerns regarding representation, but these concerns do not prevent Congress from fulfilling the fundamental requirements of a representative body.

Consider the key topic debate and debate summary as well as any new evidence you can find. Do you agree or disagree with this evaluative view?

Congressional voting factors

A key way in which members of Congress represent their constituents is by making key decisions on bills, amendments, presidential appointments or treaties. Why does a member of Congress vote *for* a bill rather than *against* it? Voting factors refers to the different causes of the way in which a member of Congress votes. We will now examine the arguments for and against the influence of the main voting factors.

KEY TOPIC DEBATE: ARE CONSTITUENTS, PARTIES, CAUCUSES AND INTEREST GROUPS INFLUENTIAL IN DETERMINING THE WAY IN WHICH MEMBERS OF CONGRESS VOTE?

Constituents

✓ The US Constitution creates a strong link between voters and members of Congress. The separation of powers gives a specific mandate to members of Congress distinct from the president's mandate. Representatives and senators, therefore, must respond to constituency needs to get re-elected. Also, House terms are very short, ensuring a constant threat of removal in the lower chamber. All of this suggests that members of Congress are responsive to public need.

» In 2020 there were sixteen crossover districts where voters chose a presidential candidate from one party and voted for a member of the House from the other party. Nine Republicans won House seats even though the majority in those districts voted for Democrat President Joe Biden. A further six districts gave Trump a majority of the vote but returned a Democrat to the House. Those Democrats knew that they would have to pursue moderate or conservative policies to get re-elected.

✗ Constituents might be ignored as a result of pressure groups and the need for funding for elections. Interest groups such as the National Rifle Association, the American Federation of Labor and corporations all make major donations at elections time. In addition, opposing the measures of the other party appears to have become an automatic reaction for members of Congress. This suggests that constituency views can become a secondary consideration where there is a conflict between the view of the constituency and party. The increased level of party loyalty is covered in the 'Partisanship' section later in this chapter.

Parties

✓ Politicians identify with a party because of their own personal values, and members of a party tend to vote in the same way. In addition, party leaders in Congress can influence the way in which members of the party caucus votes. They have authority to try to bring their party together to have collective power in Congress. Party leaders do have some patronage power, especially in the House, in which the House Speaker has a strong say in who chairs key committees. Loyalty can be rewarded with greater positions of power. One of the most significant political changes in recent years is increased partisanship, in which parties have become more unified. There is an increasing lack of willingness for a Democrat to compromise with a Republican and vice versa. Parties, then, are very influential over voting behaviour and are increasingly important.

» Party line voting was the cause of the Federal Government shutdown in December 2018/January 2019, in which Democrats and Republicans could not agree on government spending plans, for particularly Trump's request for $4.4 billion for border wall funding. A Congressional Quarterly study showed that in 2019, on average, the thirty House Democrats in Trump districts voted with the Democrat caucus on 93.6% of votes, only slightly lower than the party average.

✗ Party unity is limited by other pressures on a member of Congress such as the view of voters or pressure group lobbying. It is also limited by the personal ideology of the politician. In many cases there is bipartisan (cross-party) support for a bill where members from both parties work together. This suggests that the party is not the most important consideration.

» The Republican Party has become increasingly divided over US support for Ukraine. This marks an ideological division within the Party in which conservative Republicans oppose further funding for the country. In September 2023, this was led by Republican Matt Gaetz who proposed an amendment to the Defense Funding bill by ending all further aid to Ukraine. The amendment failed but Republicans were split with 93 Republicans supporting this measure and 126 more moderate Republicans opposing it.

Congressional caucuses

✓ **Congressional caucuses** (not to be confused with the caucus election in the primary election process) refer to *organised* groups in Congress. Whilst we can refer to a party caucus (such as all Republicans in the House) there are many other caucuses with distinct policy goals, regular caucus meetings and a leader. Caucuses often aim to influence the direction of a party or vote as a collective bloc on a bill and can be more influential than party membership in determining voting outcomes.

» The House Freedom Caucus, chaired by Representative Scott Perry, comprises approximately thirty right-wing Republicans who try to shift the Republican position further to the right, especially on economic issues. It was the more radical members of the House Freedom Caucus who forced conservative Republican Kevin McCarthy from his position as House Speaker in 2023 because they did not see him as sufficiently conservative. In 2021, despite some support from Republicans, all House Freedom Caucus members voted against funding for Biden's vaccine mandate, which would require all health workers and workers in companies with over 100 employees to have a vaccine.

» The Congressional Black Caucus is committed to raising racial minority issues in the House, sometimes opposing specific legislation. Its leaders held White House meetings with Biden on several occasions in 2021 and 2022, particularly to discuss the nature of Biden's infrastructure plan and also to shape voting rights legislation that passed the House as the For the People Act.

> **Spec key term**
>
> **Congressional caucuses:** Organised groups of legislators who share special interests and meet to pursue common legislative objectives, for example Black caucus, women's caucus, Hispanic caucus.

✗ Different caucuses will hold different levels of party unity. There is no requirement for caucus members to vote the same way. Different ideological caucuses within a party often compromise to ensure party unity. Caucuses may threaten to vote against a bill proposed by their party leadership but often step back from this when it comes to the final vote. As with each voting factor, there are other competing factors that may restrict the influence of any one factor such as caucuses.

> **Definition**
>
> **Lobbying:** The process of contacting and persuading politicians.

Interest groups and lobbyists

✓ Pressure groups exert influence through **lobbying** politicians and organising publicity on key votes. Pressure groups can play a critical role at election time, providing positive or negative publicity for a candidate. In addition, pressure groups may provide much-needed funding for a politician's campaign with critics arguing that this is effectively buying policy. This is dealt with in more detail in Chapter 7, 'Political Parties and Interest Groups'.

» Medical corporations are a very influential interest group. In the 2018 mid-term elections, pharmaceutical companies donated to 416 of the 435 members elected to the House. In addition, health sector businesses spent a record $594 million in 2019 on lobbying. This enormous sum was spent mainly on persuading members of Congress to vote in a certain way, especially in successfully fighting off Democrat-led efforts to regulate drug prices. Whilst ideologically many Democrats support drug price regulations and President Biden pushed for this in 2023, there has been insufficient support within the party to pass any meaningful legislation.

✖ It is easy to overemphasise the influence of interest groups. Despite their enormous efforts, interest groups cannot force a member of Congress to vote in a certain way. Interest groups are unlikely to persuade a member of Congress to oppose public opinion in their state or district. In addition, many pressure groups are donating money to politicians who already support their views. They do this to help supporters of their interest group to stay in power. Interest groups may have some influence over politicians in marginal constituencies, or over politicians who are moderate, but they are unlikely to change the voting behaviour of most politicians.

» Despite consistent pressure on members of Congress through lobbying and demonstrations, racial rights groups such as the National Association for the Advancement of Colored People (NAACP) and Black Lives Matter have been unable to persuade any Republicans to support the For the People Act, which Democrats have been fighting for in 2023. The Act would give greater protection to voting rights, especially for racial minorities. These groups were also unsuccessful in influencing Democrat Senators Manchin and Sinema, both elected in conservative leaning states, to support measures that would help the bill to pass. These pressure groups could not overcome ideology or influence of the public on these senators.

Key Topic Debate Summary: Are constituents, parties, caucuses and interest groups influential in determining the way in which members of Congress vote?

FOR	KEY CRITERIA	AGAINST
✓ Members of Congress are highly sensitive to public opinion largely due to the separation of powers and the need to get-re-elected. ✓ Party leaders have limited patronage power of members of Congress, meaning that they are more loyal to their constituents than any party/party leader consideration.	Are **constituents** influential?	✗ Partisanship has become so strong that members of a party appear to automatically oppose the opposing party, regardless of what constituents think. ✗ Interest groups may exert considerable influence via election campaigns forcing politicians to prioritise the interest group over the constituency view.
✓ Members of a party will naturally be inclined to agree with similar policies. ✓ Party leaders have a degree of patronage power within Congress.	Are **parties** influential?	✗ There is a lot of evidence of bipartisan (cross-party) cooperation on bills. ✗ Party leaders have limited control over individual politicians. ✗ Unity within caucuses may be stronger than unity within a party.
✓ Members of a caucus may share a common value or interest and therefore vote together regardless of party. ✓ Some caucuses have a requirement that all members vote together as a bloc in Congress.	Are **caucuses** influential?	✗ Other factors may be more influential, with caucuses within a party often compromising to ensure party unity. ✗ Not all caucuses have strong internal loyalty or a requirement to vote as a collective bloc.

FOR	CRITERIA	AGAINST
✓ Interest groups and lobbying can put enormous pressure on members of Congress. ✓ Interest groups provide much-needed funding. Parties only provide a small amount of funding for a candidate's election campaign.	Are **interest groups** influential?	✗ Interest groups cannot force a politician to vote in a certain way. ✗ Interest groups will be unable to persuade politicians who have strongly conflicting values to the group. ✗ Where an individual member votes in favour of an interest group goal, this is probably caused by party or ideological considerations not pressure from the interest group.

Exam Tip: Improving AO2 Analysis and AO3 Evaluation

The importance of a factor may depend on the issue. For example, on moral policies, the personal view of the politician might hold more sway than the party view. Some factors may not act in opposition to each other. It is often the case that the majority in a constituency have clear support for one party. A member of Congress is merely reflecting that support when they vote. In these cases, is this party or public the influencing factor? How do these points affect you final evaluation?

CASE STUDY 3.1: THE VIOLENCE AGAINST WOMEN ACT (VAWA)

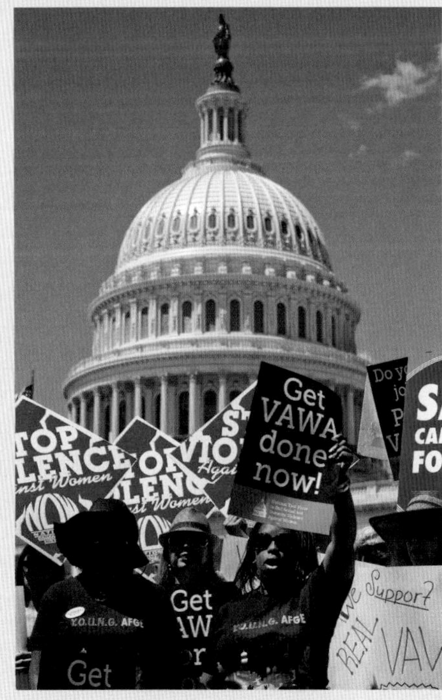

Source: JIM WATSON / Staff via Getty Images

Photo 3.3 Campaigners hold a rally supporting reauthorisation of the Violence Against Women Act outside the Capitol

Overview

First passed in 1994, and reauthorised regularly since, the Violence Against Women Act (VAWA) was not renewed in 2018. Despite efforts by Democrats and President Biden, the Act therefore could not operate until reauthorisation finally occurred in 2022. In the House, Republicans preferred reauthorisation without any amendments to the original VAWA. The Republican House minority leader at the time, Kevin McCarthy, accused then Speaker Nancy Pelosi of politicising the bill by adding provisions to provide greater protection for Native American women, transgender rights and gun provisions to restrict access to guns for those found guilty of domestic abuse. The bill eventually passed the House with the Democrat amendments largely intact. The bill then failed to pass in the Republican-led Senate in 2021, with the Republican and Democrats refusing to compromise on the dispute over the Democrat amendments passed in the House. In the Senate, Dianne Feinstein (Democrat, California) tried to get consent to vote on the House-passed VAWA bill by the end of the year, including allowing both sides to offer two amendments. Senator Joni Ernst (Republican, Iowa), who has introduced her own VAWA reauthorisation, objected to setting up the vote on the bill, arguing that the House legislation could not pass the Republican-controlled Senate.

Congress and partisanship

Between the two parties there is a lack of willingness to make compromises. This is evidence of high and increased partisanship – Democrats and Republicans in Congress have agreed on this bill in the past. The bill was reintroduced after the 2020 elections, passing the House where the Democrats had a clear majority but failing to get enough support in the Senate due to a small Democrat majority. It eventually passed the Senate in 2022.

Parties and differences

The example shows how Democrats and Republicans have opposing views and differ on key issues such as race and gender. Democrats are keen to have the highest possible protections against discrimination on the grounds of gender and race. Its reauthorisation in 2022, as part of a bigger budget package, shows some degree of bipartisanship between Democrats and Republicans.

Presidential elections

VAWA was not a major campaign issue in the 2020 election. Biden strongly supports VAWA and had a notable lead amongst women in the 2020 election over Trump. This was bigger than normal for Democrats. Trump's support amongst women collapsed in 2020 gaining only 42% of the female vote to Biden's 57%.

Congress and representation

The majority-male Congress took four years to reauthorise this legislation that would protect females from violence. This suggests that there is a concern over social representation in Congress with policy outcomes favouring some groups and ignoring others.

Congress and legislation

Congress was unable to legislate, which could be used as evidence of its ineffectiveness in this role. It shows how it is hard to pass laws through Congress. This is due to party differences but also conflict between the House and Senate. It also shows that both chambers must agree for a law to pass.

Learning Review

1. What is meant by the terms incumbency, incumbency advantage and gerrymandering?
2. What are the main arguments suggesting that Congress is representative?
3. What are the main arguments suggesting that Congress is not representative?
4. What are the four main factors that affect the way in which members of Congress vote?
5. What are the arguments that suggest each of these four main factors are influential over a member of Congress?

LEGISLATION

We will now move on to discuss the second key function of Congress: passing laws. A huge amount of congressional time is spent legislating with individual members of Congress proposing bills, committees considering them in detail and often amending them, as well as debates and votes taking place in the main chambers. Through the making of new laws, Congress has a massive impact on US citizens. So how does it work in the United States and what does a 'good' legislative process look like? You can see an outline of the legislative process in Figure 3.3. There is no need to learn every stage in this process in huge detail, however. Instead, understanding some key features of the process can be more helpful.

Localism

The separation of powers means that individuals in Congress are under pressure to deliver legislative benefits to their constituents. This has led to **pork-barrel legislation** – which complicates the legislative process as lawmakers add a huge array of amendments to legislation to benefit their constituency. This has led to high levels of federal expenditure, troubling fiscal conservatives in particular. It could also lead to the prioritisation of local, not national, needs in the legislative process.

> **Definition**
>
> **Pork-barrel legislation:** Amendments to bills proposed by a member of Congress that will bring benefits to their constituency (jobs, money, infrastructure).

Relations with the executive branch

The US Constitution makes Congress the sole legislative body but also requires presidential approval for bills passed to become law. The US Constitution, especially the separation of powers, restricts the domination of the executive branch that tends to occur in parliamentary systems such as the United Kingdom. This is illustrated in Figure 3.4. This makes Congress a very powerful legislative branch compared to the governments of other countries. Rather than simply reacting to executive (presidential) proposals, Congress is active in developing its own legislative agenda. Legislation can be initiated by any one of the three bodies, and sometimes there are rival versions of a bill being considered in the House and Senate (or even within one chamber) at the same time. Any legislation that passes one of the two chambers still has to pass the other.

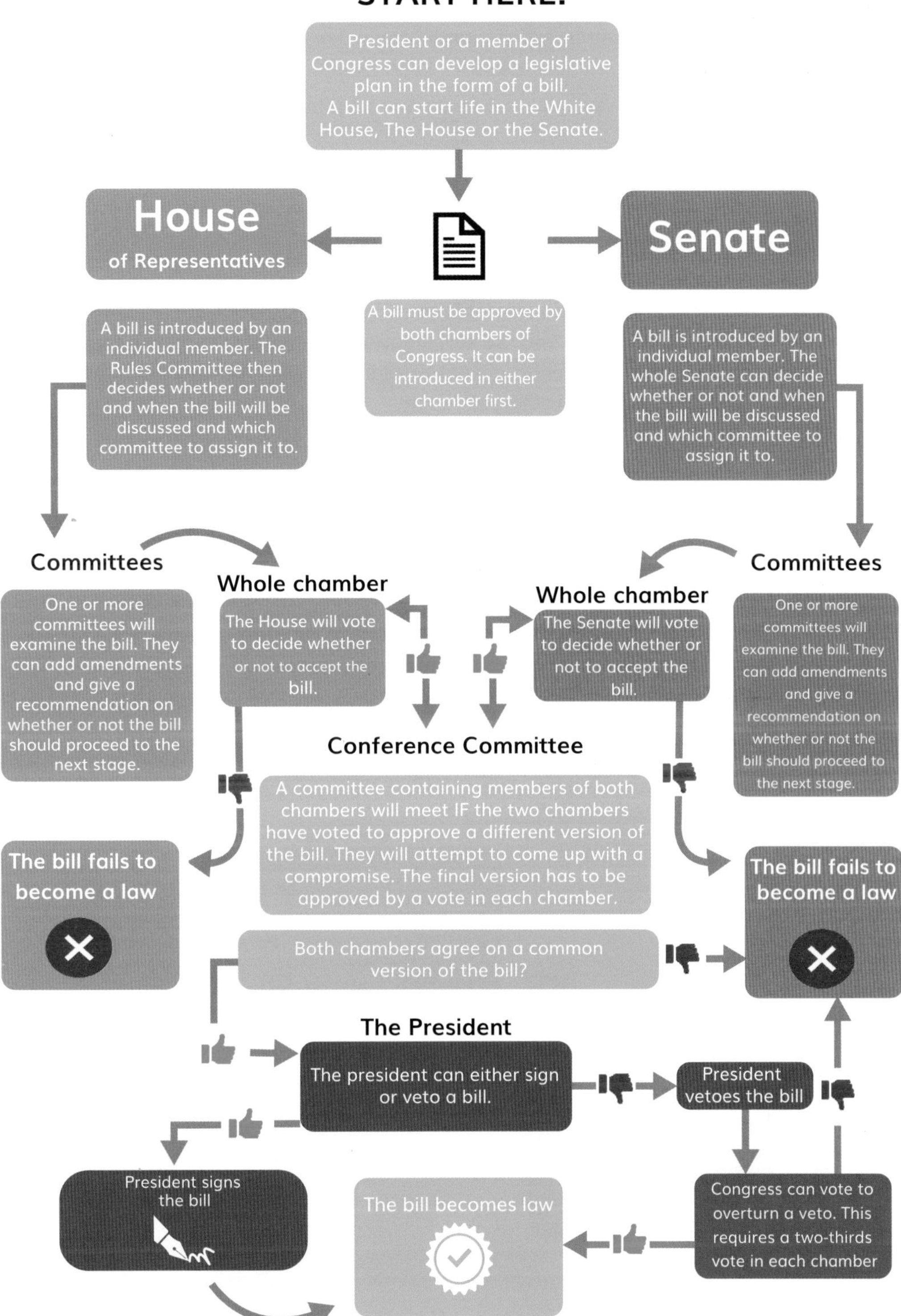

Figure 3.3 **The legislative process in Congress**

Checks and balances within Congress

The legislative process is marked by lots of checks and balances within Congress with a huge number of obstacles to passing legislation. In this sense Congress is a very conservative body; it is easier to keep existing laws than to create new ones. The House and Senate are coequal legislative partners – both must agree to identical versions of a bill. Congressional committees also play a powerful role in amending and even blocking legislation. Table 3.8 shows the organisation and role of congressional committees.

Table 3.8 **Congressional committees**

How are they organised?	The House and Senate have separate committees. For example, there is both a House Agriculture Committee and a Senate Agriculture Committee. Most committees are known as standing committees and are policy-based (such as agriculture). Committee membership is shared between both parties in proportion to the number of seats a party has in the main chamber. In other words, if the Republican Party has a majority in the Senate, they will be the majority party on all Senate committees.
What do they do?	Committees will deal with relevant legislation and oversight of the executive branch in that particular area. For example, the House Intelligence Committee will examine any security legislation but also investigate all security bodies for the executive branch, such as the Department of Homeland Security, the National Security Council and the Federal Bureau of Investigation. Committees can amend legislation, mark-up bills (award funding for projects) and investigate the executive branch. Some committees have special functions. As we have already seen, the House Rules Committee controls the agenda of the House and how/when bills are assed. Appropriations committees in each chamber are very powerful because they determine funding for any bill. Two committees in the Senate are particularly noteworthy because they conduct the hearings for exclusive power of the Senate. The Senate Foreign Relations committee will consider presidential treaties before making a recommendation to the full Senate (as well as scrutinising the commander in chief of the most powerful country in the world). The Senate Judiciary committee will conduct hearings for all presidential nominations to the judiciary, including the Supreme Court.

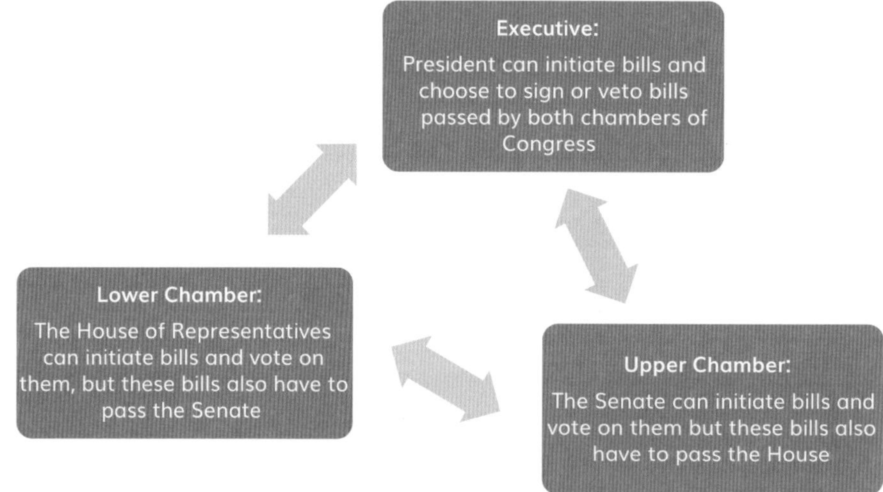

Figure 3.4 **The non-linear process for legislation in Congress – start anywhere!**

Spec key term

Divided government: When the House of Representatives, Senate and presidency are not all controlled by one party.

Partisanship

Partisanship has a major impact on the legislative process, mainly by making cross-party compromise unlikely. There has been a significant increase in partisanship since the 1990s leading to a lack of compromise between the two main parties and greater determination to directly attack the other party. The impact of partisanship can vary depending on the nature of the party majority in the House, Senate and presidency. Typically, the United States has divided government, in which more than one party controls these three institutions. In the far more unusual situation of one party controlling all three bodies, partisanship makes it easier to pass legislation.

Gridlock

A combination of some of the key features covered so far have all contributed to an inability for Congress to pass legislation. This is known as gridlock: a situation in which the three main decision-making powers cannot come to an agreement and therefore nothing gets done. This gridlock has caused Federal Government shutdown. Unless the president and Congress can agree an annual budget before the start of the next financial year, then there is effectively no money allocated for spending by the Federal Government causing the shutdown of many federal institutions and workers being unable to work.

Spec key term

Gridlock: A situation in US politics where the president and Congress are constantly preventing each other from acting, resulting in difficulty passing legislation.

House–Senate legislative differences

There are significant similarities in the legislative role of both the House and the Senate. In particular, both chambers can, and do, initiate, amend and vote to accept or reject legislation. There are, however, a few notable differences, as outlined in Table 3.9.

Table 3.9 House–Senate legislative differences

1. The House Rules Committee versus the Senate Committee of the full chamber	
House	**Senate**
In general, there are more centralised procedures in place in the House to make it easier for the party leadership and the majority to push legislation through the House. Bills are introduced by the Rules Committee. The largest party in the House has a majority of seats on the committee and therefore controls the decisions it makes. The Rules Committee determines whether a bill will be debated, the timing of such debates and the rules under which the bill can be addressed, for example whether amendment proposals are allowed.	A Committee of the whole chamber must determine whether legislation can be introduced onto the floor of the chamber. At this stage a Senate vote could block a bill before debate even begins. To make this process more efficient, the Senate often makes use of unanimous consent. All senators are asked on the floor if they wish to take up the bill and if no one speaks out against it then the bill can move to the next stage, having received unanimous consent. If one individual objects, then the Senate must go through the lengthier process of voting before a bill can be introduced.
2. A more regulated process in the House and the power of an individual member	
House	**Senate**
Amendment and debate processes are more easily regulated with limits usually placed on debate time or the number of amendments allowed. The House Rules Committee may put time limits or even amendment limits on a bill.	Regulation of debate is less apparent in the Senate, making it easier for individual senators to offer amendments or debate as long as they want to. A senator can continue talking as long as they wish. This process is known as the filibuster when it prevents a vote from taking place, thus blocking a piece of legislation.
3. Other key differences	
We have already seen how the House may respond to short-term or popular considerations more than the Senate, which might take a long-term view. House members, due to their smaller districts and more frequent elections, are arguably more sensitive to public opinion than Senate members and more likely to engage in pork-barrel legislation. However, pork-barrel legislation and a sensitivity to public opinion are also features of the legislative process in both chambers.	

Spec key term

Unanimous consent: A process in which senators are given the chance to object verbally to a motion such as moving a bill to the next stage of the legislative process. If no senator objects, then the motion is carried out without the need for all senators to vote on it.

Spec key term

Filibuster: When a senator gives a prolonged speech on the floor of the Senate to obstruct legislative progress of a bill or confirmation of appointments to the executive or judiciary.

The filibuster

The filibuster allows any individual senator to keep talking for as long as they want to, thus preventing a vote from taking place on a bill. As such, the filibuster can effectively act as a veto against a piece of legislation. The filibuster can be overcome with sixty votes in the Senate. This is through a **motion of cloture** – a motion to say that the Senate would like to end a debate and move on to vote. This means that any bill which is filibustered will require sixty votes to pass rather than 50% plus.

Definition

Motion of cloture: A motion to end debate and move to a vote of the full chamber, thus stopping a filibuster.

The filibuster was originally used only rarely, when a senator felt that a bill was a major threat to their state. In the partisan age, the use of the filibuster has increased hugely. It is often uses by a senator to block the passage of a bill proposed by a president of the opposing party. With huge increases in attempts to filibuster there are also more motions of cloture proposed to end debate and stop the filibuster. There is no official count of filibusters but the number of motions of cloture (see Figure 3.5) are a rough guide. The filibuster was created under the rules of Congress not the Constitution. This means that the Senate could change the filibuster rule and remove it altogether with a 50% vote.

» In 2021 Biden was unable to pass many of his key policies through the Senate given that the Democrats have fifty seats in the upper chamber. The For the People Act, designed to promote stronger voting rights, was blocked by filibuster. Biden called for a rule change to reduce the ability to use the filibuster and Democrats tried to make an exception so that civil rights bills were not subject to a filibuster. This measure failed with fifty-two senators opposing the idea, including two Democrats, Senators Manchin and Sinema.

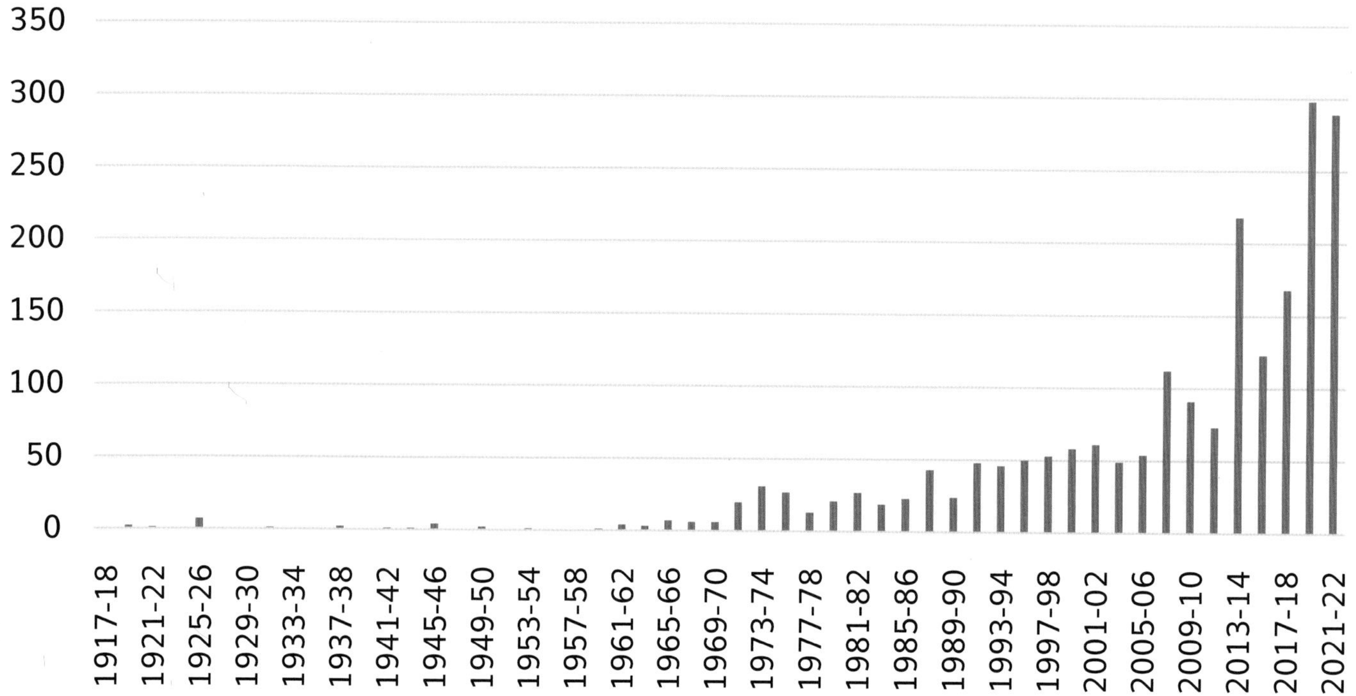

Figure 3.5 **Senate votes on cloture to end a filibuster**

POLICY SIGNIFICANCE OF CONGRESS

Congress has an enormous impact on the daily lives of people in the United States. It creates new policies by passing laws that influence every aspect of US society.

Areas on which Congress can have a significant impact include:

- Social policy such as health and welfare
- Economic policy including taxation, expenditure and regulation
- Immigration reforms
- Civil liberties and electoral processes
- Foreign policy
- Executive power
- Federalism and state ability to control their own affairs

You can find evidence and explanations of the impact of a selection of congressional acts in Table 3.10.

Table 3.10 **The impact of some recent congressional Acts**

Policy area	Congressional act	Details and impact
Public health	Affordable Care Act 2010	A bill which required all citizens to have health insurance, states to provide health insurance exchanges for citizens and for subsidies for those on low or no income. The bill, whilst being compromised on heavily, provided health benefits to millions of previously uninsured Americans. It also allowed Obama to demonstrate his ability to provide leadership in getting a much-opposed bill through Congress.
Law and order	Bipartisan Safer Communities Act 2022	This created new gun control regulations after twenty-one people were killed at a shooting at the Robb Elementary School in Texas. The bill has an important impact because it expands an existing law that prevents people convicted of domestic abuse from owning a gun to include dating partners (rather than just spouses and former spouses). It also provides greater funding for mental health services and education programmes on gun violence. Its impact was limited by the need for compromise, as Democrats had only a slim majority in the Senate. Many Democrats who supported the bill had also called for a ban on assault-style rifles for people under 21 and banning certain high-capacity gun magazines.
	Violence Against Women Act reauthorisation 2022	Having expired in 2018, the Act repeatedly failed to get enough votes to pass again until a vote in 2022. Reauthorising all current VAWA grant programmes until 2027 and, in many cases, increasing its coverage. It expands special criminal jurisdiction of tribal courts to cover non-Native perpetrators of sexual assault, which is hugely significant given the high incidence of violence against Native American women. It includes added support for LGBTQ+ survivors of domestic violence, and dating violence, and establishes a federal civil court procedure for individuals whose intimate visual images are disclosed without their consent.
Foreign policy	Iran Resolution February 2020	The congressional resolution directs the president to terminate any US military action against Iran unless explicitly authorised by Congress. Its impact was nullified when Trump vetoed the resolution. He claimed that was 'a very insulting resolution' designed by Democrats to divide the Republicans and increase the chance of Democrat success in the November 2020 elections.
The economy	American Rescue Plan Act 2021	This was Biden's first major bill as president, which passed on a party line vote, narrowly securing Senate support by 50–49. This was a massive expenditure bill, spending an additional $1.9 trillion addressing the impact of COVID-19, especially on the

Continued

Table 3.10 **Continued**

Policy area	Congressional act	Details and impact
		economy. The final bill includes one-off direct payments of $1,400 to be sent off to most Americans. It extends weekly jobless benefit payments of $300 until later in that year and gave, $14 billion for vaccine distribution. Measures to raise the national minimum wage from $7.25 to $15 per hour were stripped from the bill primarily because of the lack of sufficient support amongst Senate Democrats, with Joe Manchin refusing to support the rise.
The economy	Debt Ceiling Agreement 2023	The bill lifted the debt ceiling, increasing the amount of money the US government can borrow, preventing a default until at least November 2025. The bill provides a new cap on non-defence spending and makes it more difficult to gain access to some welfare benefits such as SNAP food stamps.
	Federal Shutdown 2018–19	President Trump and the Democrat majority in the House of Representatives failed to agree on a federal budget leading to a government shutdown. A major part of the dispute was funding for a border wall. The Congressional Budget Office calculated that this cost the US economy $11 billion in direct costs. Democrats proposed a stop-gap measure to overcome the impasse with short-term funding, including wall expenditure. Senate Democrats filibustered this bill. Trump's approval rating dropped during the shutdown, with more Americans blaming him rather than Congress.
Economy and environment	Inflation Reduction Act 2022	The Act focuses on environmental protection and other measures to improve the US economy. It allocates $369 billion to reducing greenhouse gas emissions and investing in renewable energy sources and includes a new corporate minimum tax of 15%. The final Senate vote was 51–50, with every Democrat supporting the bill while all fifty of their Republican colleagues opposed the legislation. With the Senate evenly divided on the bill's passage, Vice President Kamala Harris cast the tie-breaking vote. The bill was created as a replacement for the failed Build Back Better Act, which was effectively blocked by Manchin in the Senate. He wanted the government to spend less and focus on reducing Inflation. The Inflation Reduction Act has a narrower focus, which frustrated some progressives such as Senator Sanders. Compromises meant that the Act helped protect oil and gas companies. The legislation was created to secure support from a top recipient of oil and gas donations, Senator Manchin. The law means that if the Biden administration wants solar and wind on public lands, it must offer new oil and gas leases first.

LIMITATIONS ON THE POLICY SIGNIFICANCE OF CONGRESS

Congress's impact on policy can be limited by several considerations:

The legislative process

We have already seen how the need for widespread agreement between the House and Senate, as well as the many obstacles faced within each chamber, make it difficult to pass legislation. This legislative inaction (and a consequent reduction in Congress's impact) has become more marked in recent years as a result of increased partisanship. Failing to pass a law may be seen as a failure to address a particular need in society. On the other hand, blocking an undesirable law could be seen as positive. Much depends on ideological perspective.

Executive power

The president can limit the impact of Congress via the use of the veto, which blocks a bill.

1. **Presidential veto.** Vetoes tend to occur more when the president and congressional majority are from opposing parties.
2. **Signing statements.** These are often issued by a president when signing a bill, stating that they will not enforce or support a certain measure, often claiming they are unconstitutional. President Trump issued a signing statement after signing the National Defense Authorisation Act of 2018 objecting to over fifty clauses, most of which sought to limit his ability to initiate military action. This set up an ongoing battle between Trump and Congress over war powers.

Definition

Presidential veto: The ability of the president to stop a congressional bill from becoming law.

Signing statement: An additional document issued by the president when signing a bill. This statement can give more details on how the president might interpret and act upon the bill.

Constitutional limits

Congress is restrained from passing laws that go beyond what is permitted by the Constitution. This may include:

1. Policy that is in the remit of state governments (federalism).
2. Laws that would undermine constitutional rights, such as those guaranteed by the Bill of Rights.
3. Powers given exclusively to the president.

Sometimes Congress has its impact restricted by Supreme Court rulings that overturn acts or parts of acts. In 2010 the *Shelby v Holder* case overturned the Voting Rights Act 1965, which sought to prevent racial discrimination in voting practices. Also, in 2010 the Supreme Court heard the case of *Citizens United v FEC*, which eventually overturned key elements of the Bipartisan Campaign Reform Act. The Act limited the role of the money in elections. The Supreme Court prevented Congress from having an impact by stating that money spent during election campaigns was covered by the First Amendment, freedom of speech protections.

KEY TOPIC DEBATE: IS THE LEGISLATIVE PROCESS IN CONGRESS FIT FOR PURPOSE?

The legislative process can be evaluated **using three criteria**:

Quality legislation

✓ Are laws carefully thought out, meeting the needs of the day? This will often be a subjective judgement based on ideology. There are, however, many processes that should provide quality legislation. The checks and balances within Congress should mean that bills are carefully considered from different perspectives. In addition, congressional committees can provide expertise with some members of Congress having long-standing involvement in a specific policy.

» Legislation such as the Affordable Care Act (which passed) and the American Care Act 2017 (which attempted to repeal and replace Obamacare but failed) spent several months being scrutinised by Congress. A huge array of amendments were voted on and detailed analysis of the health and economic implications of every part of the bill were analysed.

✗ On the other hand, the process of passing a bill can become incoherent with so many different viewpoints influencing the outcome. Rather than reflecting a considered strategy, bills often contain undesirable compromises or unhelpful amendments. Even though Congress has been accused of ineffectiveness there are times when it has arguably rushed legislation. This has led to badly considered laws.

» Defence bills often contain what many argue is unnecessary spending. The National Defense Authorisation Act 2019 was accused of being high-cost and low-result. Additional M1-Abrams tanks and littoral combat ships were ordered even though the US Army and Navy, respectively, did not ask for them and expressed concerns about their use.

Effective government

✓ Congress has regularly shown its ability to be effective in passing laws which are needed for US society. It can and does pass legislation and can be particularly effective when the president commands a majority in both chambers. Even under divided government, cross-party agreement has been secured for bills, especially in times of crisis. In addition, it could be argued that Congress is *sufficiently* effective. The Founding Fathers deliberately made it difficult to pass legislation, making compromise between interests and limited government key priorities. As such passing lots of bills each year might not be desirable.

» In early 2020, Congress passed four major COVID-19 bills ranging from health measures to economic protection in a matter of a few months, and President Biden was quickly able to add to this with a Coronavirus Relief Bill in 2021. The fiscal 2020 bills passed the Senate in December 2019, avoiding a repeat of the 35-day federal shutdown of 2018–19. This legislation passed despite the House and Senate being controlled by different parties.

✗ Congress, however, is often unable to pass laws and pass them in a timely fashion, meaning that the needs of the American people are often not met by their political leaders. The House, Senate and president need to agree on a bill, and a filibuster makes even more difficult to pass laws through the Senate. In addition, increased polarisation and partisanship means that, unless all three bodies are controlled by one party, it becomes almost impossible to pass legislation.

» Standard and Poor reported that the Federal Government shutdown for 35 days in 2018–19 cost the US economy $3.6 billion. Congress continued to argue over the Violence Against Women Act after it expired in 2018 failing to agree to its reauthorisation until 2022.

Democracy

✓ The legislative process promotes democracy in several different ways, ensuring that legislation responds to the wishes and interests of the public. The separation of powers means that members of Congress are highly sensitive to public opinion and will respond to the public needs when passing laws. In addition, the process itself allows individual members of Congress to propose amendments that might be particularly beneficial to their constituency, for example protecting or subsidising a key state industry.

» The 2019 National Defense Authorisation Act contained increased military funding and benefits for military corporations, but also promoted the interests of the general public by providing parental leave for federal workers and a repeal of the military 'widow's tax'. In this example, Congress is providing pluralist democracy, promoting the interests of different groups in society.

✗ Congress may focus on representing the interests of individual constituencies rather than the wishes and interests of the United States as a whole. Pork-barrelling can be seen as undemocratic because it leads to the *over-representation* of local interests. Also, Congress is strongly influenced by lobbying, especially from wealthy organisations including corporations. This means that, rather than reflecting the wishes and interests of the general public, Congress is only representing a small elite in US society; legislative outcomes benefit the few not the many. The close relationship between corporations and politicians is developed through the funding of party election campaigns by the wealthy. In addition, many politicians are former heads of business or can use their political influence to pursue a corporate career if they move away from politics. It is common for former advisers of politicians to work for professional lobbyists to influence congressional laws on behalf of corporate interests.

» In April 2020 Ocasio Cortez accused Congress of not supporting the average American but instead giving major bailouts to wealthy corporations in its response to the coronavirus crisis. Other examples can be seen in the 'Representation' section earlier in this chapter, with examples such as big Pharma donations to members of Congress and their failure to tackle drug pricing issues.

Key Topic Debate Summary: Is the legislative process in Congress fit for purpose?

FOR	KEY CRITERIA	AGAINST
✓ The high levels of checks and balances within the legislative process ensures that legislation is carefully considered. ✓ Bills are not rushed through or driven through by one party or a dominant executive but are carefully assessed with lots of amendments.	Can Congress develop high-**quality legislation?**	✗ The process is so fragmented that there is no rational overview. Bills are often a collection of disparate ideas that do not make up a coherent whole. ✗ In addition, some bills are rushed and ill considered, especially under a unified government.
✓ Congress can pass laws and regularly achieves legislative goals. ✓ Congress is especially able to pass laws in emergency situations. ✓ Passing lots of laws is not necessarily desirable; the Founding Fathers and US public favour limited government and have deliberately made it difficult to pass new laws.	Does the legislative process allow for **effective government** in which decisions can be made?	✗ Excessive checks within Congress and increased partisanship have led to an inability to get anything done. This legislative sclerosis means that Congress is often unable to legislate to meet the developing needs of society. ✗ There have been many examples of major failures to make critical decisions for the United States with gridlock taking place. Specifically, federal shutdowns are a major concern.
✓ Both the House and Senate are elected and have high levels of control over the legislative process. ✓ They are responsive to constituency needs when legislating due to threat of removal.	To what extent is the process **democratic?**	✗ Bills are often subject to special interests, being strongly influenced by professional lobbyists or corporations. ✗ They are often influenced by localism or over-representation of specific districts. Individual members of Congress use pork-barrelling or position as committee chairs. ✗ Legislative outcomes do not represent the broader public or even the majority, leading to elitism rather than democracy.

Exam Tip: Improving AO2 Analysis and AO3 Evaluation

You can make a strong overall evaluative judgement by deciding which of the three criteria you think is the most important. How would you argue for this in an essay? Be sure to include this judgement in your conclusion as well as in the main body of the essay.

Learning Review

1. What are the five features of the legislative process in Congress? What is the meaning of each of these five features?
2. What is the role of congressional committees in the legislative process?
3. What are the main differences in the legislative process in the House and the Senate?
4. What is the filibuster? Why is it significant?

5. What are the ways in which Congress has had a major policy impact in recent years in the following policy areas?
   a. Public health
   b. Law and order
   c. Foreign policy
   d. The economy.
6. What are the three main limits on the policy significance (policy impact) of Congress?
7. For each of the following what are the arguments that suggest Congress' approach to legislation is positive? What are the negative arguments?
   a. Quality legislation
   b. Effective government
   c. Democracy.

CASE STUDY 3.2: 2022 MID-TERM ELECTIONS

Source: Sarah Silbiger / Stringer via Getty Images

Photo 3.4 **Kevin McCarthy at a Republican election party event on the night of the mid-term elections**

Overview

The mid-term elections of 2022 involved all 435 seats in the US House of Representatives being contested alongside 35 of the 100 seats in the Senate as well as 39 state and territorial governors races. In the run up to the mid-terms, opinion polls were suggesting a 'red wave' in which Republicans would gain a large number of seats in Congress at the expense of Democrats. In practice the Republicans only made modest gains in the House (with a net gain of only nine seats), but this was enough to allow them to replace Democrats as the majority party. In the Senate, the Republicans made a net loss of one seat, allowing the Democrats to maintain control of this chamber. In governors' races, Democrats made a net gain of two states. In the context of US history, the mid-term election results were disappointing for Republicans because the president's party typically performs much worse in mid-terms. The year 2022 was the first mid-term since 1934 in which the president's party did not lose any incumbent senators. It was also the first mid-term since 1986 in which the president's party achieved a net gain of governorships.

Presidential-congressional relations

Whilst Republicans performed less strongly than anticipated, the biggest impact of the mid-terms was the Republicans gaining a majority from the Democrats in the House of Representatives. With President Biden now lacking a majority, the United States moved from unified to divided government. The House became more aggressive in proposing an alternative legislative agenda to that of Biden and was more able to block any legislation coming from the White House. Incoming House Speaker, Kevin McCarthy vowed to pass legislation to control immigration even more strictly at US borders and reduced government expenditure. It was the new Republican majority that led to Biden issuing his first veto in March 2023, rejecting a bill which banned the Federal Government from making environmental considerations when investing in pension funds. In addition, the Republicans used their majority in the House to launch high-profile investigations into President Biden. In January 2023 the Republican-led House Oversight Committee began investigations into Biden and his family. The House Oversight website said that 'Chairman James Comer and Oversight Committee Republicans are investigating the Biden family's domestic and international business dealings to determine whether these activities compromise U.S. national security and President Biden's ability to lead with impartiality. Members of the Biden family have a pattern of peddling access to the highest levels of government to enrich themselves, often to the detriment of U.S. interests' (https://oversight.house.gov/landing/biden-family-investigation/).

Even with a Democratic Senate majority, Biden found it much harder to pass bills through Congress once his party lost control of the House. The ability of the Democrats to retain control of the Senate was still important for Biden, however. It gave him some support and momentum in Congress when seeking to pass bills and also meant that he could continue to shape the federal judiciary and get nominations passed in the Senate.

Parties

The mid-term elections continued to show sharp difference between the two parties with a strong campaign focus on abortion rights. This followed the *Dobbs v Jackson* decision in June 2022, in which the majority on the Supreme Court overturned *Roe v Wade* and ruled that abortion was not a constitutional right. This allowed states to choose whether to ban or heavily restrict abortion. Most Republican candidates supported the Dobbs decision whilst Democrats campaigned hard on this issue, arguing that it was a major restriction on women's rights. In addition, the outcome of the mid-terms highlighted significant divisions *within* the Republican Party. Kevin McCarthy announced he would run for the position of Speaker in the new Republican-led House. Many members of the Freedom Caucus, a conservative faction amongst House Republicans, did not vote for McCarthy to become Speaker. McCarthy had to face fifteen ballots over several days before he managed to secure enough votes to become Speaker with some Freedom Caucus members eventually giving their support after McCarthy made several concessions to them. McCarthy was removed as Speaker in October 2023 and replaced with an even more conservative Speaker Mike Johnson. Republican rules mean that just one House member can initiate a motion to remove the Speaker – a new rule that MCarthy had to agree to in order to get chosen to the Speaker's position in the first place.

Democracy

The elections themselves can be seen as a major exercise in democracy with congressional elections taking place every two years and politicians having to respond to public opinion. Turnout was 46.6% (the highest mid-term turnout since 1970) with almost 106 million votes for the two main parties in House elections. Democracy as an ideal was much debated during the mid-term campaign. President Biden said that the elections were a battle for 'the soul of the nation' as Republican extremists sought to undermine or even abolish democracy. This had its roots in former President Trump's rejection of the 2020 election result. He attacked Make America Great Again (MAGA) supporting Republicans. 'Make America Great Again' was Trump's campaign slogan in 2016. Biden said that not all Republicans are MAGA extremists but that the Republicans were now 'dominated, driven and intimidated' by Trump who sought to undermine US elections. A huge number of election deniers were successfully re-elected to the House and Senate in 2022.

Invisible primaries 2023–24

The mid-terms also had an impact on the 2024 presidential election race. They influenced the popularity of certain Democrats and, in particular, Republican presidential hopefuls for 2024. Partly because of Trump's prominence in the 2022 mid-terms, the relatively poor performance of the Republicans led to a decline in his influence and support within the Republican Party, damaging his chances of winning the Republican presidential primaries for the 2024 elections. On the other hand, Florida Governor Ron DeSantis won re-election with an increased share of the vote (+9 percentage points). With huge media focus on his result, DeSantis was able to position himself as a favourite to win Republican presidential primaries. Trump went on to attack DeSantis directly saying that his move to become president was very disloyal. DeSantis quickly started to attend events in states such as New Hampshire and South Carolina, which are early voting primary states, more than a year before any primary voting can take place.

OVERSIGHT

We will now move on to the third critical function of Congress: providing oversight on both the executive and judicial branches. This oversight forms a central part of the checks and balances that the Founding Fathers saw as essential to preventing tyranny. First, we will consider how Congress conducts this oversight of the executive; then we will ask whether it works to restrict the executive; finally, we will move on to the same considerations for judicial oversight.

KEY TOPIC DEBATE: CAN CONGRESS PROVIDE EFFECTIVE CHECKS ON THE EXECUTIVE BRANCH?

Spec key term

Oversight: The ability of one branch of government to supervise the work of another.

Congressional checks on the executive

Oversight is a key part of the checks and balances of the US Constitution. In terms of the executive, Congress can check the policy and operation of Federal Government departments and key politicians such as the president and cabinet members. The Constitution outlines several ways in which Congress is empowered to provide oversight of the executive.

Domestic policy

 **Legislate**

This power can be used by Congress to amend, reject or authorise presidential policy proposals. In addition, it can be used to regulate presidential power, for example by passing a law that restricts the president or requires certain actions. Whilst it is not strictly legislating, Congress can also pass resolutions that instruct or restrict presidential action.

Appropriate funds

A key part of the legislative process is the power given to Congress to determine how public money is spent. Any executive policy or action that requires funding must be authorised by Congress. There are specific appropriations committees in both the House and the Senate that examine expenditure in detail.

President's powers/limits to congressional power

Presidents can resist or overcome some of these attempts at oversight, for example, by using their veto power to reject congressional legislation. In addition, presidents have avoided scrutiny of the executive branch by refusing to allow certain members of the executive branch to testify to Congress. In other circumstances, the executive branch has refused to release documents, for example citing their sensitive national security status. Presidents may hold a majority in both chambers of Congress. This usually means that levels of oversight are very low as Congress seeks to support the president, not restrict him or her.

The imperial presidency

This theory suggests that over time presidents have developed methods to bypass the constitutional restrictions that Congress uses to regulate presidential power. These methods include the use of signing statements, executive orders, executive agreements and the president's ability to use media focus to control the political agenda and bypass Congress. This topic is dealt with in full in Chapter 4, 'The Presidency'.

Foreign policy

 **Declare war**

The president may be named in the Constitution as the Commander in Chief of the Army and Navy of the United States but Congress is given the constitutional power to declare war and as such has some control over military action the president wishes to take.

Ratify treaties (Senate only)

It is the president who negotiates treaties with other countries but the Senate that has the right to accept or reject them. This means that the president cannot easily make major foreign policy agreements without Senate support.

Unilateral foreign policy action

There is also an argument that presidents are extremely powerful in foreign policy allowing them to operate with few limitations. Some of this stems from practical considerations in the modern world, where the need for speed and secrecy allows the president considerable advantage, often resulting in them taking unilateral action, such as committing troops to war without consulting Congress.

Other presidential actions

✓ Impeachment and removal from office

Members of the executive can be impeached and removed from office by the House and Senate. This is the ultimate check, stripping people of their power if they act improperly. This was dealt with earlier in this chapter under the 'Distribution of power within Congress' heading, with the impeachment information starting on page 43.

✓ Ratify appointments (Senate only)

Presidential nominations to the judiciary as well as senior executive positions are subject to scrutiny by a Senate committee, and the full Senate has the constitutional right to reject these nominations. This can remove unsuitable nominations and might push the president to appoint executive leaders who are more closely ideologically aligned with the Senate position. This process has become more partisan in recent years with greater determination to block presidential appointments by senators from the opposing party.

✗ Impeachment and removal from office

This is very difficult to achieve. Both chambers need to agree and a two-thirds vote is required for removal from office. In addition, a president may hold a majority in one or both chambers of Congress, which is likely to reduce any desire to block presidential appointments or investigate their actions.

Limits to congressional oversight of the executive

These limitations strongly relate to the powers of the president and are dealt with above as well as in detail in Chapter 4, 'The Presidency'. Table 3.11 summarises the main methods that Congress can use to have oversight of the president as well as main limits to congressional oversight.

Table 3.11 Main methods of and limits on congressional oversight of the executive

Main methods of congressional oversight	Main limits on congressional oversight
• Legislate • Appropriate funds • Declare war • Ratify treaties (Senate only) • Ratify presidential appointments (Senate only) • Impeach and remove from office	• Imperial presidency theory • President's unilateral foreign policy power • President's powers such as the veto • Unified government in which the president holds a majority in the House and Senate

Key Topic Debate Summary: Can Congress provide effective checks on the executive branch?

FOR	KEY CRITERIA	AGAINST
✓ Congress has legislative power and can reject or amend a president's legislative agenda. ✓ Congress has budgetary control and can refuse to authorise funding for presidential policies.	Can Congress check the president in **domestic policy**?	✗ The president can use signing statements and executive orders to bypass Congress and achieve their legislative goals. ✗ Presidents with a majority in Congress may find it easy to pass legislation due to high partisanship.
✓ Congress can declare war and thus has power to deny the president the right to initiate military action. ✓ The Senate must ratify treaties signed by the president.	Can Congress check the president in **foreign policy**?	✗ The president can use executive agreements to bypass the need to ratify treaties. ✗ The president often uses their military power unilaterally without seeking congressional permission.

FOR	KEY CRITERIA	AGAINST
✓ The impeachment process can hold a president to account by allowing detailed investigation of their actions as well as possible removal from office. ✓ Congressional committees can investigate any aspect of the presidency, including direct questioning of senior members of the executive. ✓ Presidential appointments to the Supreme Court and senior executive positions must be ratified by the Senate.	Can Congress hold the president and the rest of the executive **responsible for their actions**?	✗ The impeachment process is difficult to use successfully requiring two-thirds of senators to vote to remove a president. ✗ Congressional committees can be dominated by the president's party leading to limited scrutiny. ✗ Presidents with a majority in one or both chambers of Congress may escape oversight.

Exam Tip: Improving AO2 Analysis and AO3 Evaluation

You can improve the quality of your answer by showing that power is not static; the ability of Congress to check the president will vary according to the specific political context. Consider the three factors affecting the relationship between the president and Congress below. How could these factors have a major impact on the extent to which Congress can restrict the president?

Factors affecting the relationship between the presidency and Congress

The extent to which Congress is able or is willing to provide strong oversight depends on a number of factors:

Divided or partisan government

Congressional restrictions on the president are likely to be far more aggressive if one or both chambers of Congress are controlled by the opposing party. This has become even more apparent in the era of high partisanship.

The popularity of the president (and Congress)

If a president is personally popular then this makes it more difficult for Congress to act in a restrictive way. Members of Congress, keen to get re-elected, are often influenced by public opinion.

The policy area

Relations between the president and Congress may alter depending on the area addressed, with presidents apparently more restricted in domestic policy than foreign policy. Presidents may have an advantage at times of crisis as the public, the media and even Congress may look to the president for leadership.

Congressional checks on the judiciary

The Supreme Court is mainly limited by the Constitution itself, not the specific actions or powers of Congress. The Supreme Court cannot act in the same way as Congress because the Supreme Court cannot legislate. It can only determine whether the Constitution has been broken. In this area, the Supreme Court is above Congress because it can declare congressional acts to be unconstitutional. Congress' ability to restrict the Supreme Court is limited to the following:

Amend the Constitution

Congress can effectively overturn a Supreme Court's constitutional ruling by changing the Constitution itself. Amending the Constitution is extremely difficult given the two-thirds (House and Senate) and three-quarters (states) thresholds, so in practice, this is not a significant congressional limit on the Supreme Court. We have to go back to 1970 for a clear example of Congress using this to overturn a court ruling.

» In *Oregon v Mitchell* 1970 the Supreme Court ruled that states could select their own voting age. Congress subsequently amended the Constitution to ensure that everyone could vote from the age of 18.

» The Supreme Court overturned the Flag Protection Act of 1990. Congress made several attempts in the 1990s to overturn this ruling with a flag protection amendment to the Constitution but fell short of the two-thirds in the Senate each time.

Impeach justices

Justices can be impeached and removed from office for high crimes or misdemeanours. The only justice to be impeached was Samuel Chase in 1805 after accusations of bias by President Jefferson. He was not removed but instead was acquitted by the Senate. In recent years, there have been claims that Justices have gone way beyond the meaning of the Constitution in their rulings, but nevertheless there have been no modern impeachments.

Ratify nominations

Any nominee to the court is subject to Senate oversight and requires the support of over 50% in a Senate vote. The Senate can prevent judicial nominees from making it to the bench of the Supreme Court. Whilst there have been no recent cases of a nominee failing to pass a Senate vote, justices have been withdrawn because of a lack of Senate support. In 2005 President Bush withdrew his nomination of Harriet Miers after Democrats criticised her lack of experience and some Republicans feared that she was excessively moderate.

You can see a full discussion of checks and balances on the Supreme Court in the Key topic debate in Chapter 5, 'The Supreme Court and Civil Rights', pages 129–132.

! **Exam Tip** – It is important to use evidence to show how an argument can be supported. Rather than simply describing something that happened you should *apply* your evidence to the question you are being asked – what does it tell us about the question? You can evaluate evidence by telling the reader how strong that evidence is. To illustrate – look again at the debate box above and note the point which states 'There is very little evidence, across United States history, of Congress overturning Court decisions.' It might be possible to cite Mitchell v Oregon as a case which was overturned by Congress when they amended the Constitution. On the other hand, if the most recent example of this is 1970 and there are very few examples in total, we can evaluate the evidence by stating it is not very strong in supporting the view that there are high levels of checks. This is *applying* evidence to the question.

THE EFFECTIVENESS OF CONSTITUTIONAL POWERS

The effectiveness of Congress could be evaluated by examining its three main roles of oversight, representation and legislation, all of which have a constitutional basis. This has been covered a great deal in the sections above.

An alternative way of evaluating Congress' constitutional powers is to examine three constitutional aspects of its power covered throughout this chapter. These are its power to control legislation, its power over foreign policy and the exclusive powers of each chamber, especially the Senate. This is outlined for you in the Key Debate Summary below. More details and examples can be found in both this chapter and the Presidency chapter.

Key Topic Debate Summary: Is Congress effective in carrying out its constitutional powers?

FOR	KEY CRITERIA	AGAINST
✓ Congress can and does pass legislation, especially in times of crisis. ✓ Checks and balances lead to high levels of scrutiny and good legislation. ✓ Passing lots of laws is not always desirable.	Is Congress effective in its **legislative power**?	✗ Excessive checks and balances and the separation of powers make Congress an ineffective legislative body that fails to legislate and fails to produce good quality legislation. ✗ Increased partisanship has further reduced Congress' ability to be an effective legislative body.

FOR	KEY CRITERIA	AGAINST
✓ Congress has a major influence over foreign policy through defence authorisations, such as the passing of the National Defense Authorisation Act. ✓ Congress can and does call a halt to military action, effectively controlling the president.	Is Congress effective in carrying out its **foreign policy functions**?	✗ Congress has often been passive and reactive in this area, deferring to the president. ✗ The president easily takes control of foreign policy, largely unchecked, as a result of the need for quick and secretive decisions.
✓ The Senate has used its ability to reject presidential treaties. ✓ The Senate has blocked presidential nominations to the executive and judicial branches.	Does the Senate make effective use of its **exclusive powers**?	✗ The Senate rarely rejects treaties negotiated by a president and is easily bypassed using executive agreements (see Chapter 4, 'The Presidency', pages 103 and 104).

Exam Tip: Improving AO2 Analysis and AO3 Evaluation

Notice that this question asks specifically about **constitutional powers.** Ensure that everything you discuss can be shown to have a constitutional basis. This returns to the theme of ensuring that you focus on the keyword(s) of a question and answer the question set. Also, you do not have to consistently argue for one side of the debate – Is Congress more successful in one of these areas compared to the other two? Is it effective in one area but ineffective in another? If you think this is the case, then include this in your conclusion as well as the main body of your essay.

Learning Review

1. What are the main methods that Congress can use to maintain oversight of the president?
2. What are the main arguments for and against the view that Congress can effectively check the president?
3. What are the main factors affecting the relationship between Congress and the president?
4. What are the main ways in which Congress provides a check on the Supreme Court?

CHANGING ROLES AND POWERS

Congress has experienced very few changes to its role or power as a result of constitutional changes. Essentially, its roles and powers remain largely the same as they always have. The way in which Congress performs those roles, however, has changed a great deal, mainly due to partisanship, as examined above.

The powers of Congress have evolved as a result of changing circumstances either in politics specifically or in society as a whole. A great deal of the decline in power of Congress comes about as a result of an increase in the power of the president.

Ways in which Congress has experienced a decline in power:

- The rise of presidential power. This is dealt with fully in 'The imperial presidency' section of Chapter 4 starting on page 102.
- Change in control of foreign policy. You can read more on this in Chapter 4, which covers the rise of presidential power in foreign policy (see page 111).
- Partisanship. The role of parties and the way this affects the role and power of Congress is covered in the following section, 'the changing role of parties.'

The changing role of parties in Congress

Congress can be seen as a set of 535 individuals across the House and the Senate or it can be analysed and understood by considering it as two chambers dominated by political parties. As we have already seen, parties do have an impact on the behaviour of individual politicians in Congress. Congressional politics can be viewed, therefore, as a team sport in which Democrats compete against Republicans.

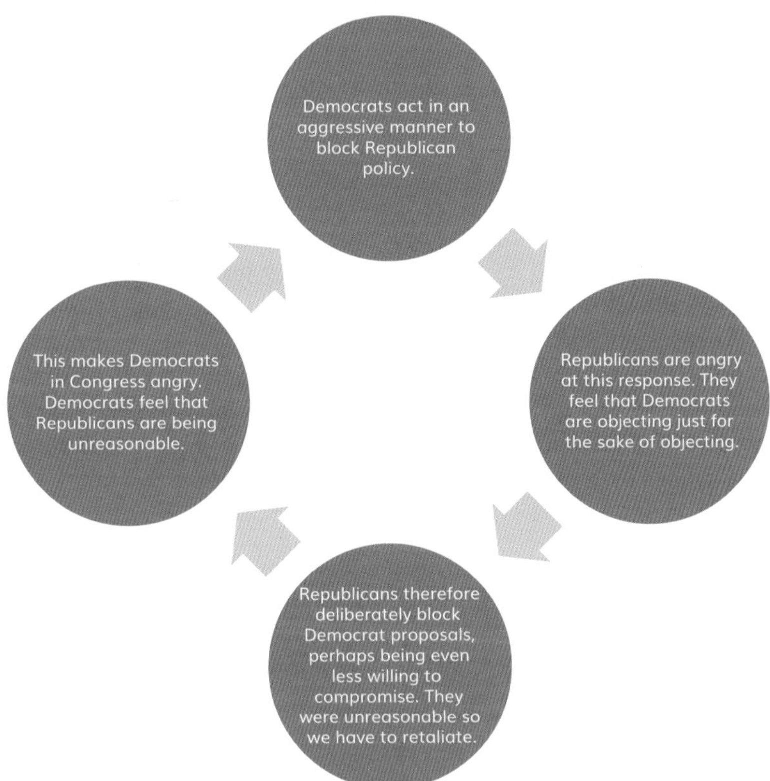

Figure 3.6 **The reinforcing effect of partisanship**

Parties have always carried out the same kind of roles in Congress. These are the same as three of the main roles of Congress: to represent, to legislate and to have oversight of the other branches of government. What has changed, quite dramatically, is *the way* in which parties and therefore Congress carry out these three roles.

Increased partisanship

There has been a trend in recent years towards parties becoming more united internally. This can be seen in the voting records of individual members of Congress. It is very common for the vast majority of Democrats to vote for a bill and the vast majority of Republicans to vote against a bill (or the other way around). The causes of this are many and complex. It is clear that partisanship has tended to encourage even greater partisanship. It is impossible to pinpoint a starting point for this or an original failure, but the reinforcing effect of partisanship can be seen in Figure 3.6.

» Increased partisanship started to emerge in the 1970s but can be seen most clearly from the 1990s onwards. In 1994, two years into the Clinton presidency, Republicans, led by new Speaker Newt Gingrich, were highly unified in opposing Clinton's policies. Gingrich developed a national campaign, the Contract with America, and used his authority to press Republicans into opposing Clinton policies and actions.

KEY TOPIC DEBATE: DO PARTIES EXERT TOO MUCH CONTROL IN CONGRESS?

This debate will be explored by investigating the three main roles of Congress. We will begin with the oversight or checks function and then move on to the other roles of legislation and representation.

Partisanship and oversight

✓ High levels of party unity have a major impact on Congress' oversight role. During times of divided government, when the president is from one party and the opposing party has a majority in at least one chamber, then oversight is likely to be strong. It means that members of the majority party will be very determined in challenging a president of the opposing party. Congress is attempting to find fault with the president and organises oversight that is unnecessary or overly aggressive. The opposite can occur when the president has a majority in Congress. The oversight function is less effective with Congress being accused of working to support anything done in the name of the party and failing to check the president.

» Trump held a majority in both chambers of Congress from 2016 to 2018 but lost that majority with Democrats capturing the House from 2018 to 2020. Despite some major concerns and questions about the Trump presidency, the Republican-led Congress organised very few investigations. Within a few months of Democrats taking control of the House in the mid-term elections, fourteen House committees had launched investigations into over fifty different aspects of the Trump presidency. These included investigations into communications between President Trump and President of Russia Vladimir Putin, security clearances at the White House, Trump's personal finances, emergency wall-building powers, separation of asylum seeking families and appointments to the Environmental Protection Agency from major corporations. The most significant investigations came with the hearings that led the House of Representative to impeach the president.

✖ Despite partisanship, Congress still performs an effective role in providing checks on the executive branch. It could be argued that they operate at the right level regardless of party majority. When the president lacks a majority, the checks are in line with the aims of the Founding Fathers to have limited government and high checks and balances. Even with a majority, presidents often find that they are strongly curtailed by Congress.

» President Biden has found it extremely difficult to pass many of his policy priorities despite a majority in the House and Senate in his first two years in office. Where policy has been passed, such as the Inflation Reduction Act in 2022, it has often required significant compromises. In this case the Inflation Reduction Act came about as a compromise bill after Biden's Build Back Better plan failed to pass Congress. Even the new Act has many compromises that Biden did not want such as protections for oil and gas companies to continue to extract CO_2-producing energy.

Partisanship and legislation

✔ When the presidency, House and Senate are controlled by the same party, partisanship can make it too easy to pass legislation. Parties then wield too much influence because a majority in Congress is likely to agree with the president on legislative packages without careful scrutiny of a bill. The

Source: ANDREW CABALLERO-REYNOLDS / Contributor via Getty Images

Photo 3.5 **Biden calls on Congress to support his Build Back Better Act in 2021**

excessive role of parties under a divided government makes the opposite occur; Congress goes too far the other way and is highly unlikely to pass legislation. This has led to a decline in the number of bills passed by Congress and created legislative gridlock. The combination of the separation of powers and partisanship results in Congress being unable to fulfil its legislative function.

» In the year after the 2018 mid-terms, the House hit a record score for party unity. Democrats voted with the majority of their party on 95% of occasions. Federal shutdown, caused by Congress being unable to pass a budget bill, has become more common in recent years with longer periods of shutdown. The three longest shutdowns in US history have all occurred since the 1990s, during a time when the president faced a majority of the opposing party in at least one chamber of Congress. These hugely harmful shutdowns are summarised in Table 3.12.

Table 3.12 **Government shutdowns**

	Total days	President	House majority
1995–96	21	Clinton (D)	Republican
2013	16	Obama (D)	Republican
2018–19	35	Trump (R)	Democrat

✗ Parties and party leaders do not have absolute control over their politicians. Parties are often considered quite weak in the United States with relatively low unity compared to the United Kingdom, for instance. Individual members of Congress can vote for legislation based on its merits not due to pressure from party leaders. As a result, there are many cases in which parties in Congress have agreed on a legislative item or compromised to allow a bill to pass. It has been the lack of complete partisanship (i.e. the lack of power of parties) that has made it difficult to pass legislation through the Senate in recent years.

» President Trump faced a Senate with a Republican majority holding just fifty-two seats and for Biden between 2020 and 2022 it was exactly 50–50. Neither president could rely on all senators from their own party giving support, making it hard to pass legislation because parties were too weak. Biden found that he lacked support from Senators Manchin and Sinema (who eventually left the Democrat Party and became an independent) on many major bills.

Partisanship and representation

✓ Partisanship can undermine representation. A member of Congress might automatically vote according to the wishes of party leaders or the majority of the party. This may lead them to ignore or contradict the wishes of their constituency. The high levels of party unity amongst Democrats in opposing President Trump suggests this has been happening.

» In 2020 there were thirty-one House Democrats representing districts where Trump got a majority of the vote in 2016. These Democrats, despite being in more conservative areas, typically voted with Democrat party leaders or against Trump. This includes the impeachment votes, border wall funding requests and attempts to repeal Obamacare.

✗ Parties do not prevent representation. High unity and polarisation between parties could be seen as responding to the wishes of the public. In the House, for example, conservative districts have become more conservative. The general public has polarised in the United States and Republican politicians are simply giving voters what they are asking for in conservative districts. It is politicians in marginal constituencies who are most likely to compromise with politicians of another party, but there are fewer of these marginal constituencies in existence.

» It is obvious Democrats such as Representative Ocasio Cortez or Senator Sanders representing particularly liberal areas of the United States, will not seek compromise with Republicans. Doing so would limit their ability to represent their constituents. It is also obvious that Democrat senators such as Senators Manchin and Sinema, representing more conservative states, will sometimes oppose Democrat proposed policies to respond to the views of their states.

Key Topic Debate Summary: Do parties exert too much control in Congress?

FOR	KEY CRITERIA	AGAINST
✓ During times of divided government, oversight is likely to be too strong. Congress is attempting to find fault with the president and organises oversight that is unnecessary or overly aggressive. ✓ Oversight function is ineffective if the president has a majority in both chambers. Congress being accused of working to support anything done in the name of the party and failing to check the president.	Do parties and partisanship undermine the **oversight role?**	✗ Despite partisanship, Congress operates at the right level regardless of party majority. ✗ Checks are in line with the aims of the Founding Fathers to have limited government and high checks and balances. ✗ Even with a majority, presidents are often strongly checked by Congress.
✓ When the presidency, House and Senate are controlled by the same party, partisanship can make it too easy to pass legislation. ✓ Under a divided government the opposite occurs; Congress goes too far the other way and is highly unlikely to pass legislation. Congress is highly ineffective in meeting the needs of the United States if it cannot legislate.	Do parties and partisanship undermine the **legislative role?**	✗ Parties are often considered quite weak in the United States, allowing individual members of Congress to vote for legislation based on its merits not due to pressure from party leaders. ✗ Congress has successfully passed legislation on a regular basis, often with compromises between parties, which can improve the quality of a bill.
✓ Partisanship can undermine representation when a member of Congress might automatically vote according to the wishes of their party rather than constituents. ✓ Under a divided government, the opposing party of the president is often united in attempting to vote against presidential proposals regardless of the public opinion in their district or state.	Do parties and partisanship undermine the **representative role?**	✗ High unity and polarisation between parties could be seen as responding to the wishes of the public not rejecting it. ✗ The general public has polarised in the United States and Republican politicians are simply giving voters what they are asking for in conservative districts. ✗ Politicians in marginal constituencies are likely to compromise with politicians of another party, showing their desire to represent public opinion in their constituency.

Exam Tip: Improving AO2 Analysis and AO3 Evaluation

There are two separate aspects to this question. Firstly, we need to understand how strong partisanship is, exactly, and secondly, how this partisanship affects each role. If partisanship is not particularly strong then it cannot have a major impact on the roles of Congress. To focus on the question, you should work out how strong partisanship is but keep your written answer concentrated on the keywords of 'too much control'. The word 'too' is deceptive. It means excessive or more than is desirable. You need to apply your AO1 knowledge to this.

Learning Review

1. What are the arguments for and against the view that Congress is effective in carrying out its constitutional powers?
2. What is meant by increased partisanship in Congress?
3. How has partisanship affected each of the three main roles of Congress? In what ways has partisanship negatively affected these roles?

Chapter Summary

- ✓ Congress is a bicameral legislature with power shared between the House and Senate. The House and the Senate can be seen as coequal legislative branches.
- ✓ Each chamber has exclusive and joint roles. Arguably the joint role of legislating is the most important, although it is relatively easy to argue that the Senate's exclusive powers are more significant than the House's exclusive powers.
- ✓ There is a high level of incumbency re-election; members of Congress find it relatively easy to get re-elected once in office.
- ✓ The main roles of Congress are to legislate, represent and conduct executive oversight.
- ✓ Congress has the potential to have a major policy impact on the United States with its ability to legislate and its high levels of independence from presidential pressure.
- ✓ Congress is strongly affected by the workings of parties and increased partisanship. Highly united parties have a major impact on the way in which Congress carries out its roles.

Exam Style Questions

- **Evaluate the view that Congress is not a sufficiently representative body. (30 marks)**
- **Evaluate the view that the Senate has a more important role to play in US politics than the House of Representatives. (30 marks)**
- **Evaluate the view that Congress is unable to regulate the president. (30 marks)**
- **Evaluate the view that partisanship has undermined Congress' ability to carry out its roles. (30 marks)**
- **Evaluate the view that the House of Representative and the Senate do not fulfil their legislative and representative functions adequately. (30 marks)**

Further Resources

The official website of Congress is a mine of information about voting records, legislative numbers, how Congress works and the latest issues which Congress is dealing with. Available at https://www.congress.gov/ (accessed 22 July 2023).

Visit *The Hill*, a news-based website devoted to all things Congress. There are separate sections under their news heading devoted to the House and the Senate. Available at https://thehill.com/ (accessed 22 July 2023).

Mounk's article in *The Atlantic* looks at the ways in which President Trump was able to sidestep congressional regulations and examines the implications of a 50–50 Senate during the first two years of the Biden presidency. See Yascha Mounk, 'The Problem with a 50–50 Senate', 6 January 2021. Available at https://www.theatlantic.com/ideas/archive/2021/01/problem-50-50-senate/617565/ (accessed 22 July 2023).

Pew Research has a host of facts of figures on Congress, including detailed analysis of the social composition of Congress. See Katherine Schaeffer, 'The Changing Face of Congress in 8 Charts', Pew Research Center, 7 February 2023. Available at https://www.pewresearch.org/fact-tank/2023/02/07/the-changing-face-of-congress/ (accessed 22 July 2023).

Visit https://bloomsbury.pub/colclough-essentials-us to access additional materials to support teaching and learning.

4 THE PRESIDENCY

Chapter Preview

The US president is the equivalent of the prime minister in the United Kingdom. Both are seen as providing the main political leadership for the whole country, acting as the driving force for their respective nations. Presidents have a significant leadership role and a great deal of authority, with enormous expectation placed upon them to lead the country. At the same time, the Founding Fathers created major constraints on their power, limiting the president's ability to act.

Given the extent of their roles and responsibilities, presidents cannot work alone. The US *presidency* refers to the roles, powers and limits of the president, as well as the support they have from other individuals and offices within the executive branch. This chapter will help you to understand presidential roles, powers and limits. You will learn what gives a president the ability to provide leadership by considering both the powers outlined in the US Constitution as well as other, informal sources of their power such as their mandate. In addition, a full understanding of the presidency requires an awareness of the relationship between the president and Congress and the Supreme Court. This will help you to appreciate the extent to which these institutions limit the president. As we saw in Chapters 2 and 3, 'The Constitution' and 'Congress', respectively, there are significant restrictions placed on the president.

Key Questions and Debates

» What are the main roles of the president outlined in the US Constitution?

» What are the informal sources of presidential power that help them to have control?

» What is the nature of the relationship between the president and Congress, and who is more powerful?

» What is the nature of the relationship between the president and Supreme Court?

» What are the main limits on presidential power and how can the power of the president vary?

» Do presidents have different power in domestic and foreign policy?

Specification Checklist

3.1 Formal sources of presidential power outlined in the US Constitution

» The role as the head of state.

» The role of head of government.

» The significance of these powers with reference to presidents since 1992.

3.2 Informal sources of presidential power

» The electoral mandate, executive orders, national events and the cabinet.

» Powers of persuasion including the nature/characteristics of each president.

» Executive Office of the President (EXOP) including the role of the National Security Council (NSC), Office of Management and Budget (OMB) and the White House Office (WHO).

» The significance of these powers with reference to presidents since 1992.

3.3 The presidency

» Relationships between the presidency and Congress and the presidency and Supreme Court, and why this varies.

» Limitations on presidential power and why this varies between presidents:

- Changing nature of power over their term in office.
- Congress, the Supreme Court and the Constitution.
- the election cycle and divided government.

» The significance of these limitations with reference to presidents since 1992.

3.4 Interpretations and debates of the US presidency with reference to presidents since 1992

» The imperial presidency.

» The extent of presidential accountability to Congress.

» How effectively they have achieved their aims.

» The role and power of the president in foreign policy.

Source: NurPhoto / Contributor via Getty Images

FORMAL SOURCES OF PRESIDENTIAL POWER

Formal sources of power are those that are clearly outlined in the US Constitution. Article 2 of the US Constitution awards the president a range of powers and roles. The two most significant, head of state and head of government, are addressed below.

HEAD OF STATE

Article 2, section 3 makes the president the head of state, acting as the chief public representative of the United States. This means that the president represents the nation and helps to provide unity for it. By meeting other heads of state and attending official ceremonies, the president provides national leadership. In addition, the president is often a focal point at times of major disasters facing the country, making visits to the scene of such events and addressing the nation. All of this, alongside the fact that presidents are nationally elected, creates a sense that they can speak for the whole United States.

- In 2023 President Biden used his annual State of The Union address in order to call for Democrats and Republicans in Congress to unite to raise the debt ceiling. This would increase the amount of money the US government could borrow and ensure they could meet all of their debts. Biden used the speech to push an economic agenda with Congress eventually approving this measure later in the year.

- In 2021 President Biden acted as a unifying figure when he led a candlelit memorial marking 500,000 people in the United States who had died of COVID-19. The president urged Americans to set aside opposing views on the matter, saying, 'We must end the politics and misinformation that has divided families, communities and the country, and has cost too many lives already. It's not Democrats and Republicans who are dying from the virus. It's our fellow Americans.'

This role does not give the president any significant powers over Congress (such as the right to veto legislation) but can still be highly significant for the power of the president because it:

Affects popularity – As the public naturally look to the president at times of difficulty, a well-handled crisis can lead to a boost in their popularity.

Allows the president to set and push a political agenda – The focus on the president allows them to take control of the political agenda in response to a crisis or through their attendance at major international events.

Is of increased importance in the media age – The role of head of state has been transformed by the development of television, internet and social media, giving the president even greater opportunity to get his message across to the public.

- President Obama gained respect from visiting Newtown, Connecticut, attending an interfaith vigil for victims of the Sandy Hook Elementary School shooting in 2012. In the days after this, President Obama received an increase in his approval ratings, taking him back up to his 2009 levels.

Spec key term

Executive branch: The executive branch is headed by the president and is one of the three main branches of government alongside the legislature (Congress) and judiciary (the Supreme Court). It is responsible for developing policy and carrying out policy and laws.

HEAD OF GOVERNMENT

The second of the two constitutional roles and powers awarded to the president is outlined in Article 2, section 1 of the US Constitution. This makes the president the head of government. Often referred to as the head of the executive, the president is awarded absolute control over the executive branch. This branch is there to assist the president, making them as effective as possible, especially in achieving policy goals and maintaining popularity. As well as the vice presidency, there are two major sections to the executive branch, the cabinet and the Executive Office of the President, with specific roles in supporting the president. The roles of these two sections of the executive are discussed later in this chapter, pages 83-90.

The president appoints approximately 4,000 positions in the executive branch and agencies, including more than 1,200 that require Senate confirmation. Incoming presidents can also create new positions or offices to reflect their specific priorities. The president will also have a senior team that helps to organise and manage the rest of the executive branch.

Source: Jeff J Mitchell / Staff via Getty Images

Photo 4.1 **John Kerry, US Special Presidential Envoy for Climate Change at the COP26 Climate Summit 2021**

» President Biden rearranged his executive branch, creating the new position of Presidential Envoy for Climate as part of the Executive Office of the President. He has also given this position a place on the National Security Council (indicating that the climate crisis is an issue affecting national security). This helped Biden both to develop and achieve his climate protection agenda, and to allow the United States to resume a major role in providing global leadership on the climate crisis. Biden appointed John Kerry, a former Secretary of State (for President Obama), Chair of the Senate Foreign Relations Committee and the US lead negotiator in the 2015 Paris Agreement on reducing global emissions.

As well as having complete authority over the executive branch, the Constitution gives the president a number of other important roles and responsibilities that fall under the head of government.

- ***Chief Diplomat*** in which the president is responsible for relationships with other countries as well as appointing those who pursue these relationships such as US ambassadors.
- ***Commander in Chief of the Armed Forces*** which gives the president the ability to direct the military. There is constitutional ambiguity here; the president is made commander in chief, yet the Constitution also states that Congress declares war. The issue of who determines military action is addressed below in 'Key topic debate: Is the president significantly restricted in foreign policy?'
- ***Setting the congressional agenda*** in which the president is influential over the legislative programme of Congress. Whilst Congress is the sole legislative branch and can ignore presidential proposals for new laws, the Constitution does give the president a specified role here when it states that 'He shall from time to time give to the Congress information of the state of the union, and recommend to their consideration such measures as he shall judge necessary and expedient.'

INFORMAL SOURCES OF PRESIDENTIAL POWER

Informal sources of presidential power refers to the way in which the president can draw power from other political processes, for example by claiming a right to govern or having the right support and advice in carrying out his or her constitutional role. Informal powers also include powers that are not

Spec key term

Informal powers: Powers of the president not listed in the Constitution.

clearly outlined in the Constitution but that the president manages to adopt. Table 4.1 provides a list of all informal powers named in the A-Level specification and where you can find more information about each of these formal powers in this chapter.

Table 4.1 Informal sources of presidential power named in the Pearson A-Level specification

Informal Source	Reference for this chapter
1. The electoral mandate **2.** The cabinet **3.** Executive Office of the President (EXOP) including the role of: **a.** The National Security Council (NSC) **b.** Office of Management Budget (OMB) **c.** The White House Office (WHO) **4.** Powers of persuasion including the nature/characteristics of each president	All covered immediately after this table below.
5. Executive orders	See 'The imperial presidency' section, page 102.
6. National events	See national events and crises in the section 'Varying power between presidencies', page 98.

Spec key term

Electoral mandate: The permission granted to a political leader or winning party to govern and act on behalf of the people. The mandate is in effect for as long as the government is in power.

ELECTORAL MANDATE

The **electoral mandate** is the cornerstone of representative democracy. It asserts that the elected politician, in this case the president, has a right to govern because he or she was elected by the people. Presidents can claim a right to expect the passage of policies that were a central part of their campaign promises. They can also claim legitimacy to pass other bills, especially when responding to changing circumstances. The extent of a mandate given to the president can depend on the way in which the election is won and the overall popularity of the winner. Some of these differences can be seen in Table 4.2.

The mandate promotes presidential power by giving the president a great deal of authority to set the political agenda and push their bills through Congress. Presidential candidates will explain their policy agenda to the public and seek consent to put that into practice. Presidents are often at their most powerful when they have just been elected and have the momentum of a successful campaign behind them, but they will find it difficult to achieve legislative goals that deviate from the ideological direction they set out during their campaign.

» Both Biden and Obama achieved some of their most important policies in their first two years in office. Obama was successfully able to pass his flagship policy, the Affordable Care Act, his main policy promise, and Biden was able to pass all three of his radical social and economic measures, the Coronavirus Aid, Relief and Economic Security Act (CARES Act), the Infrastructure Act and his social policy and environment bill, the Inflation and Reduction Act 2022.

On the other hand, some campaigns and election results lead us to question the extent to which the incoming president is legitimate. The Electoral College can cause undemocratic results in which the most popular candidate does not actually win the presidency. There are increasing concerns in the United States over the fairness of elections, with significant barriers to voting and evidence of external intervention. Democracy in the United States is in danger of becoming destabilised. Also, it is not so much the process of the mandate that determines the influence of a president but more the powers and limits of office; a president with a questionable mandate is still the president with the power to propose laws, veto legislation and utilise significant executive powers.

» Both Bush in 2000 and Trump in 2016 began with major questions about the legitimacy of their presidency. Both received fewer votes than their rival but won the election as a result of the electoral method. There were also major concerns over voting practices that cast doubt on the result. This can be seen in 2016 with fourteen states introducing new restrictive voting laws, such as photo ID requirements, which has a disproportionately negative effect on racial minority and low-income voters who typically support the Democratic Party.

Table 4.2 **Electoral mandates of presidents Biden, Trump and Bush**

Election winner	Biden (2020)	Trump (2016)	G.W. Bush (2000)
Popular vote (%)	51.3	46.0	47.9
Electoral College vote out of a total of 538	306	304	271
Mandate controversies	Trump claimed that there were voting irregularities that favoured Biden, and he requested the count be stopped before it was completed. With over 50% of the popular vote and a rejection of virtually all legal challenges, the result was confirmed and supported by senior Republicans such as Mike Pence and Mitch McConnell. Whilst the legitimacy of Biden's presidency is generally accepted, many Republican politicians, candidates and voters continue to question his position as well as the validity of US democratic processes, even in the run up to the 2024 elections.	There were concerns over Russian interference in the US election, especially in active use of social media. Trump won the election by winning the most Electoral College votes despite receiving almost 3 million fewer votes than his rival Hillary Clinton. These two factors challenged the legitimacy of Trump to carry out policies.	Bush won the election with over 50% of Electoral College votes even though his rival Al Gore had more popular votes. Florida, as the deciding state, was won by Bush by just 593 votes out of nearly 6 million. There were significant concerns about unfair voting practices but the conservative majority on the court ruled in favour of Bush. Bush's presidency divided the United States, and he remained very unpopular amongst Democrats with lots of resistance to his policy. The events of 9/11, early in his presidency, changed this with significant public approval for Bush and his actions.

CABINET

The White House website states that 'The Cabinet's role is to advise the president on any subject he or she may require relating to the duties of each member's respective office' (https://www.whitehouse.gov/administration/cabinet/). Most members of the **cabinet** are heads (Secretaries) of Executive Departments whose main role is to direct the policy and operation of their department. These departments are based on policy areas such as treasury, defence and education. In addition, the vice president and a small number of senior **Executive Office of the President (EXOP)** staff are also members of the cabinet. The existence of the cabinet is not stated in the Constitution but is established as part of long tradition of meetings of heads of departments with the president. The place of the cabinet within the executive branch can be seen Figure 4.1.

The cabinet in the United States and United Kingdom have very different levels of power. Cabinet members in the United Kingdom can act as rivals to the prime minister. They could replace the prime minister if the party decides to remove the prime minister from their position as party leader. Cabinet members can be popular amongst the parliamentary party and may have the authority to challenge prime ministerial policy. In the United States the president is not constrained by the cabinet. As the directly elected head of the executive branch, the president neither has to listen to cabinet members nor can they replace the elected president in a leadership challenge. As such the cabinet is typically a weak political body in the United States.

Definition

Cabinet: A group of senior politicians who are mainly heads of executive departments, selected by the president, who help the president to make and carry out policy.

Definition

The Executive Office of the President (EXOP): A network of offices that were created to support the president in fulfilling his or her constitutional and political roles.

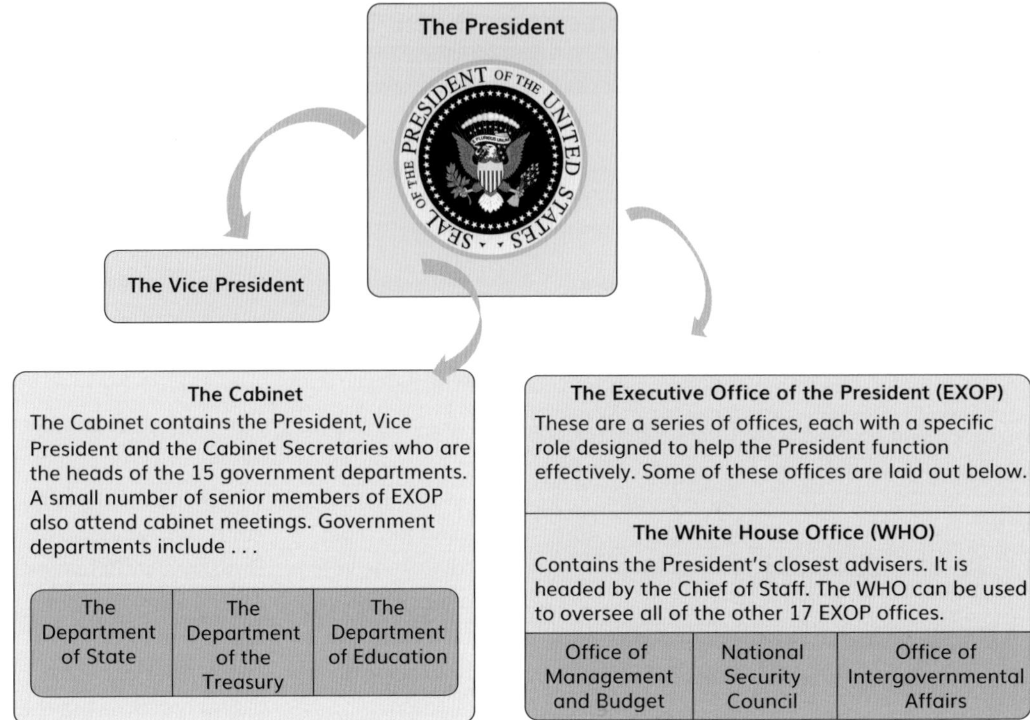

Figure 4.1 **The main offices within the executive branch**

KEY TOPIC DEBATE: DO THE CABINET AND EXECUTIVE OFFICE OF THE PRESIDENT PLAY A SIGNIFICANT POLITICAL ROLE?

✓ As a collective body

The cabinet, as a group, will meet at the president's discretion. The nature of the meeting is dependent almost entirely on the president's style. Presidents often use them to convey their message and policy priorities or to ask key members to brief the rest of the cabinet. It may serve as a forum for discussion of a policy area in which secretaries can coordinate their approach with others.

» In 2014 Obama held an emergency cabinet meeting to coordinate the US government response to an Ebola outbreak in which a Texas health-worker became infected. The two-hour meeting, which included the head of the Centre for Disease Control (CDC), ordered a review of how the outbreak began as well as directing new policy aimed at stopping its spread.

✓ As individuals

As heads of government departments, cabinet secretaries can wield huge power in their own policy area. The positions of Secretary of State (foreign secretary) and Secretary of the Treasury are hugely prestigious positions as these people play a key role in developing foreign and economic policies alongside the president.

» Biden's Secretary of the Treasury, Janet Yellen, has enormous influence over the direction and success of Biden's economic policies as well as his attempts to pass budget bills through Congress. Yellen, a former Yale University economics professor, went on to run the National Reserve before becoming Biden's pick for the Treasury position. In 2023 Yellen promised that the government would guarantee all bank deposits after the collapse of several banks including Silicon Valley Bank. Yellen and her department played a key role in developing and defending Biden's 2021 $1.9 trillion stimulus plan as well as overseeing the short-term responses of the US government to new economic challenges such as rising inflation.

✓ For presidential image

The White House website also states that 'President Biden's Cabinet reflects his pledge to appoint leaders of government agencies that reflect the country they aim to serve' (https://www.whitehouse.gov/administration/cabinet/). The cabinet can have a strong impact on the public image of the president and their administration. In such a diverse country, the social composition of the cabinet sends out a strong signal to the United States about the leadership and policy direction of the president. This in turn can have an impact on their level of public support.

» President Biden's first cabinet is more diverse than Obama's. Obama came close to reflecting the country, falling short with seven women to sixteen men, and just one Black secretary. Biden's cabinet contains the first openly gay secretary (Pete Buttigieg, Transportation) and the first Black Secretary of Defense (Lloyd Austin). In contrast to Trump's cabinet, which was dominated by white males, Biden was able to use the cabinet composition to support his drive for greater equality and inclusion in the United States. The overall social composition of the Biden cabinet can be seen in Figure 4.2, which shows membership of racial groups by percentages in the United States and in Biden's cabinet.

✖ The power and will of the president

The US Constitution gives ultimate executive power to the president who has the ability to use and ignore the cabinet as they please. Presidents rarely rely on the cabinet, especially as a collective body, to make executive policy. Presidents are free to override the policy ideas of cabinet members or to direct them to carry out presidential wishes.

» In 2021 Biden pressed ahead with his decision to withdraw troops from Afghanistan despite what insiders described as emotional pleas from the EXOP and cabinet members. He reportedly rejected advice from both Secretary of State Antony Blinken and Secretary of Defense Lloyd Austin to slow down any withdrawal.

✖ Alternative sources of advice and power

There are others who are in a better position than cabinet members to advise and direct the president. In particular, the EXOP is seen as playing a far more significant role in the life of a presidency, with presidents working more closely with senior EXOP staff positioned in the White House on a daily basis. In addition, the vice president can play a leading role in developing and delivering presidential policy.

» President Obama gave the job of developing gun control legislation and conducting relations with Congress to his vice president, Joe Biden. Rather than relying on cabinet members to make and deliver his policy priority, he entrusted Vice President Biden, former senator, with this key policy goals.

» Similarly, whilst President Biden's Secretary of Homeland Security and Secretary of State have meaningful roles, it was Vice President Kamala Harris he turned to in order to develop and deliver

Source: Chip Somodevilla / Staff via Getty Images

Photo 4.2 **Secretary of the Treasury Janet Yellen testifies at the Senate Appropriations Committee on President Biden's 2024 Budget**

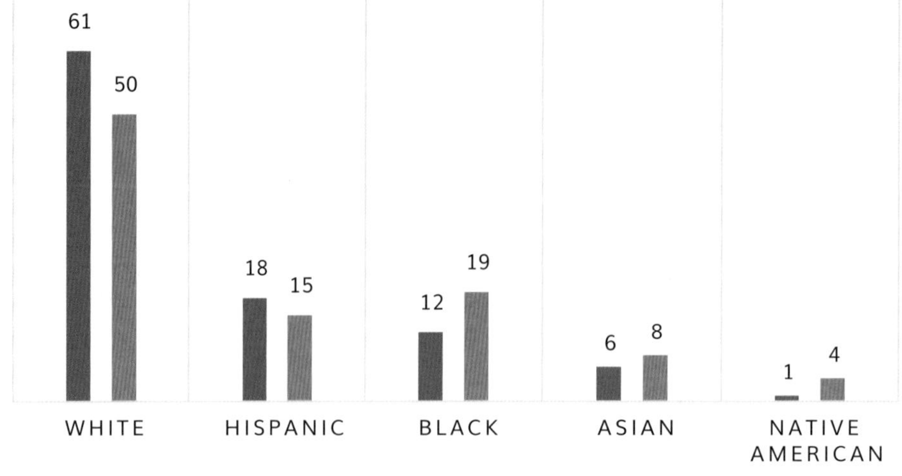

Figure 4.2 **Social composition of Biden's cabinet versus the US population**

his immigration policy. Harris was a central figure in pursuing Biden's policy to tackle the root causes of migration by working with Central American countries to stop corruption. Harris delivered an anticorruption speech in Guatemala alongside President Alejandro Giammattei. Harris pledged 500,000 coronavirus vaccines for Guatemala as well as $26 million to tackle the pandemic.

Practical limitations

The cabinet is limited by several practical factors. A large group is difficult to coordinate, and collective discussions, which include all cabinet members, can be very inefficient. It would be impossible to address the multitude of policy issues that face the United States using this full group. In addition, on any given issue, cabinet members may lack expertise, limiting the value of their contributions. As such, it makes much more sense to make decisions elsewhere in smaller, more specialist groups.

» Presidents typically reduce their cabinet meetings over time, arguably because they see limited importance in their collective role. President Obama held sixteen cabinet meetings in his first term, which dropped to twelve in his second. President Trump chaired twenty-five cabinet meetings in his one term, but eighteen of these came in his first two years.

EXECUTIVE OFFICE OF THE PRESIDENT

The Executive Office of the President (EXOP) was created in 1939 to cope with the growing demands of the Federal Government in general and the president in particular. Today it has become a series of specialist offices with each providing specific functions and advice to the president. See Table 4.3 for an outline of the EXOP offices and their leads in 2023. Despite the fact that they are not household names, the EXOP contains the president's closest advisers and often some of the most powerful political figures in the United States. Presidents are free to organise their EXOP according to their own priorities; most presidents add or take away one or two of the bodies within the EXOP to reflect their policy approach. Biden, for example, added an Office of Cyber Director to work on internet technology and the many opportunities and threats it poses for the United States.

The Biden Administration lists seventeen offices within the EXOP, roughly in line with other presidents. There are some offices that are particularly important for all presidential administrations as explained below.

The White House Office (WHO)

✓ This office contains the president's most trusted and closest advisers and is undoubtedly critical to the success of the good functioning of a presidency. This is because of its many different functions in helping the president. The WHO contains sub-offices with specialist functions such as the Office for Legislative Affairs (responsible for getting the president's legislative priorities through Congress) and the Press Office.

✓ At the head of this array of bodies is the chief of staff, who is usually seen as the key figure in any White House. The chief of staff will oversee the rest of the EXOP but is mainly involved in managing

Table 4.3 **The EXOP offices and their leads in 2023**

EXOP office	Office leader
The Council of Economic Affairs	Celia Elena Rouse
Council on Environmental Quality	Brenda Mallory
Domestic Policy Council	Susan Rice
Gender Policy Council	Jennifer Klein
National Economic Council	Brian Deese
National Security Council	Jake Sullivan
Climate Policy Office	Ali Zaidi
Office of the Intellectual Property Enforcement	Danny Marti
Office of Intergovernmental Affairs	Julie Chávez Rodríguez
Office of Management and Budget	Shalanda Young
Office of National Drug Policy	Rahul Gupta
Office of Public Engagement	Stephen Benjamin
Office of Science and Technology Policy	Arati Parabhakar
Office of the National Cyber Director	Kemba Walden
Office of the United States Trade Representative	Katherine Tai
Presidential Personnel Office	Gautam Raghavan
National Space Council	Kamala Harris

the president and helping him or her to make decisions. Presidents typically have early starts and long days, and the chief of staff has to be one step ahead of them, ready to brief them to keep them up to date on all matters. Most presidents start their day with a briefing from the National Security Council adviser and the chief of staff. President Carter's chief of staff likened his role to a javelin catcher, a perilous job in which they are charged with protecting the president from political damage.

✖ The president remains the constitutional head of the executive branch and may ignore advice or sideline White House staff. The president's governing style might mean that advice is ignored or that advisers are reluctant to challenge the president.

✖ The president may rely on other sources of advice such as the vice president or specific cabinet members. Certain members of the White House Office may have significantly more influence than others.

» President Trump had four different chiefs of staff in his single term. Relationships in the White House were often strained and Trump's impulsive and aggressive manner made it difficult for his chief of staff to carry out the important task of challenging the president when necessary and helping them to see a different perspective.

» Ron Klain, Biden's first chief of staff, played a key role in determining the policy approach of President Biden. In addition, Klain has been instrumental in negotiating with Congress, regularly calling, meeting or trying to find compromise with key Democrats to secure Biden's bills. Klain held regular phone calls with progressive Democrats, such as Progressive Caucus leader Pramila Prayapal. Progressive Democrats became anxious when Biden appointed Jeff Zients as his new chief of staff in 2023, concerned that he would not give them the same access they had with Klain.

The National Security Council (NSC)

✔ Established in 1947, this is the principal body advising the president on national and security policy. The office has become critical to the president's control over foreign policy as well as the security of the United States. This is a consequence of the power of the United States in the world and the speed and destructiveness of military technology.

✔ At the head of the NSC is the National Security Advisor, who collates security information from all departments and agencies in the United States and meets with the president for a daily security briefing. Its importance lies in its ability to shape the president's foreign policy as well as their immediate response to world events.

Source: MANDEL NGAN / Contributor via Getty Images

Photo 4.3 President Biden at an event to transition from Klain (right) to Zients (centre) as his new chief of staff

✗ The president is the head of the executive branch and can ignore advice from the NSC. A president may make use of the powerful cabinet positions of Secretary of State, Secretary of Homeland Security or Secretary of Defense, which directly relate to national security.

» President Trump's longest serving NSC Advisor, John Bolton, was seen as instrumental in pushing him into an even more aggressive approach to foreign policy, successfully persuading him to pull out of Obama's Iran nuclear deal. He also ordered the Pentagon to draw up plans for military strikes against Tehran. Bolton was eventually forced out of office after Trump started to reject some of his policy aims, for example, the bombing of Tehran and regime change.

The Office of Management and Budget (OMB)

✓ The OMB, created in 1970, is the largest of the EXOP offices with over 500 staff. Its role is to advise the president on the allocation of funds for the annual budget and to oversee the spending of government departments and agencies. The OMB can take the general policy goals of the president and turn them into specific policies, whilst advising the president on the implication of some of these choices.

✓ As a result of its financial role, all bills that are developed by and for the president are scrutinised by the OMB. The OMB tends to take on this role more than the Treasury, which is part of the cabinet. Some presidents will task the director of the OMB with congressional relations in an attempt to secure support for the president's economic policy goals.

✗ Again, the president is in a superior constitutional position, allowing them to ignore advice from the OMB. At a given time some offices in the EXOP are more powerful than others and the president might make use of economic expertise from other parts of the EXOP. Alternatively, the president may pursue their own goals, instructing the OMB to follow presidential priorities. Additionally, the president could move beyond the EXOP altogether and make use of the Secretary of the Treasury to develop legislation.

» In 2023 Shalanda D. Young, director of the OMB, was instrumental in developing Biden's budget proposal for 2024. She testified before the Senate Budget Committee to persuade senators of the merits of the bill. In this case, Young is responsible for both developing policy and helping Biden in his ability to use the power of persuasion to gain congressional support.

Key Topic Debate Summary: Do the cabinet and Executive Office of the President play a significant political role?

FOR	KEY CRITERIA	AGAINST
✓ The cabinet can play a collective role in advising the president but in particular in allowing the president to develop a coordinated policy. This can be particularly important during major crises. ✓ Individuals cabinet members can be very important in developing and executing presidential policy. ✓ The cabinet can have a strong impact on the public image of the president and their administration.	Does **the cabinet** play a significant role?	✗ The cabinet has no constitutional role and can be ignored by the president. Individual cabinet members can also be sidelined or removed by the president. ✗ There are other sources of advice and support for the president. Cabinet members, working in their departments most of the time, may be less loyal to the president than EXOP members. ✗ It is practically difficult for the cabinet to have collective influence given the constraints of time and their individual expertise on a given issue.
✓ The White House Office is critical to the success of a president through the development of policy and policy advice. This is how the president generates their legislative agenda. ✓ The chief of staff is critical in managing the president, briefing the president, helping to determine strategy and often working with other bodies such as Congress. ✓ Specific offices such as the Press Office are critical to ensure that the president can communicate their message successfully and set the direction of the political agenda.	Does **the White House Office and chief of staff** play a significant role?	✗ The president remains the constitutional head of the executive branch and may ignore advice or sideline White House staff. ✗ The Office may still be significant, but it can have a negative impact on a presidency with poor management or advice. ✗ The president's governing style might mean that advice is ignored or that advisers are reluctant to challenge the president.
✓ Specific offices play a key role in developing policy and giving advice. The two most important aspects of US government policy are economic and security policy giving the OMB and NSC fundamentally critical roles. ✓ The OMB is exceptionally influential as it is well staffed with experts, draws up the president's annual budget and briefs the president on the economy. ✓ The NSC is influential in determining the president's security policy and helps to inform the president of developments to help keep those in the United States safe.	Do other EXOP offices such as **the OMB and NSC** play a significant role?	✗ The president may use alternative sources of advice and support such as cabinet members or ignore the advice of the OMB or NSC. ✗ The NSC Advisor might find that the president prefers to rely on advice and information from their Secretaries of State or Defense. ✗ The director of the OMB could be sidelined by a prominent Secretary of the Treasury. ✗ Some members of EXOP staff may be seen as less competent and have limited impact on the presidency, sometimes resulting in their dismissal.

Exam Tip: Improving your AO2 analysis and AO3 evaluation

It is clear that some of the informal sources of presidential power in this debate are more significant than others. It is impossible to argue that the White House Office, for example, is insignificant. A stronger response will judge **the extent** to which each of these sources are significant. You could also make the distinction between positive (empowering the president) and negative (undermining the president) significance. Remember that both a positive and negative impact can be very significant. Consider how this analysis would affect your overall judgement.

Spec key term

Powers of persuasion: This is an informal power of the president in which he or she can use the prestige of their job, and other bargaining methods, to get people to do as they wish.

POWERS OF PERSUASION

In 1960, Richard Neustadt, a presidency specialist, argued in his book *Presidential Power* that the president's main power is merely 'the power to persuade'. He was referring to significant limits to the president's formal powers and the way in which the US political system provides extensive checks and balances can heavily restrict the president. This means that a president must rely on his or her informal powers of persuasion, especially in relation to Congress, to achieve their policy goals. A great deal of this is based on personal ability. A president must be a good communicator who possesses a great deal of authority in convincing others to accept his or her ideas. Different presidents will choose different leadership styles. Some may seek consensus and compromise whilst others will be more aggressive in attempting to persuade members of Congress.

The power to persuade is obviously limited by the constitutional powers of Congress to reject presidential proposals.

Regardless of their style, presidents appear to find it increasingly difficult to persuade members of the opposing party given the high levels of partisanship that now exists.

» President Trump frequently took an aggressive stance as president, singling out individuals who opposed him, often by delivering personal attacks on Twitter. During the presidential primaries, he assailed fellow Republican rivals such as Ted Cruz who he often referred to as 'Lyin' Ted'. This continued in office as Trump attacked those who did not support him. This included moderate Republican Senator Susan Collins. In one Twitter comment in 2020, after he nominated Amy Coney Barrett to the Supreme Court, he said 'There is a nasty rumor out there that @SenatorCollins of Maine will not be supporting our great United States Supreme Court Nominee. Well, she didn't support Healthcare or my opening up 5000 square miles of Ocean to Maine, so why should this be any different. Not worth the work!' Trump recognised that he needed to gain support from Republicans, however, especially in the Senate where he held a slim majority. He often toned down his rhetoric against people in his own party and met with key individuals such as Cruz when trying to repeal Obamacare in 2017.

As well as being based on personal ability, presidents have several advantages that increase their power to persuade. As a nationally elected leader they have a great deal of authority, claiming a mandate to govern. In addition, they have enormous media focus and can use this to set the political agenda, persuade the public or single out individuals in Congress for political attack. A president's ability to persuade will be influenced by the political context they operate in. Presidents who are personally popular, for example, will find it much easier to persuade members of Congress to support their policy agenda.

LIMITATIONS ON PRESIDENTIAL POWER

THE RELATIONSHIP BETWEEN THE PRESIDENT AND CONGRESS

The Founding Fathers created two political giants who push their political agendas and are often forced into compromise as they seek to achieve their policy goals. It is the president's relationship with Congress that largely determines how much power they have and, ultimately, their success as president.

As we saw in the Chapter 2, 'The Constitution', the Founding Fathers created the separation of powers, alongside extensive checks and balances to prevent a dominant executive branch, ensuring that power is shared. It does so in three main ways:

1. The president and Congress receive separate mandates allowing them both to claim the right to govern. Congress is unlikely to simply accept the president's political agenda and is active in developing and pursuing its own legislative priorities. Members of the House and Senate must be sensitive to constituent views and may vote against a president's agenda if it is unpopular in their state or district.
2. There is a possibility of bipartisan control/divided government in which the president is from one party and at least one chamber of Congress is controlled by the opposing party. This will create conflicting agendas between the president and Congress.
3. The president cannot use a threat of promotion or demotion over members of Congress to pressure them into supporting his or her policies. Even if the president has a majority in Congress he or she is not guaranteed support from members of their own party.

   It is this constitutional setting that we must bear in mind when we consider the power relationship between the president and Congress.

KEY TOPIC DEBATE: CAN THE PRESIDENT DOMINATE CONGRESS IN THE AREA OF DOMESTIC POLICY?

> **Spec key term**
>
> **Domestic Policy:** Policy focused on issues inside the United States such as health, education and economic policy. This contrasts with foreign policy, which focuses on the United States' external relationships in its dealings with other countries.

Powers of the president

✓ Setting the political agenda

Presidents can make great use of their informal sources of power, such as their mandate and their access to the Executive Office of the President, to set the political agenda and dominate both foreign and domestic policymaking. As nationally elected leaders, presidents have enormous influence, determining political and legislative priorities for Congress to consider. Presidents may have limited power in the legislative process, but they often successfully use their powers of persuasion to achieve their desired policy goals. There is an expectation, for example, that the president will set a federal budget that Congress will consider as part of the legislative process.

» Since his election in 2020 President Biden was extremely successful in setting the agenda of US politics and achieving some significant policy goals. He was elected partly on the basis of promising more measures to tackle the health aspects of COVID-19 as well as its economic impact, and he also campaigned heavily on the need for more measures to tackle the climate crisis. All these items dominated the congressional agenda since his election. In March 2021 Biden achieved his first major legislative success with the passage of the American Rescue Plan Act. This was a huge expenditure bill spending an additional $1.9 trillion addressing the impact of coronavirus, especially on the economy.

Veto congressional bills

The **regular veto** allows the president to reject bills passed through Congress. By refusing to sign a bill and sending it back to Congress, the president is signalling that they are vetoing a bill. Whilst presidents can only accept or reject a whole bill, they can use the *threat* of veto to shape legislation. Presidents sometime stat that they will not sign a bill if it contains certain measures or if key presidential priorities are missing. Table 4.4 shows how President Biden has made use of the veto and threat of the veto.

The president can use a **pocket veto** if Congress presents a bill within ten days before Congress adjourns. Congress can overturn regular vetoes with a two-thirds vote in each chamber. Pocket vetoes, however, cannot be overturned because it is considered that Congress would not have sufficient time to debate and vote. Whilst Congress may try to avoid offering bills that the president dislikes within the last ten days of a congressional session, this is not always feasible. As Table 4.4 shows, recent presidents have made use of the veto power to achieve their policy goals or to prevent Congress from achieving theirs.

» In 2016 President Obama successfully protected one of his key legislative achievements by vetoing measures passed by the Republican-led Congress that attempted to overturn the Affordable Care Act.

> **Definition**
>
> **Regular veto:** The power of the president to reject a bill passed by Congress, preventing it from becoming a law.

> **Definition**
>
> **Pocket veto:** The power of the president to issue a veto within the last ten days of a congressional session. The pocket veto cannot be overturned by Congress.

Table 4.4 **President Biden and the use of the veto**

The veto in 2024	Biden issued his first veto of 2024 in order to protect his environmental agenda and accelerate his aim of having more electric vehicles on US roads. Congress had previously authorised Federal Government expenditure of $7.5bn on electric vehicle charging stations. They subsequently passed a law which ensured that more of this $7.5bn was spent on made in America products. Biden vetoed this law, arguing that it would slow down the move towards the use of electric vehicles and that he only wanted short term imports whilst the US developed its manufacturing capacity.
The veto in 2023	Biden issued four vetoes in quick succession between March and May 2023. This increased intensity of vetoes occurred after Republicans gained a majority in the House of Representative in the mid-term elections of 2022. The Republicans successfully passed bills in Congress, gaining support from a small number of Democrat senators for some of their proposals. In 2023 President Biden issued his first veto against a Republican sponsored bill that banned the government from considering environmental impacts when making investment decisions for federal worker's retirement plans.
The veto in 2021 and 2022	Despite issuing some veto threats, if bills did not contain what he wanted, Biden did not veto at all during his first two years in office (when Democrats controlled both chambers of Congress). This shows that the use of the veto can be a sign of a weaker president. When presidents have control over Congress they are less likely to be forced into vetoing an agenda set by an opposing party in Congress.

✓ **Bypass Congress/the imperial presidency**

The president can make use of the tools of the imperial presidency to bypass Congress and take control of the political agenda. These include the use of executive agreements and signing statements. There is a detailed discussion of the imperial presidency at the start of the 'Interpretations and debates' section of this chapter.

Limits on the president

✗ **Legislative power of Congress**

The president's legislative agenda is dependent on political support from Congress. Congress can amend, reject or authorise presidential proposals. Even if presidents successfully pass legislation, they often find that they have had their policy goals undermined with amendments and alternative ideas. Congress can also regulate presidential power, for example by passing a law that restricts the president or requires certain actions. Whilst it is not strictly legislating, Congress can pass resolutions that instruct or restrict presidential action.

» The March 2021 American Recovery Act, initiated by Biden, had measures to raise the national minimum wage from $7.25 to $15 per hour stripped from the bill because it was opposed by all Republicans but also lacked sufficient support amongst Senate Democrats.

» In November 2021, Biden's Infrastructure Act only passed with significant compromises, despite a Democrat majority in both chambers, as the progressive and moderate wings of his party pushed their own agendas. Biden was unsuccessful in securing several of his environmental aims such as increasing taxes on the wealthy to provide more funding for environmental measures.

Congress is particularly unlikely to accept presidential proposals during divided government. In addition, presidents often find themselves on the back foot, with Congress setting the political agenda and the president reacting, often by being forced in to compromises or issuing vetoes.

✗ **Limits to the power of veto**

Presidential vetoes can be seen as a defensive weapon. They allow the president to block the agenda of Congress but not necessarily to achieve their own legislative aims. If a president is issuing a high number of vetoes, this is usually a sign of weakness rather than strength. Presidents are often forced into vetoes when facing a hostile congressional majority from the opposing party. In addition, the veto is a somewhat blunt weapon in which the president can only accept or reject a whole bill. The regular veto can also be overturned by a two-thirds vote in each chamber of Congress. Table 4.5 shows how often vetoes are overridden.

» President George W. Bush issued twelve vetoes, with eleven of these coming in his last two years in office. This came after the Republican Party lost their majority in the mid-terms of 2006. After this election, House Democrats, led by Speaker Pelosi, took control of the political agenda, forcing the president on the defensive.

» Similarly, Trump threatened to veto a COVID-19 relief bill unless Congress agreed to increases federal pay-out cheques from $600 to $2,000. Despite some Democrat support for this measure, Congress did not increase this figure with insufficient Republican support. Trump subsequently failed to follow through on his veto threat. Unsurprisingly in this case, he decided not to veto the whole bill, which he shaped, because of this single aspect of the bill.

Table 4.5 **Presidential vetoes 1992 to 2020**

President	Regular	Pocket	Total	Overridden
Bill Clinton	36	1	37	2
George W. Bush	12	0	12	4
Barack Obama	12	0	12	1
Donald Trump	10	0	10	1

✖ **Appropriate funds: The power of the purse**

A key part of the legislative process is the power given to Congress to determine how public money is spent. Any executive policy or action that requires funding must be authorised by Congress. There are specific appropriations committees in both the House and the Senate that can amend bills and the funding allocated to them.

» The pledge to build a border wall was at the forefront of President Trump's election campaign but it was a policy he failed to deliver on, mainly because Congress repeatedly refused to give funding to this project. In 2021 congressional Republicans vowed not to provide any funding for Biden's vaccine mandate requiring federal workers to be vaccinated.

✖ **Impeachment and removal from office**

Members of the executive can be impeached and removed from office by the House and Senate. This is the ultimate check, stripping the president of their power if they act improperly, although in reality presidents are unlikely to face an impeachment process. President Trump, however, was impeached twice during his presidency, although he was not removed from office on either occasion. For more detail on the impeachment process, see the Chapter 3, 'Congress', page 44.

Key Topic Debate Summary: Can the president dominate Congress in the area of domestic policy?

FOR	KEY CRITERIA	AGAINST
✓ The president can use their mandate and authority in office to set the political agenda for the country. ✓ They can use their power to persuade to achieve their desired policy goals, pressurising Congress to comply.	Does the president have control in **initiating and negotiating legislation** with Congress?	✗ Congress can amend, reject or authorise presidential policy proposals. ✗ Congress has the power of the purse, that is, it can determine whether the president receives funding for their policy proposal. ✗ Separation of powers means that Congress is often aggressive in initiating their own legislation or blocking the policy goals of a president.

FOR	KEY CRITERIA	AGAINST
✓ Presidents can use their regular or pocket veto to block domestic policy legislation passed by Congress. ✓ Presidents can also use the threat of veto to force Congress to compromise to achieve their domestic policy goals.	Can the president use their **veto power** to control domestic policy?	✗ The veto is a defensive weapon, allowing the president to block congressional proposals but not necessarily achieve their own. ✗ Regular vetoes can be overturned but Congress.
✓ Presidents can use executive orders to bypass Congress and achieve their desired policy goals. ✓ A president may use signing statements to effectively veto parts of a bill and refuse to put them into practice.	Can the president use the powers of the imperial presidency to **bypass Congress** altogether?	✗ There is a limit to the extent to which presidents can use executive orders and signing statements. All major policy changes requiring new laws to be passed need to be authorised by Congress. ✗ The Supreme Court may rule that the use of an executive order or signing statement is unconstitutional.

Exam Tip: Improving your AO2 analysis and AO3 evaluation

How do the following points affect your analysis and evaluation? To what extent does the nature of party majorities affect the power of the president over domestic policy? If a president is in office during a time of divided government does this make a major difference to their power? Consider what both the theory *and* the evidence tells you.

Learning Review

1. What are the two formal sources of presidential power?
2. For each source, name two ways in which this could help the president to achieve their policy goals.
3. What are the other three roles that the Constitution awards to the president?
4. What are the four informal powers covered in the section above?
5. For each of these informal powers can you name:
   a) One way in which this plays a significant political role?
   b) One way in which it is limited?
6. What are the four main limits on the power of the president?

Comparative Learning Review

1. What are the key similarities between the role of the prime minister and the role of the president?
2. What are the key differences between the role of the prime minister and the role of the president?
3. What are the key similarities between the power of the prime minister and the power of the president?
4. What are the key differences between the limits on the prime minister and the limits on the president?

THE RELATIONSHIP BETWEEN THE PRESIDENT AND SUPREME COURT

Whilst the Supreme Court rules on constitutional issues, it is the president (and Congress) who have the biggest impact on the daily lives of those living in the United States, holding control over domestic and foreign policy. The main relationship between the two is based on these two powers:

- The president can appoint individual justices when a vacancy occurs.
- The Supreme Court can review presidential action and policy if there are claims that the president has acted unconstitutionally.

KEY TOPIC DEBATE: CAN THE PRESIDENT DOMINATE THE SUPREME COURT?

Powers of the president over the Supreme Court

Presidential appointment of individual justices

Technically the president nominates rather than appoints a member of the Supreme Court. They do this when a vacancy occurs through the retirement or death of a justice. This nomination is then voted on by the Senate who have the power to reject the president's selection. This process is addressed in more detail in Chapter 5, 'The Supreme Court and Civil Rights', starting on page 124. This allows the president to influence the ideological composition of the court. For example, Republican presidents will nominate justices who are more likely to interpret the Constitution in a manner that gives conservative outcomes. Some presidents are fortunate enough to make an appointment that swings the ideological balance of the court in their favour.

» President Trump had a major influence on the court, making three appointments in his single term. The death of Ruth Bader Ginsburg, a liberal justice, allowed Trump to replace her with a significantly more conservative justice, Amy Coney Barrett, in October 2020. Justice Coney Barrett, President Trump's third appointee, was perhaps the most significant, allowing him to secure a clear conservative majority on the court.

Presidential authority

Presidents can use their authority to influence both public opinion and individual justices by supporting or opposing a position and creating the impression that a certain outcome is the only valid interpretation of the Constitution. Arguably, when they are deciding on a ruling, justices are mindful of public opinion and the presidents' criticisms of the court in previous cases.

» In 2022, President Biden publicly criticised the Supreme Court decision in *Dobbs v Jackson*, saying that the decision was a 'tragic error'. The court had previously determined that abortion was a constitutional right in *Roe v Wade* (1973) but the Dobbs ruling overturned this constitutional protection. Biden appealed to voters to return more Democrats to Congress in the mid-term elections of 2022 to provide further abortion right protections. He said that Congress could pass a law ensuring that there was a right to an abortion that all states would have to comply with. In addition, he issued an executive order direct to the Department of Health and Human Services to act within their power to maintain access to reproductive health clinics and protect the privacy of those who use them. This suggests a battle between different ideological directions on the court and a possible influence of the president in future cases where the justices might be mindful of such attacks from the president.

Amending the Constitution and court packing

Presidents could call for a constitutional amendment that overturns the Supreme Court ruling. In addition, some presidents have threatened court packing, in which they suggest that they may ask Congress to increase the number of justices on the court. The Constitution does not fix the number of justices at nine and a president could quickly add two or three more justices to give them an ideological majority on the court.

» In reality the court packing idea has never been put into action, with Franklin Roosevelt being the last president to seriously propose this in 1937. It was seen as sufficiently threatening in 2023 for Senator

Ted Cruz to call for a constitutional amendment to limit the Supreme Court to nine justices to stop President Biden from making any moves to pack the court. There have been several presidential calls for constitutional amendments to overturn a judicial opinion but none of these have been successful.

Limits on presidential power over the Supreme Court

✖ The president can only appoint a limited number of justices

The president may have the opportunity to influence the composition of the court through an *individual* appointment but appointing one or two justices does not allow the president to dominate the whole court. The president is likely to have limited impact with one appointment, especially when making a like for like replacement. Justices typically choose to retire when they have a similar ideological outlook to the person in the White House. This ensures that they will be replaced by a justice with similar views to their own.

» President Trump appointed conservative Justice Gorsuch to replace Justice Scalia. This had negligible impact on the court as the two justices share similar views and values. President Obama's appointees had little or no impact with both Sotomayor and Kagan replacing similarly liberal justices. Some presidents such as President Carter (1976–80) were unable to make any appointments.

✖ Justices are independent

The central reason why the president cannot dominate the court is because of strong levels of judicial independence. Once appointed, justices cannot be removed by a president and are free to rule against the president who appointed them. There is no sense in which a president controls their appointee. The president cannot provide a sufficient threat to the court as a whole to make them fearful of giving a ruling against the president. Presidents can and often do 'lose' Supreme Court cases.

» In *NLRB v Canning* (2012), the court ruled unanimously that President Obama did not have the power to make **recess appointments** during a short congressional break. The majority opinion included decisions from his two appointees, Justices Sotomayor and Kagan. The court was willing to challenge the president when it ruled that recess appointments could only be made when Congress was in recess for longer than ten days not the three used by Obama.

Definition

Recess appointments: Presidential appointments (for example to executive bodies) that do not require Senate approval because the congressional session has ended: Congress is on recess.

✖ Supreme Court rulings and constitutional sovereignty

As well as being independent, the Supreme Court is also responsible for upholding the sovereign Constitution. This means that it has the ability to give rulings against presidential action or policy and the president is forced to comply. The president is subject to significant constitutional limits and the court is in a position to enforce these limitations. Presidents have no formal role in changing the Constitution and it is unlikely they would reach the two-thirds vote in each chamber to overturn a court ruling.

» Both President Trump and President Biden had their new immigration policies overturned by the court on the grounds that their administrations did not follow proper procedures. President Biden sought to end a Trump-era policy (the policy, known as Migrant Protection Protocols, that required asylum seekers to remain in Mexico whilst their claim was processed). The case, *Biden v Texas* (2021), forced the Biden administration to abandon his more liberal approach of allowing asylum seekers to cross the border to process their claims and to return to more restrictive policies.

Key Topic Debate Summary: Can the president dominate the Supreme Court?

FOR	KEY CRITERIA	AGAINST
✓ Presidents can nominate individual justices to the Supreme Court and thus have influence on court rulings. ✓ Some presidents are fortunate enough to make an appointment that swings the ideological balance of the court in their favour.	Does the **appointment process** allow presidents to dominate?	✖ Presidents have little or no control over the justice they nominate. Appointments for life means that justices may deliver opinions that the president who nominated them dislikes, with no threat of removal. ✖ Presidents typically only nominate one or two justices. This rarely affects the overall balance of the court.

FOR	KEY CRITERIA	AGAINST
✓ Presidents can use their authority to influence justices by calling for a particular outcome in a court ruling or by denouncing the court if they deliver an opinion that they dislike. ✓ Presidents also have influence over public opinion, which might put pressure on justices to comply with public expectations or dominant ideas in society.	Does the president have the **authority to influence court decisions** beyond appointments?	✗ Justices are independent and unlikely to be influenced by a presidential view. They are free to use their own interpretation of the Constitution. ✗ The president will find it difficult or impossible to sway the majority of five justices needed to give a ruling which suits him or her
✓ Presidents may call for changes to the Constitution to overturn a court decision that they oppose. ✓ Presidents may threaten to pack the court with additional justices to increase their influence over Supreme Court opinions.	Can the president **change the Constitution** to get the court rulings he or she desires?	✗ The sovereign, entrenched Constitution allows the court to have significant power to regulate presidents' policy or use of their powers. Presidents have virtually no chance of changing the constitutional rulings delivered by the court. ✗ Court packing has rarely been threatened because of the damage it may do to the authority of the president or the court. The court has always had nine justices and a change is unlikely.

Exam Tip: Improving your AO2 analysis and AO3 evaluation

What does the word *dominate* mean in this context? How might your response, including your conclusion, change if we used different words such as 'influence' or 'have more power than'? Be sure to focus on the keyword of *dominate* when deciding what your overall AO3 evaluation is.

Evaluative view: Can presidents dominate the Supreme Court?

Presidents cannot dominate the court as a whole; they are unable to influence or determine the outcome of Supreme Court cases against the court's will. This is because the president has very limited powers at their disposal over the court. In addition, the high levels of independence of the court protects justices from interference from other bodies, such as the president. The main power of the president in relation to the court is making nominations, but this does not allow them to impose their will on the whole court. This does not mean that the Supreme Court is *more powerful than* the president. Presidents have a significant influence over the policy direction of the United States, which the Supreme Court does not. It is difficult to argue, however, that the president *dominates* the court.

Consider the key topic debate and debate summary as well as any new evidence you can find. Do you agree or disagree with this evaluative view

FACTORS AFFECTING PRESIDENTIAL POWER

Whilst all presidents are working with the same powers and limits (as outlined above) they can also experience considerable fluctuations in their power. This is caused by the changing political context in which they are operating. This context can refer to party majorities in Congress, levels of public support, the ideological make-up of the Supreme Court and unforeseen events or crises, as well as presidential skill and strategy in using their power to persuade. Presidential power may also vary according to the policy area with some arguing that presidents have a greater ability to control foreign policy compared to domestic policy.

Exam Tip – Any evaluation of the level of presidential power will consider the powers and limits of the president. One of the golden rules of democratic politics is that power is rarely static. Instead, the power of an individual or institution tends to vary over time. A more sophisticated evaluation could show how the power of a president may vary over time and why some presidents may be more powerful than others. Do not make the mistake of concluding 'it **all** depends'. You will need to give some sense of your overall judgement of the extent of power and show that the exact extent of this power can change over time.

VARYING POWER BETWEEN PRESIDENCIES

Table 4.6 shows how the Obama and Bush presidencies were affected by the factors of public opinion, divided government and national events or crises.

Table 4.6 Factors affecting the power of the Bush and Obama presidencies

Factor affecting presidential power	How this affected power during the Obama presidency	How this affected power during the Bush presidency	How the power of Bush and Obama compare
Public opinion	Whilst Obama's central policy platform was to achieve healthcare reform, the plan started to lose popularity once he was elected. Obama was forced to water down the bill, removing the public option (a measure that would have created a Federal Government health insurance body) and eventually passing the bill with many House Democrats voting against.	The 9/11 terror attack led to a massive increase in support for Bush in 2001, as the public united behind their leader and both his foreign and domestic policies. The level of national grief and the desire for unity made it much more difficult for Democrats to challenge Bush policies.	Both presidents experienced the same process of declining power and found it easier to achieve their policy goals in their early years in office. One major difference is the huge level of support for President Bush in the years after the 9/11 attack. He had the highest approval rating of any of the post-1992 presidents, giving him a much greater opportunity to achieve his policy goals.
Divided government	Obama started office in January 2009 with a Democrat majority in both chambers, allowing him to pass what were arguably his most significant bills of his presidency in his first two years of office: his financial stimulus package and the Affordable Care Act. After 2010, his party lost control of the House with the new Republican majority often blocking his agenda. Obama lost control of the Senate in the second of the two mid-terms during his presidency in 2010.	Bush was able to enjoy a majority for his first six years in office, eventually losing the mid-term elections of 2006. This allowed incoming speaker Nancy Pelosi and the new Democrat majority to dominate with their policy plan called the 100-hour agenda. Virtually all the Democrat policies passed Congress and Bush felt compelled to sign these bills.	Bush had a majority in Congress for six of his eight years compared to just two for Obama. This made it significantly easier for Bush to achieve his policy goals, especially on the major annual issues such as the budget. Whilst Obama struggled to pass his budgets through a Republican House, Bush's economic packages passed with some ease. Bush did not experience budget gridlock and federal shutdown as Obama did.

Continued

Table 4.6 **Continued**

Factor affecting presidential power	How this affected power during the Obama presidency	How this affected power during the Bush presidency	How the power of Bush and Obama compare
National events or crises	Obama began his term in office after the onset of the banking crisis. The need to focus on the financial slump prevented Obama from using the momentum of electoral success to push the Affordable Care Act through Congress – arguably a significant reason for the compromises he had to make to pass the bill. In 2012 Obama benefited politically from Hurricane Sandy. The election season was underway with negative attention turned on Obama's opponent Mitt Romney who was alleged to support the elimination of Federal Emergency Management Agency (FEMA), the government agency responsible for managing such natural disasters. Obama was able to appear as a uniting figure, which is likely to have aided his bid to gain re-election.	The events of 9/11 led to an unprecedented increase in public support for President Bush and allowed him to be only the second president in US history to see his party gain seats in Congress in a mid-term election. Critics at the time said that there was no basis for the invasion with Iraq not being involved in 9/11 and not possessing the weapons of mass destruction (WMDs) that Bush claimed existed. After the invasion, Bush stated that the United States could find no such evidence of WMDs. He continued to lose public support for his leadership from 2004 onwards, losing the mid-terms in 2006.	Whilst the banking crisis and Hurricane Sandy were major crises that had devastating effects, the events of 9/11 had a profound impact on so many aspects of US political life. It led to a great deal of unity amongst Americans and gave President Bush enormous amounts of power, as Democrats were reluctant to be seen to oppose him. Obama was held back from pursuing his own policy goals by the banking crisis but was given a huge political boost by Hurricane Sandy and his response to it.

KEY TOPIC DEBATE: DO DIFFERENT PRESIDENTS EXPERIENCE VERY DIFFERENT LEVELS OF POWER AS A RESULT OF THE FACTORS AFFECTING PRESIDENTIAL POWER?

✓ Public support

A president may experience low levels of public support or face significant criticism over a specific policy or event. This could cause the president and their administration to be much more defensive as they are forced to respond to regular media attacks. A president may feel more confident if they are receiving praise, making them more emboldened in pursuing their agenda. The popularity of the president is most significant, however, because it affects the response of Congress to presidential policies. As we saw in Chapter 3, members of Congress are sensitive to public opinion and their need to get re-elected. Members of Congress are more likely to reject a presidential proposal if it is unpopular in their state or district.

» In President Biden's first year in office, he was able to secure support even from Democrats in marginal states or districts, arguably because of this public support. Whilst Senator Manchin expressed significant concerns over Biden's infrastructure and COVID-19 relief bills, he still voted for them, perhaps being influenced by their popularity overall. In Trump's first two years in office, he was unable to unite all Republicans in a finely balanced Senate (fifty-two Republicans and forty-eight Democrats), for example failing to secure agreement for a replacement bill to secure his aim of repealing Obama's Affordable Care Act. This difference could be explained by the much higher opinion poll ratings for Biden compared to Trump in their respective first eighteen months of office.

✓ Divided government

The nature of party control in Congress can lead to major differences in the level of presidential power. A president with a majority in both chambers of Congress is likely to be far more powerful than a president who lacks a majority in either. If a president loses that control, this gives a renewed mandate to one chamber and often leads them to be aggressive in challenging the president's policy by proposing alternatives and/or rejecting the president's legislative agenda. Presidents who lead under unified government are in a better position to achieve policy goals but even with a small majority in a chamber in Congress, the president may find it difficult to achieve legislative success unless they can unite the party. For details of party control of the presidency and Congress see Figure 3.7.

Spec key term

Unified government: The opposite term to divided government. Both chambers of Congress, House and Senate, and the presidency are controlled by people from the same political party.

» As we can see in Table 4.6, President Bush was in a stronger position than other presidents such as Obama because Bush held a majority in both chambers for six of his eight years in office, compared to Obama's two. President Biden was more able to achieve legislative success with his American Rescue Plan Act and his CARES Act and Infrastructure Investment and Jobs Act whilst he had a majority in both chambers of Congress.

✓ National events or crises

Events, often unforeseen, can have either a positive or negative impact on the power of the president. Presidents and their administration must spend time and possibly financial resources in dealing with the crisis. It can force the creation of a new political agenda in response to the event or crisis, which may direct the president's attention from their other policy goals. Events or crises can also affect both public support for the president and the reaction of Congress to presidential policy. The nature of the event or crisis is important:

- Was it of the president's making (or seen to be)?
- Does it unite the country behind the president?
- Does it lead to major partisan divides over the most desirable response?

» The COVID-19 crisis was a major unanticipated factor affecting the power of the president. For President Trump, the crisis had a mainly negative impact on his power. There was resistance, especially in Republican areas, to mask requirements, lockdowns and restrictions on businesses. In addition, Trump was criticised for his lack of effective response in crisis management, often leaving the issue for states to deal with. This had a negative impact on the voter perception at the 2020 election and contributed to Trump's defeat. A contrasting event was 9/11, which saw a major rise in George W. Bush's level of public support and reduced any resistance from both Democrats and Republicans to his foreign policy agenda.

Key Topic Debate Summary: Do different presidents experience very different levels of power as a result of the factors affecting presidential power?

FOR	KEY CRITERIA	AGAINST
✓ Public support can have a major impact on the president's confidence and willingness to take action. ✓ Changes in popularity affect the authority a president has, for example, with president's potentially losing confidence if unpopular. ✓ Popularity has a significant impact on the extent of congressional support for the president's policies.	Does **public opinion** have a major impact on presidential power?	✗ It is the formal powers and limits on the president that determine their power, not public opinion. ✗ High levels of partisanship means that levels of support are not likely to change amongst the president's own party. ✗ Powers of proposal, agenda-setting and veto remain constant for all presidents.

FOR	KEY CRITERIA	AGAINST
✓ This factor has a considerable impact on the power of the president because it determines the extent to which Congress is likely to support his or her bills. ✓ Presidents often experience a considerable depreciation of power after mid-term elections. ✓ Imperial presidency powers are limited and cannot overcome the restrictions of divided government. The imperial presidency is explained on page 102.	Does **divided government/ party** majorities have a major impact on presidential power?	✗ It does but this does not account for major differences between presidents as they almost always face divided government at some point. ✗ President Bush was unusual as he maintained a majority for six of his eight years in office, whereas presidents Clinton, Obama, Trump and Biden all lost a majority after just two years in office. ✗ Imperial presidency powers can overcome loss of power with a president bypassing Congress and making more use of executive orders, executive agreements and unilateral military action.
✓ Events or crises can lead to major changes in public support for the president. They have an *indirect* effect on presidential power. ✓ Events or crises and the resulting impact on public opinion can increase or decrease Congress's willingness to support the president. ✓ This factor can force a change in policy priorities or force a president to shift focus from their main agenda.	Do **events or crises** have a major impact?	✗ Some presidents or presidential terms face crises of a limited nature or no major crisis at all. ✗ Presidents can offset crises using their powers and leadership, resulting in a lack of change in their support levels.

Exam Tip: Improving your AO2 analysis and your AO3 evaluation

Focus on the keyword(s) of the question. In this case we are asked if the factors lead to very different levels of power. Whilst these factors will change the level of presidential power, we can try to show the extent to which they do and show that and make a useful distinction between minor differences between the power of different presidents and major differences which would relate directly to the word 'very'.

VARYING POWER WITHIN THEIR TERM IN OFFICE

Presidents will typically experience fluctuations in their power level within their term in office. This is caused by the same three factors addressed above as well as by the **election cycle**. A typical profile for a president is that they experience most power at the start of their presidency, with later stages of the cycle leading to a decline in their ability to achieve their policy goals as seen in Table 4.7.

Definition

Election cycle: The different stages of a presidency as they move through their time in office.

Learning Review

1. What are the three main ways in which the president can influence the Supreme Court?
2. What are the three limits on presidential power over the Supreme Court?
3. What are the three main factors affecting the power of a president?
4. What is the election cycle and what are the different stages within it?

Definition

Lame-duck presidency: The final months of a president's second term in which the president loses authority and power as attention is turned to the next set of presidential elections.

Table 4.7 **Stages in the election cycle**

Stage in the election cycle	Typically characterised by . . .
1. After the presidential election	Presidents are usually at their most influential. They have just received a public mandate, are usually at their most popular and often have a majority in Congress.
2. Mid-term elections	The president's party typically loses control of one or more chambers in these congressional elections, leading to a major decline in their ability to pass legislation. All post-1992 presidents have moved from a position of having a majority in both chambers to losing control of at least one.
3. Throughout a term	Presidents usually experience a steady decline in popularity, facing increased criticism and often reduced willingness from congressional politicians to support their policies.
4. The end phase of a two-term presidency	The last six to twelve months of a presidents second term is often when the president is described as a **lame duck**, meaning one who finds it difficult to move forward politically. Everyone is aware that the presidency will soon be over and there is greater focus amongst politicians on potential successors and upcoming elections. The presidency can lose momentum often marking the weakest point of a presidency.

Spec key term

Imperial presidency: An over-powerful president who carries out policy whilst avoiding constitutional checks and balances.

Executive order: A direction to the federal bureaucracy on how the president would like a piece of legislation to be implemented.

INTERPRETATIONS AND DEBATES

THE IMPERIAL PRESIDENCY

The term **imperial presidency** was used by Arthur J. Schlesinger in his 1973 book *The Imperial Presidency*, a critique of the excessive use of power during the Nixon presidency of the time. The phrase specifically refers to the idea that presidents are extremely powerful *as a result of being able to overcome constitutional restrictions on their power.* He argues that Nixon was able to escape the checks and balances intended by the Founding Fathers and to act in a largely unrestrained manner. Presidents have several possible actions at their disposal to achieve this. These are explored throughout this section and are:

- Executive orders and signing statements
- Executive agreements
- Unilateral action in foreign policy.

KEY TOPIC DEBATE: DOES THE UNITED STATES HAVE AN IMPERIAL PRESIDENCY?

✓ Executive orders and signing statements

The president can instruct members of the executive branch and executive agencies to carry out policies or practices. An **executive order** does not require a vote in Congress. The use of this power may seem uncontroversial and well within the president's rightful powers. President Biden, for example, signed executive orders to set up a White House Gender Policy Council that had 200 days to produce policy ideas to create greater gender equity in the United States. On the other hand, presidents could effectively be using these orders to put a new policy in place without going through the legislative process. Congress then does not have the chance to reject a president's proposal. Table 4.8 gives examples of the use of executive orders by Biden. Presidents can also issue **signing statements**, which explain that a president agrees to the bill but will not enforce certain provisions, arguing that they are unconstitutional, for example. This effectively acts as a line-item veto in which a president rejects part of a bill only.

Table 4.8 **A selection of executive orders signed by President Biden**

Policy area	Executive order
Economy and work	• 2024, requires tech companies to provide detailed information on advanced AI projects to the Commerce Department. • 2023, an executive order to help reduce childcare and senior care costs, with government agencies taking over fifty separate actions to reduce costs for families. • 2022, Biden forgives $10,000 of student debt for anyone earning less than $125,000 per year. Challenged in the Supreme Court in *Nebraska v Biden* (2023). • 2021, the COVID-19 vaccine mandate required that workers in companies with over 100 people had to be vaccinated. The Supreme Court ruled that Biden did not have the authority to create this mandate in *NFIB v Department of Labor* (2022).
Guns	• 2023, increase the regulations around background checks so that more sellers are forced to complete criminal checks on the buyer. Biden said that the Bipartisan Safer Communities Act 2022 gave him the authority to do this. • 2022, six measures to restrict guns including a rule to help stop the proliferation of 'ghost guns', which are homemade guns with no serial numbers.
Rights	• 2022, the Department of State sets up a group to respond quickly to international violations of LGBTQ+ rights. • 2021, reverse the Trump ban on transgender Americans in the military.

✗ Executive orders and signing statements are limited

Executive orders and signing statements are limited in their scope; presidents must still propose legislation to Congress for the policies that usually matter to them the most and cannot issue a signing statement without some constitutional justification for disregarding part of a bill. It would be unthinkable for President Trump to achieve a whole border wall or for President Biden to pass his infrastructure plan through executive orders. In addition, executive orders and signing statements are often subject to legal challenges, usually stating the president has exceeded their authority.

» As we saw in the Supreme Court section of this chapter, Presidents Trump and Biden both had executive orders overturned by the court and more evidence can be seen in Table 4.7 in which Biden's vaccine mandate was overturned.

✓ Executive agreements

These are agreements between the president and another country. The president may negotiate a deal or common policy approach with a foreign leader and declare this as US policy. Presidents can use this to bypass the need for the Senate to ratify a treaty. Executive agreements can be seen as treaties in disguise; by naming them executive agreements, the president can evade traditional checks and balances and disregard the views of the Senate.

» President Trump passed only one treaty throughout his presidency, an eighty-nine to ten vote that accepted a new trade deal between the United States, Canada and Mexico. At the same time, he entered into a significant number of executive agreements including a digital trade deal with Japan.

Executive agreements are limited

Executive agreements are limited in the sense that they are only agreements between a *president* and another country and not, officially, an agreement with the United States as a whole. New presidents are not bound by such executive agreements. Also, whilst presidents may be able to play around with the meaning of words, some foreign policy agreements are so important that it is unlikely that the president would be willing to try to bypass the Senate.

» Senators wrote to the Iranian government in response to Obama's Iran deal executive order saying that the agreement was not part of US law. The Senate has rejected treaty proposals such as the Disability Treaty, signed by Obama, which fell short of the two-thirds requirement in the Senate.

Foreign policy and unilateral action

Presidents have been increasingly willing to initiate significant military action without seeking congressional approval. The Constitution is unclear when it says that the president is the commander in chief of the armed forces, but also that Congress has the power to declare war. Presidents have focused on the meaning of constitutional words, committing military action but saying that this is very different from a war. Technological changes have allowed presidents to assert much more control and to bypass Congress in military policy saying that, as they are using jets, drones and missiles but not committing troops to a country, their actions do not constitute a war. As such, according to successive presidents, Congress does not have to be consulted. In practice, the president acts without consultation, rendering Congress virtually powerless.

» In 2011 President Obama initiated major air strikes on Libya, seeking to overthrow the regime of the Libyan leader Colonel Gaddafi, who was captured and killed by Libyan opposition forces after the attack. Conversely in 2020, President Trump's administration signed a deal with the Taliban to withdraw troops from Afghanistan within fourteen months without a vote in Congress.

Foreign policy limits

There are significant constitutional restrictions on the foreign policy power of the president. Not only does the Constitution award Congress the power to declare war, Congress has attempted to reassert this power through the War Power Act of 1973, which requires the president to seek approval for 'hostilities' abroad. In addition, Congress controls military funding, allowing them to limit the power of the president further. The extent to which Congress can restrict the president's foreign policy power is addressed in the foreign policy section, page 111.

» In 2020 Congress took pre-emptive action against President Trump, passing a resolution that blocked funding for any future strike on Iran. Congress feared presidential aggression in his final months in office, although Trump issued a successful veto against this bill.

THE IMPERILLED PRESIDENCY

In contrast to the imperial presidency theory, the **imperilled presidency** theory suggests that presidents cannot carry out their policy wishes as they are continually blocked, particularly by Congress. This is partly because of the high levels of checks and balances created by the Founding Fathers. The theory of the imperilled presidency has gained more support in recent years, suggesting that recent presidents have become weaker or *more imperilled*. This change coincides with the rise in partisanship, in which members of one party are reluctant to compromise with a president from another. The combination of separation of powers, checks and balances and high levels of partisanship results in a president who is largely powerless to act.

» This can be seen in the final six years in office of former presidents Clinton and Obama, when they both faced a hostile Republican majority. Both found it difficult to pass their budgets and both experienced significant federal shutdowns because they could not get their financial packages passed through Congress. Obama spent a great deal of political energy in the rest of his term on defending his healthcare policy passed in his first two years, rather than adding lots of new policy successes to his name.

Spec key term

Imperilled presidency: This is the contrasting theory to that of an imperial presidency. It argues that the president does not have enough power to be an effective leader.

Key Topic Debate Summary: Does the United States have an imperial presidency?

FOR	KEY CRITERIA	AGAINST
✓ The president can use executive orders to bypass Congress and achieve policy goals. ✓ The president can also use signing statements to confirm he or she will not enforce parts of a bill they see as unconstitutional. This effectively acts as an enhanced veto power. ✓ Presidents can use their informal powers such as the authority they have via their mandate to set a legislative agenda and successfully use executive orders and signing statements.	Can the president use **executive orders and signing statements** to bypass Congress?	✗ Executive orders and signing statements are limited in scope and could be challenged in court. Most policy will require legislative approval from Congress, and the Supreme Court can block any abuse of executive order power. ✗ The separation of powers and high levels of checks and balances make it very difficult for the president to achieve policy goals. ✗ The frequency of divided government, coupled with high levels of partisanship makes it increasingly difficult for presidents to achieve many or any of their policy goals.
✓ The president can use executive agreements to bypass the need for Senate approval of treaties. ✓ Executive orders are sometimes used to ensure that the United States complies with international agreements. These are not voted on in Congress.	Can the president use **executive agreements** without consulting the Senate?	✗ Most international agreements are so important that presidents would feel compelled to request a treaty vote. ✗ Congress could pass resolutions that prevent an executive order from taking place.
✓ Presidents often initiate military action without seeking permission from Congress. ✓ This power has become increasingly important as foreign policy decisions require speed and secrecy, giving the president greater control.	Can the president conduct other **foreign policy** without limits from Congress?	✗ Congress holds the power to declare war and has reinforced its control over military action with the War Powers Act 1973. ✗ Congress has budgetary control over military matters and can curtail presidential policy by withholding funding.

Exam Tip: Improving your AO2 analysis and AO3 evaluation

The extent to which Congress wishes to restrict the president depends on the nature of party control. If the president has a majority in the House and Senate then they are likely to be much more powerful. When facing divided government, with a hostile majority in at least one chamber of Congress, can the president still successfully achieve their policy goals? How will these points and questions affect your evaluation of an imperial versus imperilled presidency?

CASE STUDY 4.1: BIDEN AND IMMIGRATION POLICY

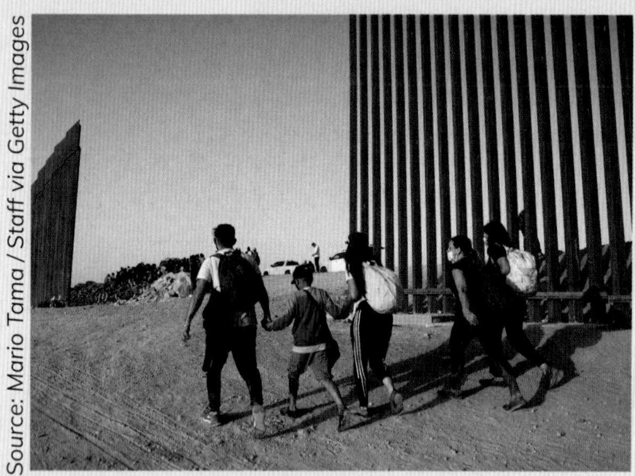

Source: Mario Tama / Staff via Getty Images

Photo 4.4 **Migrants cross through a gap in the US–Mexico border**

Outline

Pew Research estimated that there were 10.5 million illegal immigrants in the United States in 2020 out of a total population of 321 million. In 2021 the US Border Patrol reported 1.6 million encounters with migrants along the US–Mexico border, more than quadruple the number in the previous year and the largest total on record. Republicans have typically responded to this by giving more power to law enforcement offices such as the Department of Homeland Security and creating laws that would make it easier to detain and deport illegal immigrants. In addition, many Republicans have attempted to create a more hostile environment for those seeking to become immigrants by claiming asylum. In 2018 President Trump began a policy of separating families who attempted to enter the United States, by detaining children separately from their parents. Democrats opposed this and what they saw as additional inhumane treatment.

President Biden initially took a more liberal approach to the issue of immigration, but in 2023 reverted to some Trump-era conservative policies. Democrats have tended to make it easier for individuals to successfully claim for asylum. In addition, they argue that it is both impractical and undesirable to attempt to detect and deport illegal immigrants. Instead, they have attempted to resolve the social and economic issues related to illegal immigrant status. For example, Obama favoured the DREAM Act, which would allow all illegal immigrants to be granted a right to remain (but not automatic citizenship), allowing illegal immigrants greater access to jobs, education and healthcare. When this policy failed to pass Congress, he issued two highly controversial executive orders bypassing Congress. Deferred Action for Childhood arrivals (DACA), for example, allowed anyone who arrived in the United States before their 18th birthday to remain in the United States.

Executive orders

President Biden immediately reversed several Trump-era immigration policies by issuing executive orders that stopped the building of the Mexican border wall and removed the Trump travel ban on people arriving to the United States from fourteen specific countries including Iran, Iraq and Nigeria. President Trump stated that this was necessary for national security reasons, with many Democrats arguing that it was unnecessary and appeared to be targeted at Muslim-majority countries in particular. Biden also used executive orders to establish new policies, such as a requirement that immigration rights were respected without discrimination on the grounds of gender, sexuality or gender identity. In 2023 Biden issued new executive orders making it harder for asylum seekers to have the right to apply for the right to remain in the United States, creating a presumption that anyone who enters illegally is not eligible for asylum status. These executive orders could be seen as evidence of an imperial presidency because they involve making major policy changes without consulting Congress.

Role of the EXOP

The EXOP played a key role in determining the exact approach to immigration taken by the Biden presidency. Its involvement shows how complex the decision-making process is and how many different government agencies are involved, often with conflicting interests or viewpoints. Major increases in attempts to cross the border resulted in growing public criticism of the Biden approach. This led to disputes amongst senior White House advisers about how fast Trump-era border restrictions should be removed. Biden used Klain, his chief of staff, to push his policy agenda within the executive branch. Klain held a meeting with senior EXOP staff including Susan Rice, domestic policy adviser, and Elizabeth Sherwood-Randall, Homeland Security Advisor. Klain told them that they must do more to retain Trump-era regulations where possible. This added to ongoing conflicts between those in the administration pushing for Biden's liberal policy as outlined in his election campaign, and those who took a more practical approach in the face of growing immigration numbers.

Supreme Court

Biden attempted to end Trump's 'remain in Mexico policy', returning to a policy of processing claims inside the United States. This was blocked by the Supreme Court in 2021 on a technicality (the Biden administration had not followed all required procedures to assess the impact of the policy). The Supreme Court later reversed its decision in 2022, with the Department of Homeland Security saying that it would begin work on making changes to the policy immediately. In a separate ruling in 2022, the Supreme Court also overruled the Biden policy of prioritising those who had committed more dangerous crimes for deportation. This was challenged by some conservative states that argued that this allowed the Federal Government to overlook some illegal immigrants when prioritising others. The court sided with the state, saying that the Federal Government does not have discretion on whom to deport. This case, the first involving Justice Ketanji Brown Jackson, was an emergency ruling that the court has already agreed to review.

Parties

Republicans criticised the Biden administration for encouraging greater immigration into the United States, creating even more social, economic and humanitarian problems. After the mid-term elections of 2022, Republicans started to use the majority they gained in the House of Representatives to limit immigration, promising construction of the border wall, a policy that is not supported by a single Democrat in Congress. In 2023 House Republican Chip Roy initiated the Border Safety and Security Act. The bill, which would effectively stop asylum seekers from remaining in the United States, had limited chances of passing Congress. The issue of immigration has had some cross-party consensus in the past. In 2013, fourteen Senate Republicans voted for an Obama policy that would allow more illegal immigrants to have a right to remain. Today, this topic marks an area of high partisan divisions between the two parties, with the anti-immigrant rhetoric of the Trump presidency increasing this divide. There are also some divisions *within* the Democrat Party on the issue. Progressive Democrats, such as Pramila Jayapal, have attempted to push Biden further, saying that he should go beyond simply reversing Trump policies but also push for greater citizen rights for illegal immigrants. Moderate Democrats in marginal states are much more cautious, however, fearing that Biden's reversal of many Trump-style policies will cause them to lose seats in upcoming congressional elections.

HOW EFFECTIVELY HAVE PRESIDENTS ACHIEVED THEIR POLICY AIMS?

The success with which presidents achieve their aims requires us to have a clear sense of what those aims are in the first place. In addition, we can consider how important those policy aims were to the president involved as well as how ambitious those plans were. Presidential electoral campaigns can help us to determine the policy goals of a president. The following points will help you to sharpen your analysis when evaluating the extent to which the president has achieved their policy aims.

- **Power, limits and the constitutional context** – US presidents are subject to extensive checks and balances. They are arguably more constrained than any other political leader and we would not expect them to achieve policy aims with the same success of say a British prime minister or a dictator.
- **It is relative** – one way to make sense of the success levels of a president is to compare different presidents. If this falls within the remit of an A-Level question, this can enhance your analysis. A president may not have achieved as many of their goals as a dictator but if they appear to achieve a lot more than other presidents then this tells us something significant about that president. In addition, you might consider how ambitious the presidents' aims are. Have a look at pages 108–109 to see a comparison of how effectively four recent US presidents have achieved their policy aims.

HOW EFFECTIVELY HAVE PRESIDENTS ACHIEVED THEIR POLICY AIMS

	Election Result 	Congress Majority	Context 
President Clinton 1992 – 2000  Ira Wyman / Contributor via Getty Images	Clinton was elected with 43% and 49% of the vote in his two elections, partly as a result of a strong third-party candidate Ross Perot.	Clinton had a majority in both chambers from 1992 to 1994 but lost control of both chambers with a Republican majority for his final six years in office.	Clinton beat a one-term president, George H.W. Bush, at a time when the economy had gone into recession. He was also the first president elected after the end of the Cold War.
President Obama 2008 – 2016 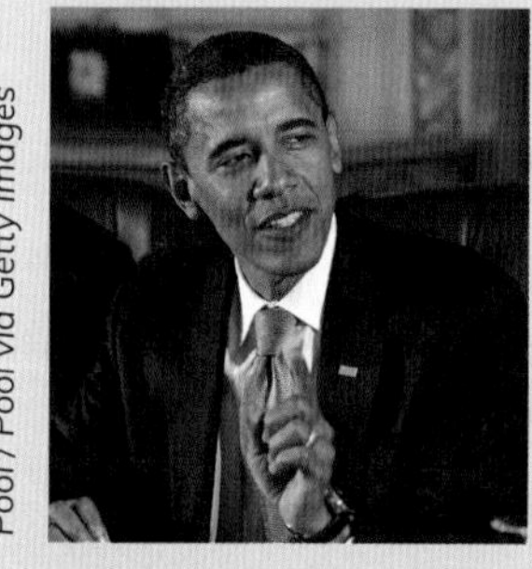 Pool / Pool via Getty Images	Obama secured clear electoral victories in both elections with nearly 53% of the vote in 2008 and 51% in 2012.	Obama won with a majority of Democrats in both chambers of Congress. This majority ended in the House in the mid-terms of 2010, forcing Obama to be far more defensive in the face of an uncompromising Republican majority. The Democrats also lost control of the Senate in 2014.	The focal point of the election campaign was the Iraq War and Bush's troop surge of 2007, as well as the failure to find WMDs in Iraq. The election campaign also had to focus on the collapse of various banks. This led to an economic crisis that engulfed much of the world, with the impact felt throughout the Obama presidency.
President Trump 2016 – 2020  Anna Moneymaker / Staff via Getty Images	President Trump gained 46.1% of the popular vote, with 2.8 million fewer votes than his opponent Hillary Clinton, despite gaining a majority of Electoral College votes.	President Trump held a majority in both chambers for his first two years in office with the Democrats securing a majority in the House in the 2018 mid-term elections.	The central focus of his campaign was his brand of populist nationalism in which he sought to put 'America First'. The main symbol of this was his promise to build a wall across the length of the US–Mexico border. During his election campaign, he focused on deregulating businesses and cutting tax as well as repealing many of President Obama's policies, including the Affordable Care Act.
President Biden 2020 – present  Source: Pool / Pool via Getty Images	Biden won with 51% of the vote.	The Democrats retained control of Congress, although the Senate had a 50–50 split making it a challenge for Biden to secure agreement from this chamber.	The election was fought in the setting of the health and economic crisis of the COVID-19 pandemic. As with most election campaigns, the policy and actions of the outgoing president, in this case Trump, formed a focal point for the election campaign. Biden campaigned to reverse many of Trump's policies, especially in relation to issues such as immigration, race relations and police reform.

Policy Success 	Policy Failure 
✓ He achieved substantial gun reform with the Brady Act of 1993, keeping a key policy promise from the 1992 election. ✓ He passed the North American Free Trade Agreement (NAFTA) through Congress, although this was negotiated and supported by his predecessor. ✓ He achieved a great deal of his goals to be involved in the prevention of conflict in other countries such as Rwanda and Somalia. This was a policy established by Clinton more clearly after the election in 1992, where he focused almost entirely on economic policy.	✗ His inability to achieve healthcare reform, the central policy goal in his 1992 campaign. Unlike Obama, his failure to compromise and manage the development of the policy led to its downfall. ✗ His biggest regret was not doing more to stop the war in Rwanda, wishing he had acted faster to prevent the genocide that took place. ✗ He advocated ending the ban on gay and lesbian soldiers in the military. Instead, due to major military resistance, he ended up with a compromise policy whereby military applicants were not asked about their sexuality, called 'Don't Ask, Don't Tell.'
✓ He successfully passed the Affordable Care Act (his central policy promise), though he did have to compromise heavily despite a Democrat majority. ✓ He achieved his stimulus package, a measure that led to a $787 billion injection of spending into the economy. ✓ A long-standing opponent of US involvement in Iraq, Obama pledged to end the Iraq War and withdrew troops in his first term.	✗ He failed to gain sufficient support for his immigration reform policy, the DREAM Act. This would have given illegal immigrants the right to remain in the United States, but his attempts to pass legislation failed, mainly due to Senate filibusters. ✗ Obama also pledged to close Guantanamo Bay, but his measures were rejected in bipartisan opposition from members of Congress who feared the impact of bringing suspected terrorists back to mainland United States. Obama was criticised by some progressive Democrats for not closing the camp by executive order. ✗ He was limited in his ability to achieve economic and social policy due to a Republican majority in Congress. The lack of agreement between Obama and Congress on the budget led to federal shutdown.
✓ The 2017 budget passed Congress with massive cuts to corporate federal tax rates from 35% to 21%. ✓ Trump was able to deregulate the economy mainly through a long list of executive orders. These included orders ending the Clean Power Plan, designed to reduce CO_2 emissions in electricity production, and overturning measures intended to protect wildlife. ✓ He had some success in creating a more hostile environment for immigrants and asylum seekers, introducing the Remain in Mexico Policy. ✓ His appointment of federal judges, including three Supreme Court justices in just one term, creating an enduring legacy of a conservative majority on the bench. He appointed more appeal court judges than any other recent president in their first term and achieved almost as many as Obama did in eight years.	✗ He was unable to repeal and replace the Affordable Care Act. He removed the individual mandate that required individuals to have health insurance but not the funding programme. ✗ In failing to secure funding to build the border wall, Trump was unable to achieve the one policy with which he most identified. Trump even tried to declare a national emergency to secure more funding but had this declaration overturned by a bipartisan vote in Congress. ✗ As one of a small number of presidents to fail to secure re-election he was then unable to pursue more of his policy goals.
✓ The American Rescue Plan Act 2021 and the Infrastructure Act 2021 increased federal expenditure to tackle the economic impact of COVID-19, develop more infrastructure and spend more on protecting the environment. ✓ Biden had a quick impact on his pledges to reduce CO_2 emissions by re-signing the Paris Treaty and successfully including major environmental measures in his Infrastructure Act. ✓ The Inflation Reduction Act 2022 allowed Biden to spend over $1 trillion on energy and climate change, to lower prescription drug prices for consumers and also to protect healthcare expenditure.	✗ Biden has repeatedly sought to pass the For the People Act to expand voting rights and reduce the role of money in US elections. The bill passed the House but was filibustered in the Senate. ✗ Biden promised to extend Obamacare by reintroducing the public option in which the Federal Government would directly offer health insurance but has not had this bill debated in Congress. ✗ Biden has had mixed success with his aim to stop the spread of COVID-19, instituting increased testing and a vaccine mandate for federal workers. He missed his target of getting 75% of adults vaccinated by 4 July 2021, instead reaching this milestone a month later.

Learning Review

1. What is the imperial presidency?
2. What are the main ways in which a president can act as an imperial president?
3. What are the main limits on these actions of a president?
4. What is the imperilled presidency?
5. For the following presidents, give examples of them achieving their policy aims (successes) and examples of them failing to achieve their policy aims.
   a) Clinton
   b) Bush
   c) Obama
   d) Trump
   e) Biden

THE EXTENT OF ACCOUNTABILITY TO CONGRESS

Congress has a range of methods and powers that they can use to hold a president to account. The effectiveness of the methods and powers Congress can use to restrain the president was explored in detail in the 'Oversight' section of Chapter 3, page 67. This section provides a summary of these methods as well as a key topic debate summary in order to help you see the arguments for and against in one place.

KEY TOPIC DEBATE: CAN CONGRESS HOLD THE PRESIDENT TO ACCOUNT?

The extent to which the president is accountable to Congress is not only dependent on the powers of Congress but also the extent to which Congress are willing to use these powers. Table 4.9 lists the main methods that Congress can use to restrict the president as well as selected examples from presidents since 1992.

Table 4.9 **Selected examples showing how presidents since 1992 have been held to account by Congress**

Method or power of Congress	Examples of presidents since 1992
Vote on or amend a president's legislative proposals	**Biden, 2021.** President Biden found that the American Rescue Plan Act 2021, his financial response to the COVID-19 crisis, was amended significantly, despite him holding a majority in both chambers of Congress with his aim to increase the federal minimum wage rejected.
Budgetary control	**Obama, 2013.** President Obama could not secure congressional support from the Republican-led house for his 2013 budget. Their insistence on stopping the Affordable Care Act by withdrawing funding led to a sixteen-day federal shutdown. The president eventually protected the ACA but was forced into other compromises on tax and expenditure.
Initiate and pass laws	**Trump, 2019.** The Democrat-led House consistently passed bills designed to push the United States in a different direction than that intended by Trump, or bills that deliberately restricted the power of the president. In 2019, this included bills to lower prescription drugs costs, tighten up controls on guns and end US involvement in the war in Yemen.

Continued

Table 4.9 **Continued**

Method or power of Congress	Examples of presidents since 1992
Overturn presidential vetoes	**Trump, 2020.** Congress passed the National Defense Authorization Act in 2020 with President Trump issuing a veto partly because he objected to clauses that stopped him from withdrawing troops from Afghanistan. Congress successfully overturned the veto, affirming the budget and limiting presidential power (although Trump later agreed a deal with the Taliban to withdraw troops from Afghanistan without a vote in Congress).
Declare war	**Bush, 2003.** Whilst Congress has not declared war since it declared war on Romania in the Second World War, it has voted to accept or reject military action. In 2003 President Bush had to work hard to secure support for the Iraq War and could only act with their approval.
Impeach and remove a president	**Trump, 2019 and 2020.** President Trump was impeached for changing US foreign policy in an attempt to get a foreign government to interfere to help him win the 2020 presidential election. He was also impeached for inciting an insurrection against the government in the run up to the 6 January 2021 attacks on the Capitol. The Senate acquitted Trump on both occasions.
Ratify Treaties (Senate only)	**Clinton, 1999.** The Senate voted against the Comprehensive Nuclear-Test-Ban Treaty designed to stop the testing and further development of nuclear missiles. Clinton was held accountable and prevented from joining this treaty and indicating a different priority for US foreign policy.
Ratify presidential appointments (Senate only)	**Bush, 2005.** President Bush's nomination of Harriet Miers to the Supreme Court had to be withdrawn as a result of a lack of Senate support. Some senators were concerned about her lack of judicial experience with others questioning her ability to be independent once on the court as she was the acting legal counsel for Bush at the time.

As we saw earlier in the chapter, the president can attempt to avoid or overcome these methods of accountability using:

a) Their main powers.
b) The actions of an imperial president.

It is these main powers and actions of an imperial president that suggest that Congress cannot hold the president to account. The material for this debate has been covered throughout this chapter and is summarised here.

THE ROLE AND POWER OF THE PRESIDENT IN FOREIGN POLICY

Presidents are given a high degree of authority in this area both politically because they are nationally elected, and constitutionally because of the powers given to them by the Constitution. The Constitution grants the president the positions of head of state and the commander in chief of the armed services. All of this gives the president a leading role in foreign policy. As well as setting the general approach the United States takes to foreign policy, they also take the lead in times of foreign and security crisis.

Key Topic Debate Summary: Can Congress hold the president to account?

FOR	KEY CRITERIA	AGAINST
✓ The separation of powers creates separate mandates for the president and Congress and restricts presidential patronage. Congress often has a strong desire to hold the president to account rather than deferring to them. ✓ Congress has legislative power and restricts the president by amending and rejecting presidential bills. ✓ Congress controls the budget and can pass laws to defund presidential projects.	Can Congress restrict the president's **domestic legislative agenda**?	✗ Presidents have a great deal of authority over legislation given their national mandate and the media attention they attract, allowing them to dominate the political narrative and use their power to persuade. ✗ Presidents can issue vetoes to protect their policies or to prevent Congress from passing laws they do not like, helping the president to escape attempted congressional restrictions. ✗ Presidents can use signing statements and executive orders to bypass potential congressional restrictions and achieve their policy goals.
✓ Congress has specific foreign policy powers such as the power to declare war and the power to accept or reject requests from the president to attack other countries as stated in the War Powers Act. ✓ The Senate has the power to reject presidential treaties and therefore thwart some of the president's key policy goals. ✓ Congress can and does vote against the president on foreign policy matters.	Can Congress control the president's **foreign policy agenda**?	✗ The president is the head of state and commander in chief and has high levels of constitutional authority in the area of foreign policy. ✗ The president can use executive agreements to bypass the need for Senate approval of treaties. ✗ As a result of changes in technology and the need for speed of action and secrecy, Congress has become deferential in this area whilst presidents have become more willing to act without consulting Congress.
✓ The Senate can reject presidential nominations to key executive positions such as Secretary of State or head of the Office of Management and Budget. ✓ Ultimately the president can be removed from office if they are impeached by the House and then removed by the Senate.	Can Congress determine **the personnel of the executive branch?**	✗ Presidents can appoint cabinet members as well as ambassadors and diplomats, allowing them to decide who makes policy and how it will be made. ✗ Presidents can create new offices of the EXOP to push their policy priorities. ✗ Presidents can also evade the need for ratification by the Senate through recess appointments.

Exam Tip: Improve you AO2 analysis and AO3 evaluation

As with all evaluations of the relationship between the president and Congress, we have to weigh up the competing powers and limits. It is also essential to acknowledge the significance of party control and whether the president has a majority in Congress. How would this affect Congress' response to the president for each of the powers in the table above and how would this affect your overall evaluation?

Another dimension to the foreign policy debate revolves around the extent to which the United States should adopt an aggressive stance or use peaceful means to achieve its goal. Foreign policy hawks (named after the bird of prey) are more likely to advocate military attacks on other countries. Foreign policy doves (named after the bird that symbolises peace) are more likely to support diplomatic or other non-violent approaches to international relations. Table 4.10 outlines the ethos and policy of recent US presidents in the areas of foreign policy.

Table 4.10 The foreign policy and ethos of recent presidents

President Clinton 1992–2000 Nation-building	President Clinton, operating in the years following the end of the Cold War, developed the concept of 'nation-building'. The United States, he argued, should use its status as the sole superpower for ethical rather than self-interested reasons. This involved US involvement in preventing wars around the world, especially civil wars, to prevent genocide and humanitarian crisis. Clinton deployed troops to these ends in Rwanda, Haiti, Somalia and Kosovo to prevent bloodshed and attempt to create national unity and democracy. Clinton continued to face congressional resistance to his policies, especially where it led to the deaths of US soldiers.
President Bush 2000–2006 The Bush Doctrine	After the attacks of 9/11, President Bush was in a powerful position to determine the direction of US foreign policy. He did this by outlining 'The Bush Doctrine', in which he stated that the United States was the defeater of fascism and communism and was uniquely placed to be a dominant force in the world. He asserted a right to launch pre-emptive strikes on enemies of the United States. It is this doctrine that underpinned the US attack on Iraq and the removal of its leader Saddam Hussain. The initial phase of the attack was a massive air- and sea-launched bombing campaign, known as 'shock and awe', which killed over 6,000 civilians in its initial phase. Bush regularly used the phrase 'war on terror' to justify the opening of the Guantanamo Bay detention camp for those captured in Iraq or Afghanistan. The facility was created using an executive order and criticised for its lack of respect for human rights.
President Obama 2008–16 Pragmatic and piecemeal	Obama inherited two post-9/11 wars in Afghanistan and Iraq alongside the war on terror, campaigning to end involvement in Iraq. He appeared to make policy on a case-by-case basis, responding to the political context of the day, without being completely attached to a driving philosophy in the way that Bush or Clinton were. Obama engaged in several peace deals with countries traditionally seen as enemies of the United States, such as Cuba and Iran, upsetting conservatives and foreign policy hawks. At the same time, he was criticised when he bypassed Congress and took an aggressive stance in bombing Libya in 2011 in support of a popular uprising against the dictator Colonel Gaddafi. Despite calling for a similar regime change in Syria in 2012 as a result of government atrocities in a Syrian civil war, Obama backed down, influenced perhaps by the political fallout from his actions in Libya. Obama ordered more drone attacks than his predecessors, with strikes in countries such as Yemen, Somalia and Pakistan (1,878 strikes in total). None of these were sent to Congress for approval. In 2011 Obama ordered the assassination of Osama bin Laden, as the person held responsible for the 9/11 terrorist attacks on the United States. Bin Laden was killed in Pakistan without Congress or the Pakistani authorities being consulted beforehand.
President Trump 2016–20 Hawkish unilateralism	President Trump placed American interest and American nationalism at the heart of his foreign policy, alongside his dislike of tying the United States into international agreements. These agreements were seen by Trump as a limit on US sovereignty and self-interest. The hawk is the symbol of aggression in foreign policy, in contrast with the dove which represents peace. He quickly left the Paris Agreement and made critical remarks about the North Atlantic Treaty Organization (NATO), threating to leave the alliance that was a cornerstone of US and Western security policy. He also cancelled the Iran agreement and launched bombing raids on a Syrian airbase and ordered the assassination of Qasem Soleimani, an Iranian military general. Trump ordered 2,243 drone strikes in his first two years of office and issued an executive order saying that the government was no longer required to report these drones strikes to the public.

Continued

Table 4.10 **Continued**

President Biden 2020– **Diplomacy and democracy**	President Biden began his presidency stressing the importance of international cooperation to make the United States stronger in the world, in contrast to President Trump's more aggressive and unilateral approach. Biden talked of the need for 'global cooperation to face existential threat' of environmental destruction and his desire to 'unite democratic values with our diplomatic leadership'. One of Biden's first acts as president was to reengage with other countries by signing the Paris Agreement, thereby committing the United States to meeting internationally agreed standards to reduce CO_2 emissions. Whilst he has strengthened diplomatic ties he has also, like all recent presidents, ordered extensive airstrikes. In 2022 he ordered drone strikes that killed the leader of the Islamic State in Syria, Maher al-Agal. Biden also honoured the agreement between the Trump administration and the Taliban in Afghanistan to withdraw troops, within fourteen months of the 2020 agreement. Biden signalled a contrast with both Clinton's and Bush's foreign policy when he said that the era of major military operations to remake other countries is over. The removal of troops was met with major criticism after the Taliban took control of the Afghanistan capital Kabul just eleven days after the US withdrawal.

KEY TOPIC DEBATE: IS THE PRESIDENT SIGNIFICANTLY RESTRICTED IN FOREIGN POLICY?

Modern foreign policy presidents

War has become faster, more complex and more deadly. First jet engines, then nuclear missiles, satellites, computer technology and drones have all contributed and this has centralised power in the presidency. All of this means that the United States now requires fast decision-making, secrecy and major and diverse expertise to deal with the dangers it faces. It is the president and their National Security Council that can achieve this and not Congress. Congress has been forced into a more passive role, having to trust the president's security information or accept that presidents had to act quickly and not consult Congress.

» In 2003, President Bush sought permission for an invasion of Iraq, citing a potential threat to the United States from Iraq's weapon of mass destruction. The president and his security advisers could not share details of their intelligence for reasons of national security. Congress was left in a position of having to trust the president. If the president's claims were true then the consequences of inaction were potentially disastrous. Given this, alongside public grief and anger at the 9/11 terror attack, almost half of Democrats in Congress joined Republicans in authorizing a military campaign.

Continuing restraints

Congress retains significant powers, which it can use to restrict the president in foreign policy such as the power to declare war, budgetary power and the Senate ratification of treaties. Congress can and does continue to curtail a president's foreign policy agenda. Also, while the president may be more able to act at times of perceived emergency, a great deal of foreign policy does not require the speed and secrecy of decision-making best suited to presidential action. For example, there are no practical reasons why Congress cannot be involved in foreign policy decisions on climate change or trade agreements.

» President Obama backed down from his planned military strike in Syria even after he had introduced a bill into Congress to authorise military strikes in 2013 against the regime of President Assad. Instead of ordering military strikes immediately, he decided to seek congressional approval for the measures. This was perhaps a result of the heavy criticism he faced for his lack of congressional consultation before bombing the Libyan capital.

Constitutional powers of the president

The Constitution awards the president significant powers that allow them to dominate foreign policy. As commander in chief, the president can order military action and argue that they have the right to act unilaterally. All post-1992 presidents have initiated military action without seeking congressional approval. They have also ignored the War Powers Act, discussed below, rejecting the right of Congress to assert control over the initiation of military action. The president is in the driving seat and Congress is often a mere passenger. Finally, the president can use executive agreements to pursue deals with other countries and bypass the Senate's constitutional power to ratify treaties. These constitutional powers, alongside the changing nature of modern foreign policy, allow the president to have largely unrivalled power.

» In 2011, President Obama ordered airstrikes on Libya without consulting Congress. He rejected claims that he should have consulted Congress because there was no military invasion but only airstrikes. President Biden ordered air strikes in 2021 against Syrian militia groups on the border with Iraq. Biden was criticised, particularly by Democrats, who stated that the president lacked constitutional authority to make such decisions without consulting Congress.

Constitutional powers of Congress

Congress is granted the power to declare war, and whilst the technical process of declaring war has not happened since the Second World War, Congress can argue that the intent of the Founding Fathers was clearly to give them control over the initiation of military action. Congress attempted to reassert this power by passing the War Powers Act that requires the president to consult with Congress where possible before military action and gives Congress the power to order the withdrawal of troops within ninety days. This act was passed to restrain Nixon after his unilateral decision to invade Laos and Cambodia as part of the Vietnam War effort. Congress also has funding power, in which they can limit military action through the power of the purse.

Key Topic Debate Summary: Is the president significantly restricted in foreign policy?

FOR	KEY CRITERIA	AGAINST
✓ Congress can continue to place restraints in foreign policy using the power to declare war, budgetary power and the Senate ratification of treaties. ✓ A great deal of foreign policy does not require unilateral presidential action. There are no practical reasons why Congress cannot be involved in foreign policy decisions on climate change or trade agreements.	Does the nature of **modern foreign policy** allow Congress to restrict the president?	✗ Modern military policy is much faster and more deadly, which means that the president must be free to act without always consulting Congress. ✗ The increased complexity and secrecy requited means that the president, with access to superior sources of information such as the NSC, is better placed to make decisions.
✓ Congress has specific foreign policy powers such as the power to declare war and the power to accept or reject requests from the president to attack other countries as stated in the War Powers Act. ✓ The Senate has the power to reject presidential treaties and therefore thwart some of the president's key policy goals.	Does **the Constitution** give Congress sufficient power to restrict the president's foreign policy agenda?	✗ As commander in chief, the president can order military action and argue that he or she has the right to act unilaterally. ✗ Presidents have ignored the War Powers Act, rejecting the right of Congress to assert control over the initiation of military action. ✗ Finally, the president can use executive agreements to make deals with other countries and bypass the need for Senate ratification of treaties.
✓ Individual members of Congress can claim a mandate and will want to represent the views of their constituents on foreign policy issues. ✓ Ultimately Congress can claim a stronger mandate than the president after a mid-term election, especially where the president's party loses a majority.	Does Congress have **political advantages** that allow it to restrict the president in the area of foreign policy?	✗ As the nationally elected head of government, the president can avoid foreign policy restraint and use the authority of their national mandate to determine US-wide policy. ✗ Members of Congress only possess a local mandate and have less authority to speak on international issues.

Exam Tip: Improve your AO2 analysis and AO3 advanced evaluation

Don't make assumptions about words that seem to have an obvious meaning. The concept of 'foreign policy' is a great case in point. There is a major difference between a short-term military raid, a long-term invasion of a country, negotiating a budget deal with neighbouring countries or securing an environmental treaty. The president will have more or less control in each of these scenarios and you could bring this in to add to your analysis and evaluation.

Evaluative view: Do presidents dominate foreign policy?

On balance, the president is given greater constitutional power than Congress, which allows him or her to be the dominant force in foreign policy. Most importantly, in the modern era, the power of the president in this area has evolved as military policy has become fast moving and more deadly. This has led to a significant imbalance of power in which the president is able to dominate. Whilst Congress has attempted to limit the president, it has often failed to do so. Much of the evidence that is used to demonstrate congressional control ends with presidents prevailing in the end. Even though the Constitution aims to create many checks and balances in the area of foreign policy, contemporary evidence strongly supports the view that the president dominates foreign policy.

Consider the key topic debate and debate summary as well as any new evidence you can find. Do you agree or disagree with this evaluative view?

» Congress passed several resolutions in the last two years of the Trump presidency, by forbidding him from taking military action in specific countries such as Iran. They also passed a bipartisan bill to ban arms sales to Saudi Arabia, which had been approved by the Trump administration. Members of Congress took this stand to oppose Saudi Arabian involvement in civil war in Yemen.

Political powers given to the president

As the nationally elected head of government, the president can avoid foreign policy restraint. Their national mandate allows the president to speak for the whole of the United States, placing them in a better position to determine international matters than members of the Senate or, in particular, members of the House, who only have a district-based mandate. Especially at times of international crisis it is natural for citizens to look to the president for solutions with Congress taking a more passive role in providing foreign policy leadership.

» In the mid-term elections of 2018, Nancy Pelosi and House Democrats campaigned mainly on the local and national matters that directly affected the daily lives of their constituents. This gave House Democrats a domestic policy mandate when they took control of the House, in which they focused their attentions on measures such as raising the minimum wage.

Political powers of Congress

At the same time Congress is elected and has democratic legitimacy. In addition, members of Congress have to respond to constituency views in order to be returned to office at election time. They are likely to vote against presidential foreign policies if those policies are unpopular in their state or district. Congress can limit the president more aggressively after a mid-term election especially if the president's party loses a majority. Congress can claim a renewed mandate and a greater right to set foreign policy direction.

» After the 2006 mid-term elections, the Democrats took control of the House of Representatives. Incoming Democrat speaker, Nancy Pelosi, used this new mandate to push foreign as well as domestic policy by challenging the continued presence of US troops in Iraq and asking for the president to assume a new direction.

Learning Review

1. What are the main methods that Congress can use to hold the president to account?
2. Why might each of these methods fail to hold the president to account?
3. For each of the following presidents how would you describe their approach to foreign policy? What are the examples of their specific foreign policies?
   a) Clinton
   b) Bush
   c) Obama
   d) Trump
   e) Biden
4. What are the reasons why the president might be powerful in the area of foreign policy?
5. What are the main limits to the president's foreign policy power?

Comparative Learning Review

1. What are the similarities in the ways in which the president and prime minister can be held to account by the legislature (Congress and Parliament)?
2. What are the differences in the ways in which the president and prime minister can be held to account by the legislature (Congress and Parliament)?

Chapter Summary

- ✓ The president is given several specific powers and roles by the Constitution including head of state, commander in chief and head of the executive branch.
- ✓ The president has a number of informal sources of power including their mandate as well as the resources provided to them by the cabinet and the Executive Office of the President.
- ✓ The separation of powers and checks and balances should mean that there are significant restrictions on the president in both domestic and foreign policy.
- ✓ The imperial presidency suggests that the president is extremely powerful and can overcome constitutional limitations.
- ✓ Checks and balances also operate between the president and Supreme Court.
- ✓ The power of the president can vary both within and between presidencies.

Exam Style Questions

- **Evaluate the view that the presidents' constitutional roles give them major political power. (30 marks)**
- **Evaluate the view that the cabinet and the Executive Office of the President play a significant role in influencing the policy and actions of the president. (30 marks)**
- **Evaluate the view that presidents are more powerful in foreign policy than domestic policy. (30 marks)**
- **Evaluate the view that the president can dominate the Supreme Court. (30 marks)**
- **Evaluate the view that mid-term elections are the most important factor that causes changes to presidential power. (30 marks)**

Further Resources

Greenberg, M. and Tait, D. (2020) *Obama: The Historic Presidency of Barack Obama* – Updated Edition (New York: Sterling).

Wolf, M. (2021) *The Final Days of The Trump Presidency* (New York: The Bridge Street Press).

Woodward, B. (2019) *Fear: Trump in the White House* (New York: Schuster).

The official White House website has an overview of all the EXOP offices and personnel as well as the latest news from the presidential office. Available at https://www.whitehouse.gov/ (accessed 23 July 2023).

A brilliant insight into decision-making and conflict within the Biden administration on the issue of immigration is Zolan Kanno-Youngs, Michael D. Shear and Eileen Sullivan, 'How Infighting over the Border Divided the Biden White House', *The New York Times*, 9 April 2022. Available at https://www.nytimes.com/2022/04/09/us/politics/biden-border-immigration.html (accessed 23 July 2023).

Visit https://bloomsbury.pub/colclough-essentials-us to access additional materials to support teaching and learning.

5 THE SUPREME COURT AND CIVIL RIGHTS

Chapter Preview

The enormous power of the Supreme Court is derived from the written and sovereign Constitution of the United States. This allows the court to decide whether the Constitution has been broken and makes the court far more powerful than the Supreme Court in the United Kingdom. Parliamentary sovereignty prevents the UK Supreme Court from overturning acts of Parliament whereas the US court can overturn laws passed by Congress as well as actions of the president.

The power of the court means that it has a major impact not only on US politics and politicians but also on the daily lives of all who live in the United States. In recent years, the court has cancelled abortion rights, extended the right to carry a gun in public and limited laws designed to prevent racial discrimination in US elections. It has protected gay rights in the workplace, allowed a ban on transgender individuals serving in the military, as well as limited the ability of the Federal Government to regulate carbon emissions and curb global warming.

To evaluate the many aspects of the Supreme Court we will explore several court rulings since 2005. You will find that a specific court case can be used to support different arguments. As such, this chapter makes use of a single court case several times, helping you to learn the case and also see how it can be applied to different parts of the A-Level Politics specification.

This chapter also includes coverage of the issue of civil rights, in particular the extent to which racial rights groups have been successful in ensuring greater levels of equality in the United States.

Key Questions and Debates

- Is the Supreme Court nomination process fit for purpose?
- What is the extent of the impact of the Supreme Court on public policy?
- Is judicial restraint a better approach than judicial activism?
- How effectively has the Supreme Court protected civil rights?
- Is the Supreme Court best described as a political or judicial body?
- Is the living constitution approach to interpreting the US Constitution more desirable than an originalist approach?
- Have racial rights campaigns made a significant difference to racial equality?

Specification Checklist

4.1 The nature and role of the Supreme Court

- The US Constitution.
- The independent nature of the Supreme Court.
- The judicial review process.

4.2 The appointment process for the Supreme Court

- Strengths and weaknesses of the process.
- Factors influencing the president's choice of nominee.
- The current composition and ideological balance.

4.3 The Supreme Court and public policy

- Impact on public policy including a wide range of examples since 2005.
- The role of judicial activism and judicial restraint and criticisms of each.

4.4 The protection of civil liberties and rights in the US today

- Rights protected by the Constitution and by rulings of the court.

4.5 Race and rights in contemporary US politics

- The methods, influence and effectiveness of racial rights campaigns and the impact on current domestic policy: voting rights, affirmative action and representation.

4.6 Interpretations and debates of the US Supreme Court and civil rights

- The political versus judicial nature of the Supreme Court.
- Living constitution ideology and originalism.
- How effectively civil and constitutional rights have been upheld by the Supreme Court and the effectiveness of this protection.
- The extent of their powers and the effectiveness of checks and balances.
- The successes and failures of measures to promote equality, including affirmative action and immigration reform.

Source: Andrew Lichtenstein / Contributor via Getty Images

THE NATURE AND ROLE OF THE SUPREME COURT

Whilst the US Constitution establishes a Supreme Court, it does not give many details on the nature, role or extent of power of the court. As we will see, the rightful role of the court is much debated with questions regarding both how much power it should have and the most desirable way to interpret and apply the Constitution.

THE SUPREME COURT AND THE CONSTITUTION

The roles, powers and limits of the US Constitution are outlined in Article III of the Constitution in three very short sections. Only the first two of these are of importance to us:

Article III, section 1

- Establishes the existence of a Supreme Court.
- Establishes that justices are appointed for life.

Article III, section 2

- The court can determine the outcome of all cases brought to it under the Constitution.
- All justices are nominated by the president and have to be ratified by the Senate.

In addition, ***other parts of the Constitution*** allow Congress to:

- Establish the structure of lower courts.
- Establish the total number of justices (this has been kept at nine since the Civil War).

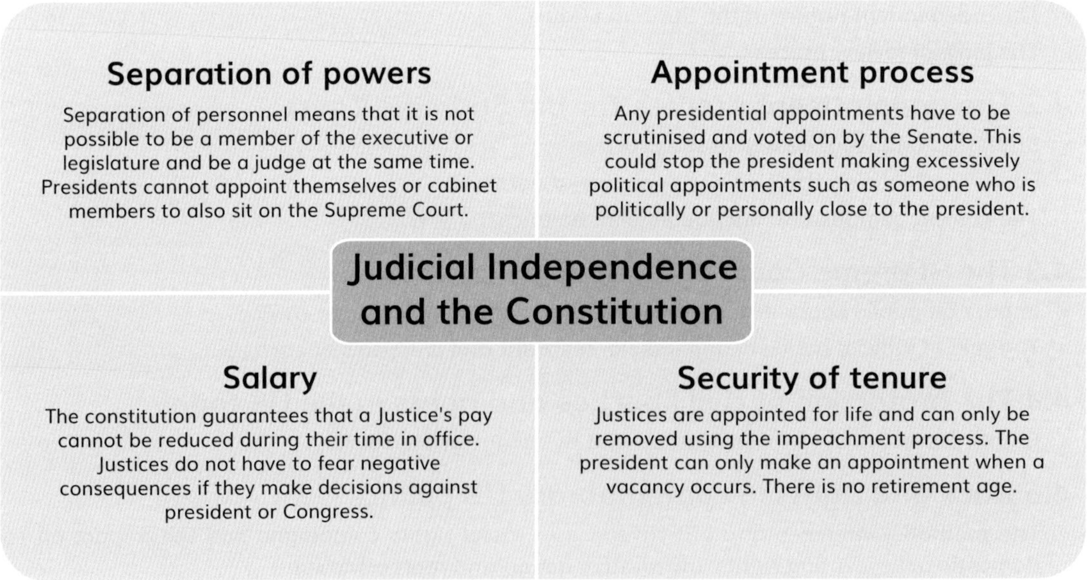

Judicial Independence and the Constitution

Separation of powers

Separation of personnel means that it is not possible to be a member of the executive or legislature and be a judge at the same time. Presidents cannot appoint themselves or cabinet members to also sit on the Supreme Court.

Appointment process

Any presidential appointments have to be scrutinised and voted on by the Senate. This could stop the president making excessively political appointments such as someone who is politically or personally close to the president.

Salary

The constitution guarantees that a Justice's pay cannot be reduced during their time in office. Justices do not have to fear negative consequences if they make decisions against president or Congress.

Security of tenure

Justices are appointed for life and can only be removed using the impeachment process. The president can only make an appointment when a vacancy occurs. There is no retirement age.

Figure 5.1 **The independence of the Supreme Court**

INDEPENDENT NATURE

To uphold the principles of the **rule of law** and **judicial neutrality** it is essential that a court is independent from other bodies, especially powerful political institutions. Independence means that the court is free from external influence. The processes that promote and protect the independence of the court are set out in Figure 5.1.

> **Definition**
>
> **Rule of law:** The principle that all people and bodies, including government, must follow the law and, if they do not, can be held to account through fair legal processes.
>
> **Judicial neutrality:** The principle that judges should make decisions based on the meaning of the law and not based on their own personal values.

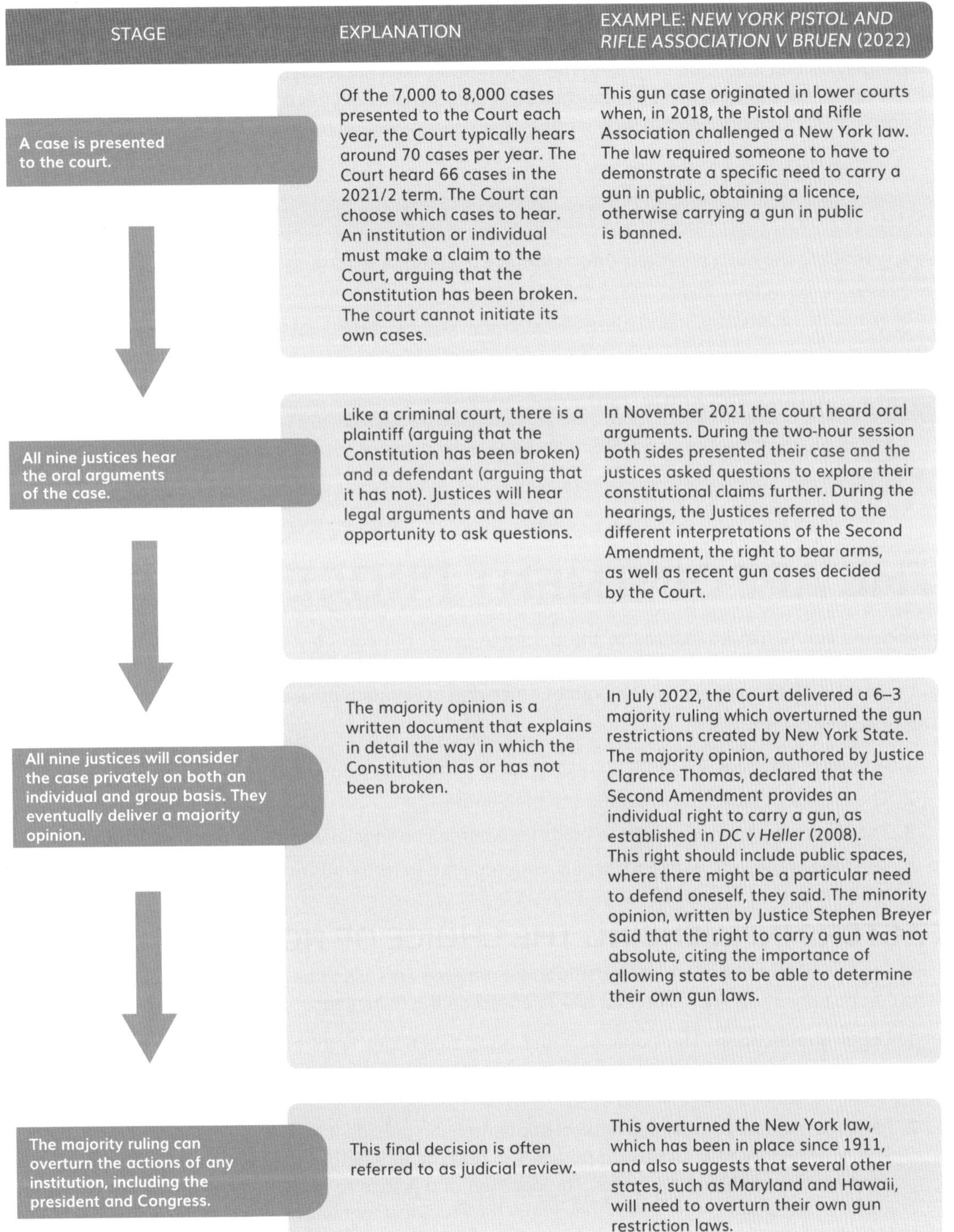

STAGE	EXPLANATION	EXAMPLE: *NEW YORK PISTOL AND RIFLE ASSOCIATION V BRUEN* (2022)
A case is presented to the court.	Of the 7,000 to 8,000 cases presented to the Court each year, the Court typically hears around 70 cases per year. The Court heard 66 cases in the 2021/2 term. The Court can choose which cases to hear. An institution or individual must make a claim to the Court, arguing that the Constitution has been broken. The court cannot initiate its own cases.	This gun case originated in lower courts when, in 2018, the Pistol and Rifle Association challenged a New York law. The law required someone to have to demonstrate a specific need to carry a gun in public, obtaining a licence, otherwise carrying a gun in public is banned.
All nine justices hear the oral arguments of the case.	Like a criminal court, there is a plaintiff (arguing that the Constitution has been broken) and a defendant (arguing that it has not). Justices will hear legal arguments and have an opportunity to ask questions.	In November 2021 the court heard oral arguments. During the two-hour session both sides presented their case and the justices asked questions to explore their constitutional claims further. During the hearings, the Justices referred to the different interpretations of the Second Amendment, the right to bear arms, as well as recent gun cases decided by the Court.
All nine justices will consider the case privately on both an individual and group basis. They eventually deliver a majority opinion.	The majority opinion is a written document that explains in detail the way in which the Constitution has or has not been broken.	In July 2022, the Court delivered a 6–3 majority ruling which overturned the gun restrictions created by New York State. The majority opinion, authored by Justice Clarence Thomas, declared that the Second Amendment provides an individual right to carry a gun, as established in *DC v Heller* (2008). This right should include public spaces, where there might be a particular need to defend oneself, they said. The minority opinion, written by Justice Stephen Breyer said that the right to carry a gun was not absolute, citing the importance of allowing states to be able to determine their own gun laws.
The majority ruling can overturn the actions of any institution, including the president and Congress.	This final decision is often referred to as judicial review.	This overturned the New York law, which has been in place since 1911, and also suggests that several other states, such as Maryland and Hawaii, will need to overturn their own gun restriction laws.

Figure 5.2 **The judicial review process**

JUDICIAL REVIEW PROCESS

This is the process by which the court determines whether the Constitution has been broken. The court has the power to overturn the actions of any other institution if, in the eyes of the court, those actions have broken the Constitution. This effectively gives the Supreme Court the final say in all constitutional cases. The process is outlined in Figure 5.2.

The Constitution is not completely clear on the extent of power of the Supreme Court. In a landmark case, *Marbury v Madison* (1803), the court declared that it has the power of judicial review and could overturn Congress. It also determined that it had the power to overturn state law by doing so for the first time in *Fletcher v Peck* (1810). It may seem logical that a Supreme Court should have this power; it is a largely settled idea that, in making the Constitution itself supreme and giving the court the power to rule on constitutional issues, the court has the final say. It could be argued, however, that this is not apparent in the Constitution but was a power the court assumed for itself.

Spec key term

Judicial review: The ability of the Supreme Court to declare acts of Congress, and acts or actions of the presidency, unconstitutional and therefore null and void.

Learning Review

1. What are the main provisions made in the Constitution regarding the Supreme Court?
2. How is the independence of the Supreme Court upheld?
3. What is judicial review and what are the main stages of the judicial review process?

Comparative Learning Review

1. What are the similarities and difference between the independence of the US and UK supreme courts?

THE APPOINTMENT PROCESS

Presidents can nominate Justices to the Supreme Court but can only do so once a vacancy occurs. There is no retirement age for a justice. Vacancies come about through a justice's decision to retire, but several justices have been forced out of office due to ill health or several have died whilst in office.

The appointment process:

1. A team of advisers will draw up a shortlist of candidates who are considered and interviewed.
2. The president makes a nomination to the Senate.
3. The Senate Judiciary Committee holds committee hearings in which the nominee is questioned.
4. The full Senate vote with a 50% plus vote required to ratify this nomination.

FACTORS INFLUENCING THE CHOICE OF NOMINEES

Unlike the president, there are no constitutional requirements (such as age or nationality) regulating who can be appointed. A presidential pick is based on the following:

1. ***Legal qualification***: The nominee must have significant legal expertise and experience. The Senate is unlikely to ratify someone who is not legally qualified, and such an appointment would receive huge negative publicity.
2. ***Ideology:*** Instead of making a neutral appointment a president is strongly influenced by ideology. The case history of a judge can be used to determine whether they typically give rulings with conservative or liberal outcomes. The decision of a justice to retire is often a political one, with justices choosing to retire when they know their replacement will be selected by a president who shares similar values to them.
3. ***Additional considerations***: These include the social characteristics of the nominee and presidential popularity. President Biden pledged, as part of his election campaign, that he would nominate the Supreme Court's first black female should he be given the opportunity to do so. He honoured this pledge when he nominated Ketanji Brown Jackson in 2022. The desire for diversity might be the primary goal for some presidents but can also be a way of securing support from a key

voter base. President Obama appointed the first female Hispanic member of the court, Sonia Sotomayor. Whilst the reasons for this are varied, he received an increased share of the Hispanic vote in his bid for re-election in 2012. There is no constitutional requirement to promote diversity. President Trump did not select any racial minority members to the court.

THE CURRENT COURT

Courts are referred to by the name of their current chief justice. The Roberts Court began with his appointment to the position of chief justice in 2005. It has typically had a conservative majority and has proven itself to be far more conservative than the Warren Court (1953–69) which delivered several liberal landmark rulings, such as the desegregation ruling in *Brown v Board* (1954). The composition of the court can be seen in Table 5.1.

Extent of impact of appointments

Limited: Some appointments will have a limited impact on the court because they do not affect the overall ideological balance. If a **liberal justice** dies or retires whilst the incumbent president is a Democrat then they will simply be replaced by a justice with a similar liberal outlook. Stephen Breyer chose to resign in 2021 knowing that he would be replaced with a like-minded liberal justice appointed by President Biden.

Moderate: Appointments have a much greater impact when the sitting president does not share the same ideology as the justice who is retiring. This happened in 2020 when liberal Justice Ruth Bader Ginsburg died and was replaced by a Trump nominee, **conservative Justice** Amy Coney Barrett.

High: The largest impact occurs when there is a change of ideology of a justice **and** there is a change in the ideological balance of the court overall. If the court swings from 5–4 in favour of liberals to 5–4 in favour of conservatives this can have a huge effect on the type of constitutional rulings the court will give. The nomination of Kavanaugh was highly significant because, at the time of his appointment, the court had four liberals and four conservatives with retiring Justice Kennedy acting as a **swing justice**. Whilst he was best described as conservative, Kennedy would sometimes side with the liberal four especially on critical cases. This often prevented the conservatives from making radical decisions in areas such as abortion with Kennedy even contributing to a ruling in which gay marriage was constitutionally protected. Coney Barrett's addition as a conservative justice, replacing a liberal sealed a clear conservative majority on the court. We can refer to a post-Trump Roberts Court to describe the clear conservative majority created by his three nominations.

Visit the companion website for a case study on the nomination of Ketanji Brown Jackson.

Spec key term

Liberal justice: A justice who typically interprets the Constitution in a manner that produces liberal outcomes.

Conservative justice: A justice who typically interprets the Constitution in a manner that produces conservative outcomes.

Swing justice: An informal name for the justice on the Supreme Court who falls ideologically in the centre of the nine current justices.

Table 5.1 **Composition of the Supreme Court in 2023**

Justice	Year of appointment	Appointing president	Ideology	Senate vote	Senate majority	Replaced justice	Ideology
Clarence Thomas	1991	Bush, Sr	Conservative	52–48	D	Thurgood Marshall	Liberal
John G. Roberts (chief justice)	2005	Bush, Jr	Conservative	78–22	R	William Rehnquist	Conservative
Samuel A. Alito	2006	Bush, Jr	Conservative	58–42	R	Sandra Day O'Connor	Conservative – moderate
Sonia Sotomayor	2009	Obama	Liberal	68–31	D	David H, Souter	Conservative – moderate
Elena Kagan	2010	Obama	Liberal	63–37	D	John Paul Stevens	Liberal
Neil M. Gorsuch	2017	Trump	Conservative	54–45	R	Antonin Scalia	Conservative
Brett M. Kavanaugh	2018	Trump	Conservative	50–48	R	Anthony M. Kennedy	Conservative-moderate
Amy Coney Barrett	2020	Trump	Conservative	52–48	R	Ruth Bader Ginsburg	Liberal
Ketanji Brown Jackson	2022	Biden	Liberal	53–47	D	Stephen G. Breyer	Liberal

Source: Alex Wong / Staff via Getty Images

Photo 5.1 **The Roberts Court in 2023. Back row left to right: Amy Coney Barrett, Neil Gorsuch, Brett Kavanaugh and Ketanji Brown Jackson. Front row left to right: Sonia Sotomayor, Clarence Thomas, Chief Justice John Roberts, Samuel Alito and Elena Kagan**

KEY TOPIC DEBATE: IS THE SUPREME COURT NOMINATION PROCESS FIT FOR PURPOSE?

The presidential nomination

✓ The president is entitled to make their own decision regarding the Supreme Court as justified by the Constitution and also their elected mandate. It is desirable for elected politicians such as the president to have some influence over the court, reflecting the values of the public in their choice.

✓ In practice, the president will choose a well-qualified individual with all recent nominees having extensive legal experience and high levels of legal education.

» On the current court, eight of the nine justices have Ivy League law degrees, with six having experience as a clerk for a previous justice. In addition, eight of the nine justices held senior judicial posts before joining the Supreme Court. The one justice who lacked this judicial experience, Elena Kagan, was both the Dean of Harvard Law School and the solicitor general to Barack Obama.

Committee hearings

✓ The requirement for nominees to face several rounds of questioning before the Senate Judiciary Committee should help to ensure that the appointed person has the essential characteristics of judicial ability, neutrality, independence and personal integrity which are needed to be a justice. This ensures that the president is careful to pick someone with the right qualities – a kind of deterrent effect.

✓ The bipartisan committee will scrutinise the justice's judicial record as well as their personal background and any concerns about their character.

» Whilst Ketanji Brown Jackson was quizzed in person by senators for more than twenty-four hours over three days in 2022, there were an additional 379 questions plus sub-questions that she was asked to respond to in writing. These questions explored, in huge detail, her judicial philosophy and concerns about potential bias.

Senate confirmation vote

✓ The requirement to gain approval from the Senate should prevent the president from nominating unsuitable justices. Any overtly political decisions, in which the president chooses someone who is personally or politically close to them, are likely to be rejected. Significant concerns about their judicial experience or personal character could also lead to failure in the Senate vote.

✓ The Senate provides a deterrent effect but has rejected presidential nominations. In other cases, nominations have been withdrawn when it looked unlikely that the nominee would obtain sufficient Senate support.

» In 2005 President Bush, Jr was forced to withdraw the nomination of Harriet Miers after Democrats expressed concerns over her lack of judicial experience and her proximity to Bush in acting as his legal adviser. The last nominee to fail in a Senate vote was Robert Bork in 1987 when the majority of senators rejected his nomination on the grounds of excessive conservative bias.

The presidential nomination

✗ The presidential choice is based on ideology rather than making a neutral appointment. This injects bias into the court undermining its ability to interpret the Constitution in a neutral manner. This political approach has become prominent since the 1980s when President Reagan publicly stated that he wanted justices who would deliver conservative outcomes, reversing many of the liberal rulings delivered by the court in the decades before this.

✗ In turn, the court is seen as a partisan body, which undermines its legitimacy as the guardian of constitutional rules.

» The Federalist Society, a conservative judicial pressure group, was highly influential in President Trump's nominations, giving him a shortlist of the ideal conservative justices which he picked from. In his 2016 election campaign Trump pledged to nominate an anti-abortion justice, politicising his nomination even before he had chosen someone.

Committee hearings

✗ The committee hearings are a highly partisan process. There are concerns that the opposing party goes too far in its questioning and moves beyond a focus on the judicial ability of the nominee. Senators from the president's own party often appear to be cheerleaders for the nominee, not careful scrutinisers.

✗ Increasingly nominees have developed a strategy of not answering questions about their views on the meaning of specific parts of the Constitution or on previous cases. In particular, they avoid hot topics such as abortion, gun rights or gay marriage. Nominees repeatedly state that they cannot comment on a case that might come before the court because this would damage their independence, or that all the facts have to be considered before any interpretation can be given.

» In 2022 after the *Dobbs v Jackson* abortion ruling, some moderate Republican senators such as Lisa Murkowski and Susan Collins criticised the ruling. The latter said that the interpretations made by both Gorsuch and Kavanaugh, which overturned the constitutional protection of the right to abortion, was at odds with their answers given to the Senate Judiciary Committee during the nomination process. It is common for nominees to give bland or generalised answers to secure their position. Once nominated, they cannot be removed even if it is true that their responses were misleading during the Senate judiciary hearings.

Senate confirmation vote

✖ Increased partisanship has meant that voting takes place largely along party lines. This means that senators automatically vote for or against a nominee based on the president who nominated them and not on their judicial ability or personal integrity. This is a major concern for the quality of the justice appointed as well as their level of neutrality.

» In 1993 Ruth Bader Ginsburg was nominated in a bipartisan vote with ninety-six votes in her favour and just three Republicans voting against her. Since then, only Sotomayor and Roberts have received more than five votes from the opposing party. When Obama had the opportunity to replace the conservative Scalia after his death in 2016, the Republican majority in the Senate refused to vote on his nomination at all, leaving the court with a vacancy until after the 2016 election. Republicans argued that it was too close to the presidential election. When President Trump won the 2016 election, he was able to nominate a conservative justice, Gorsuch.

Key Topic Debate Summary: Is the Supreme Court nomination process fit for purpose?

FOR	KEY CRITERIA	AGAINST
✓ The president has a mandate. It is good for politicians to have some control over judges. ✓ The president will choose a well-qualified individual.	Is the **president's role** desirable?	✗ The president's choice is political and infects the judiciary with political bias. ✗ The president's mandate is short-lived and justices are appointed for life, when values may have changed.
✓ The Senate Judiciary Committee ensures in-depth consideration of a nominee. ✓ Justices are carefully scrutinised judicially, politically and personally.	Are **committee hearings** effective in scrutinising a nominee?	✗ The committee hearings are highly partisan. ✗ There are excessive checks from one party and insufficient checks from the other.
✓ The Senate can prevent a nominee who is: ◦ excessively political ◦ unqualified ◦ personally unsuitable.	Does the **Senate confirmation vote** play a positive role in the process?	✗ The Senate vote is excessively partisan. ✗ If a president has a majority then the Senate is merely a rubber stamp. ✗ If a president lacks a majority then there can be deliberate obstructionism.

Exam Tip: Improving your AO2 analysis and AO3 evaluation

You can add sophistication to your answer by considering different political contexts, showing how the process might be more or less desirable in different situations. The process is affected by partisan politics. Is it more desirable when the president has a Senate majority or when he does not? You could also show a longer-term trend in which the process has become more partisan. Does this suggest that the process was once suitable but is not fit for purpose in the age of partisan politics?

Evaluative view:

The process for appointing justices as outlined in the Constitution has several key strengths, which, overall, means that the process is fit for purpose. The main aim of any judicial appointment process is to ensure that high-quality, well-experienced justices are in place and that significant checks and balances and scrutiny achieve this. It is true that the bias of the process causes problems, but this is not strictly the fault of the process outlined in the Constitution. It is caused by the wider issue of polarisation and the actions of presidents in choosing justices. Presidents used to make fewer partisan decisions showing that the process can work and is therefore fit for purpose.

Consider the key topic debate and debate summary as well as any new evidence you can find. Do you agree or disagree with this evaluative view?

Learning Review

1. How are justices of the Supreme Court appointed?
2. What are the main factors influencing a president's choice of justice?
3. How many of the current justices were appointed by Republicans and how many were appointed by Democrats?
4. Which justices on the court are considered to be liberal and which have a conservative approach to interpreting the Constitution?
5. What are the circumstances that cause high, medium and low impact of an individual appointment?
6. What are the arguments for the nomination process?
7. What are the arguments against the nomination process?

THE EXTENT OF THEIR POWERS AND THE EFFECTIVENESS OF CHECKS AND BALANCES

The court plays a critical role in checks and balances by enforcing constitutional rules. They can deliver opinions that limit the president and/or Congress, ensuring that they act within the Constitution. This can involve adjudicating in constitutional disputes between the president and Congress. Table 5.2 shows how one branch can affect the other.

Exam Tip – Power is a word that students use frequently without always having a clear understanding of what it means. When discussing the powers of the Supreme Court, try to move beyond explaining what that power is. You can improve your analysis and evaluation by demonstrating the *impact* that this power has. What changes as a result of the court's decision? A possible approach is to compare the US Supreme Court to the president and Congress. To work out which of the three branches is the most powerful, consider which one has the biggest impact on the daily lives of those who live in the United States.

Table 5.2 **Checks and balances between the Supreme Court, President and Congress**

Institution	Checks and balances
Supreme Court	Uses judicial review to regulate presidential actions and acts of Congress.
President	Can appoint justices to the Supreme Court when there is a vacancy.
Congress	Can overturn Supreme Court decisions, alongside the states, by amending the Constitution. Can impeach and remove individual justices if they commit high crimes or misdemeanours.

KEY TOPIC DEBATE: ARE THERE ONLY LIMITED CHECKS ON THE SUPREME COURT WHICH PROVIDE FEW RESTRICTIONS ON JUSTICES?

Powers of the court

The Supreme Court may escape checks and balances as a result of the following key powers that it holds:

As we have already seen, the most significant power of the court allows them to overturn the actions, policies and laws of any other US institution. In this sense the court is above president and Congress as it can overturn any of their actions that are deemed unconstitutional. In addition, the court has had a major impact on the power of the Federal Government versus the states and the extent to which civil liberties are protected in the United States. Examples of this power in action can be seen in Table 5.3.

Table 5.3 Selected Roberts Court cases that limit presidential, congressional or state power

Case	Issue	Ruling against
Department of Homeland v Texas (2024)	The federal government removed some of the razor wire placed along parts of the Texas- Mexico border, by Texas officials. The Supreme Court issued a 5–4 ruling rejecting the objections raised by Texas.	States
Biden v Nebraska (2023)	Biden used an executive order to forgive student loan debt of up to $10,000. The Court ruled along typical ideological lines with a 6-3 ruling saying that the president did not have the authority to do this. The Higher Education Relief Opportunities for Students Act 2003 allowed the president to modify financial assistance programmes but not cancel them.	President
NFIB v Department of Labor (2022)	The court ruled against President Biden's COVID-19 vaccine mandate. The mandate required that workers in companies with over 100 people had to be vaccinated.	President
Obergefell v Hodges (2015)	The majority on the court used its power of interpretation to rule that gay marriage was protected by the Constitution under the Fourteenth Amendment due process clause. Chief Justice Roberts opposed the ruling saying it was an 'act of will, not legal judgement'. All fifty states were required to comply, with many having to change their laws after the ruling.	States
NLRB v Canning (2014)	President Obama made two recess appointments. These are appointments to executive posts made when Congress is on recess (not sitting), meaning that the president does not have to seek Senate approval. The court ruled that the three-day break of Congress was not long enough to be counted as a recess thereby nullifying Obama's appointments.	President
Shelby v Holder (2013)	The Voting Rights Act 1965 was put in place to stop racial discrimination in elections. Many southern states had made a series of laws to deter racial minority voting or deliberately drew up constituency boundaries to limit it. The 5–4 majority opinion ruled that there was no longer a justification for limiting states' rights by allowing the Federal Government to check and overturn state voting procedure. The majority stated that they could not see sufficient evidence of racism in US electoral practice.	Congress President Obama publicly supported the law and was critical of the court for removing it.
Citizens United v FEC (2010)	The Bipartisan Campaign Reform Act 2002 regulates the use of money in US elections. This court ruling overturned key sections of the act by limiting First Amendment rights to free speech.	Congress The Act was signed by President George W. Bush in 2002 and was supported by President Obama in 2010.

✓ Interpretation

The power of judicial review is magnified by the vagueness of the US Constitution. Justices have a degree of freedom to achieve their preferred ideological outcomes because the US Constitution is short and often ambiguous. In other countries, which have sovereign, entrenched constitutions, the Constitution is very detailed, allowing justices judicial review but limiting their options when it comes to interpretation of the wording. There are many areas of the US Constitution that are highly ambiguous, one example of this is *Obergefell v Hodges* (2015), outlined in Table 5.3.

✓ Independence

The independence of the court protects its power to use judicial review. If the Supreme Court is to deliver rulings that overturn powerful institutions then it must be free from any negative consequences. The independence of the court was explored in more detail in Figure 5.1. Evidence for its independence can be seen in Table 5.3, which gives examples of powerful institutions losing cases.

Limits to Supreme Court power

On the other hand, there are significant checks placed on the court as a result of the following:

✗ Scope

Whereas the president and Congress can initiate policy in any area, the Supreme Court merely reacts to the actions of other institutions *if* it is a constitutional matter. In recent years, the president and Congress have made policy decisions in a wide range of areas including foreign policy, the budget, including tax and expenditure, environmental regulations, COVID-19 regulations and foreign policy decisions over Ukraine. The Supreme Court does not enjoy this breadth of control.

✗ Constitutional wording

Justices do not have the freedom to interpret the Constitution in any way they please and must operate within the boundaries of justifiable meaning. This is reflected in Supreme Court rulings in the Roberts Court in which unanimous cases are the most common outcome. The Constitution is clear, at least in these areas. The principle of stare decisis limits the current court in its ability to use its own judgement, requiring it to adopt previous judicial rulings. Different Justices, however, adhere to this principle to very different extents and the court can ignore precedent.

✗ External constraints

Despite its independence, there are several external constraints on the court. The ultimate limit is Congress' ability to overturn the court's decisions by amending the Constitution, although the entrenched Constitution means that this is not a regular occurrence. In addition, the president and Congress often use their authority to exert influence over the court, publicly arguing for a particular outcome before the court delivers its ruling. Although the president and Senate oversee the appointment of individual justices, as the Exam Tip explains, this is not a major check on the court as a whole or even on an individual justice.

Exam Tip – Many students cite the appointment process as a limit on the Supreme Court. This is not a strong point. The limits presented here are far more useful. The president typically only appoints one or two justices, which does not necessarily affect the majority decision. Most importantly, once appointed, a justice is not under the power of the president. Individual justices can and do give rulings opposing the president who appointed them.

Spec key term

Stare decisis: An approach in which justices stand by decided cases, upholding precedents and maintaining former adjudications.

Key Topic Debate Summary: Are there only limited checks on the Supreme Court which provide few restrictions on Justices?

FOR	KEY CRITERIA	AGAINST
✓ Judicial review allows the court to have the final say over the president or Congress. The president and Congress must accept the court's rulings with no checks on the court's majority opinion. ✓ Judicial review is not explicitly stated in the Constitution – it was self-awarded in *Marbury v Madison*.	Are checks on **judicial review** only very limited?	✗ The court is limited by its constitutional scope. Whilst it has the final say, it can only address constitutional issues. ✗ This gives it a much narrower remit than that of the president and Congress, meaning that its power is restricted or checked well by the Constitution.

✓ The Constitution is incredibly vague and therefore provides few limitations on the Supreme Court's ability to determine their own rulings. ✓ The court can become a policymaker, making decisions beyond purely constitutional issues and can ignore stare decisis.	Are the checks on their **scope of interpretation** only very limited?	✗ The wording of the Constitution is not completely elastic. There is a limit to how far the meaning can be stretched. ✗ The convention of stare decisis limits the ability of the court to make personal/biased decisions.
✓ Justices have near complete independence from the president and Congress as they are appointed for life. The appointment process itself provides no realistic checks once a justice is in office. Justices can easily ignore the president, Congress or public opinion.	Does the extent of their **independence** mean that checks on the court are very limited?	✗ Justices can be impeached for high crimes or misdemeanours. ✗ Justices still operate in contemporary society and will be aware of dominant values, election results and the views of the president and Congress.

Exam Tip: Improving your AO2 analysis and AO3 evaluation

Supreme Court questions might involve a focus on individual justices or the court as a whole. You may even cover both in one essay. There can be a difference between a limit on the court as a whole and a limit placed on an individual justice. Think carefully about this difference so that you are aware of what, exactly, a question is asking. This will help to sharpen your analysis and evaluation.

Definition

Judicial philosophy: A specific approach, taken by a justice, that determines the way in which they interpret the Constitution.

Learning Review

1. What are the main powers of the Supreme Court?
2. What are the main limits on the Supreme Court?

Comparative Learning Review

1. What are the main differences in the power of the US and UK supreme courts?

Spec key term

Judicial restraint: An approach to judicial decision-making that holds that a justice should defer to the executive and legislative branches, which are politically accountable to the people. It can also refer to the idea that justices should accept the ruling established in previous court decisions.

THE SUPREME COURT AND PUBLIC POLICY

JUDICIAL ACTIVISM AND JUDICIAL RESTRAINT

Activism and restraint are two opposing **judicial philosophies**. They address the extent to which a justice should overturn the actions and policies of elected politicians.

Judicial restraint involves a Justice being reluctant to overturn elected bodies or established judicial precedent. A justice, in their ruling, tends to defer to politicians, based on the idea that elected politicians, not unelected judges, should make policy.

Justice John Roberts is associated with the philosophy of judicial restraint. The 2012 *NFIB v Sebelius* reviewed the acceptability of the Affordable Care Act (ACA), especially in imposing legal requirements on states to provide health insurance. Roberts took a very different approach to all other justices. He classified the ACA as a federal tax and, given federal tax is allowed under constitutional rules, that the law was acceptable. Given this unusual interpretation and the expectation that Roberts would side with the conservative bloc against Obamacare, it seems likely that the chief justice did not think it acceptable to overturn the flagship policy of the elected president.

» This is consistent with other rulings by Roberts. In *Dobbs v Jackson* (2022), he criticised the conservative majority for going too far in overturning *Roe v Wade* (1973). Roe set a constitutional precedent stating that abortion is a constitutional right. Roberts argued, 'surely we should adhere closely to principles of judicial restraint here, where the broader path the Court chooses entails repudiating a constitutional right we have not only previously recognised, but also expressly reaffirmed applying the doctrine of stare decisis'.

Judicial activism is a contrasting approach to judicial restraint. Activism means that justices apply their own personal ideology and give rulings which overrule elected politicians or established judicial precedent. Activism is not exactly the same as bias. It is having a bias *and* using it to overturn politicians or precedents.

Spec key term

Judicial activism: An approach to judicial decision-making that holds that a justice should use their position to promote desirable social ends.

Activism can be used to achieve liberal or conservative goals depending on what is being reviewed. The Warren Court in the 1950s and 1960s was seen as practising liberal activism. It delivered a series of liberal rulings that overturned southern state practice. More recently, the court has been accused of liberal activism, for example in *Roe v Wade* (1973) (guaranteeing the right to abortion) and in *Obergefell v Hodges* (2015) (stating that gay marriage was constitutionally protected). In both instances, the court 'found' rights that are not explicitly listed in the Constitution and forced all states to comply with these liberal values.

Since the Supreme Court became dominated by conservatives, with a 6–3 majority after the three Trump appointees, there has been more evidence of conservative activism. This can be seen in the Roberts Court reaction to the freedom of religion clauses of the First Amendment. This amendment allows the right of individuals to hold their own religious beliefs and also forbids the establishment of an official state religion. The amendment has been used to ban prayer in government schools to prevent any government from supporting a specific religion. The Roberts Court, arguably acting in a judicially active manner, has frequently protected conservative and Christian values in its interpretation of the Constitution in this area, overturning state law. This can be seen in Table 5.4.

Table 5.4 Selected Roberts Court rulings on First Amendment religious rights

Case	Outcome
Fulton v Philadelphia (2021)	The State of Philadelphia allows certified organisations to provide foster care services. To promote equality, the state would not allow the Catholic Church to be involved in this process because the church would not allow same-sex couples to adopt. The court ruled 9–0 in favour of the church, ruling that the ban contradicted the Free Exercise of Religion clause of the First Amendment.
Carson v Maikin (2022)	The State of Maine provided educational funding in the form of school vouchers, which parents could use to contribute to payment for private school fees. But they did not allow the vouchers to be used in religious-based schools. The **majority opinion** of the court ruled 6–3 that this violated the Free Exercise of Religion clause. The **minority opinion** interpreted in favour of Maine, stating that the majority was wrong because it broke the established principle of separation of church and state. The ruling was constitutionally mistaken, they said, because it required state governments to fund religious institutions.
Kennedy v Bremerton School District (2022)	Joseph Kennedy, a school football coach, regularly held prayers on the pitch after matches and was asked to stop doing this by the school. After he refused, he was dismissed. The court ruled 6–3 in favour of Kennedy, protecting his First Amendment right to freedom of expression. There was no violation of the separation of church and state requirement of the First Amendment as the prayers were held after the game was over. Sotomayor, writing the minority opinion, cited the established precedent of *Engel v Vitale* (1962), saying the court has consistently recognised that school officials leading prayer is constitutionally impermissible. She wrote that 'Official-led prayer strikes at the core of our constitutional protections for the religious liberty of students and their parents, as embodied in ... The First Amendment.'

KEY TOPIC DEBATE: IS JUDICIAL RESTRAINT SUPERIOR TO JUDICIAL ACTIVISM?

Judicial restraint is superior

Judicial restraint can be supported by pointing out the flaws in judicial restraint, which make restraint a preferable approach to delivering rulings.

✓ **Constitutional duty**

Judicial activism involves justices overstepping their rightful constitutional role. This approach involves judges being active in overturning elected politicians, which undermines representative democracy. Restraint is superior because unaccountable justices should not establish important principles for society for decades to come. This is the constitutional duty of elected politicians.

» The restraint shown by Roberts in *NLRB v Sebelius* was far more desirable than an activist approach. Roberts, in deferring to Obama and Congress over the Affordable Care Act, allowed the elected politicians to establish a policy that they were democratically elected to deliver.

✓ **Authority of the court**

Restraint promotes public confidence in the court whereas activism can damage the court's reputation. This is because activism can give the appearance that the court has lost any sense of neutrality. Without respect for the Constitution there is a danger of a breakdown of consensus about the political process and the potential for more violent conflict. An activist court is easily dismissed as non-objective, leading to a breakdown in faith in the rules of politics.

» The Supreme Court came under a huge amount of criticism after the *Roe v Wade* ruling of 1973, as many saw this as a ruling based on values rather than one based in the Constitution. Perhaps paradoxically, the authority of the court and the Constitution was then undermined further when the court overturned this decision in *Dobbs v Jackson* (2022). Ignoring the established precedent of Roe, based on what most perceive as ideological bias, suggests that the Constitution has no objective authority; it means merely whatever the justices wish it to be. This is exactly what Roberts appears to be concerned about when he criticises his fellow conservatives for going too far in overturning *Roe v Wade*.

Spec key term

Imperial judiciary: A judiciary that is all-powerful and on which checks and balances are ineffective.

✓ **Ideological bias**

Judicial activism is ideologically motivated. Justices are not applying the law neutrally but are using their own personal judgement. This undoubtedly goes beyond their prescribed role as neutral arbiters of the Constitution. The use of activism has led to critics referring to an **imperial judiciary**: justices can achieve their own ideological goals, limiting other public bodies without being constrained by the Constitution. The wording of the Constitution is so vague that justices are free to act without constitutional constraint.

» The Roberts Court appears to be pursuing conservative Christian values, especially since the appointments of Kavanaugh and Coney Barrett. In doing so they are undermining the role of the Constitution in ensuring that governments stay out of religion and allow individuals to choose.

Judicial activism is superior

On the other hand, there are significant concerns with judicial restraint, which may mean that it is not superior to activism.

✗ **Failure of constitutional duty**

Restraint can lead to a failure of the court to carry out its duty to uphold the Constitution. Deferring to politicians may go too far and allow them to break fundamental constitutional principles. Judicial restraint is often supported as a method of promoting democracy, by allowing the elected politicians to have the final say, but the US Constitution does not place the will of the majority as its highest priority. Higher priorities required by the Constitution are the provision of checks and balances and the regulation of politicians by ensuring they follow constitutional rules. These can fail to operate if the court is dominated by restrained thinking.

» Despite the provision of constitutional rights and checks and balances, the court has often deferred to the president. This ranges from presidents' unilateral decisions to initiate military action even without congressional support; major laws such as the Patriot Act, which arguably undermine a number of constitutional rights such as the right to privacy; and President Trump's so-called 'Muslim ban', which the court upheld.

✖ Power and rights

Restraint gives an advantage to powerful institutions and can limit rights. When there is restraint, the less powerful body or individual will almost always lose out. This is particularly true in the area of civil liberties, which involves individuals challenging the major powers of the US system such as the president, Congress or state legislatures. Restraint can allow powerful federal politicians to infringe individual or state rights that should be constitutionally guaranteed.

» The Supreme Court has also faced criticism for restraint in the area of federalism where, between 1936 and 1995, it allowed a major expansion of federal power. The Federal Government won every federal–state dispute between those years when the state complained about limits to their commerce powers. By showing restraint when the Federal Government passed new laws, the court has arguably allowed the undermining of the key constitutional principle of federalism.

✖ Ideological bias

Restraint is often based on a conservative bias. Whilst restraint is often justified because it is more neutral than activism, a decision to be restrained may not actually be genuine restraint. Justices are not holding back despite their true values and allowing the president and Congress to act even when they disagree with them. In reality, justices accept decisions made by politicians because those members of the bench are ideologically supportive of the policy or action. Liberal justices are not being restrained when they do not overturn a law made by a Democratic Congress and president.

» When the Supreme Court ruled in favour of Trump in *Karnoski v Trump* (2019), we should not assume that this was an example of judicial restraint; more likely it was conservative bias. In allowing Trump to ban transgender individuals from the military, the court delivered a conservative ruling. It is likely that they did this because of their conservative values and not because they were restraining themselves to allow the elected president to have the final say.

Key Topic Debate Summary: Is Judicial restraint superior to judicial activism?

FOR	KEY CRITERIA	AGAINST
✓ Restraint allows elected politicians to have greater control. Justices should not be overturning decisions made by politicians unless they are unambiguously unconstitutional. ✓ This is more democratic. It promotes representative democracy. ✓ The Founding Fathers did not necessarily intend the Supreme Court to have the final say – this was an assumed power created during *Marbury v Madison*.	Which approach best allows the court to carry out its **constitutional duty?**	✖ Restraint can lead to a failure of the court to carry out its constitutional duty in regulating politicians. ✖ Restraint means that the court fails to regulate the president especially in the area of foreign and security policy. ✖ The Founding Fathers did not place democracy as the highest or sole consideration – politicians must conform to constitutional standards and activism best ensures courts promote checks and balances.
✓ Restraint promotes greater confidence in the court and its objectivity. ✓ Activism can equally be used to undermine rights where they are already established by court precedent or acts of Congress.	Which approach best promotes the **authority of the court and the Constitution?**	✖ Restraint may lead to concerns that powerful institutions are not being regulated and that rights are not protected. ✖ Activism can be used to promote modern values and respect support for emerging rights.

FOR	KEY CRITERIA	AGAINST
✓ Activism is by definition biased and will always be less neutral than restraint. ✓ Activism has been practised by both conservatives and liberal justices who have sought to enforce their own political agenda. ✓ This has led to claims of an imperial judiciary.	Which approach is the most **neutral or least biased?**	✗ Apparent restraint often masks judicial bias. Justices are motivated more by achieving their goals than being restrained – upholding politician's views or precedent when it fits their value system. ✗ Activism can be acceptable when it reflects majority public opinion or modern values.

Exam Tip: Improving your AO2 analysis and AO3 evaluation

In this debate we have examined the desirability of activism **versus** restraint. You must always remember to answer the question set – is one better than the other? In this question, you may well conclude that neither is more desirable because they are both extreme/unacceptable judicial philosophies. Equally you can demonstrate how support for activism is often biased. Liberals may support liberal activism but oppose conservative activism.

IMPACT ON PUBLIC POLICY

Spec key term

Public policy: Legislation and judicial decisions made on any policy that affect the whole of the US population.

The Supreme Court's power allows them to have a major impact on public policy. Public policy relates to any government policy that has an impact on society. This covers health, education, law and order, and economic policy. By delivering rulings, the Supreme Court could affect public policy by:

- Overturning existing public policy, stating that is it unconstitutional.
- Upholding existing public policy as established by politicians.
- Effectively creating new public policy via judicial interpretation.

Public policy is often challenged on constitutional grounds such as constitutional rights, federalism or the extent of presidential power. Overturning or upholding an existing policy both have an impact. By overturning a law that forbids gay marriage, for example, the court is effectively changing public policy by legalising gay marriage.

The final bullet point, creating new public policy, is closely associated with judicial activism. This has led to claims that the Supreme Court is a policymaker on a par with traditional policymakers such as

Source: Chip Somodevilla / Staff via Getty Images

Photo 5.2 **Supreme Court justice nominee Ketanji Brown Jackson during the Senate judiciary confirmation hearings 2022**

the president or Congress. This is based on the idea that the Constitution is so vague that justices can give rulings in every major aspect of public policy including health, education, the environment, transport policy, law and order, and the economy. Activist justices have shown a determination to use this power to achieve their own policy goals. The Obergefell and Roe cases are cited as examples, as are the recent Roberts Court rulings protecting Christian religious values. Table 5.5 gives examples of how the Supreme Court has changed public policy.

Table 5.5 Court cases and their impact on public policy

Public policy area	Case name	Impact on public policy
Health and welfare	*NFIB v Sebelius* (2012)	This had a low impact on public policy in the sense that it upheld Obamacare as the established law in place. Roberts appeared to use judicial restraint to deliberately ensure the court did not change public policy made by the president and Congress.
	National Federation of Independent Business v Department of Labor (2022)	The ruling overturned President Biden's policy that required all workers in a large company to have a vaccine. This had a high impact on public policy by limiting the government's attempt to protect people's health.
Gay rights	*Obergefell v Hodges* (2015)	This had an extremely high impact by declaring that gay marriage is a constitutional right. Like Roe, this established a new public policy requirement for all states. Chief Justice Roberts accused the majority of acting beyond the Constitution.
	Bostock v Clayton (2020)	The court declared that the Civil Rights Act provided employment protection rights based on sex and that this includes sexuality. This had a high impact because it forced all states to apply the same standard of public policy in the area of LGBTQ+ rights in the workplace.
Guns	*DC v Heller* (2008)	This ruling overturned a DC law that banned handguns in the home. This had a high impact because it was the first time the Supreme Court has declared the right to bear arms to be an individual right not a state right to have militias. Its impact was arguably not as strong as *Bostock v Clayton*.
	New York Pistol and Rifle Association v Bruen (2022)	This ruling overturned New York state laws that required individuals to demonstrate a need to carry a gun in public and thus gain a licence. The ruling is expected to change the law in several states, making it significantly easier for individuals to carry guns in public, having a major impact on policy.
Abortion	*Roe v Wade* (1973)	This ruling established that the right to choose was a constitutional right. This changed laws in a wide range of states, forcing them to allow abortion services.
	Dobbs v Jackson (2022)	This ruling overturned *Roe v Wade* (1973). Whilst some states continue to provide abortion facilities, many states immediately closed all such facilities or banned abortion. At the time of the Dobbs ruling, thirteen states had passed trigger laws, allowing the immediate ban of abortion in almost all cases should Roe be repealed.

During her confirmation hearings in 2022, Ketanji Jackson Brown argued that justices were not the same as members of Congress and did not make policy. She stated that 'Judges are not policymakers. That we have a constitutional duty to decide only cases and controversies that are presented before us. Within that framework, judges exercise their authority to interpret the law, and not make the law.'

Exam Tip – The powers and limits of the Supreme Court can provide you with a plan for several different questions. It could be applied to allow you to evaluate views about the Supreme Court in a range of different areas, such as the extent to which the court protects civil liberties. Bear in mind that you must always answer the question set. Think carefully about whether the powers and limits list is relevant. The extent to which the court has an impact on public policy is one such example. You could *apply* the powers and limits to public policy giving you a plan for this essay. Alternatively, evaluating the impact of the court on public policy could be completed by evaluating each of the three limits on the policy impact of the court below.

The court is limited in its ability to have an impact on public policy:

- Justices **cannot initiate a new policy** in the way that the president and Congress can. They must wait for a constitutional challenge to be presented to the court.
- The court can **only rule on constitutional issues**. Unlike the president and Congress, it can only review policy that might contradict the Constitution. It has limited jurisdiction, unlike a true policymaker.
- The court can also limit its own policy impact if it **uses judicial restraint** rather than judicial activism.

Learning Review

1. What is the difference between judicial activism and judicial restraint?
2. What are the arguments in favour of restraint (or against activism)?
3. What are the arguments in favour of activism (or against restraint)?
4. What are the main ways in which the Supreme Court can have an impact on public policy?
5. How is the Supreme Court limited in its impact on public policy?

THE PROTECTION OF CIVIL LIBERTIES

Civil liberties are the freedoms of the individual that are protected, especially from restriction by powerful institutions. The specific phrase 'civil rights' usually relates to the idea of freedom from discrimination, especially on the grounds of social characteristics such as race, gender or sexuality. In addition to this there are several other rights or liberties such as freedom of speech, the right to vote, freedom of religion, the right to privacy and the right to a fair trial.

Spec key term

Constitutional rights: Those rights that are legally protected by the Constitution.

Constitutional rights are those civil liberties that are protected by the Constitution. The original US Constitution is largely silent on the issue of the rights of the individual and is instead focused on the powers (and limits) of political institutions. It establishes, for example, state rights. Civil liberties are protected by subsequent amendments to the Constitution, notably the first ten amendments, which constitute the Bill of Rights, and the Fourteenth Amendment, which granted citizenship and equal civil and legal rights to African Americans and enslaved people. Table 5.6 outlines the key constitutional amendments that protect rights and gives examples of relevant court cases.

In the United States today, there is an ongoing struggle for civil rights for individuals based on their social identity. For example, there are major concerns about state laws that undermine racial minority voting rights and criticisms of racial discrimination by the police. There are also ongoing concerns about attacks on gay and transgender rights as well as direct attacks on individuals. Whilst there has been some support amongst Republicans and self-described conservatives for gay and transgender rights, they have often strongly opposed measures proposed by Democrats to promote gay and transgender rights.

Table 5.6 Constitutional coverage of rights and related Supreme Court cases

Amendment	Right	Court cases	Outcome
		Bill of Rights	
First Amendment	Freedom of expression	*Kennedy v Bremerton* (2022)	A football coach has the First Amendment right to lead prayers after a game.
First Amendment	Freedom of religion	*Fulton v Philadelphia* (2021)	Catholic groups are allowed to hold their religious views against homosexuality by continuing to provide state adoption services but refusing to support adoption by gay couples.
Second Amendment	Right to bear arms	*DC v Heller* (2008); *New York Pistol and Rifle v Bruen* (2022)	Heller set a precedent that the Second Amendment refers to the individual right to carry a gun. The case overturned laws limiting possession of handguns in the home. New York Pistol extended this to the right to carry in public.
Fourth Amendment	Right to privacy	*Riley v California* (2014)	Police cannot search the cell phone of an individual without a warrant.
Eighth Amendment	Freedom from cruel and unusual punishment	*Panetti v Quarterman* (2007)	Reaffirmed that a person who is mentally ill is entitled to Eighth Amendment protection if they do not have a rational understanding of the reason for their execution.
Tenth Amendment	State rights – reserved power of states	*Shelby v Holder* (2010)	Many of the restrictions on state control of voting processes imposed by the Voting Rights Act 1965 were lifted by the court on the grounds of state rights.
Further amendments	**Right**	**Court cases**	**Outcome**
Fourteenth Amendment	Due process clause; Equal treatment clause	*Brown v Board* (1954)	Declared racial segregation was unconstitutional.
		Roe v Wade (1963)	Guaranteed abortion rights.
		Dobbs v Jackson (2022)	Overturned abortion rights provided by Roe.
		Gratz v Bollinger (2003)	Restricted the use of affirmative action.
		Obergefell v Hodges (2015)	Promoted gay rights – right to marry.

Arguably the Supreme Court is in a better position than any other institution to protect civil rights because it can use its power of judicial review to defend rights listed in the Constitution. Indeed, the Supreme Court has been the driving force for major developments in the protection of civil liberties in the United States. It has issued landmark historical rulings such as *Brown v Board* (1953) (which declared that racial segregation was unconstitutional) and *Roe v Wade* (1973) (which guaranteed the right to an abortion) alongside more recent cases such as *Bostock v Clayton* (2020) (which prevented labour market discrimination on the grounds of sexuality).

Brandon Bell / Staff via Getty Images

Photo 5.3 **Protesters hold a candlelit vigil at the Supreme Court following its 2022 decision to overturn *Roe v Wade***

Yet, the court has also been accused of failing to protect rights when it has a duty to do so. For example, in the cases of *Shelby v Holder* (2013), the court overturned key components of the Voting Rights Act. This allowed states to take greater control of voting regulations and led to new laws that have undermined the extent to which racial minorities can or do take part in elections. Many states have introduced voter ID laws or have not created sufficient numbers of polling stations or staff, leading to a disproportionate reduction in racial minority individuals having access to voting.

From another perspective the court has also been criticised for protecting or finding rights that do not exist in the Constitution. *Obergefell v Hodges* (2015) delivered a 5–4 ruling and gave constitutional protection to gay marriage. Whilst this enhances civil liberties, the justices in the minority argued that this was a constitutionally incorrect ruling as gay rights are not stated in the 1787 Constitution or any subsequent amendments.

In exploring this debate, there is an important distinction between:

1. The extent to which the Supreme Court has the *ability* to protect civil liberties – this relates to the powers and limits of the court.
2. The extent to which it is *willing* to protect civil liberties – this relates to both its values (liberal or conservative) and its judicial philosophy (activist versus retrained).

KEY TOPIC DEBATE: DOES THE SUPREME COURT PROVIDE EFFECTIVE PROTECTION OF CIVIL LIBERTIES?

The Supreme Court is in a very strong position to uphold civil liberties. Here are the arguments that suggest it provides effective protection. You can make use of Table 5.6, which provides evidence of court cases involving rights.

Power and limits

✓ The courts power of judicial review, based on a sovereign entrenched constitution, gives the court considerable power to protect civil liberties. They have the ability to act as the guardians of constitutional rights by annulling laws or stopping actions of politicians which limit rights. This is protected by their independence, which allows them to challenge powerful politicians free from negative consequences.

✓ The Constitution, mainly through the Bill of Rights and Fourteenth Amendment, provides an extensive list of legally enforceable rights, as outlined in Table 5.7.

Interpretation and ideology

✓ The vagueness of the Constitution has allowed the Supreme Court a great deal of freedom to maximise the protection all civil liberties.

✓ As well as protecting rights that are clearly enumerated in the Constitution, the Supreme Court has also used the vagueness of the due process clause and the equal treatment clause of the Fourteenth Amendment to establish new rights. Whilst it may be difficult to add new rights through constitutional amendments, the Supreme Court has been able to add so-called **interpretive amendments** that protect civil liberties.

» It has protected other rights such as the right to privacy in *Riley v California* (2014) when it ruled unanimously that the police cannot search an arrested person's cell phone without a warrant.

Spec key term

Interpretive amendments: Supreme Court rulings that appear to add new constitutional standards as a result of an interpretation of the court. These are not official amendments to the Constitution and do not change its wording.

Activism and restraint

✓ An activist court could have a major impact on civil liberties, especially where the court has a liberal activist court committed to protecting rights even if this involves overturning political institutions.

✓ There are times when judicial restraint can lead to higher levels of rights protection, especially when there is established court precedent that protects a right.

» The Supreme Court's decision to find gay rights in the Constitution at key points in history have led to major advances in rights protection. In *Obergefell v Hodges*, Chief Justice Roberts accused the majority of an act of will, using judicial activism to establish the right to gay marriage. If the Supreme Court now uses restraint, accepting Obergefell as precedent, then this right will continue to be protected.

On the other hand, there are a number of reasons why the Supreme Court might not be providing effective protection of civil liberties.

Power and limits

✗ The Supreme Court could be limited in its power to protect civil liberties by the possibility of Congress amending the Constitution to overturn court rulings. Given the difficulty of changing the Constitution this is unlikely to happen.

✗ Perhaps the biggest limit on the courts power to protect civil rights is its constitutional jurisdiction. The court cannot protect rights that are not stated in the Constitution.

» Many states continued to create significant restrictions on abortion after the Roe v *Wade* ruling of 1973, leading to a series of follow up cases in which specific state restrictions (not bans) had to be reviewed by the court. The court ruled in *Dobbs v Jackson* (2022) that the wording of the Constitution did not guarantee abortion rights.

Interpretation and ideology

✗ The court may have the power to protect civil liberties but this does not mean that it will necessarily choose to provide those protections. Justices have a great deal of discretion to interpret the Constitution in this area in particular. For example, what is the correct interpretation if freedom of expression clashes with another civil liberty such as freedom from discrimination?

✗ The extent to which civil liberties are protected in practice depends on the way in which justices choose to interpret the Constitution. A more conservative court is likely to find in favour of those in authority and is less likely to produce outcomes that protect civil liberties than a liberal majority court.

» The Roberts Court has delivered a series of rulings that have undermined civil liberties. As well as the Dobbs ruling in 2022, which revoked abortion rights, the Supreme Court has undermined the rights of racial minorities in *Shelby v Holder* and transgender rights in *Karnoski v Trump*.

Activism and restraint

✖ The court may take a judicially restrained approach, which can lead to a lack of rights protection. In cases where the president, Congress or the states might limit the rights of the individual, judicial restraint could encourage justices to allow the limitations to continue.
✖ Conservative justices might choose to use judicial restraint because it is likely to lead to conservative outcomes in civil rights cases.

» In *Trump v Hawaii* (2018) the Supreme Court used judicial restraint to uphold the right of the president to ban travel to the United States from seven Muslim-majority countries. The president argued that the ban was to protect national security. Justice Sotomayor, writing for the minority, argued to the ban was an unconstitutional act of religious discrimination. She pointed to several speeches during President Trump's election campaign in which he attacked Muslims.

Key Topic Debate Summary: Does the Supreme Court provide effective protection of civil liberties?

FOR	KEY CRITERIA	AGAINST
✓ The Constitution covers a wide range of civil liberties that are granted legal protection. ✓ The Supreme Court is extremely powerful in using judicial review to overturn other institutions that limit rights.	Does the court have the **power** to protect rights?	✖ The court is limited by its ability to enforce rulings and sometimes faces resistance from states. ✖ Court rulings could be overturned by constitutional amendments. ✖ The court can only protect rights that are outlined in the Constitution. There are some rights, such as assisted suicide and abortion, that are not enumerated.
✓ The vagueness of the Constitution gives justices lots of freedom to protect rights. ✓ This vagueness means that rights protection can be applied to modern circumstances or standards. ✓ Justices can use the ambiguity of the Constitution to establish new rights in the form of interpretive amendments.	Does the scope for **interpretation** lead to effective rights protection?	✖ The court may lack the willingness to protect rights as a result of its ideological bias. ✖ Conservative courts are less likely to protect civil liberties and may even undermine them. ✖ The current court is dominated by conservatives leading to a reduction in rights protection in practice.
✓ Activist courts are more likely to protect civil liberties as they are more willing to challenge politicians. ✓ At times, restraint, respecting judicial precedent can help to promote rights.	Does the choice of **activist or restrained** judicial philosophy make a difference?	✖ Judicial restraint is likely to lead to outcomes which allow powerful politicians to restrict rights ✖ Restraint can be connected to conservatism in which justices place less emphasis on the need to protect civil liberties and more on protecting the authority of the president or Congress.

Exam Tip: Improving your AO2 analysis and AO3 evaluation

As with many Supreme Court questions, the answer to this is dynamic. In other words, the extent to which the court protects rights can change over time. The Roberts Court has become gradually more conservative, arguably protecting rights to a lesser extent. You can give some sense of this in your answer by giving an overview of what has happened in recent years. You could also consider the difference between rights favoured by conservatives and rights favoured by liberals. Are some rights being better protected than others?

Learning Review

1. Which amendments to the Constitution protect which civil liberties?
2. What are the main ways in which the Supreme Court can protect civil liberties?
3. What are the main limits on the Supreme Court's protection of civil liberties?

Comparative Learning Review

1. What are the main differences in the ability of the US and UK supreme courts to protect civil liberties?
2. What are the main similarities in the ability of the US and UK supreme courts to protect civil liberties?

THE POLITICAL VERSUS JUDICIAL NATURE OF THE SUPREME COURT

Although the Supreme Court is part of the judicial branch, the court has been accused of being more like a political branch or a third legislative chamber. This is based on its apparent bias and its enormous political impact as a constitutional court. The key to evaluating this debate is to have a clear idea of some of the key differences between a political and judicial body.

Three important distinctions:

1. Are decisions made based on a neutral application of the Constitution/law or based on ideological considerations?
2. Is the body independent (from politicians and public opinion) or subject to political pressure?
3. Does the body have limited scope, restricted to interpreting the laws given to them by politicians, or does it have unlimited scope to make policy in all areas?

KEY TOPIC DEBATE: IS THE SUPREME COURT A JUDICIAL BODY RATHER THAN A POLITICAL BODY?

Neutrality

✓ A judicial body should be ideologically neutral, basing its decisions on the law and the Constitution not their own personal views. Justices deliver a detailed written opinion on the wording of the US Constitution to justify their interpretations.

✓ The use of precedent and respect for *stare decisis* could be used to reduce personal judicial bias.

✓ Supreme Court proceedings operate as we would expect for a judicial body. There is a legal debate outlined by each side and a chance for justices to question the lawyers.

✓ The most common court split for the Roberts Court is 9–0. This suggests that, at least in these cases, the Constitution is directing justices.

» The *Snyder v Phelps* case reviewed a state ban on Westboro Baptist Church protests. The protesters picketed military funerals, claiming that the deaths were God's punishment on America for supporting homosexuality. The 8–1 ruling overturned the state ban on the protests on the grounds of First Amendment rights, even though all the eight justices, especially the four liberals, would have serious personal reservations about homophobic protests. This shows how the Constitution directs the outcome, not the personal views of justices.

✖ Justices are ideologically biased. Presidents often make statements about what kind of justice they would like to see on the bench, and politicians in Congress react strongly for or against a nominee depending on party and ideology.

✖ Ideological consistency can also be seen within the rulings of an individual justice over time. A specific justice typically interprets the Constitution to produce liberal or conservative outcomes.

» On controversial cases in 2022 and 2023, the common split of the court was 6–3, with the six Republican-appointed justices delivering conservative majority opinions in cases such as *New York Pistol and Rifle and NFIB v Department of Labor.*

Independence from political processes

✔ The Supreme Court is well placed to act in a judicial capacity given its high level of independence. The court is not elected, and justices are appointed for life. This has allowed justices to make decisions that oppose the president suggesting they can act in an independent neutral manner.

✔ The court has often led the way on rulings that political bodies are reluctant to address because the issues involved are controversial and involve strongly held public views. The court has given decisions that oppose dominant views of the day. It is undoubtedly the case that justices do not have to respond to public opinion in the way that a political body would do. It was the court, not Congress, that ruled against separate facilities on the grounds of race in 1954.

» All recent presidents have lost major court cases. Obama lost several cases including *NLRB v Canning* in which all justices ruled to limit the use of his recess appointment power. *National Federation of Independent Business (NFIB) v Department of Labor* (2022) limited President Biden's ability to require COVID-19 vaccines to protect public health.

✖ Justices are subject to external pressure from other political institutions. The president and Congress have a great deal of authority and may publicly criticise justices or urge for certain rulings while the case is being heard.

✖ Justices appears to respond to public opinion in a similar way to politicians. They may be influenced by strongly held or dominant views in society and cannot escape from being aware of the dominant norms of the day.

Limited scope

✔ Justices can be described as judicial not political as they have limited scope to make decisions. Justices can only give rulings based on the law or constitution, not all political issues, and are unable to initiate cases.

✔ Unlike politicians, there are a large range of areas that they have no input on, such as tax rates, government expenditure and foreign policy. Most recent decisions made by the president and Congress cannot be reviewed by the courts.

» President Biden and Congress have dealt with a wide range of issues in recent years, including infrastructure funding, the federal minimum wage, police reform and a $40 billion Ukraine aid bill. The Supreme Court cannot deal with or develop policies in any of these areas as this is beyond the scope of its constitutional jurisdiction.

✖ In reality, the Constitution is so vague that the Supreme Court can make decisions in virtually all areas of policy in the same way that politicians can. Even health, immigration and economic and foreign policies can be reviewed by the court as there are almost always constitutional implications.

✖ There is evidence of judicial activism in which justices deliberately make policy. Justices use the vagueness of the Constitution to achieve their own public policy goals leading to criticisms that they are an imperial judiciary.

» In recent years, the Supreme Court has influenced healthcare policy in a number of different cases. It upheld the Affordable Care Act in *NFIB v Sebelius (2012), as well as undermining some specific provisions in later cases. It has also overturned a major part of President Biden's vaccine mandate requirement in NFIB v Department of Labor (2022) and in Biden v Nebraska (2023) the court gave a ruling on Biden's policy of forgiving some student debt.*

Key Topic Debate Summary: Is the Supreme Court a judicial body rather than a political body?

FOR	KEY CRITERIA	AGAINST
✓ Justices neutrally interpret the Constitution and justify their rulings using the constitutional text. ✓ Justices give rulings that they may personally disagree with. ✓ Unanimous rulings suggest neutrality.	Are justices ideologically **biased or neutral** interpreters of the Constitution?	✗ Justices use personal bias when interpreting the Constitution. ✗ This can be seen in the consistency with which a justice rules.
✓ Justices are free to make neutral rulings free from external pressure. ✓ They have strong mechanisms to protect independence.	Are justices **independent** from political pressures and processes?	✗ Justices are subject to external pressure from other political institutions. ✗ Justices appears to respond to public opinion in a similar way to politicians.
✓ Justices are judicial because they can only make decisions in the narrow area of the Constitution. ✓ There is a limit to the elasticity of the Constitution.	Does the Supreme Court have a limited **scope**, focusing on constitutional matters only?	✗ The Constitution is so vague that the Supreme Court can make decisions in virtually all areas of policy in the same way that politicians can. ✗ There is evidence of judicial activism in which justices deliberately make policy.

Exam Tip: Improving your AO2 analysis and AO3 evaluation

You can show good AO1 knowledge if you demonstrate an awareness of individual justices and their actions or ideology in a given case. This can also be used to good effect to improve analysis and evaluation; you could argue that some justices or some approaches are more political than others.

LIVING CONSTITUTION VERSUS ORIGINALISM

The US Constitution contains around 4,500 words written at a convention by the fifty-five Founding Fathers in 1787. There are many different approaches to interpreting an historical text such as this, to determine what, exactly, this text means. Should we, for example, consider the intentions of the person who wrote it? In this section we will examine two competing approaches of the living constitution and originalism.

Spec key term

Originalism: The belief that the interpretation of the US Constitution should be based on the intended meaning of the Founding Fathers/authors of constitutional amendments and/or the common understanding of people of the day.

ORIGINALISM

Originalism requires a justice to give rulings based on either the intention of the people who wrote the US Constitution or commonly held understandings of the wording at the time it was written. The meaning of the Constitution is determined by working out what the authors were trying to achieve.

Originalism is associated with Justices Gorsuch and Thomas in particular. Thomas has applied this method by looking at commonly held meanings of the day in which the Constitution was written. He has used this to conclude, for example, that First Amendment rights do not apply to minors because in the 1780s it would be parents who had control over their children. The originalist position is associated with conservatism. The dominant values in the 1780s were far more conservative than those held today. Adopting an originalist approach can lead to conservative positions because the authors of the Constitution were typically more conservative than the dominant values in current US society.

LIVING CONSTITUTION

This alternative approach to originalism is based on the idea that the Constitution must be applied to modern circumstances. In part, this is based on a view that the Founding Fathers intended the Constitution to be an organic or living document. Society and its values change requiring the Constitution to be updated in the interpretation process. The **living constitution** approach is seen as a form of **loose constructionism**. Loose construction allows justices significant freedom in applying their interpretation of the meaning of words in the Constitution.

The living constitution approach is associated with liberal justices who have sought to state that the Constitution protects rights that are not specifically listed in the Constitution and that would not have been recognised or supported by the authors of the Constitution. Both Roe and Obergefell can be seen as exemplifications of the living constitution, given that the Founding Fathers and the authors of the Fourteenth Amendment would not have supported gay rights or abortion. Chief Justice Earl Warren adopted this approach to interpretations in the 1950s and 1960s. In one death penalty case, he stated that the meaning of the Eighth Amendment is not fixed but 'must draw its meaning from the evolving standards of decency that mark the progress of a maturing society'. What people understood to be 'cruel' at the time the Constitution was written is different from our understanding today.

Spec key term

Living constitution: The idea that the Constitution is an evolutionary document that can change over time through reinterpretation by the Supreme Court.

Loose constructionism: A legal philosophy that favours a broad interpretation of a document's language. This term is often used to contrast with strict construction, a philosophy that favours looking solely at the written text of the law.

KEY TOPIC DEBATE: IS THE LIVING CONSTITUTION APPROACH SUPERIOR TO ORIGINALISM?

Modern society versus history

✓ The living constitution promotes an up-to-date constitution that is suitable for modern circumstances. For example, it may have been acceptable in the past for the president to consult Congress before military action. The advent of nuclear missiles and jet engines may make such requirements less palatable. Originalism cannot cope with changes in society such as technology.

✓ Over time the Supreme Court has allowed a major growth in the power of the Federal Government over the states, with no changes to the wording of the Constitution. In this sense, the Constitution is living and has to be.

» The growth of a national and international economy requires far more centralised planning and control, meaning that more power must be given to the Federal Government. As a result of a socio-economic crisis in the United States in the 1930s there was a major increase in federal regulation in the economy, which the Supreme Court allowed. Every case taken to the court between 1936 and 1995, based on the Interstate Commerce Clause, was won by the Federal Government not the states. The Supreme Court recognised the need to allow a change to the application of the wording of the Constitution.

✗ Originalism can easily be applied to modern circumstances. Fourth Amendment freedoms can be applied to cell phones as well as houses. Free speech can mean the written word or published internet. The *principles* remain the same.

✗ Like any historical text, it is possible to gain an appreciation of the meaning of the authors as well as the commonly held views of the people of the day.

» In *Riley v California* (2014), the Supreme Court gave a ruling preventing the police from searching the contents of a person's cell phone without a warrant. An originalist approach can easily be applied to the Fourth Amendment right to privacy. Even though the technology is new, the intentions of the Founding Fathers are clear and can still be applied. The aim was to protect individuals from unreasonable searches of their private domain. This typically referred to the home but, as the justices noted, a cell phone can contain a huge amount of personal information and should be protected.

Objectivity and bias

✓ The living constitution approach is just as objective as originalism. Originalists choose to be originalists because it tends to yield conservative outcomes.

> **!**
> **Exam Tip** – Students sometimes produce unclear response to questions in this area. This happens when they introduce consideration of liberal and conservative ideology into an already complex debate. When evaluating the two approaches it is important not to switch the debate into one of liberal values versus conservative values. This debate is about two different approaches to interpretation, not whether liberalism is superior to conservatism. Indeed, whilst originalism is associated with conservatism, it does not have to produce conservative results. The same applies to a living constitution approach that could lead to conservative outcomes.

✓ The living constitution protects the authority of the document by making it more relevant to modern society.

✓ It is impossible to discern the intentions of the Founding Father and therefore difficult to claim authority when stating that a ruling was based on those intentions.

» There is considerable debate about the originalist interpretation of the text of the Second Amendment right to bear arms, which states 'A well-regulated Militia, being necessary to the security of a free State, the right of the people to keep and bear Arms, shall not be infringed.' A commonly held view is that the Founding Fathers intended to allow people to keep and bear arms as part of being in a state militia. In other words, an originalist could argue that the Second Amendment was designed to allow states to have militias and does not grant an individual right to carry a gun. Some originalists dispute this argument, however, and say that there was clearly an intention to allow individuals to keep and bear arms. This shows how, in practice, it is very difficult to adopt an originalist approach.

✗ The living constitution approach is biased. Originalism takes the views of the authors of the Constitution, not the views of the justices. Liberals adopt a living constitution approach to get the liberal outcomes they want.

✗ The living constitution undermines the authority of the document due to obvious bias.

» The Supreme Court has undermined its authority when using a living constitution approach to 'find' new rights such as abortion in Roe and gay marriage in Obergefell. This has fuelled conflict rather than settled dispute. It is only politicians who should use their own personal values to make decisions about such matters.

Rights protection

✓ Accepting the values of the Founding Fathers risks wiping out major developments in rights especially in relation to race, gender and sexuality. We cannot accept the personal values of the Founding Fathers in this area.

✓ Interpretive amendments are essential because the US Constitution is excessively difficult to change. The Constitution would be out of touch with modern values on rights if the court did not update its meaning for society today.

» Cases such as Roe and Obergefell protect fundamental rights and must be respected by the US legal system. By taking an originalist approach in Dobbs, women have lost an essential right, forcing many women into unacceptable positions where they lose control over their own body and life.

✗ Originalism can deliver liberal or conservative results. It is not biased.

✗ It is not the job of justices to deliver what we think is good or right but to protect constitutional rules until they are changed by politicians.

» Justices cannot make up rights that simply do not exist in the Constitution, such as gay rights or abortion. In Dobbs, the court did not ban abortion using an originalist position but said that there is no guarantee of this right in the Constitution. Supporters of the right to choose should focus their criticism on those politicians who choose to ban abortion, not on the majority opinion of the court.

Key Topic Debate Summary: Is the living constitution approach superior to originalism?

FOR	KEY CRITERIA	AGAINST
✓ It promotes an up-to-date constitution that is suitable for modern circumstances. ✓ Originalism cannot cope with changes in society such as technology. ✓ It is impossible to know what the intentions of the Founding Fathers were.	Can the approach cope with the demands of **modern society**?	✗ Originalism can easily be applied to modern circumstances. The Fourth Amendment freedoms can be applied to cell phones as well as houses. Free speech can mean the written word or published internet, the principles remain the same. ✗ Like any historical text, it is possible to gain an appreciation of the meaning of the authors as well as the commonly held views of the people of the day.
✓ Originalism is no more objective than a living constitution approach. ✓ Originalists choose to be originalists *because* it tends to yield conservative outcomes. ✓ The living constitution protects the authority of the document by making it more relevant to modern society.	Is the living constitution more **objective?**	✗ The living constitution approach is biased. Originalism takes the views of the Constitution's authors, not the views of the justices. Liberals adopt a living constitution approach to get the liberal outcomes they want. ✗ The living constitution undermines the authority of the document due to obvious bias.
✓ Accepting the values of the Founding Fathers risks wiping out major developments in rights especially in relation to race, gender and sexuality. ✓ Interpretive amendments are essential given the difficulty in changing the Constitution.	Does the living constitution better promote **modern values and rights?**	✗ Originalism can deliver liberal or conservative results. As such neither approach is superior in protecting rights. ✗ It is not the job of justices to deliver what we think is good or right but to protect constitutional rules until they are changed by politicians.

Exam Tip: Improving your AO2 analysis and AO3 evaluation

This is challenging area of the topic. It is very useful to review the Supreme Court cases above to ensure that you know how a case interpretation could be seen as being based on originalism or the living constitution. Do not assume that a conservative justice is an originalist. It will add complexity to your answer if you can show that, whilst originalism if favoured by conservative justices, it could lead to liberal results.

Learning Review

1. What are the main theoretical differences between a political and a judicial body?
2. In what ways can the Supreme Court be described as political?
3. In what ways can the Supreme Court be described as judicial?
4. What is the difference between originalism and the living constitution?
5. What are the advantages of originalism?
6. What are the advantages of the living constitution?

RACE AND RIGHTS IN CONTEMPORARY US POLITICS

Race has long been a major issue in US politics. Slavery and segregation are part of US history, and racial discrimination and conflict still occur in the US today in a variety of forms. There are laws that have a disproportionately negative effect on racial minorities, and there are concerns about racism in the criminal justice system. In this section we will explore the extent of success of racial right groups in promoting equality.

The Fourteenth Amendment was designed to overcome racial discrimination. Despite constitutional change the persistence of racial discrimination and inequality means that there are many groups fighting to overcome this in the US today. Figure 5.3 shows how three different groups have attempted to promote equality.

CASE STUDY 5.1: NATIVE AMERICANS AND RACIAL EQUALITY IN THE UNITED STATES

Source: Pete Marovich / Stringer via Getty Images

Photo 5.4 President Joe Biden speaks at the White House Tribal Nations Summit 2022

Overview

Native Americans or First Americans, once 100% of the population of the area now known as the United States, now make up just 2.9% of people there. Native Americans faced a drastic population decline with the loss of whole tribal groups and languages as a result of ethnic cleansing by Europeans and the introduction of new diseases, starting in 1492. The main approach of the colonists was to segregate Native Americans by creating reservations in which Native Americans could have some autonomy. Native Americans were often pushed on to marginalised land and were not given a share of the natural resources on the majority of the land that was taken by Europeans. At the end of the 1800s, there began a stronger move to assimilate First Americans to reduce or remove their native culture and identity. One such approach began with the Federal Bureau of Indian Affairs programme to provide schooling for Native Americans in day or boarding schools based on a desire to remove Native identity and preach Christianity.

Approximately 20% of Native Americans live on one of the 574 federally recognised tribal reservations today with many living in other rural areas. Only 5% of Native American reservation land is owned privately by Native Americans, with much of the remainder being held in trust by the Federal Government. Firstly, this perpetuates the racist assumption that Native Americans are not able to govern themselves or take control of resources. Secondly, Native Americans cannot mortgage their assets to gain loans like other Americans. This makes it difficult to gain home ownership and also to start a business to help prosperity in the area. Native Americans are far less likely to own property than other racial groups and are significantly more likely to live in poverty (26.2% compared to white poverty rates of 8.1%). During the first twelve months of the COVID-19 pandemic in 2020, Native Americans were twice as likely to die compared to the white population.

The president and Congress

President Joe Biden, in his socio-economic legislation packages, proposed measures designed to tackle inequality and address Native American issues. Biden's American Rescue Plan Act contained $30 billion in additional funding for tribal issues and also included a plan to vaccinate as many Native Americans as possible through the Bureau of Native American Affairs. Biden cited the need to target support given the extremely high contraction and death rate amongst Native Americans. The Act passed on partisan lines. Biden's successful infrastructure package also contained $13 billion in funding to tackle droughts affecting Native Americans.

Presidency

President Biden appointed several Native Americans to key federal positions, increasing minority representation in the executive, including Deb Haaland as Interior Secretary. In 2021 Haaland announced a new bureau to investigate missing and murdered Native Americans as well as an investigation into the abuse faced by some Native Americans in federal boarding schools. Biden has also reinstated the Annual Tribal Nations Summit in which tribal leaders and executive leaders meet to discuss policy and issues facing Native Americans.

Parties

Of the two parties, the Democrats are most likely to produce policies that Native Americans regard as favourable. Their general socio-economic policies are more likely to overcome disadvantage compared to the Republicans, and Democrats are keen to provide measures that tackle racial discrimination specifically. Whilst the American Rescue Plan Act 2021 was about broader issues, it contained many measures specifically designed to help Native Americans. All Republicans voted against the bill showing high levels of partisanship. Biden also reinstated the Tribal Nations summit that was begun by President Obama but suspended by President Trump.

Elections

The use of first-past-the-post voting and the relatively small number of Native Americans in the United States could lead parties to consider that First Americans are not a significant electoral force. It is common practice to list racial groups in voter analyses but Native Americans are typically not mentioned. CNN, reporting on the 2020 election, upset many Native Americans when it simply placed all Native Americans in the category of 'other'. Despite this, there is evidence to suggest that Native Americans can have a significant impact on election outcomes. Biden won Arizona, the first time a Democrat has done so since 1996, by just 5,457 votes. Even excluding other Native American groups, Navajo make up 67,000 people of voting age in Arizona with Biden gaining approximately 80% of the Navajo vote. It is clear that the Native vote made the difference here and possibly in other states marginally won by Biden, such as Wisconsin (which Biden won back from Republicans by just 20,000 votes).

Like other racial minority groups, Native Americans are increasingly restricted in their ability to vote, for example as a result of photo ID laws.

Pressure groups

There are a range of groups campaigning for social justice for First Americans. Groups such as the National Congress of American Indians have campaigned against the ongoing injustice caused by the creation of Native American reservations. Most Native American reservation land is still owned and managed by the Federal Government on behalf of Native Americans. Native American groups have been unsuccessful in making fundamental changes to these and many other laws that limit the ability of Native Americans to prosper. Another pressure group, NARF, serves as a legal advocate in the US court system to assist the 574 federally recognised tribal nations seeking land return, protection for sacred places, access for subsistence hunting and fishing, and other issues like defending the right of Native people to vote.

The Supreme Court

The Supreme Court heard two cases involving Native American issues in 2023. *Department of the Interior v Navajo Nation* was fought over a Navajo claim that the Federal Government and state government had mismanaged water resources of the Colorado River, which are part of the agreed homeland of the Navajo Nation. *Haaland v Brackeen* tested the Indian Child Welfare Act 1978, which bans the placement of Native American children with non-native families. Pressure groups such as the Native American Rights Fund have successfully fought cases in the Supreme Court. One such case was *Cobell v Salazar* (2009), which fought against the Department of the Interior's mismanagement of federally run Native trust funds. This led to a $3.4 billion payment to Native American reservations. Native Americans have suffered significant losses in the court. Whilst Native American courts have been given the power to prosecute non-natives who commit crimes on reservations, this power was reduced in *Oklahoma v Castro Huerta* (2022), when the court ruled 5–4 that state governments have the right to prosecute cases involving non-native Americans on tribal land. Native American women have suffered huge amounts of abuse; a National Institute of Justice report found that 4 out of 5 Native American women were the victim of violence, and 96% of them described their attacker as non-native American.

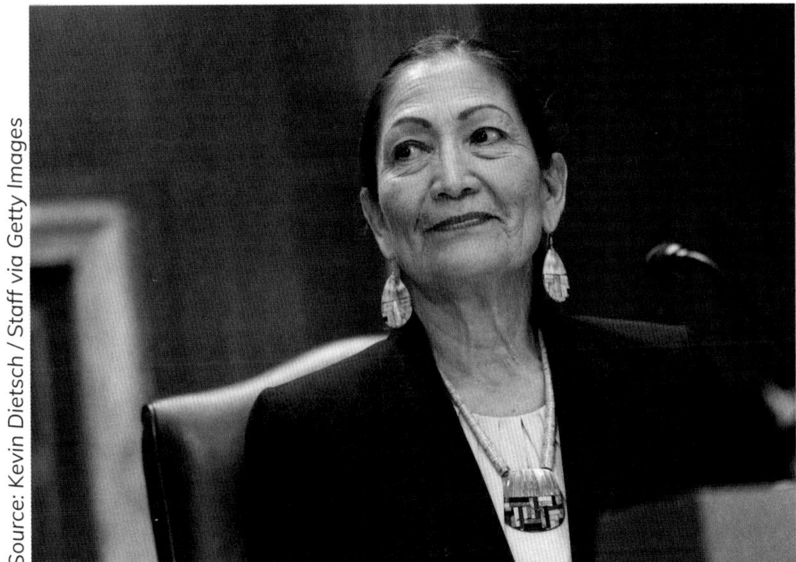
Source: Kevin Dietsch / Staff via Getty Images

Photo 5.5 **US Interior Secretary Deb Haaland at the Senate confirmation hearing in 2021**

NARF

Source: ©Native American Rights Fund

The Native American Rights Fund holds governments accountable to upholding the legal rights of Native peoples, and to fulfilling the terms of treaties the Federal Government negotiated with tribes. NARF serves as a legal advocate in the US court system to assist the 574 federally recognised tribal nations seeking land return, protection for sacred places, access for subsistence hunting and fishing, and other issues such as defending the right of Native people to vote. NARF sued the United States in 2018 for issuing the Keystone XL pipeline permit, as the planned route encroached on tribal lands and threatened tribal water resources and sacred places. In 2023, NARF represented tribes working to protect the Bears Ears National Monument in Utah, which the Federal Government created after years of tribal advocacy to safeguard the sacred places and artefacts.

NAACP

The National Association for the Advancement of Colored People is the oldest racial rights group in the United States. The NAACP have a Legal Defense Fund, not only fighting cases in court but also completing a great deal of lobbying and protests. They have campaigned against voter registration restrictions and have organised a series of demonstrations called Moral Mondays. In 2023 the group organised rallies in Washington as part of their campaign to forgive student debt of up to $50,000, going beyond the $10,000 agreed to by President Biden.

Black Lives Matter (BLM)

Formed in 2013, this group calls for non-violent civil disobedience in protests against police discrimination and violence against Black people. It developed after a series of high-profile killings of Black people by police. The groups became more prominent after the killing of George Floyd in 2020 and organised a series of protests across the United States. They campaign for reduced police funding, a national register of police violence complaints and held a get out the vote campaign to maximise Black turnout at the 2020 election.

Figure 5.3 **Three racial rights groups in the United States**

SOME METHODS USED BY RACIAL RIGHTS CAMPAIGNS

Litigation

Groups take the government or other authorities to court, including the Supreme Court. NARF have a legal wing responsible for successful cases such as *Cobell v Salzar* (2009). The court declared that the Federal Government had mismanaged Native American land and other assets and were forced to pay compensation to Native American tribes.

Protests

There has been a long history of peaceful civil disobedience, such as sit ins, to overcome racial discrimination. The NAACPs Moral Mondays campaign blocked access to state legislatures or occupied their entrance areas. Black Lives Matter organised several demonstrations after the death of George Floyd in 2020.

Get out the vote (GOTV) campaigns

Racial minority groups have worked hard to gain and keep access to voting and are active in ensuring that minority members can and do use their vote. Black Lives Matter held a WhatMatters2020 campaign in which they helped people to register to vote and the NAACP contacted 675,000 Black voters in ten swing states during the 2020 elections to promote turnout.

THE EFFECTIVENESS OF RACIAL RIGHTS CAMPAIGNS

The success of racial rights groups can be explored by examining the extent to which they have achieved their goals. You could, for example, evaluate the success of the three groups in Figure 5.3 – to what extent has each one achieved their aims? The A-Level Politics specification lists three areas that you could use to judge their effectiveness: affirmative action, voting rights and minority representation.

> **Spec key term**
>
> **Affirmative action:** A policy of favouring historically disadvantaged members of a community.

Affirmative action

Affirmative action is any attempt to overcome the effects of previous discrimination. It goes beyond creating legal equality to give additional support or benefits to groups historically discriminated against. It was introduced in the 1960s as an acknowledgement that legal equality did not do enough to overcome major social and economic equality; racial minority groups disadvantage will continue to cause disadvantage. This policy takes different forms. It began with provision from President Kennedy in 1961 to ensure that the Federal Government took more care to utilise racial minority companies. Since then, it grew in use by Federal Government employment, housing and education. Quotas in education have been used as one form of affirmative action reserving a fixed number of places to members of a racial minority group. The success of affirmative action can be measured by the extent to which it has helped to reduce socio-economic inequality on racial grounds.

Voting rights

Voting rights have been a major battle for racial minority groups. Although the right to vote was extended to all men with the Fifteenth Amendment of 1870, and to all women with the Nineteenth Amendment of 1920, there have been repeated attempts to restrict voting by race. States introduced a number of practices from the 1920s onwards to attempt to restrict minority voting. These included:

1. **Gerrymandering on racial lines**. This can be done by drawing boundaries to ensure that areas with high racial minority populations are split into separate constituencies to dilute their political influence. It has also involved drawing boundaries to ensure that a constituency with a high percentage of racial minority member has a lot more people than the average. In this way 'white constituencies' get much greater representation than 'Hispanic or Black constituencies'.
2. **Literacy tests**. It was common to impose literacy test, but these were often used in areas with higher concentrations of minority citizens.

3. **Felony voting restrictions**. People in prison are banned from voting and, in many states, voting restrictions continue after a prison sentence has been fulfilled. Given the higher incarceration rates particularly of Black males, felony voting restrictions have a disproportionately negative effect on access to voting of racial minorities.

Minority representation

Racial minority groups have been hugely underrepresented in positions of power. This includes representation in businesses and in the media as well as political office. This may mean that policy outcomes do not always reflect the interests of racial minorities, and also perpetuates ideas and stereotypes about who can take powerful positions in society.

KEY TOPIC DEBATE: HAVE RACIAL RIGHTS GROUPS BEEN EFFECTIVE IN ACHIEVING RACIAL EQUALITY?

Affirmative action

Groups such as the NAACP have actively campaigned for states to maintain affirmative action and have provided legal expertise in Fourteenth Amendment Supreme Court cases on the matter.

✓ Affirmative action had a major positive impact by providing social opportunities for racial minorities after the social deprivation caused by slavery and the systematic discrimination of separate facilities.

✓ There is a great deal of evidence to show that affirmative action has reduced the income and employment gap between majority and minority workers.

✓ It provides greater social mixing, social acceptance and racial minority role models for future generations.

» In the first thirty years of its use since 1965, the percentage of Black people who graduated from university grew from 5% to 15%. President Clinton remarked that it had been good for America and that it was time to 'mend it not end it'. As can be seen in Table 5.7, however, there is still a major socio-economic gap between racial groups. Disparities in wealth and home ownership have a reinforcing effect. White families have wealth that is passed on to the next generation to a much greater extent than is the case with Black, Hispanic or Native American families. Home ownership in itself has generated wealth for homeowners as house prices have increased hugely over recent decades.

✗ Affirmative action has faced a major decline in recent years. Despite NAACP support, the Supreme Court effectively ended the use of quotas, reduced the scope of other approaches to affirmative action and many states, including California, have banned affirmative action in any form. The American Civil Rights Institute has long campaigned for state-based bans and has successfully organised several state initiatives to remove affirmative action.

✗ From a different perspective affirmative action can be criticised as racist, causing inequality between races to persist. Justice Clarence Thomas opposes affirmative action saying that there is a 'moral equivalence' between laws designed to discriminate against a race and laws designed to give benefits to a racial group to achieve equality.

» In 2023, in *Students for Fair Admissions v Harvard*, the Supreme Court effectively ended the use of affirmative action in University admissions processes. The 6-3 ruling said that such racial considerations broke the 14th amendment. Justice Ketanji Jackson Brown issued a strong dissenting view on the impact of the ruling which would mean that it would 'take longer for racism to leave us'. Quoted in *The Guardian* June 2023.

» A study by Harvard Kennedy School investigated the impact of the ending of affirmative action and found that, once it was repealed in four states studied between 1990 and 2009, minorities working in state or local government decreased. Hispanic men's participation decreased by 7%, Black women's decreased by 4%, and Asian women's decreased by 37%. This suggests that affirmative action works in terms of achieving social goals but that it is failing because it has been scaled back so much. As Table 5.7 shows, there is still a major disparity in the life chances of different racial groups.

Table 5.7 **Poverty and home ownership rates of selected racial groups**

	White	Native American	Black	Hispanic
Poverty rate (%) 2020	8.1	26.2	14.6	14.0
Home ownership rate (%) 2021	74.2	51.0	44.6	47.5

Source: Census Bureau 2021.

Voting rights

✓ Voting righting for racial minorities had developed enormously in the United States with legal protections for voting rights such as the Voting Rights Act of 1965. This act outlaws any provisions that deny or restrict the right of racial minorities to vote. It bans specific practices by name such as literacy tests. The Act also required states with a history of racial discrimination to seek permission from the Federal Government if they wanted to change electoral laws.

✓ Racial rights groups have successfully boosted turnout with get out the vote campaigns aimed at educating the public in both voter registration and key political issues. Groups such as BLM, NARF and NAACP have been campaigning to ensure that there are no legal barriers to voting, attacking legal restrictions on voting and also seeking to maximise minority turnout during election campaigns.

» Black voter turnout steadily grew from the mid-1990s until 2012. In the 2012 election Black turnout exceeded white turnout for the first time in the election of the first Black president of the United States.

✗ *Shelby v Holder* (2013) overturned key provisions of the Voting Rights Act with states no longer required to seek approval from Federal Government to make changes to their electoral laws.

✗ This has led to a huge increase in state laws that depress voter turnout amongst racial minority voters. There is a systematic attempt by many states to disenfranchise voters with a series of practices that work together to restrict voting. The American Civil Liberties website lists and explain these, with the group successfully challenging some, but not all, of these restrictions in the Supreme Court. The American Civil Liberties Union state that since Shelby, more than 400 anti-voter bills have been introduced in thirty-eight states.

✗ Felony voting restrictions continue to exist with people in many states being unable to vote even once they have finished their prison sentence. This has a disproportionately negative effect on Black men in the United States.

» According to the Sentencing Project, African Americans are 3.7 times more likely to be disenfranchised by felony voting restrictions than non-African Americans. Over 6.2% of the adult African American population is disenfranchised compared to 1.7% of the non-African American population. Voting restrictions after the Shelby ruling appear to be having a negative impact on racial minorities with Black turnout dropping by 7.1 percentage points between 2012 and 2016 (white turnout increased between these elections) and Black turnout dropping below white turnout again.

Representation

✓ The civil rights movement of the 1950s and 1960s as well as the Voting Rights Act have led to an increase in minority representation in Congress. Minority representation has also increased in the executive branch with an increase in racial minority members in cabinet. The year 2008 saw a huge breakthrough with the first Black president, Obama; the first Black vice president, Kamal Harris, followed in 2020.

✓ In the United States, there is stronger minority representation in the House of Representatives than the Senate. All states have a majority white population with senators being elected in the whole state. Members of the House are elected in districts (usually smaller areas within a state) with sixty districts in the United States in which a single racial minority group makes up more than 50% of the population.

✓ Table 5.8 can be interpreted to show a positive view of representation in Congress, with Black representation in the House being roughly proportional to the population as a whole. Minority representation has increased with each election in recent years.

✗ Racial minorities are still underrepresented in the legislative branches in recent years, particularly in the Senate, and Hispanics are underrepresented in both chambers.

✗ Minority representation in the executive has improved but has been uneven. Whilst 40% of Biden's cabinet are drawn from racial minority groups, the figure was only 20% during the Trump presidency.

Table 5.8 **Racial minority representation in Congress 2022 election**

Social group	House (%)	Senate (%)	US population (%)
Hispanic	10.6	6	18.9
Native American	0.9	1	2.9
Black	12.8	3	14.2

Key Topic Debate Summary: Have racial rights groups been successful in achieving racial equality?

FOR	KEY CRITERIA	AGAINST
✓ Affirmative action programmes make a considerable difference to education and income for racial minorities with longer-term generational impacts. ✓ It undermines informal segregation and creates role models.	Does **affirmative action** contribute to racial equality?	✗ Affirmative action has been limited in its use and is on the decline. ✗ Affirmative action is a form of racism, discriminating against white people.
✓ There has been huge progress in legal protections for racial minorities in relation to voting, especially with the Voting Rights Act 1965. ✓ Campaign groups have successfully protected the right to vote and mobilised minority voting.	Are **voting rights** respected equally for all racial groups?	✗ Main legal protections have been significantly weakened with the Shelby ruling, which interest groups have been powerless to stop. ✗ Many states have systematically attempted to restrict minority voting.
✓ There has been a major increase in minority representation in the executive, legislature and judiciary. ✓ Black representation in the House of Representatives is roughly proportional the population as whole.	Do racial minority groups have **equal representation** in positions of power?	✗ There is still severe underrepresentation of racial minority groups especially in the Senate. ✗ The executive branch has seen uneven representation of minorities in recent years.

Exam Tip: Improving your AO2 analysis and AO3 evaluation

It is obvious that all minority groups are not represented and protected equally. Some groups have been more successful in achieving equality than others. You could show the distinctions between different racial minority groups in your response.

We have spent time evaluating the extent to which measures to promote equality have been successful in relation to voting rights and affirmative action. A further area that could be evaluated is the policies and practices surrounding immigration in the United States in recent years.

IMMIGRATION REFORM

The United States has the highest number of immigrants than any country in the world standing at over 40 million in 2023. It is particularly the development of unauthorised immigration, however, that has been a major social, economic and political issue in recent years.

The Pew Research Center estimates that there were 10.7 million unauthorised immigrants in the United States at the start of the Trump presidency and 10.5 million at the start of the Biden presidency. President Obama protected around 700,000 children and young adults with an order not to deport anyone who arrived as a minor in an executive order called Deferred Action for Childhood Arrivals (DACA). In addition, immigrants from some countries have temporary protected status (TPS) due to the levels of violence in the countries they left.

Illegal immigration is a driver of inequality in US society for several reasons:

- Socio-economic poverty caused by people not being able to work legally. This leads to low wages, maltreatment and unemployment. Illegal immigrants will find it much harder to gain access to health, welfare and education, although it is common for states to provide education for undocumented immigrants.
- Law and order issues. The immigration process itself is tied up with smuggling, kidnapping and murder. High levels of poverty also connect with high rates of crime.

The Democratic and Republican parties have typically taken very different approaches to the issue. On the whole Democrats have sought a more liberal or permissive approach, attempting to solve the problems outlined above by making it easier for illegal immigrants to gain citizenship or the right to remain in the United States. In addition, there has been more humanitarian assistance provided by Democrats. Republicans tend to favour greater restrictions on illegal immigration putting more emphasis on preventing people from coming to the United States and providing a harsher environment to discourage illegal border crossings. Whilst there is overlap amongst moderate Democrats and Republicans, Table 5.9 shows how the two parties have approached this differently, as typified by Obama and Trump.

Table 5.9 Obama and Trump approaches to illegal immigration

Obama	Trump
DREAM Act – a measure aimed to allow a path to citizenship for virtually all illegal immigrants. This failed to pass Congress.	Pledge to build a border wall across the entire length of the US–Mexico border and make Mexico pay for it.
DACA executive order – allowed any illegal immigrant to remain in the United States if they arrived as a minor. DAPA then allowed the parents of children with the right to remain to stay in the United States legally.	Opposed DAPA and DACA. Instead talked negatively for example, in 2016 referring to immigrants from Mexico by saying 'they're sending people that have lots of problems, and they're bringing those problems with us. They're bringing drugs. They're bringing crime. They're rapists. And some, I assume, are good people.'
Maximised temporary protected status to prevent deportations.	Family separation at the border, separating children from their parents and holding children separately, a policy strongly criticised by Democrats and some Republicans as inhumane.
Record number of deportations for any president, including Trump.	Created a 'remain in Mexico' policy for all asylum seekers. This meant that asylum seekers had to stay in detention areas in Mexico while the US government assessed their asylum claims. Biden ended this plan.

Success of the policies

The success of these policies continues to be debated and largely falls along partisan lines:

- Democrats claim that their approach is the only one that will solve social and economic issues surrounding illegal immigration. The United States has around 10 million illegal immigrants and it is impossible to remove a significant number of these. Granting legal status will make huge progress in overcoming inequality and social issues by giving people easier access to healthcare, education and jobs.
- In addition, Democrats emphasise the need to treat people more humanely in the immigration process, protecting fundamental human rights and providing for basic human necessities.
- Republicans argue that Democrats are making the problem worse by encouraging more immigrants to come to the United States. This is backed up by figures showing a major increase in people trying to cross the border at the start of the Biden presidency, including a rise in children who are not accompanied by an adult.
- The Republican Governor of Texas has been strongly critical of the Biden administration on this issue and has taken a tougher line, revoking housing shelter licences to any organisation in Texas that houses unaccompanied migrant children.

Learning Review

1. What are the main methods used by racial rights groups?
2. What is affirmative action?
3. In what ways have racial rights groups been successful in overcoming racism and inequality?
4. In what ways have racial rights groups failed to be successful?
5. How has immigration policy been reformed in recent years? How does the response of Democrats and Republicans differ?
6. How have these reforms been successful or unsuccessful?

Comparative Learning Review

1. How effective are interest groups in protecting rights in the United States and United Kingdom? Are they more effective in one country than the other?

Chapter Summary

- ✓ The Supreme Court is the body that determines whether the Constitution has been broken.
- ✓ The nine justice possess the considerable power of judicial review, allowing them to overturn actions of the president and Congress.
- ✓ The appointment process, involving the president and Senate, is criticised for politicising the court.
- ✓ The Supreme Court has a major impact on public policy and the level of rights protection in the United States.
- ✓ There are conflicting views about the merits of different judicial philosophies such as activism versus restraint and originalism versus the living constitution.
- ✓ There is a debate about the extent to which the court is best described as a political not judicial body.
- ✓ Civil rights are an ongoing area of controversy in the United States with contemporary concerns about the lack of racial equality.

Exam Style Questions

- **Evaluate the view that Supreme Court justices are politicians in disguise. (30 marks)**
- **Evaluate the view that the appointment process for justices is not fit for purpose. (30 marks)**
- **Evaluate the view that Supreme Court justices should interpret the law and the Constitution based on the intent of the people who wrote it. (30 marks)**
- **Evaluate the view that the Roberts Court has failed to protect civil liberties. (30 marks)**
- **Evaluate the view that the Roberts Court is a major disappointment to conservatives. (30 marks)**
- **Evaluate the view that racial equality has been achieved in the United States. (30 marks)**

Further Resources

Cohen, A. (2021) *Supreme Inequality: The Supreme Court's Fifty-Year Battle for a More Unjust America* (London: Penguin Publishing).

Gorsuch, N. (2018) *A Republic: If You Can Keep It* (New York: Random House).

Greenhouse, L. (2017) *The US Supreme Court: A Very Short Introduction* (Oxford: Oxford University Press).

Loewen, J.W. (2018) *Lies My Teacher Told Me: Everything Your American History Textbook Got Wrong* (New York: New Press).

Wilkins, D.E and Stark, H. (2017) *American Indian Politics and the American Political System* (New York: Rowman & Littlefield).

A must read for Supreme Court nerds is Empirical SCOTUS, visit https://empiricalscotus.com/ (accessed 27 July 2023). This website covers Supreme Court decisions but its analysis trends in court rulings and the responses of individual justices.

For excellent research and analysis on public opinion, visit Pew Research Center, 'Immigration & Migration', available at https://www.pewresearch.org/topics/immigration/ (accessed 27 July 2023) or 'Race and Ethnicity in the Local News Ecosystem', Pew Research Center, 5 March 2015, available at https://www.pewresearch.org/topics/race-and-ethnicity/ (accessed 27 July 2023).

Visit https://bloomsbury.pub/colclough-essentials-us to access additional materials to support teaching and learning.

6 ELECTIONS

Chapter Preview

In 2000, President Bush was elected to be the president of the United States even though his rival, Democrat Vice President Al Gore, received more votes from the public. In 2016, the same thing happened again; Donald Trump became the 45th president despite Hillary Clinton attracting 2.8 million more votes. How did this happen? What does it say about democracy in the United States?

In this chapter we will explore the many issues, debates and processes surrounding the election of the president of the United States. Presidential elections, taking place every four years, are the starting point for one person, nationally elected, to attempt to lead the country and achieve their policy agenda. The method for electing the president, the Electoral College, is the same system created for the United States by the Founding Fathers and first used in 1788. It is accused of being based on outdated principles. In this chapter you will appreciate a number of critical processes surrounding the presidential election itself, which make up the hugely intense and lengthy election period.

We will also explore the role of money in US politics in the form of campaign finance. The way in which money is donated, raised and spent during election campaigns has also raised many concerns. By the end of the chapter you will be in a position to evaluate the extent to which campaign finance laws have done enough to regulate money and address those concerns.

Key Questions and Debates

- What are invisible primaries and why are they significant?
- What are primaries and caucuses and how desirable are they?
- How is the president elected and what are the main advantages and disadvantages of the electoral method used?
- What are national party conventions and do they make a difference?
- Do presidents have an incumbency advantage when seeking a second term?
- What is the role of money in the form of campaign finance and how well regulated is it?

Specification Checklist

5.1 Electoral systems in the United States

5.1.1 The main processes to elect a US president, including:

- **The constitutional requirements**
- **The invisible primary**
- **Primaries and caucuses**
- **The role of national party conventions**
- **The Electoral College**
- **The resulting party system**
- **The importance of incumbency on a president seeking a second term.**

5.1.2 The role of campaign finance and the current legislation including the McCain-Feingold Act 2002 and *Citizens United v FEC* (2010)

Source: Peter Dazeley via Getty Images

ELECTORAL SYSTEMS IN THE USA

There are two main stages of voting in presidential election which can be seen in Figure 6.1 – primaries and caucuses, and the Electoral College.

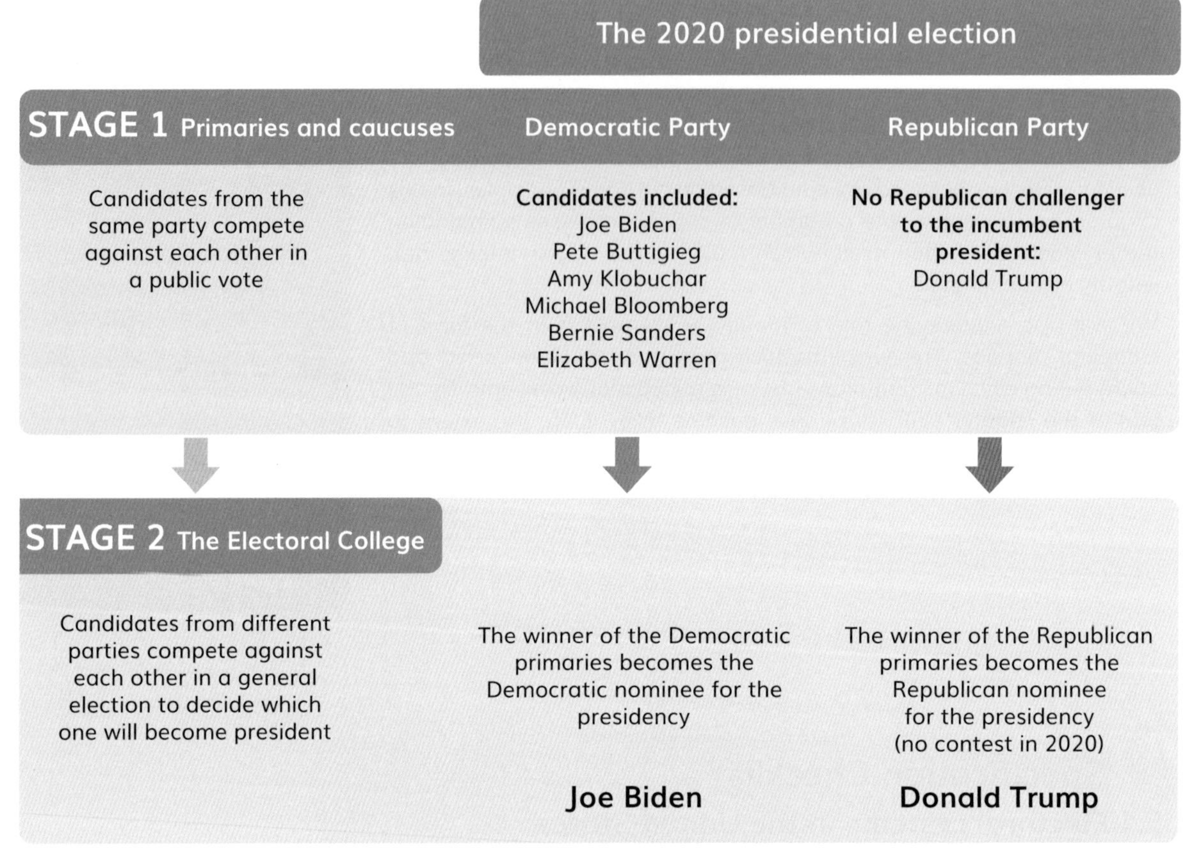

Figure 6.1 **The two stages of voting in presidential elections**

PRIMARIES AND CAUCUSES

Primaries and caucuses, usually referred to simply as primaries, are not mentioned in the Constitution but were created by political parties: the first national party primaries for the presidency took place in 1968. Candidates from the same party compete against each other in a public vote. This means that there are often two sets of primaries in a presidential election year: one for the Democratic Party and one for the Republican Party.

Presidential primaries cover a range of complex processes. There are variations in rules and procedures for each party and each state. We will explore first the fundamentals and then further features of primaries, covering everything you need to know. Once you understand each of the five main steps, then you have grasped the most important aspects of the primary process. Figure 6.2 demonstrates these steps and how they unfolded in 2020.

WHO CAN VOTE AND HOW

Different states have different rules that determine who can vote and how. Firstly, there is a distinction between the two main types of voting known as primaries or caucuses. Most states use primaries, in which voters attend a voting centre and privately cast a vote. A small number of states use caucuses. Caucus states hold a public meeting in which people have to attend a debate before voting occurs. Voting takes place publicly with a show of hands or standing in a certain area of a room.

How they work	How it happened in 2020

1. Candidates from the same party compete against each other in a public vote.

In some election years there are two primaries – one for the Democrats and one for the Republicans. A voter is allowed to vote in one party's primary only. In other election years only one party holds a primary. It is unusual for anyone inside the party to challenge a sitting president who plans to run for a second term. The party of the sitting presidency tends not to have a primary, therefore.

Ballotpedia lists twenty-eight candidates who were active during the campaign and seventeen who were effective enough to appear on ballots in five or more states. Almost all these candidates announced their presidential intentions in 2019. This field covered candidates with a range of ideological outlooks ranging from socialists (Sanders), progressives (Warren) and moderates (Biden).

2. Different states hold their primaries on different dates.

The presidential election takes place in November with primary voting typically starting in February. By tradition, the first two states to hold primaries are always Iowa then New Hampshire.

Many of the twenty-eight candidates dropped out of the race before voting began. There were twelve candidates remaining on the day of the vote in the first state – Iowa. The first four results were as follows:

3 February – *Iowa won by Buttigieg*
11 February – *New Hampshire won by Sanders*
22 February – *Nevada won by Sanders*
29 February – *South Carolina won by Biden*

3. Some states choose to hold their primaries on the same day as each other to maximise their influence.

The most significant example of this is known as Super Tuesday in which lots of states hold their primary on the same day.

The fifth date in the calendar was **Super Tuesday** on 3 March in which fourteen states voted, electing a total of 1,344 delegates on one day.

3 March *Super Tuesday; thirteen states plus one Territory voted, with nine states won by Biden and four by Sanders.*

4. How does a candidate win the election overall? Candidates compete in each state to win delegates.

Each state is given a number of 'delegates' reflecting its population. Delegates are party activists. They pledge to go to a meeting (the party convention) that takes place after all states have voted. Delegates vote for a specific candidate reflecting how the voters in their state voted.

By winning in a state, a candidate wins delegates (you can think of them as points) which are added up as candidates compete in more states. *In most cases*, there is a proportional rule. If a candidate achieves 20% of the vote in a state, they receive 20% of the delegates from that state.

Here is an example of the allocation of delegates for Nevada:

Candidate	Votes (%)	Delegates won (36 total)
Sanders	40.5	24
Biden	18.9	9
Buttigieg	17.3	3
Warren	7.1	0

5. Any candidate who gets over 50% of all delegates wins – they become the official presidential candidate for that party.

This is confirmed at the party convention at the end of the voting process. All delegates meet and cast their votes to make the result official.

To win the nomination, a Democratic candidate needed to get over 50% of the 3,979 delegates (1,990+)

Biden: 2,716 **Sanders: 1,112**

Figure 6.2 **How primaries work and how it happened in 2020**

Open primaries

Who can vote? In states with open primaries anyone registered to vote can choose to vote in either the Republican Primary or the Democrat Primary (but not both).

Which states use open primaries? Twenty-two states held open primaries in the 2020 elections. This includes Alabama, Alaska and Texas.

What are the implications?

✓ Open primaries maximise the choice of voters. Anyone can vote in either party's primary. This can be particularly important in those years in which only one party has a primary because it allows a voter to participate in a primary even if they are not a registered supporter of that party.

✓ They can be beneficial to political parties by attracting more moderate voters. For example, independents are allowed to vote and moderate Republicans might vote in the Democrat primaries.

✗ Open primaries can be subject to spoiling tactics. Republican voters might vote in the Democratic primaries to damage the chances of the Democrats winning the presidential election. This might involve voting for the second- or third-placed candidate so that the eventual winner must keep running until the very end, expending precious resources.

✗ It could be argued that open primaries are unnecessary and that only supporters of the party should be allowed to vote in the primary.

Closed primaries

Who can vote? In states with closed primaries, a person can only vote in a party primary if they are registered as a supporter of that party. This typically requires someone to tick a box declaring they are a supporter of a particular party when they register to vote.

Which states use closed primaries? In 2020 fourteen states held closed primaries, including Nevada, New Mexico and New York.

What are the implications? Closed primaries preserve a party's freedom of association by better ensuring that only members of the party influence outcome.

✓ Closed primaries can prevent spoiling tactics in which supporters of one party use negative voting in another party.

✓ Closed primaries protect the identity of a party ensuring that only members of the party influence that result.

✗ Closed primaries prevent independents from voting which might damage the electoral chances of a political party. They are less likely to promote the success of moderate candidates. In this sense open primaries may be more desirable for a party.

✗ Closed primaries are particularly unfair in those election years in which only one party holds a primary.

KEY TOPIC DEBATE: DO PRIMARIES PLAY A POSITIVE ROLE IN US POLITICS?

Voter choice/democracy

✓ Primaries increase voter power by adding another set of elections to the process of selecting a president. Voters are given a choice between candidates from the same party rather than party leaders imposing the candidate.

✓ Voters can choose from a range of competing policies and ideologies within a political party. Candidates from all factions of the party will typically run in a primary. This choice is widest in open primaries in particular.

✓ In addition, primaries can offer choice by social characteristic, giving voters the opportunity to select not only by ideology but also by diverse characteristics such as race, gender or region.

» In the 2020 Democrat primaries, twenty-eight candidates declared their intention to run with twelve remaining on the day of the first vote. This field covered candidates with a range of ideological outlooks ranging from socialists (Sanders), progressives (Warren) and moderate candidates such as Biden, Klobuchar and Buttigieg. In addition there was a range of social groups represented with several female candidates (such as Harris and Klobuchar), several racial minority candidates (Yang and Harris) and the first openly gay candidate to run for the presidency (Buttigieg).

✖ The use of voting in different states on different dates creates a major democratic flaw in the primary system. Voters in earlier states have a much greater level of influence on the outcome, influencing voting in later states. Choice in earlier states is much greater than later states.

✖ Voter choice can also be harmed by the use of 'unbound delegates'. In some states, these delegates are free to vote however they want to in the eventual party convention regardless of public voting in that state. In essence, public voting provides nothing more than an advisory role that can be ignored.

» In the 2024 Republican primaries prominent candidates Ron DeSantis and Vivek Ramaswamy dropped out after Iowa, the first state to vote. DeSantis, one of the favourites to win the whole primary process, dropped out after coming second to Trump. Voters in Iowa had greater levels of choice (four candidates) than voters in later states who only had a choice of Trump and moderate Republican Nikki Haley. This political inequality contradicts the basic principles of democracy.

Policy awareness and participation

✔ The primary process allows people to develop much greater political awareness of policies and issues with competition between candidates. This is particularly apparent in the TV debates throughout the process.

✔ Primaries create an ideas factory for the party as a whole, generating new policy ideas and putting them to the test before voters.

✔ This greater awareness can encourage political participation, with voters being better equipped to make effective choices at the ballot box.

» Whilst Bush defeated McCain in a closely fought primary race in 2000, McCain's policy of campaign finance reform gained attention and popularity and was passed into law.

✖ The numbers watching the TV debates in primaries is not particularly high. In caucus states, with the requirement to attend a debate, turnout is particularly low.

✖ Voting in different states on different dates causes a critical problem for voter participation. Voters in late states are often left unable to vote, becoming disenfranchised because one candidate has already reached over 50% of the delegates by that point in the race. It is unacceptable in a democratic system to deny people the right to vote.

✖ The existence of closed primaries also restricts participation, especially in those election years where only one party is holding the primary.

» In the 2020 democratic primaries, the race finished when Sanders dropped out and Biden was the only person remaining. Voters in the remaining twenty-six states were not allowed to participate in the competition. No state in 2020 had a turnout above 50%: Montana reached 45% but North Dakota was the lowest at just 2.6%.

Parties

✔ Primaries represent a major advantage for political parties. They put candidates from their party through a political test in real elections. This shows which candidates perform strongest while campaigning, in turn helping the party to select candidates with the proven ability to win elections.

✔ Throughout the primaries themselves, any personal issues or concerns with a candidate can be aired. This means that not only does the strongest candidate win but there are less chances of damaging revelations during the real presidential election.

» In 2016 the Republican establishment would almost certainly have chosen an established insider such as Ted Cruz or Jeb Bush. The primaries instead led to a clear winner in Trump who was arguably better equipped to win the presidency for the Republicans than either of the former candidates. The primaries quickly showed that whilst Bush has huge fund-raising capacity he lacked resonance with voters.

✖ Primaries can also do a great deal of damage to a political party as a result of the intense conflict between candidates from the same party. By exposing divisions, people might lose faith in the party or a particular candidate.

✖ The eventual winner of the primary can be strongly politically damaged by the process, having been heavily scrutinised and attacked by people within their own party. This may damage the chances of the eventual winner from securing the presidency.

✖ This can be a particular problem in single primary years. Candidates fighting primaries come under a great deal of attack and have to spend huge resources to win this competition. The presidential candidate who is running for a second term may face no such primary contest, saving those resources for the real presidential election.

» In 2016 Sanders spent a great deal of the primaries attacking Clinton's Washington insider status and elitism, focusing on her connections with Wall Street and the $625,000 she was paid in speaking fees from Goldman Sachs. Trump was able to win the election by attracting support from traditional working-class Democrats saying that he represented their values more than Clinton, building on Sanders' arguments. This arguably contributed to Trump's eventual success in swing states such as Wisconsin and Pennsylvania.

Key Topic Debate Summary: Do primaries play a positive role in US elections?

FOR	KEY CRITERIA	AGAINST
✓ Primaries increase voter power, with voters given choices between candidates from the same party. ✓ Voters can choose from a range of competing policies and ideologies within a political party. ✓ Primaries can offer choice by social characteristic, giving voters the opportunity to support candidates of a particular race, gender or region.	Do primaries promote **voter choice and democracy**?	✖ Voters in earlier states have a much greater level of influence and choice undermining democracy. ✖ Voter choice can also be harmed by the use of unbound delegates. ✖ In a given year only one party might hold a primary, limiting voter choice.
✓ The primary process allows people to develop much greater political awareness of policies and issues. ✓ Primaries can generate new policy ideas. ✓ Greater awareness can encourage political participation, with voters being better equipped to make effective choices at the ballot box.	Do primaries enhance **voter education and participation**?	✖ The numbers watching the TV debates or participating in primaries are not particularly high. Caucus states have low turnout in particular. ✖ Voting in different states on different dates causes a critical problem for voter participation. Voters in late states are often disenfranchised. ✖ The existence of closed primaries also restricts participation.
✓ Primaries put candidates to the test in real elections. This helps the party to select a candidate with the proven ability to win elections. ✓ Personal issues or political concerns about a candidate can be dealt with in public at this time, allowing candidates to focus on other things during the presidential election.	Are primaries **beneficial for parties**?	✖ Primaries expose divisions within parties, undermining public confidence. ✖ The eventual winner of the primary can be damaged by the process, restricting their chances of winning the presidency. ✖ This can be a particular problem in single primary years where candidates from one party face internal conflict.

Exam Tip: Improving your AO2 analysis and AO3 evaluation

There is a useful distinction between criticisms of a primary process in general (all primaries will tend to do this) and the specific system of the United States (this is a problem caused by the way that the United States does primaries). You can help your evaluation by working out whether you support the idea of primaries in general and also whether you are supportive of the approach taken in practice.

Evaluative view:

Primaries could play a positive role in US politics, especially in enhancing democracy. At the moment they fail to do this mainly because of primaries are held on different dates. Primaries are best evaluated as party-based elections, however, and should be judged on the extent to which they cause harm or bring benefits to a party. Despite setbacks for a party such as cost or internal party conflict, primaries have an overall benefit in allowing a party to choose the most electable candidate available to them.

Consider the key topic debate and debate summary as well as any new evidence you can find. Do you agree or disagree with this evaluative view?

Spec key term

Invisible primaries: A period before primary voting takes place in which candidates attempt to build a strong foundation of funding, public support and staffing, to allow them to run a successful primary campaign.

INVISIBLE PRIMARIES

The **invisible primaries** are a process that takes place before any primary votes are cast. Potential presidential candidates attempt to establish themselves as powerful candidates for the upcoming primary race. Potential candidates will attempt to gain public support, build up election funding and establish an effective campaign team. Invisible primaries begin when any of these activities start to take place for a potential candidate. The invisible primaries become more intense as the primaries approach with the main attempts to gain popularity and raise funds taking place in the second half of the year before the presidential race. You can see some key facts, candidates and dates for the 2019/20 and 2023/24 invisible primaries in Table 6.1.

Table 6.1 Invisible primaries in 2019/20 and 2023/24: Key facts, candidates and dates

2019/2020 Democrats	2023/2024 Republicans
Key facts	
• Only one party, the Democrats, held a competitive primary. • Twenty-eight candidates declared they would be running in the primaries, the widest field ever. • There were seven televised Democratic primary debates which took place before first voting in Iowa.	• The first TV debate was held in August 2023 in Milwaukee, Wisconsin. • Moderate Republican candidate Christie dropped out in January 2024 just days before voting in the Iowa caucus. Opinion polls showed that he had limited support and was considerably less popular than moderate Nikki Haley. He was excluded from the final primary tv debate before dropping out. • Florida Governor Ron DeSantis visited early states such as Iowa and Alabama before he had declared his candidacy in May 2023. He spent time directly attacking Trump and positioned himself further to the right of Trump on social and moral issues to attract Republican activist voters.
When candidates officially announced they would run	**Early declarations**
• November 2017 – Andrew Yang announces candidacy. • 9 February 2019 – Elizabeth Warren announces candidacy. • 19 February 2019 – Bernie Sanders announces candidacy. • April 2019 – Pete Buttigieg announces candidacy. • April 2019 – Joe Biden announces candidacy. • And some invisible primary dropouts: o November 2019 – Beto O'Rourke. o December 2019 – Kamala Harris.	• November 2022 – former President Trump announces that he would run in the primaries. • February 2023 – Nikki Haley, former South Carolina governor and former US ambassador to the United Nations, announces her candidacy for president. • May 2023 – Florida Governor Ron DeSantis announces his candidacy on a Twitter Spaces event, which was delayed due to technical errors. • November 2023 – Republican Senator Tim Scott suspended his campaign after he struggled to gain enough popularity and funding to qualify for the third set of primary TV debates. This came after former Mike Pence dropped out of the contest in October 2023 with poor showings in opinion polls.

Whilst there is no actual voting, invisible primaries can have an impact on the real primary race. Candidates will follow their opinion poll ratings, especially in the all-important early states. See Figure 6.3 for opinion polls during the invisible primaries of 2019/20. In addition, they will also be aware of how much funding they have raised (and spent). A poor performance in opinion polls or funding terms may force a candidate to drop out of the race, realising they have little or no chance of success when primary voting begins. The funding and polling information is public knowledge and can also affect the confidence that voters have in certain candidates.

Source: Scott Olson / Staff via Getty Images

Source: Bill Clark / Contributor via Getty Images

Source: Scott Olson / Staff via Getty Images

Source: Scott Olson / Staff via Getty Images

Photo 6.1 **A selection of Republican Party invisible primary candidates, left to right: Ron DeSantis speaks at a campaign rally in Iowa in May 2023; Nikki Haley announces she is running in the Republican primaries at an event in South Carolina in February 2023; Mike Pence announces his candidacy at an event in Iowa on 7 June 2023; Donald Trump speaks at an Iowa event on 13 March 2023**

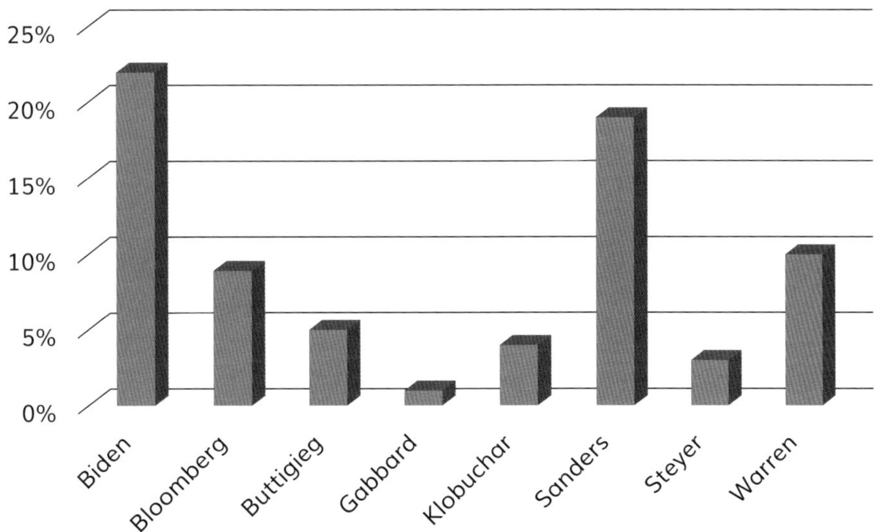

Figure 6.3 **Opinion polling during the invisible primaries 2020: Candidate figures immediately before going to the Iowa polls**

KEY TOPIC DEBATE: DO INVISIBLE PRIMARIES PLAY A SIGNIFICANT ROLE IN THE PRIMARY PROCESS?

Narrowing the field

✓ Invisible primaries can play an important role by reducing the total number of candidates in the race. They have an impact on some candidates who are forced to drop out as a result of poor public opinion ratings or a lack of finance.

✓ This also has implications for democracy by reducing the level of choice that voters have when the real primaries begin.

✓ Invisible primaries can play a particularly important role when a large number of candidates decide that they wish to run within a party. Invisible primaries help to remove less able candidates, giving voters more of a realistic range of candidates to choose from.

» In 2024 the invisible primaries had a major impact with significant drop outs. The most prominent of these was Mike Pence who left the race in October 2023. Despite being a well-known figure and performing well in the early TV debates he failed to raise sufficient funds or gain enough public support to suggest he could win early state primaries.

✗ Invisible primaries may do little to narrow the field of candidates when few or no candidates drop out. Later stages such as early primary state voting can have a much greater impact on candidates and their chances of retiring from the election.

✗ They have a particularly limited impact for those primaries in which only a small number of candidates declare that they are running. In these primaries it is unlikely that there will be many or any dropouts during invisible primaries.

» Whilst the field was narrowed in the 2020 Democratic primaries there was still a significant number of candidates left in the race so the level of choice remained high. Invisible primaries played a limited role in the 2016 Democratic primaries with only two candidates (Sanders and Clinton), making serious declarations during the invisible primary period.

Outsiders

✓ The invisible primary has its most substantial significance when it helps to establish a candidate and allows them to develop media exposure, funding and a campaign team. This period can be critical because it can allow unknown candidates to emerge as possible winners and therefore be competitive in the primaries.

✓ Lesser-known, lesser-funded candidates can use this time period to visit states, attend debates and fundraise. Without the invisible primaries they may not have the chance to build momentum and compete effectively.

» In 2008, the invisible primary allowed unknown Democrat candidate Barack Obama to gradually emerge. He was seen as a viable candidate by the end of the invisible primaries and had emerged as the main rival to clear favourite Hillary Clinton.

✗ Outsiders rarely establish themselves through invisible primaries. In practice, the invisible primaries are dominated by well-known, well-funded establishment figures with lesser-known candidates often being forced to drop out.

✗ Invisible primaries lengthen the campaign and can increase the total resources required. Better known, better financed candidates are in a stronger position to cope with these resource demands and attract further funding during this period.

Exam Tip – You should always *apply* your evidence to the question you are answering. Focus on explaining what the example tells you about the question, and minimise the time spent simply explaining what happened. One way of evaluating evidence is to say how typical it is. There may be some evidence to support an argument, but it might be atypical: most of the evidence, therefore, still supports the alternative view. Obama's success in the invisible primaries is an example of this.

» The Obama evidence of 2008 is not typical. In 2020 there were many lesser-known candidates who did not gain traction. People such as Seth Moulton and John Hickenlooper remained relatively anonymous as invisible primary dropouts.

Determine the winner or most likely winners

✓ Invisible primaries often give a clear indication of the likely winner or the two or three candidates who will be competitive. It is usually only the two or three candidates who have the highest public opinion ratings and finances by the end of the invisible primaries who have a realistic chance of winning.

✓ It is often the case that the winner of the invisible primaries proves to be the eventual winner of the primary voting itself. Invisible primaries could therefore be seen as more important than the primaries themselves, with the later primary stage merely confirming what voters have already learned.

» In 2016 both Clinton and Trump were the clear invisible primary winners with very high fund-raising and the most favourable public opinion ratings within their parties. In 2020 Biden was the clear front runner in public opinion terms. His success in the invisible primaries allowed him to survive the threat of losing the first three states and go on to win the nomination.

✗ Invisible primaries cannot tell us with any certainty who the winner or likely winners will be. With no actual voting taking place, invisible primaries are far less significant than the actual primary voting.

» In 2016 Jeb Bush raised record sums of money during the Republican invisible primaries and was one of the favourites as judged by public opinion polls. Bush performed very badly in early primary states and was forced to drop out of the race during this stage. In the Democrat race of 2016 it was difficult to judge who would win at the end of the invisible primaries with Clinton being the slight favourite in public opinion terms and Sanders managing to raise more funds than her.

Key Topic Debate Summary: Do invisible primaries play a significant role in US primaries?

FOR	KEY CRITERIA	AGAINST
✓ Invisible primaries can reduce the total number of candidates in the race as poorly performing candidates drop out. ✓ This reduces voter choice. ✓ They can play a key role if there is a large number of candidates, giving voters more of a realistic range of candidates to choose from.	Do they **narrow the field** and reduce choice?	✗ There may be few or no dropouts during this electoral phase. ✗ They have a particularly limited impact for primaries in which only a small number of candidates choose to run.
✓ The invisible primary allows a candidate to establish themselves and allows them to develop media exposure, funding and a campaign team. ✓ Lesser-known, lesser-funded candidates, can use this time period to visit states, attend debates and fundraise.	Do they give **outsiders** a better chance to succeed?	✗ With no actual voting taking place invisible primaries are far less significant for the actual primary voting. ✗ Candidates could perform well in the invisible primaries but not when voters go to the polls.

FOR	KEY CRITERIA	AGAINST
✓ Invisible primaries can give an indication of the likely winner or the few candidates who will be competitive. ✓ The winner of the invisible primaries often proves to be the eventual winner of the primary voting itself with the later primary stage confirming what we have already learned.	Do they **determine winners** or most likely winners?	✗ Invisible primaries cannot tell us with any certainty who the winner or likely winners will be – there is no actual voting. ✗ Candidates can sometimes do well in the invisible primaries only to flounder when voting takes place.

Exam Tip: Improving your AO2 analysis and AO3 evaluation

Stronger answers will focus on and apply the keyword of this question. In this case we have examined the *significance* of invisible primaries. This can be evaluated by considering the *impact* that they have. How would primaries be different if there were no invisible primaries? Focus your analysis and evaluation on this impact.

Learning Review

1. What are the main processes involved in primary elections? How do they work?
2. What are the differences between open and closed primaries and caucuses?
3. What are the main arguments for and against the US primary process?
4. What are invisible primaries?
5. What are the main ways in which invisible primaries are significant?
6. What are the main ways in which invisible primaries are not significant?

NATIONAL PARTY CONVENTIONS

National party conventions take place for each party in a presidential election year at the end of the primary process. They are often seen as the starting point for the presidential election campaign, marking a time when a candidate can move on from the primaries, use the huge focus that party conventions create and focus their attentions on defeating the other main candidate.

In theory, the main role of national party conventions is to choose the parties' nominees for the presidency. In addition, national party conventions are attended by party activists from around the country who meet to determine the party **policy platform** (effectively a manifesto) going into the presidential election race. The creation of national party primaries in 1968, however, has essentially removed these roles in any meaningful way. It is now the primary process that selects the presidential nominee with the convention acting as a rubber stamp.

Presidential candidates will hope for a nationwide **poll bounce** in which they improve their poll ratings. Conventions are also used to boost popularity in a single state; it is common for party conventions to be held in swing states as candidates try to capture or maintain these states. The Republican convention of 2016 was held in Cleveland, Ohio – a key swing state – in a basketball arena with a capacity of 20,000. In a 2008 convention in swing state Colorado, the Democrats took the unprecedented step of using a football stadium for Obama's acceptance speech with a capacity of 100,000 generating an impressive spectacle of support. You can see more details of the 2020 conventions in Table 6.2.

Whilst an evaluation of the significance of party conventions can be judged by the way in which they carry out their traditional roles, the main focus should be on the *impact that they have on the ensuing presidential elections*. Parties and presidential candidates use the party convention as a way of launching presidential campaigns

Definition

Policy platform: A phrase used to describe the policy pledges made by a candidate or party at election time.

Poll bounce: An increase in positive opinion-poll ratings.

Table 6.2 Democratic and Republican Party conventions 2020

Democrats	Republicans
Key facts	
Milwaukee, Wisconsin, 17–20 August + virtually across the United States.	Charlotte, North Carolina, 24–27 August + presidential address from White House South Lawn.
The convention confirmed Joe Biden as the presidential nominee and Kamala Harris as Biden's choice of running mate. The convention was postponed and downsized from the planned meeting in July due to the COVID-19 pandemic. Both Biden and Harris gave remote speeches rather than the traditional stage speech. Biden made no direct reference to Trump, deliberately choosing not to use his name. Sanders and Biden created a 'Unity Task Force' to draft the party platform that was presented and voted on at the convention. Losing primary candidates Sanders, Warren, Buttigieg and Yang all spoke in support of Biden at the convention. There were also speeches from both Barack and Michelle Obama, with the latter spending a great deal of her speech attacking President Trump's record. She criticised his lack of leadership during the COVID-19 pandemic and Trump's divisive nature, referring to the 'emboldening of torch bearing white supremacists'. Billie Eilish, Jennifer Hudson and Prince Royce all performed during the convention, attracting more publicity.	Trump was unable to hold the event in the original venue as a result of state regulations on COVID-19. A total of 2,550 delegates were scheduled to attend the nomination but only 336 were able to. A large venue with crowds was still used. During the convention, the first and second families mixed with large crowds without masks. Trump's acceptance speech on the South Lawn at the White House attracted criticism for the use of the presidential residence as part of his campaign. Trump mentioned Biden by name forty-one times attacking him as a 'Trojan horse for socialism'. The Republican Party reused the same platform as the one agreed in 2016. This created some negative publicity as it left in references criticising 'this president', which were words previously aimed at Obama. There were speeches from many senior Republicans and from Trump's wife, Ivanka, and daughter, Melania.
Impact: Final night viewing figures: 24.6 million There was no evidence of a poll bounce after the convention although some polling showed that Biden received a boost in his personal favourability ratings. **Biden regained the State of Wisconsin in the presidential elections. In 2016, Trump had been the first republican to win the state since 1984.**	**Impact:** Final night viewing figures: 23.8 million. There was no evidence of a poll bounce after the convention. An ABC poll found no increase in Trump's favourability ratings. **Obama won this swing state in 2008. Trump won in 2016 and managed to retain this state in 2020.**

Source: Anadolu Agency / Contributor via Getty Images

Source: Charles Ommanney/ Contributor via Getty Images

Photo 6.2 Republican Party Convention 2016 (*left*), Cleveland Ohio and Democratic Party Convention 2008, Denver Colorado (*right*)

KEY TOPIC DEBATE: DO PARTY CONVENTIONS HAVE ANY POLITICAL SIGNIFICANCE?

Traditional roles

✓ Party conventions are the formal meeting that select the presidential and vice presidential candidates for the party with delegates voting to decide presidential and vice presidential nominee. The rules of each party state that a candidate requires over 50% of delegates.

✓ Delegates debate and vote to determine the platform (and therefore in theory, the candidate) for the presidential election.

✓ If no candidate achieves this, a brokered convention takes place requiring more rounds of voting. If this happens then primary results become less important. Delegates from many states are then allowed to switch their vote to another candidate and in both parties super-delegates, party officials such as chairs of state parties or former presidents, are allowed to vote to determine the party nominee.

In 2020 there was an official vote to confirm Biden as the party nominee and the policy plan developed by Sanders and Biden was voted on. It included:

- A universal public health insurance option.
- Allowing Medicare to negotiate for lower prescription drug prices.
- Universal free COVID-19 testing, treatment and vaccines.
- Eliminating carbon emissions from power plants by 2035.
- Increasing the federal minimum wage to $15 per hour.

✗ It is the primary process and the convention that decides who will represent the party in the presidential election. The winner is known well in advance of the convention which is stage managed to allow the winning candidate to maximise their chances of winning the presidency.

✗ In turn, the winning candidate will choose their own platform and are in no way bound by a policy platform made by the party committee. If there is a difference between the party platform and the winning candidate, the candidate can easily ignore the platform.

✗ There has never been a brokered convention, meaning that it is the primaries and not an additional vote including senior party members that determines who the presidential candidate is.

Publicity and activism

✓ Party conventions can be judged by the impact that they have on the ensuing presidential election. Candidates may receive positive publicity as a result of presenting themselves and their policies or seeking to undermine their opponent. Candidates may receive a poll bounce, boosting their election campaign.

✓ Party conventions can be used to enthuse activists and core supporters. This helps a campaign by ensuring that supporters are motivated to vote (rather than not voting at all) and that activists will be effective in working to campaign for the candidate.

» The 2020 Democratic convention used key people and speech themes to attract publicity, enthuse activists and motivate core voters to go out to vote. Speeches by Barack and Michelle Obama were seen as particularly influential.

✗ The conventions form just one small part of an intense and expensive campaign. As such they are unlikely to play a significant role in determining voting behaviour. Other stages and events such as the TV debates between the candidates are likely to have a greater impact, especially as they are held closer to the election itself and have much higher viewing figures. These viewing figures can be seen in Figure 6.4.

✗ Many voters will be strong supporters of one party over another or will have already made their decision at this point and therefore are not going to be influenced by the convention.

✗ The two conventions can effectively cancel each other out. It is unlikely that one convention would be extremely effective with the other gaining significant negative publicity.

» As we saw in Figure 6.3, there was no evidence of a poll bounce for either candidate after the 2020 party conventions. Poll bounces appear to be on the decline.

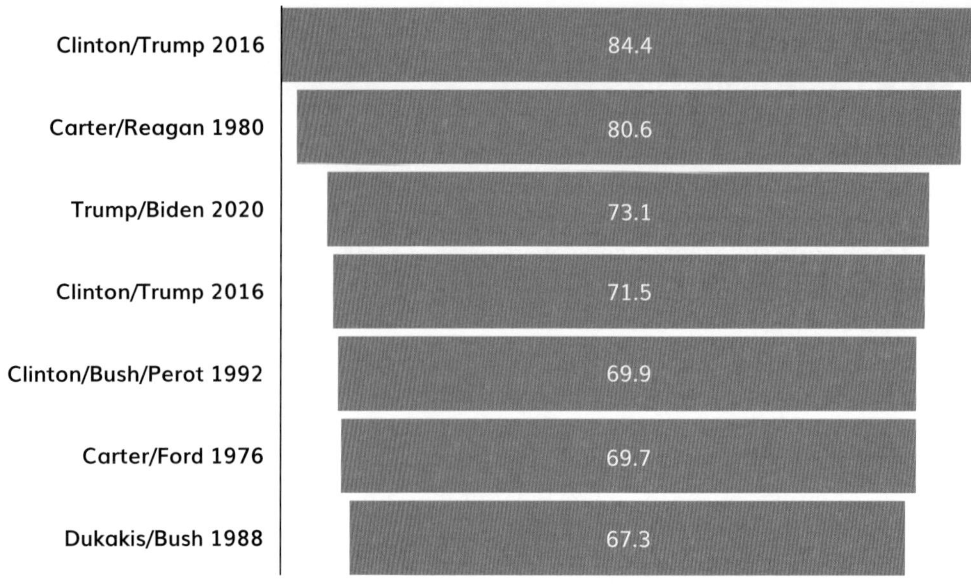

Figure 6.4 Viewing figures (millions) for the most-watched presidential TV debates

Source: Statista.

Reunite party

✓ Party conventions play a very important role in reuniting a party after the internal party conflict of primaries. Reuniting the party can help to boost the popularity of the party and the winning candidate. Losing candidates in the primary process often give speeches to declare their support for the winner.

✓ Failing to reunite the party may reveal divisions and make the party or winning candidate look weak. This could have a major negative significance for a candidate in the presidential election.

» In 2016 Trump's main primary rival, Ted Cruz, gave a speech but failed to give his endorsement to Trump, instead urging people to 'vote your conscience'. This led to audible booing and negative media coverage. The Democrat convention of 2020 agreed policies based on a Unity Task Force headed by Biden and losing candidate Sanders. Losing primary candidates Sanders, Warren, Buttigieg and Yang all spoke in support of Biden at the convention, helping to show unity.

✗ Whilst a convention is used to unite a party, this may have limited impact on voting behaviour. Voters may have developed support or opposition to certain candidates during the primaries. Any ongoing divisions are unlikely to make a voter switch party away from the divided party. The Cruz speech did not do enough to cause Trump to lose the election, for example.

✗ People often vote for their party out of principle, believing that this is better than the opposing party gaining power. As such, conventions have a limited role in causing a voter to switch allegiance.

» In both 2016 and 2020 voters held strong views on the candidates themselves. In 2020 more voters had a strong opinion regarding Trump than any incumbent since 1980, and more voters held a strong opinion on Biden than any challenger to an incumbent since at least 1980. By May 2020, 69% stated they had a strongly favourable or strongly unfavourable rating of Trump, suggesting fewer swing voters than in other years. This, alongside the reduced nature of the conventions due to COVID-19, suggests the conventions have a limited impact on the views of voters. It is independent voters who often swing an election, and Biden held a large lead among independents even before the 2020 convention. As such he was unlikely to get a poll bounce at the convention.

Key Topic Debate Summary: Do party conventions play a significant role in US politics?

FOR	KEY CRITERIA	AGAINST
✓ Party conventions technically select the presidential and vice presidential candidates for the party. ✓ Delegates debate and vote to determine the platform for the presidential election. ✓ If no candidate achieves this a brokered convention takes place requiring more rounds of voting.	Do party conventions have an impact through their **traditional roles**?	✗ Primaries (not the convention) determine the winner of the presidential nomination. ✗ The winning candidate determines their own platform, which receives most focus. ✗ There has never been a brokered convention meaning the delegates have never had a critical say in who the candidate will be.
✓ Party conventions launch the presidential campaign. They provide major publicity and the hope of a poll bounce. ✓ Party conventions can be used to enthuse activists and core supporters who go on to campaign and/or vote for the party.	Do party conventions have an impact on **elections and election outcomes**?	✗ The conventions have a limited impact on public opinion in practice. Other stages of the election are likely to have a greater impact. ✗ Many voters have made their decision before party conventions. ✗ It is unlikely that one convention is extremely effective whilst another generates significant negative publicity.
✓ Party conventions reunite a party after the internal party conflict of primaries. This can boost the popularity of the party and the winning candidate. ✓ Not reuniting the party may reveal divisions and make the party or winning candidate look weak.	Do party conventions have an impact on **parties**?	✗ Uniting the party may have a limited impact on voting behaviour. Any ongoing divisions within a party are unlikely to make a voter switch party. ✗ People from one party are unlikely to vote for the other and will vote for their party out of principle.

Exam Tip: Improving AO2 analysis and AO3 evaluation

Consider the idea of positive and negative impact to make your analysis and evaluation more complex. Remember that if the convention has a negative impact on a candidate this is still an impact. Do not make the mistake of arguing that this is not an impact.

Learning Review

1. What are party conventions and what is their traditional role?
2. In what ways can party conventions have a significant political impact?
3. What are the arguments which suggest that party conventions lack impact?

THE ELECTORAL COLLEGE

Rather than having a system in which people vote in the country as a whole, awarding the presidency to the winner, the voting process in the United States is more complicated, using an electoral college. This process was created in 1787 by the Founding Fathers who were keen to protect the power of states and were also concerned about giving too much power to an uneducated mass of people. This has led to significant criticisms that **the Electoral College** is entirely inappropriate in a modern democracy. You can see the essentials of the process in Figure 6.5.

Definition

The Electoral College: The name of the process used to elect the president.

Basic process	How it happened in 2020
People vote in states (not in the United States as a whole) with each state being given a value or number of points.	• Each state represents a number of 'points' with larger states given larger values. • For example, the value of California is 55 and Wyoming is 3. • People vote for the individual presidential candidates in each state. In 2020, the leading candidates were Trump and Biden.

A winner-takes-all system is used – the candidate who gets the most votes in a state wins the whole value of that state.	• Biden got the most votes in California (63%) and won all 55 points. The points are known as Electoral College votes or ECV. • Trump won the most votes in Florida (51%) and won all 29 ECV. • The state with the smallest population, Wyoming, was won by Trump (70%), gaining him 3 ECV.

To become the president, one candidate needs to get over 50% of the points from all the states.	• The total value of all states is 538 ECV, with 270 points or more needed to win. • The popular vote (the votes of the people) was translated into an ECV for the whole country. • All states plus Washington DC voted and awarded ECV. • Biden secured 306 ECV compared to Trump's 232, making Biden the president of the United States.

Figure 6.5 **The essentials of the presidential election system**

There are two other important features that you will need to understand before you evaluate the Electoral College:

ALLOCATION OF ELECTORAL COLLEGE VOTES (ECV) TO A STATE

The number of ECV awarded to a state is not entirely proportional to the population of a state. The value for each state is equal to the number of members of the House of Representatives for each state, which gives a roughly proportional allocation of ECV to each state. So far, there is a fair allocation according to population. The Constitution also awards additional ECV points for each state, giving all states +2 ECV (equal to the number of Senators per state) regardless of population. California is given +2 state even though it has the same +2 value as Wyoming, the state with the fewest residents. This was a deliberate measure by the Founding Fathers to increase the power of smaller states.

THE ROLE OF DELEGATES

The ECV value refers to a number of people known as delegates. In 2024 The Electoral College values for each state were adjusted with California dropping to 54. Instead of winning 54 ECV in California, the candidate who wins there secures 54 delegates. These are people appointed by the state to vote within the Electoral College. It has become an expectation or convention that the Electoral College delegates will vote according to the wishes of their state and reflect public opinion. It is a legal requirement in thirty-three states plus DC that delegates vote according to majority public opinion in their state. This leaves seventeen states that allow their Electoral College delegates to ignore the popular vote.

These two provisions (of the use of delegates and the allocation of an Electoral College value to states) are outlined in the Constitution. The Constitution makes no mention of party conventions or primaries. These are processes created by parties themselves. Further details of constitutional provisions of the presidential election process can be seen in Figure 6.6.

» Presidential elections take place every four years on the Tuesday after the first Monday in November.
» To run for presidency an individual must be a natural born citizen of the US, over 35 and a US resident.
» The Constitution requires that this is a state-based voting system with states allocating delegates or ECV to presidential candidates.
» Each state has a value equal to the number of congresspersons and senators for that state.
» To become president, a candidate requires 50% plus of total ECV (270/538 currently).
» If no candidate has 50% plus ECV then the House decides but states vote in blocks.
» The Twenty-third Amendment gave three Electoral College votes to Washington DC in 1961. Previously residents of DC had no right to participate in presidential elections.
» The voting age was reduced from 21 to 18 by the Twenty-sixth Amendment in 1971.
» There is nothing in the Constitution that explains how states translate the popular vote into the Electoral College votes for that state. All states have chosen to use a winner-takes-all system. Most states do this on a whole state basis – whoever wins the popular vote in the state wins all the votes for the state. Maine and Nebraska are the only two states that award some of their Electoral College delegates based on which presidential candidate wins in House Districts.

Figure 6.6 **Constitutional provisions of the presidential election system**

KEY TOPIC DEBATE: IS THE ELECTORAL COLLEGE AN ACCEPTABLE PROCESS FOR SELECTING THE PRESIDENT TODAY?

Given that the system was created by the Founding Fathers as part of the original US Constitution of 1787, it is unsurprising that the Electoral College has been heavily criticised. In recent years there has been a great deal of evidence that can be used to support the reform of this voting system. Chief amongst these are the two elections in which the winner of the popular vote did not go on to become the president because they did not win the Electoral College vote.

Democracy

✓ The Electoral College is broadly democratic, with both parties competing under agreed rules. The system requires candidates to win in a series of fair, state-based elections. The winning candidate is almost always the one with most of the popular vote.

✓ The system often produces a clear winner as it tends to exaggerate popular support. By coming first in lots of states by a small margin, a candidate can still capture a very high total of ECV. Giving the winner such a boost can add to their legitimacy and allow them to deliver on their election promises. This promotes majoritarian democracy in which the majority gets what they voted for.

» In 1992 President Bill Clinton received 69% of the Electoral College votes based on only 43% of the popular vote. In 2020 President Biden received 51% of the vote but 57% of the Electoral College votes. This could increase the ability of both presidents to fulfil the platform they were elected for by depicting them as popular presidents with a clear mandate to govern.

✗ Over-representing a presidential candidate through ECVs is not aiding democracy. It does not reflect the wishes of the United States in general and has a limited impact on a president's power. Other factors, such as popularity and a majority in Congress, determine a president's ability to carry out policy promises and not the impression of a clear mandate.

✗ The most significant democratic concern, however, is that the most popular candidate (in terms of the number of actual votes) can lose the election. This is unacceptable in a democracy yet has now occurred twice in recent elections (2000 and 2016). This destroys basic principles of a representative democracy and the concept of an electoral mandate. The reason for this can be seen using the election results from two states in Table 6.3.

Clinton gained nothing from winning by a large margin. If she had come first in the State of Maryland with 47% of the votes, she would have received fewer popular votes than she did but still captured

Table 6.3 **Election result in two states in 2016**

State	ECV	Won by	Vote (%)	Total votes (millions)
Wisconsin	10	Trump	47.22	1.405
Maryland	10	Clinton	60.33	1.677

the 10 ECV from that state. Trump was able to win the election with fewer popular votes than Clinton because he won lots of states by a small margin and Clinton won many other states by big margins.

The states

✓ The Electoral College protects smaller states from being dominated by the interests of those states with the highest populations. The Founding Fathers deliberately over-rewarded small states through the allocation of more ECVs, giving them a stronger political voice.

✓ What was perhaps an unintended consequence of the Electoral College is that it protects the voting power of low turnout states. A state maintains its Electoral College value regardless of how many people turnout to vote. Given that turnout often relates to education and income, this could protect the interests of lower income, lower educated areas.

» In 2020 Minnesota had the highest turnout at 80%, whereas Oklahoma produced the lowest at just 55%. Despite this disparity in turnout, Oklahoma maintained its 3 ECVs and Minnesota its 10.

✗ Elections should not be based around state interests but the wishes and interests of individuals. The Electoral College is unfair because of the over-representation of smaller states. The way in which ECV are allocated to states means that individual voters in Wyoming are given more power than those in California.

✗ In practice, it is **swing states** that are hugely significant in the race to win the presidency. Voters in these states therefore end up with more power. Candidates spend almost all of their campaign on just a few states. Instead of trying to win as many votes as possible, across the whole United States, parties can ignore safe states and focus on a small number of voters. A presidential candidate can often win an election if they can gain just five or six states compared to how their party fared at the last election.

» Twelve states accounted for 96% of the 2020 general election campaign events involving the presidential and vice presidential candidates. Figure 6.7 shows how much money the candidates spent on TV advertisements in swing states in 2016.

Definition

Swing states: States that could feasibly be won by either party because a party last won by a small margin. The winning party could easily change in the next set of elections.

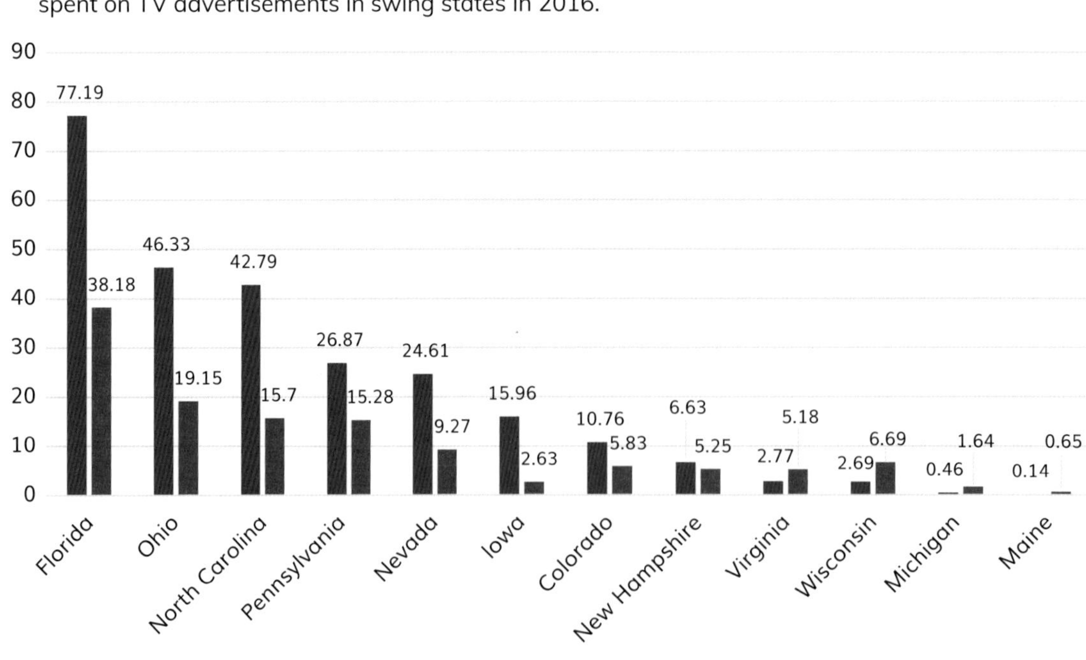

Figure 6.7 **TV advertisement spending in swing states in 2020 ($ millions)**

Source: *Advertising Analytics.*

Delegates

✓ The Electoral College creates delegates or electors who can make the final decision. This was an intentional decision by the Founding Fathers to act as a check on public opinion. Today, the delegates could prevent an unsuitable individual from becoming the president.

✓ The role of delegates could be defended by pointing out that the majority are legally obliged to vote according to the election outcome for their state. In addition, it is very unlikely that delegates would deliberately seek to undermine public opinion and reject the most popular candidates.

✗ The continued use of delegates is a major concern with the possibility that rogue delegates could subvert the wishes of the public.

✗ Delegates are not qualified to make decisions on behalf of the people and instead represent an outdated idea that does not have a place in a modern democracy.

» Faithless or rogue electors have never changed the outcome of a presidential election and incidents of rogue electors are not common. In 2016 there were seven rogue electors. Two of these were delegates who should have voted for Trump, with Clinton losing five delegates who ignored public opinion in their states. One of Clinton's delegates cast a vote for Faith Spotted Eagle, a Native American campaigner who has sought to protect the environment as well as the interests of the Sioux Nation.

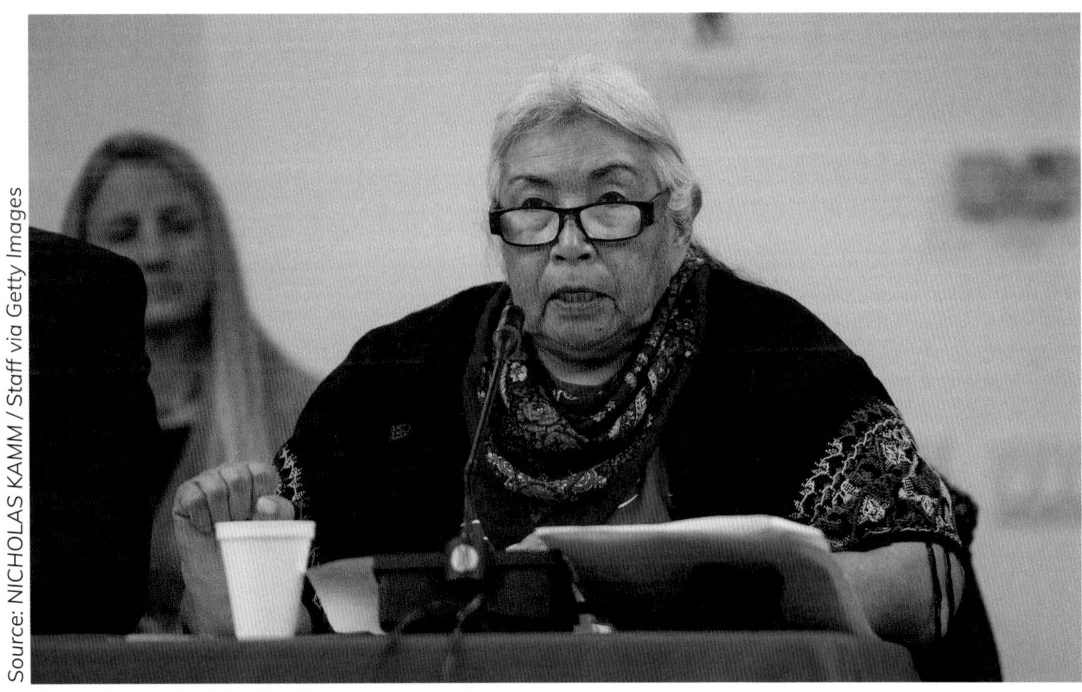

Source: NICHOLAS KAMM / Staff via Getty Images

Photo 6.3 **Faith Spotted Eagle, the only Native American to receive an Electoral College Vote**

Key Topic Debate Summary: Is the Electoral College fit for purpose?

FOR	KEY CRITERIA	AGAINST
✓ The Electoral College is broadly democratic with both parties competing under agreed rules. ✓ The system often produces a clear winner, promoting a strong leader and majoritarian democracy.	Is the process **democratic**?	✗ The Electoral College process is undemocratic, usually over-representing the winner in ECV terms. ✗ The most popular candidate can lose the election, which is unacceptable in a democracy.
✓ The Electoral College protects smaller states and thus voters in smaller states from being dominated by the interests of those states with the highest populations. ✓ The Electoral College protects the voting power of low turnout states – this could protect the interests of lower income, lower educated areas.	Does the process benefit **states**?	✗ Elections should not be based around state interests but the wishes and interests of individuals. The over-representation of smaller states is not democratic. ✗ In practice the system awards far too much power to a few swing states.
✓ Delegates were created by the Founding Fathers to act as a check on public opinion. Delegates could prevent an unsuitable individual from becoming the president. ✓ The majority of delegates are legally obliged to vote according to the election outcome for their state.	Is the role of **delegates** acceptable?	✗ There is the possibility that rogue delegates could subvert the wishes of the public – their existence is undemocratic. ✗ Delegates are not qualified to make decisions on behalf of the people.

Exam Tip: Improving AO2 analysis and AO3 evaluation

Evaluation requires you to come to a clear and well-supported judgement based on a consideration of different viewpoints. A strong answer here will take a position and then strongly support that view. Whilst you must show an awareness of different viewpoints, do not be afraid to push your argument strongly throughout your answer.

Learning Review

1. What are the main stages in the basic process of the Electoral College (presidential elections)?
2. How are Electoral College votes allocated to a state?
3. What role do Electoral College delegates play in the election process?
4. What are the main criticisms of the Electoral College?
5. What are the main arguments in favour of the Electoral College?

CASE STUDY 6.1: 2020 PRESIDENTIAL ELECTION

Source: Pool / Pool via Getty Images

Photo 6.4 **Donald Trump and Joe Biden participate in their final debate before the presidential election**

Overview

As with many other presidential elections, the 2020 election focused a huge amount on the record of the president trying to gain re-election. The Trump presidency was highly divisive with an aggressive approach to those who opposed him. He regularly issued hostile tweets or personal attacks in speeches and sought to divide more than seek consensus. He was the first president to seek a second term after losing an impeachment vote in the House of Representatives. His brand of nationalism with the slogan, 'Keep America Great', and his moral conservatism in areas such as immigration, racial rights or gay and transgender rights gave him a loyal activist following. Trump's opponent, a hugely experienced former vice president, Joe Biden, was a moderate Democrat whose election campaign was fought on the issues of COVID-19, the economy and the record of Trump himself.

This was very much a COVID-19 election with the pandemic hitting the United States to full effect in January 2020. By the day of the election more than 250,000 Americans had died from COVID-19, more than in any other country in the world. Trump turned what could have been a hugely uniting force in the United States into a divisive political issue. Having ordered lockdown, he was quicker than most national leaders to oppose COVID-19 restrictions and defy medical advice. Even mask wearing became a divisive political issue with Trump using anti-mask rhetoric from around May 2020, connecting the issue with personal freedom. During one TV debate he mocked Biden for wearing a mask. Trump opposed mail-in ballot voting, which became more common as a result of the crisis, saying that it helped to rig the election.

The result

It was the heaviest defeat for a sitting president since 1932. Whilst Trump's populist nationalism, social conservatism and aggressive style gave him a loyal and activist voter base, opinion polls in the run up to the election showed more people feeling very strongly for or against the president than for any previous president. Crucially he failed to gain support from moderate and swing voters losing ground to Biden amongst key voter groups and in swing states. Biden won the election by flipping five states which Trump won in 2016. He regained traditional Democrat states of Michigan, Pennsylvania and Wisconsin but also won two traditionally Republican states, Arizona and Georgia. The issue of COVID-19 was inevitably high on people's list of issues and polls regularly put Biden ahead when the public were asked who would handle the COVID-19 crisis better with a Pew Research poll putting Biden 17 percentage points ahead on this issue.

Parties and coalition of supporters

President Trump failed to gain support beyond his core voter base and struggled to attract swing voters. This was no surprise given his aggressive approach to governing with personal and aggressive attacks on political opponents both beyond and within his party. He lost support amongst white male voters, especially those with lower levels of education. While he received more votes than Biden in this group, this undermined his considerable strength in winning the 2016 campaign. Biden as a Democrat maintained solid support amongst Black voters (87% support) and Hispanic voters (65%), which are almost identical to support from these groups for Clinton in 2016.

Parties and party policy

Joe Biden won the Democrat primaries as a relatively moderate candidate, defeating more left-wing progressives such as Sanders and Warren. He campaigned for additions to Obamacare to extend provision but stopped short of adopting the progressive wing policy of Single Payer (or Medicare For All) in which the government would provide universal healthcare insurance. He focused the campaign on policies to ensure that more people were vaccinated, rebuilding the economy with greater government investment and a push towards a green economy. He pledged to increase tax on high earners and corporations and spend money on green infrastructure. As such, Biden continued with the tradition of Democrats in challenging socio-economic inequality and promoting the interests of those on lower and middle incomes. Having said that, progressives in his own party such as Ocasio Cortez, Sanders or Warren, whilst supportive of Joe Biden during the campaign, did not see his policies as doing anywhere near enough to tackle the major problems of poverty and inequality. Trump stood in opposition to all of these policies and continued to focus on the nationalist populist 'America First' agenda he was identified with since the 2016 election. His campaign paid less attention to policy detail, but Trump was able to stand on his record of cutting corporation tax and taking a harder line on immigration. This included his remain in Mexico policy in which asylum seekers were required to complete their asylum application from outside the United States as well as his family separation policy in which families who crossed the border were held in separate facilities with children being removed from their parents. In contrast to Biden, he rejected pro-environment policies, pulling the United States out of the Paris Agreement and deregulating to allow for greater use of oil and gas resources. Trump's policies remained consistent with the values of the Republican Party, typically finding more favour with the conservative and evangelical factions.

Electoral College

Whilst Biden was consistently ahead in national polls, the use of the Electoral College meant that the candidates were focused on swing states. For Biden it was important to win back traditionally blue (Democrat) states such as Wisconsin, Pennsylvania, Michigan and Ohio. In addition, red (Republican) marginal states were also a focus with states such as Arizona and Florida being targeted. A great deal of resources and campaign time was spent in these states. Whilst Biden failed to make any ground in Ohio or Florida, he was able to capture two states won by Republicans in 2016 (Arizona and Georgia) as well as regaining Wisconsin, Pennsylvania and Michigan. Biden therefore won by gaining five states more than Clinton in 2016. With 81,283,501 votes, Biden received the largest support of any presidential candidate based on the highest turnout (66.7%) since 1900.

Democracy

The 2020 election may well be seen as a turning point for US democracy with the values of democracy severely challenged. During election night, when early counting showed Trump ahead, he issued a series of tweets often with the phrase 'stop the count', saying that voting irregularities meant that the vote was unfair. After President Trump lost the election in 2020, he rejected the result and he and other Republicans continued to attempt to stop Biden from becoming president. This culminated in the events of 6 January 2021 in which 2,000 people stormed the congressional building in an attempt to prevent Biden from becoming president. Trump encouraged protests giving a speech on 6 January that ended with the words 'We fight. We fight like hell and if you don't fight like hell, you're not going to have a country anymore.' A gallows was erected outside the Capitol, and some shouted 'Hang Mike Pence' after the vice president refused to attempt to reject the election result. Five police officers died while trying to prevent the attack.

Since the election there has been an increasing movement challenging the concept of democracy. Trump has sometimes made comments that were critical of democracy suggesting he would prefer to remove it. Some conservatives, including senior Republicans, are questioning the idea that the United States should be a democracy. In 2020 Republican Senator Mike Lee repeatedly questioned the desirability of democracy. He stated that 'democracy isn't the objective; liberty, peace, and prosperity are'. Lee continued to point out that the word democracy is not in the Constitution, and argued there was never any intention for the United States to be a democracy. He won re-election to the Senate in 2022.

Campaign finance

As with all recent elections, neither candidate accepted federal funding for their campaign and, as such, neither could be subject to campaign expenditure limits. Whilst Trump began the election with incumbency advantage, the Biden campaign outraised and outspent the Trump campaign. This could be used to support claims that money helps to buy an election with the biggest spender taking the White House. On the other hand, it could be argued that the cause–effect relationship is the other way around. Biden raised more money because he was more popular. Democrats raised over half of their money from small online donations, but this did not stop major concerns being raised about big money donations to both parties and the potential influence of major donors.

Super PACs continued to play a major role in this election, being able to raise and spend money with no donation or expenditure limits. Republican mega-donor Sheldon Adelson gave $75 million to Preserve American in 2020, a new super PAC focused on attacking Biden. The Biden campaign benefited from FutureForward USA a new super PAC that spent over $100 million during the 2020 campaign. The money was spent mainly on attack ads criticising Trump, which were run in swing states. Open Secrets reported that whilst the group is partly funded by Dustin Moskovitz, co-founder of Facebook, most of the money donated to the group cannot be traced. There are fears that such major tech donations to the Biden campaign wields significant policy influence. At the same time, the secrecy surrounding donations leads to a lack of accountability and ability to monitor potential influences.

THE PARTY SYSTEM

The United States has a very strong two-party system with the Democratic Party and the Republican Party dominating the political system. At any one point in time, Congress is likely to contain politicians from the main two parties only. Elections, therefore, are almost exclusively contests between these two groups. Third parties have virtually no impact on US politics.

The two-party system is encouraged by the use of first-past-the-post or winner-takes-all elections. This, alongside the established nature of the Democratic and Republican parties, discourages people from voting for third parties. The Democrats and Republicans have the brand recognition, the political expertise of recently elected politicians and the fund-raising capabilities to help maintain their dominance.

Spec key term

Party system: The number of parties that exist *and* have significant political power.

INCUMBENCY

The idea of incumbency advantage suggests that the person in office will find it easier to win the next election compared to their challenger. This can be seen throughout the history of US presidential elections; when a president has attempted to gain re-election almost 70% of these have resulted in success (22 out of 32). Table 6.4 shows the outcomes of recent presidential elections where the sitting president has run for re-election.

The evidence also shows that success is far from guaranteed; it is possible for challengers to unseat the sitting president. President Trump was the latest incumbent to lose office. After his first term, Trump was able to maintain support amongst his core voter base, and even expand his total support, but lost support amongst swing voters. He carried thirty states in 2016, but this fell back to twenty-five in 2020.

Table 6.4 Outcomes of recent presidential elections with an incumbent candidate

Year	Incumbent	Incumbent: win or lose	2nd term challenger	Previous political office
1980	Carter	lose	Ronald Reagan	Governor
1984	Reagan	win	Walter Mondale	Vice president
1992	Bush Sr	lose	Bill Clinton	Governor
1996	Clinton	win	Bob Dole	Senator
2004	Bush Jr	win	John Kerry	Senator
2008	Obama	win	Mitt Romney	Governor
2020	Trump	lose	Joe Biden	Vice president

KEY TOPIC DEBATE: DO PRESIDENTIAL INCUMBENTS HAVE A SIGNIFICANT ADVANTAGE WHEN SEEKING RE-ELECTION?

Executive control and experience

✓ Presidents can use their position to deliver specific policy benefits to key voting groups and swing states. Presidents may attempt to stimulate the economy or give strategic economic handouts as elections approach.

✓ Presidents may inspire greater confidence as they have White House experience. Their challenger may be untested at a national executive level. The president could be seen as a safe pair of hands.

✓ The office of president may give significant authority. As commander in chief, the president has enormous responsibility for the security of the nation with the incumbent benefiting from this image.

» In office, Obama rewarded key voting blocs, such as Hispanic people, with executive orders on immigration and the appointment of the first Hispanic justice on the Supreme Court. Mitt Romney, his Republican opponent, had none of these opportunities. Similarly, President Bush remained popular after his response to 9/11 and the unity this created within the United States after the attack. It was this that helped his re-election in 2004.

✖ Presidents can be judged on their record and may have policy mistakes or personal misjudgements to their name. Presidents can take the praise but can also be blamed when things go wrong.

✖ If there are major events during a presidency this can improve the individual in office's reputation if handled well or undermine support for them if handled badly. Major economic and social crises, wars and the COVID-19 pandemic have all impacted the power of the president.

» President Trump was strongly criticised for his lack of leadership during the COVID-19 crisis. Instead of attempting to unite the country under his leadership, he politicised the issue. His approach was to downplay the extent of the problem, often deriding those who wore masks and being part of events (such as the Republican Party convention) where leading Republicans did not appear to follow mask and social distancing guidelines. Exit polls for the 2020 election showed that COVID-19 was high on voters' priorities and that Biden was seen as the better candidate to address the issue.

Media focus and recognition

✔ Presidents will find it easy to gain media attention and can speak from the White House directly to voters. This allows them to attract publicity and sell their message to the country. The Rose Garden strategy, in which the president gives an address to the nation from the garden of the White House, is commonly used in the run up to elections.

✔ US elections are extremely expensive, but a president can attract free publicity using social media or news outlets. Challengers to a president will find it difficult to get this level of publicity to sell their political agenda and attack their opponent.

» Obama's speech on the death of US officials in the Benghazi attacks in September 2012 highlighted his role as commander in chief at a time of great national significance. In 2011 Obama announced the withdrawal of troops from Afghanistan with the main withdrawal of 24,000 planned for the summer of 2012, in the months leading up to the election.

✖ This factor does not give the president a monopoly over the media. Presidential TV debates provide an opportunity for an incumbent to impress upon the voters their communication, leadership and policy advantages over a president.

✖ As with the executive control argument, a president may be subject to a great deal of negative publicity that may undermine them. Presidents come under intense media scrutiny, with any flaws or failures quickly highlighted by the media and other politicians.

» President Trump has broken from many norms when it comes to media use. Whilst this gained attention, it has often undermined the extent to which he looks presidential in using the office to govern and represent the United States as a whole and unify the nation. His regular use of aggressive tweets, his intense use of Rose Garden speeches to attack Biden and his use of the White House to deliver a party convention speech were all seen as breaking with the tradition of US presidents.

Elections

✔ Having already won one presidential election, the president has an established campaign team with a proven track record. Incumbents also typically outspend their opponents, giving them an electoral edge because they find it easier to raise funds.

✔ Incumbent presidents tend not to face primary challenges giving them a major advantage over their opponent. The sitting president can continue to raise funds and not spend them whilst the other party faces an internal party battle for the nomination in which candidates from one party spend time and money attacking each other.

Figure 6.8 shows campaign expenditure for recent elections with the incumbent typically outspending the challenger. Bill Clinton (1996), George W. Bush (2004) and Barack Obama (2012) were all incumbent presidents who spent more than their rivals and won the election.

✖ Money is no guarantee of success; the candidate who raises the most money will not necessarily win the election. In addition, challengers could raise and spend more money than the incumbent.

✖ The incumbent president may face a competitive primary. This could create greater political damage than the primary process creates for the challenger. It is unusual for a president to face a primary, but if it happens it exposes high levels of criticism from the president's own party, further undermining their authority.

» Of the last four incumbent presidents to lose a presidential election, three faced competitive primaries, damaging their ability to successfully fight for re-election. President Trump is the only president to lose office whilst not facing such a primary challenge. In the 2020 election, the campaign for Joe Biden raised and spent more than the campaign for Trump.

Key Topic Debate Summary: Is there an incumbency advantage for presidents?

FOR	KEY CRITERIA	AGAINST
✓ Presidents can deliver specific policy benefits to key voting groups and swing states. ✓ Incumbents may inspire greater confidence with the challenger lacking national executive experience. ✓ The office of president may give the president significant authority, given their role as commander in chief, for example.	Can the president make use of their **executive experience**?	✗ Incumbents may have a poor track record as president, making policy mistakes or personal gaffes. ✗ Economic and social crises, wars and COVID-19 have all impacted on the president, who could be blamed for significant problems in society.
✓ Presidents gain media attention and can speak from the White House directly to voters, attracting publicity. The Rose Garden strategy is often used by presidents. ✓ Presidents can attract free publicity, whereas challengers find it difficult to get this level of publicity in which they sell their political agenda and attack their opponent.	Do presidents have a **media advantage**?	✗ Presidential TV debates provide an opportunity for an incumbent to impress voters. ✗ A president may be subject to a great deal of negative publicity that may undermine them. Presidents come under intense media scrutiny, with any flaws or failures quickly being highlighted by the media and other politicians.
✓ A president has an established campaign team with a proven track record of winning. Incumbents typically outspend their opponents. ✓ Incumbent presidents tend not to face primary challenges, giving an advantage over their opponent.	Do presidents have a better ability to fight an **election campaign**?	✗ Money is no guarantee of success; the candidate who raises the most money will not necessarily win the election. ✗ Challengers could raise and spend more money than the incumbent. ✗ The incumbent president may face a competitive primary, creating the risk of high levels of political damage.

Exam Tip: Improving AO2 analysis and AO3 evaluation

For this particular debate there is some clear and well-defined evidence. Making use of the overall statistics on presidential re-election rates as well as applying evidence from three or four different elections will help to support your overall judgement.

Learning Review

1. What type of party system does the United States have?
2. What is meant by incumbency?
3. What are the main advantages for an incumbent president at election time?

Comparative Learning Review

1. In what ways are the party systems of the United States and United Kingdom different?
2. In what ways are the party systems of the United States and United Kingdom similar?

CAMPAIGN FINANCE

Money plays a major role in US elections. Candidates and parties raise enormous sums of money to spend on their campaigns, creating several concerns. There are claims, for example, that elections are a money contest in which the candidate with the highest funds has the best chance of winning the election. In addition, there are also concerns over the influence that major donors may have over the politicians they donate to. To restrict the role of money in US elections, there have been many campaign finance regulations created. In the rest of this section, we will explore both the concerns about the role of money in presidential elections and the extent to which **campaign finance regulations** have successfully resolved these issues.

Spec key term

Campaign finance: Any money raised or spent to influence the outcome of elections.

Definition

Campaign finance regulation: Laws that regulate the way in which money is donated, raised or spent in elections.

Definition

Soft money: Money that can be raised or spent during elections but cannot be regulated by any existing laws. Hard money refers to money that can be regulated.

CAMPAIGN FINANCE REGULATIONS

The first major attempt to regulate money in US elections came in 1971 and 1974 with the Federal Election Campaign Act (FECA). It has the following provisions:

- Places legal limits on campaign contributions. A private individual can only donate $1,000 and a group can only donate $2,500. These figures have been adjusted slightly since 1974.
- Creates federal funding of presidential elections. This works on a matching funds basis (for every dollar a candidate raises, they are given a dollar by the Federal Government). To qualify, a party must receive 5% plus of the vote in the previous election. It was anticipated that all candidates would want take advantage of this federal funding resource. If the maximum expenditure limit was $100 million then the Federal Government would provide $50 million and the candidate would raise $50 million. There would be no point raising more than this as candidates are limited to a maximum spend of $100 million.
- Sets a maximum expenditure limit for each candidate. This only applies to all candidates who take matching funds/federal funding.
- Requires candidates to disclose sources of campaign contributions and campaign expenditure.
- Created the Federal Election Commission (FEC). The FEC is a six-member bipartisan committee that oversees the election, and regulates and seeks prosecution in the courts if rules are broken.
- Requires the creation of Political Action Committees (PACs). A PAC must be created by any group that wants to donate money to a campaign. Businesses and pressure groups create their own PAC, which is registered with the FEC. The PAC is legally responsible for complying with all campaign finance laws.

These regulations were only partially successful as parties, politicians and donors found ways of donating or spending that were not covered by FECA regulations. In addition, many legal challenges undermined the workings of FECA. Attempts to spend money that could not be regulated became known as **soft money** (with money that is regulated being referred to as hard money). Since then, the ability to raise and spend soft money has increased enormously, undermining attempts to regulate money in elections. For example, court decisions ruled that money donated to or spent by national party committees (as opposed to candidates) should be largely unregulated, even though national party committees were raising money and spending it in support of their presidential candidate.

Another major blow to campaign finance regulations was the effective end of the maximum expenditure limits. This began in 2000 when George W. Bush became the first Democrat or Republican candidate who decided not to take federal funding. Bush calculated that he could raise and spend more than the federal maximum limit and by not taking federal funding he was allowed to spend as much as he could raise. Obama was the next presidential candidate to do this which meant that the 2000, 2004 and 2008 elections saw one candidate limited to a maximum expenditure whilst their opponent could exceed this limit. You can see the inequalities in expenditure between candidates in these elections in Figure 6.8. No candidate has taken federal funding from the 2012 elections onwards.

In an attempt to reduce the influence of soft money, Congress passed the second major piece of campaign finance regulations, the Bipartisan Campaign Reform Act (BCRA), in 2002. It is often known as the McCain-Feingold Act after its two principal sponsors. Two provisions are particularly important:

- National party committees became subject to campaign finance regulations in addition to presidential candidates. Therefore, FECA rules on raising and spending of money now applied to parties.
- Issues advertisements were included as donations to an election campaign. Pressure groups or businesses would run TV issue adverts in which they outline a social issue and made the

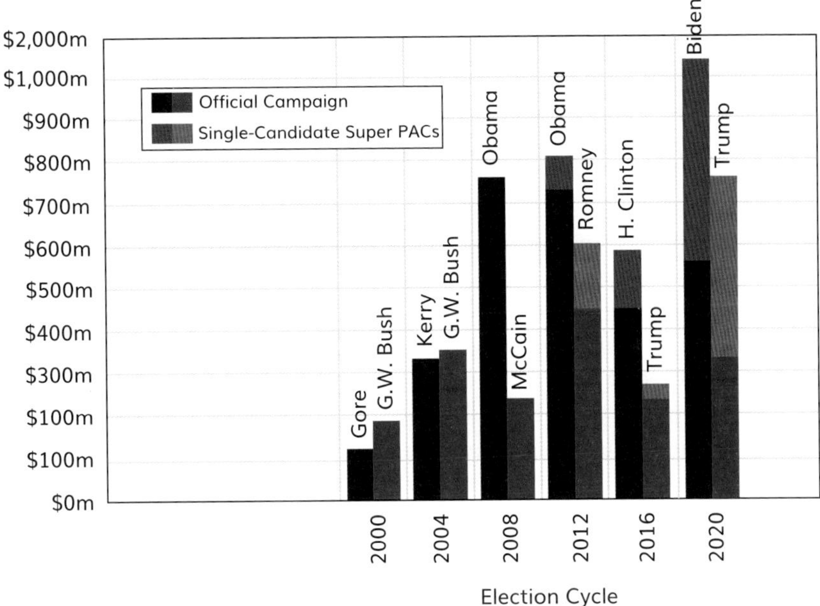

Figure 6.8 **Campaign expenditure in presidential elections 1999–2016**

Source: open secrets.org.

presidential candidate's views clear. No money would be directly donated to a campaign in this instance, meaning that groups could spend unlimited sums of money to promote or attack a candidate without the expenditure counting towards the candidate's campaign total. The BCRA defined all issues adverts within sixty days of an election as 'electioneering communications' and prohibited them during this period.

THE SUPREME COURT RESPONSE

Overall, the Supreme Court, usually responding to First Amendment free speech cases, has undermined the major laws regulating money in elections. *Citizens United v FEC* (2010) had a particularly significant impact, overturning most of the important regulations of the BCRA. In particular, the court gave a 5–4 ruling which stated that the ban on issue adverts during election campaigns broke the First Amendment. This led to not only the return of issue adverts but also the creation of super PACs. These super PACs raise major concerns about the influence of major donors as well as secrecy and are discussed in full in Chapter 7.

DIFFICULTY IN ACHIEVING REFORM

Attempts to regulate money in US elections have hit some serious obstacles which means that regulations overall have a limited impact:

- Effectively politicians are regulating themselves and are reluctant to limit their ability to raise and spend money. Whilst there was some cross-party support for the BCRA, there is now a more partisan approach to the issue, in which Democrats have been more likely to favour regulations but are often blocked by Republicans in Congress.
- The Supreme Court has delivered rulings that, in the name of the First Amendment, overturn campaign finance regulations. The conservative majority on the court in recent years means that majority opinion is unlikely to support new regulations.
- Soft money expenditure is common due to the complexity of campaign finance laws, allowing politicians, pressure groups and wealthy individuals to evade the regulations.

KEY TOPIC DEBATE: HAS CAMPAIGN FINANCE REGULATION BEEN EFFECTIVE?

The success of campaign finance regulation can be evaluated by examining what it is trying to achieve. There are three main concerns surrounding money and elections that the regulations seek to overcome:

Excessive influence of major donors

✓ FECA and the BCRA sought to limit maximum donations. Regulations on donations still exist today, with groups obliged to comply with maximum donation limitations. This should prevent major donors from having excess of influence over individual politicians.

✓ Making campaign donations public is also a way of limiting political influence. It exposes any politicians who appear to be responding to donations by delivering policy benefits to the groups or individuals who have donated to them.

✗ The existence of soft money shows that there are many ways of donating money without being limited by campaign finance regulations. In practice, many groups or individuals find ways to donate significant sums of money to election campaigns.

✗ Super PACs have allowed wealthy individuals or groups to donate huge sums of money that cannot be regulated. By donating to a super PAC rather than a candidate, donors can evade restrictions. This has led to a major growth in large donations.

» Republican megadonor Sheldon Adelson gave $75 million to Preserve America in 2020, a new super PAC focused on attacking Biden. The concern is that, had Trump won, Adelson would expect policy benefits in return. In addition, politicians may fear that to keep campaign finance money flowing they need to deliver policy benefits to the donors or potential donors such as Adelson.

Secrecy surrounding who is donating and receiving cash

To prevent corruption, it is critical that donations and expenditure are made public and accounted for. Having a transparent system with public declaration is also essential if campaign finance regulations ought to be enforced.

✓ FECA regulations have been successful in preventing secrecy, requiring all organisations that donate money to set up political action committees and to declare all money they have donated. Equally, parties and candidates have a legal obligation to disclose where the funding has come from.

✓ The Federal Election Commission can investigate pressure groups, businesses and politicians in relation to campaign finance activity.

✓ Whilst this is not a formal part of the campaign finance regulation system, interest groups or journalists such as Opensecrets.org have played critical role in monitoring campaign finance and bringing to light any concerns.

✗ The main concern surrounding secrecy over campaign finance has developed since the Citizens United ruling and the creation of super PACs. In many cases the money donated to super PACs does not have to be disclosed because it is not going directly to a candidate's campaign fund. This allows wealthy donors to spend millions funding super PACs who then go on to campaign for a particular candidate without working directly with them.

» Future Forward USA spent nearly $100 million backing Biden and attacking President Trump in TV adverts. According to OpenSecrets around $60 million of that expenditure comes from 'dark money', namely undisclosed sources.

Inequality of expenditure between candidates or parties

✓ FECA in particular reduces the likelihood of inequality of expenditure between the big two parties or candidates by providing matching funds and maximum expenditure limits. Limiting donations can also help to ensure that one party does not receive a concentration of campaign finance from a small number of major donors. This makes elections more competitive, with a democratic contest on a level playing field.

✓ FECA could also help smaller parties to compete by providing federal funding once a party has secured 5% of votes in a federal election.

✓ We could also argue that the extent of inequality of expenditure between Democrats and Republicans is not a cause for concern. Money is not a guarantee of electoral success, with the loser sometimes spending more money than the rival. In addition, it is important to consider what is the cause and what is the effect in this scenario. It may be the case that it is simply the candidate who is the most popular who can attract the highest campaign finance contributions.

✖ FECA regulations have largely failed as the federal funding system and maximum expenditure limitations no longer effectively operate in practise. Inequality of expenditure between the Democratic and Republican parties has increased in recent years with the collapse of campaign finance regulations.

✖ The collapse of campaign finance regulations, especially federal funding, maximum expenditure limits and the increase in total expenditure on presidential elections, has made it even more difficult for smaller parties to compete.

» Between 1976 to 2000, under the regulation of FECA, the main two candidates typically spent similar amounts of money on campaigning, largely as a result of a maximum expenditure figure. Since then, US elections have seen great disparities in expenditure between the two main parties. This was particularly the case in the 2008 presidential election when Obama massively outspent McCain ($760 million versus $358 million). On the other hand, there have been many elections in which both candidates raised and spent similar amounts. In the 2016 election Clinton outspent Trump by a significant margin but still ended up as the losing candidate.

Key Topic Debate Summary: Has campaign finance regulation been effective?

FOR	KEY CRITERIA	AGAINST
✓ Regulations on donations still exist today, which should prevent major donors from having excess of influence over individual politicians. ✓ Most campaign donations are a matter of public record creating accountability.	Have regulations resolved concerns about **the excessive influence of donors**?	✖ The growing role of soft money makes it very difficult to regulate donations and therefore the influence of donors. ✖ Since 2010 super PACs have made it virtually impossible to prevent large single donations from wealthy individuals.
✓ There are significant campaign finance regulations requiring disclosure to the FEC with all records published on their website. ✓ Interest groups such as Opensecrets.org work hard to monitor the use of money and expose concerns.	Have regulations resolved concerns about **secrecy**?	✖ The main concerns have developed since the creation of super PACs, which do not always need to declare the source of their funding.
✓ Public funding of parties during elections helps to reduce inequality of expenditure. ✓ Inequality is not a concern and often simply reflects the popularity of the candidates.	Have regulations resolved concerns about **inequality of expenditure between parties or candidates**?	✖ The federal funding system has collapsed as candidates no longer accept this, with major inequalities in expenditure in each election. ✖ This harms third parties who already found it hard to compete with the two well-funded main parties.

Exam Tip: Improving AO2 analysis ad AO3 evaluation

There is a difference between legal theory and political practice in this debate. You can improve your evaluation by stating which one you think is more important and why. In addition, try to use evidence to show that a concern is real rather than just assuming there is a problem based on theory.

Learning Review

1. What is the difference between campaign finance and campaign finance regulation?
2. What are the two main laws regulating money in elections and what are their main provisions?
3. Why is it difficult to add further reforms/regulations to money in US elections?
4. In what ways has campaign finance regulation been effective?
5. In what ways has campaign finance regulation been ineffective?

Chapter Summary

✓ The US presidential election process is a complex one with many different stages.

✓ Presidential elections are preceded by primaries in which the public can vote to decide which candidate will represent the party in presidential elections.

✓ The campaign season is very long, beginning with invisible primaries. At this stage candidates from the same party attempt to gain campaign finance and public support in preparation for the primaries.

✓ National party conventions take place at the end of the primary season and launch a presidential campaign.

✓ Incumbents have a significant advantage over their rivals.

✓ The role of money in the form of campaign finance plays a significant role with limited regulation.

Exam Style Questions

- Evaluate the view that presidential primary and caucus elections are undemocratic. (30 marks)
- Evaluate the view that invisible primaries have a major effect on primary outcomes. (30 marks)
- Evaluate the view that the Electoral College has no place in a modern democracy. (30 marks)
- Evaluate the view that national party conventions play a significant role in US elections. (30 marks)
- Evaluate the view that incumbent presidents have a major advantage over their rival when running for re-election. (30 marks)
- Evaluate the view that campaign finance reform has largely failed. (30 marks)

Further Resources

Boden, M. and Teague, M. (2022) *The Steal: The Attempt to Overturn the 2020 US Election* (London: Grove Press).

Guelzo, A. (2023) 'In Defense of the Electoral College', *National Affairs*, no. 56 (summer), available at https://www.nationalaffairs.com/publications/detail/in-defense-of-the-electoral-college (accessed 27 July 2023).

For a documentary covering recent US elections and voter suppression, see *All In: The Fight For Democracy* (2020), directed by Lisa Cortes and Liz Garbus (USA: Story Syndicate). Available on Amazon Prime.

Visit https://bloomsbury.pub/colclough-essentials-us to access additional materials to support teaching and learning.

7 POLITICAL PARTIES AND INTEREST GROUPS

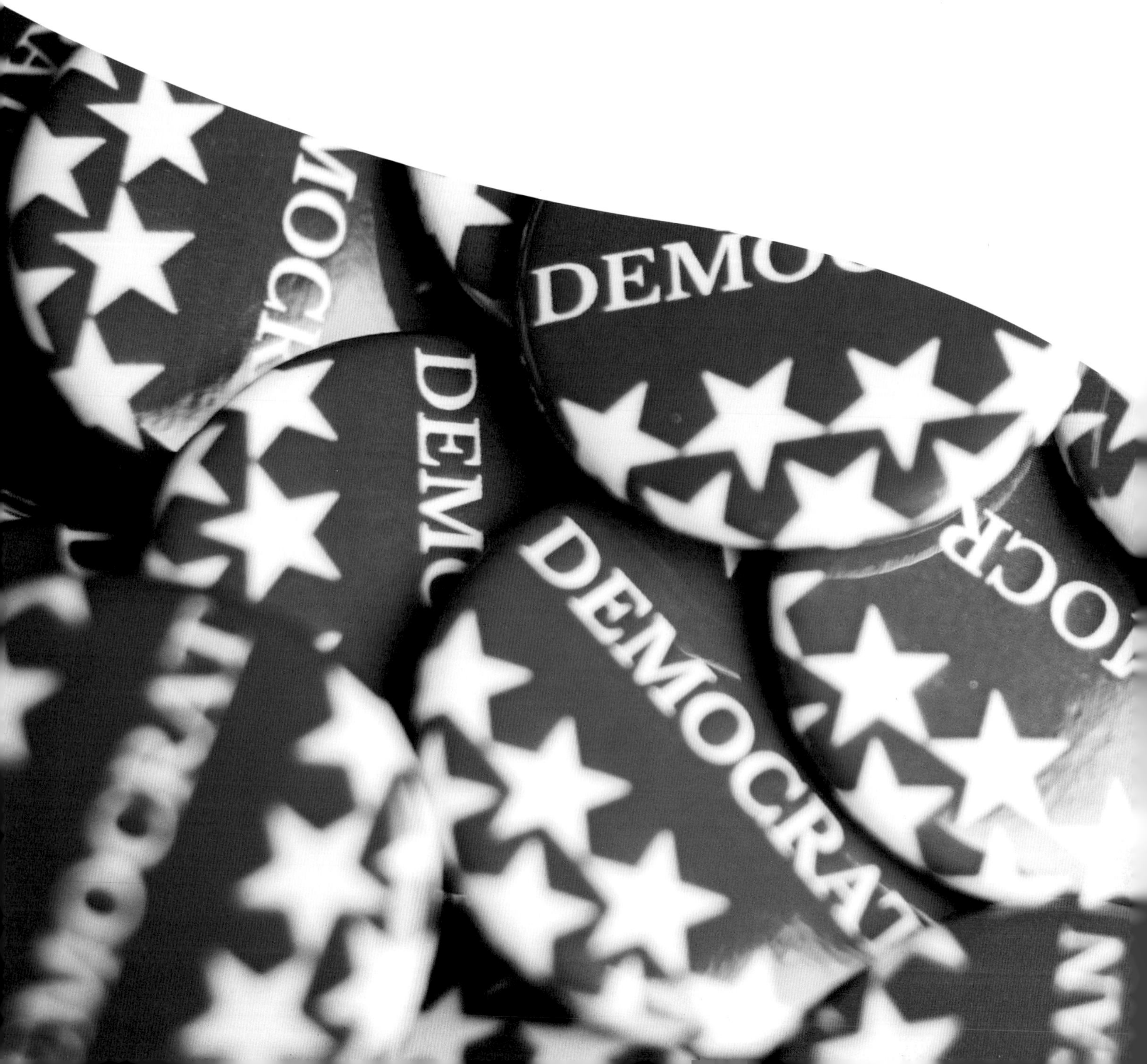

Chapter Preview

Parties and interest groups play a central role in representing the public and have a major impact on democracy. Additionally, they both generate and push for policy ideas that, when put into practice, have a major impact on the lives of the 332 million people in the United States as well as people around the world. In this chapter we will examine their contribution to both democracy and policymaking in the United States.

In a similar fashion to the United Kingdom, the United States is dominated by two main parties. The Democratic Party is the more left wing of the two parties whilst the Republican Party is further to the right. This chapter will allow you to evaluate the extent to which the two parties share similar or conflicting values and policies. The US parties are often described as broad church movements: there is a wide range of views within each party. The Democrats and Republicans are organised into factions (subgroups) that often compete to attempt to dominate the policy direction of the party which they are part of.

Interest groups are a hugely powerful force in the United States, with significant influence over politicians. This chapter will explore some of their causes and the conflicts over issues such as abortion, gun rights, gay and transgender equality, racial equality, the environment and the power of trade unions and corporations. We will examine the tactics used by interest groups; how much influence they have over the president, Congress and the Supreme Court; and the positive and negative impact of interest groups on US democracy. In this chapter (and the book as a whole) the terms interest group and pressure group are both used and mean the same thing.

Key Questions and Debates

- What are the main policies of the Democratic and Republican parties?
- What are the main conflicts between different factions *within* each party?
- What are the resources and tactics of interest groups?
- What is their influence on democracy?
- What are PACs and super PACs and how do they use money to influence politics?
- How do interest groups influence the main branches of government?

Specification Checklist

5.2 The key ideas and principles of the Democratic and Republican parties

- **The distribution of power between parties.**
- **The changing significance of the Democratic and Republican parties with regards to:**
  - **Social and moral issues.**
  - **The national economy.**
  - **Social welfare.**
- **The current conflicts and tendencies and the changing power and influence that exist within the parties:**
  - **Democrats: liberals, moderates and conservatives.**
  - **Republicans: moderates, social conservatives and fiscal conservatives.**
- **Coalition of supporters for each party:**
  - **How and why race, religion, gender and education are likely to influence voting patterns in relation to one recent presidential election campaign (since 2000).**

5.3 Interest groups in the United States

- **Their significance, resources and tactics.**
- **The influence, methods and power of at least one single-interest group, professional group or policy group.**
- **Their influence on democracy.**

5.4 Interpretations and debates

- **The ways in which interest groups influence the three branches of government and policy creation including the role of PACs and super PACs and their impact on democracy.**

Source: istock.com/adamkaz

KEY IDEAS AND PRINCIPLES OF THE DEMOCRATIC AND REPUBLICAN PARTIES

The Democratic and Republican parties are often locked in policy battle, each seeking to impose their political agenda on the United States through success at the ballot box. The Democrats are typically pushing for greater protection of civil rights such as racial or gender rights, greater environmental regulation and the promotion of welfare through government intervention. In the United States it is common to label these positions as liberal. The Republicans, often referred to as the Grand Old Party or GOP, are more likely to favour lower levels of government involvement in the economy and welfare and have often opposed calls for greater rights protection in relation to race, gender or transgender. The positions they hold are usually described as conservative.

THE DISTRIBUTION OF POWER BETWEEN THE PARTIES

The party system in the United States is characterised by the Democratic and Republican parties, they dominate creating a very strong two-party system. Congress is typically 100% Democrat and Republican, with the occasional independent. In presidential elections, they are the only two parties that have a realistic chance of winning, capturing over 98% of the vote in all but one presidential election since 2000.

KEY TOPIC DEBATE: DO DEMOCRATS AND REPUBLICANS HAVE STRONGLY CONFLICTING VALUES AND POLICIES?

There is evidence that the two parties have polarised in recent years, moving further apart ideologically with fewer overlaps in policy or values. There has also been a major increase in partisanship, meaning there is a lack of willingness of politicians in each party to seek compromise with those from another party. All of this suggests that the two main parties are far from similar. For more details on partisanship, see Chapter 3, 'Congress', pages 72–76.

Source: Win McNamee / Staff via Getty Images

Photo 7.1 **Mike Johnson receives the gavel, becoming the new House Speaker in 2023**

Social and moral policy

✓ This policy area marks a significant level of conflict between the two parties regarding race, gender and transgender rights, illegal drugs, immigration and police power. Republicans tend to emphasise the need to maintain a strong authority of regulatory laws and high police power, whereas Democrats tend to promote the rights of the individual to a much greater extent. This forms part of what has become known as the culture wars in the United States, in which there is a clash between liberal and conservative values across the country. You can read more about culture wars in the United States in the 'Getting Started on US Politics' chapter at the start of this book.

» The election of Mike Johnson to be the new Republican House Speaker in October 2023, suggests that the Republicans have moved even further to the right on social and moral policy. Johnson has frequently supported anti-abortion policies as well as restrictions on transgender and gay rights. He championed the closure of abortion clinics in his home state, Louisiana and defended the state's same-sex marriage ban. Earlier in 2023 The Republican majority House of Representatives voted to overturn a Pentagon policy guaranteeing abortion access to armed forces members and also voted to prevent the military's health plan from covering gender-affirming hormone therapy. Almost all Democrats opposed these measures.

✗ There are basic similarities, with most or all Democrats and Republicans supporting basic or fundamental rights protections. This is true of agreements over major legislation such as the Civil Rights Act 1964, which attempted to prevent racial discrimination. There are also overlaps between the two parties in which some conservative or moderate Democrats support mainstream Republican policy or moderate Republicans align with Democrats. This can be seen, for example, with a small number of pro-choice Republicans and pro-life Democrats.

» The Senate unanimously passed the Emmett Till Antilynching Act 2021–2, which was then signed by President Biden. It made lynching a federal hate crime. This was a highly symbolic vote promoting racial equality, targeting the racist practice of lynching in the United States. It passed with every member of Congress supporting it, with the exception of three house Republicans. Similar bills have been proposed and failed for over 100 years in US politics.

The national economy

✓ The two main parties attempt to move the United States in very different ideological directions regarding economic policy. Republicans call for a much more restricted government. Their policies are based on the need for individual freedom from government control and the view that **free market economics** is the most efficient way of delivering economic success. Democrats on the other hand argue for greater government intervention to overcome socio-economic inequality. Democrats are far more critical of free market economics than Republicans, typically aiming to increase federal expenditure and taxes on the wealthy.

» The extent of conflict can be seen in the **federal shutdowns** of 2018 (thirty-five days) and 2013 (sixteen days). Under divided government, Democrats and Republicans refused to compromise despite major negative economic consequences. Before 1990, federal shutdowns never lasted more than a day, but since then there have been six shutdowns lasting over three days, revealing the increased conflict between the two main parties. Republicans, attempting to reduce Federal Government involvement, typically oppose what they see as excessive government expenditure.

✗ As with social and moral policy, there is some overall party consensus as well as an overlap between the two parties. Despite their apparent differences, some have argued that Democrats promote capitalist and business interests in a similar way to the Republican Party. This theory is supported by the role of PACS and super PACS (see page 218) in which corporations donate huge sums of money to both Democrat and Republican Party campaigns and expect favourable policy outcomes in return.

» The Democrats banking regulation reform, the Dodd Franks Act of 2009, was challenged for its limited attempt to regulate banking in the face of a major global economic crisis caused by the failure of banks and banking regulation. Critics argued that the Democrats were not serious about regulating the banking industry, approaching the issue in a similar manner to the Republican Party.

Definition

Free market economics: An approach to economic policy in which the government seeks to have very low regulation of the economy and avoids government intervention in the economy.

Federal shutdown: This occurs when the president and Congress cannot agree on the federal budget. With no budget agreed, as a new financial year starts, all non-essential Federal Government offices close down and workers are sent home until a resolution is found.

Social welfare

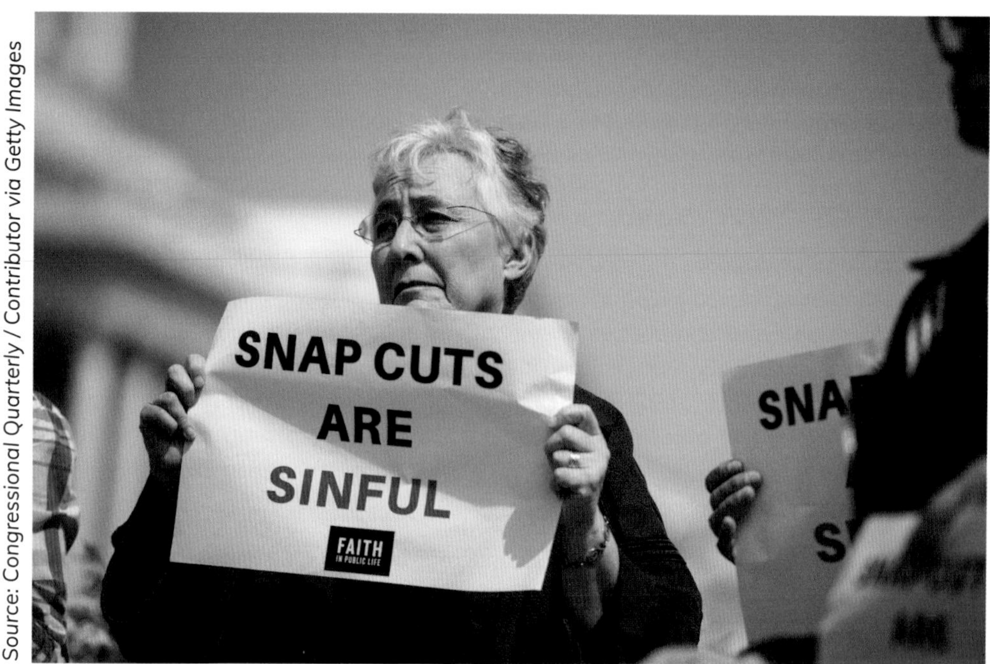

Source: Congressional Quarterly / Contributor via Getty Images

Photo 7.2 **Democrats campaign against food stamp cut proposals in 2018**

> **Exam Tip** – Avoid relying on generalised policy differences (such as stating that Democrats want higher taxes on the wealthy and Republicans want to cut such taxes). As well as explaining general policy goals, you should use contemporary evidence of *specific* party policies. Showing a knowledge of specific examples and congressional politicians can boost your AO1 knowledge levels but also give you a better feel for the extent of disagreement, boosting your analysis and evaluation.

The two main parties take opposing stances on health and welfare benefits. Republicans emphasise the need for self-reliance and individual liberty from government control, often reducing government expenditure and federal welfare programmes. Democrats argue that the socio-economic system gives many individuals limited control over their circumstances in a system that causes unfair levels of inequality. This can be seen in the ongoing battle between Democrats and Republicans over healthcare since Obama managed to pass the Affordable Care Act 2010. This bill ensured that all US citizens had healthcare insurance with subsidies for low-paid workers and those with no income. All Republicans voted against the bill and have since made several (unsuccessful) attempts to repeal it.

» There is an ongoing tussle between Democrats and Republicans over the Supplemental Nutrition Assistance Program (SNAP), in which the Federal Government provides food stamps to those who would otherwise be in food poverty. Republicans have often reduced expenditure on this provision. In 2021 President Biden issued an executive order to make major increases in individual SNAP payments, which, according to the US Agriculture Department, now covers 42 million people. In 2023 the Republican majority House of Representatives forced Democrats into a compromise during the debate on the wider economic issue of raising the debt ceiling. Some Democrats voted for the overall package whilst also being critical of a Republican amendment to SNAP eligibility. Previously 18-50 year olds had to be in work to receive SNAP but Republicans lifted this age range to 55.

As with the other policy areas, there are some underlying agreements as both political parties favour some level of federal provision for welfare. In addition, both parties have responded to the social emergencies such as the COVID-19 pandemic with extensive welfare provisions. Most notably, both parties favour social security spending for the elderly in the form of Medicare. Arguably for Democrats, this is part of their value-based agenda whereas Republicans may be more motivated by the knowledge that older people make up a large and politically active part of their voter base.

» Some overlap can be seen in healthcare policy with a small number of moderate Republicans such as Senator Susan Collins effectively supporting the Affordable Care Act by refusing to vote in favour of Republican proposals to abolish it. During the COVID-19 pandemic in 2021, Democrats and Republicans both agreed to the need for federal intervention. They agreed, for example, on $600 payments for each adult, partly to give funding to those in need but also to stimulate spending in the economy. President Trump and Democrat House Speaker Nancy Pelosi both argued in favour of a higher pay-out cheques of $2,000, although this policy was not agreed by Congress as a whole.

Key Topic Debate Summary: Do Democrats and Republicans have strongly conflicting values and policies?

FOR	KEY CRITERIA	AGAINST
✓ Democrats are far more liberal on issues of social and moral policy than the Republican Party. ✓ There is significant conflict between the two parties in areas such as racial minority, gender and transgender rights, illegal drugs, immigration and police power. ✓ Republicans emphasise the need to maintain strong authority via police power, whereas Democrats tend to promote the rights and power of the individual to a greater extent.	Do the two parties hold conflicting values and policies relating to **moral and social policy?**	✗ There is a consensus between Democrats and Republicans over the protection of certain rights viewed as fundamental. ✗ This particularly relates to legal equality on the grounds of race and a growing consensus supporting gay marriage. ✗ There is some overlap between centre ground Democrats and Republicans, especially with pro-gun Democrats and pro-choice Republicans.
✓ Republicans favour a decreased role for the government in the economy whereas Democrats push for greater federal expenditure and increased taxes on the wealthy. ✓ Democrats are far more critical of free market economics than Republicans.	Do the two parties hold conflicting values and policies relating to **the national economy?**	✗ Both political parties favour free market capitalist economics. ✗ Left-wing critics see both the Republicans and Democrats as protectors of corporate interests. ✗ Democrat and Republicans in Congress have supported similar policies in times of crisis such as global banking crisis in 2000 and the more recent COVID-19 pandemic.
✓ Democrats emphasise the unfairness of socio-economic inequality, whereas Republicans focus on individual responsibility and self-reliance. ✓ Democrats have introduced many federal welfare programmes such as healthcare reform and food stamps. Republicans have typically opposed or attempted to reduce such initiatives.	Do the two parties hold conflicting values and policies relating to **social welfare?**	✗ Both parties favour some form of welfare provision, especially in the form of welfare for the elderly. ✗ There is some overlap, with moderate Republicans seeking to protect Democrat welfare initiatives. ✗ In times of crisis both parties support provision of social welfare.

Exam Tip: Improving AO2 Analysis and AO3 Evaluation

There is a useful distinction between policies driven by values or policies created by pragmatic considerations. A party may get pushed into support for a policy that they would not normally support because of practical or pragmatic reasons such as strongly held public opinion or short-term emergencies. It is possible to argue that this does not represent a real or significant similarity between the two parties. There is a short-term policy agreement but not a long-term ideological one. Consider how you could apply this to different parties, politicians or policies.

Learning Review

1. What are the three main policy areas that are used to explore similarities and differences between the Democratic and Republican parties?
2. What are the main differences in policy between Democrats and Republicans in each of these three policy areas? Can you name specific policy examples to illustrate each difference?
3. What are the main similarities in policy between Democrats and Republicans in each of these three policy areas? Can you name specific policy examples to illustrate each similarity?

CONFLICTS WITHIN PARTIES

The Democratic and Republican parties each have a great deal of ideological diversity within them, covering a range of opinions in the United States. The two parties are often seen as weak in the sense that they are internally divided. In addition, party leaders within Congress have limited powers to control party politicians. Political rivalry within a party is often organised around **factions** who compete to determine the policy direction of the party. Many of these factions are organised into congressional caucuses that are organised groups with leaders, regular meetings and agreed strategies.

Definition

Factions: Subgroups of a political party often based on a distinctive ideology or set of policies.

KEY TOPIC DEBATE: ARE EACH OF THE MAIN FACTIONS IN THE DEMOCRATIC PARTY POWERFUL?

The Democratic Party is characterised by a significant, ongoing division between two main factions. Liberals, often referred to as progressives, are the more left wing of the two factions. They compete with moderates, who aim to shift the party to the centre ground of US politics. This ongoing battle is often reflected in presidential primaries for the Democratic Party in which liberals/progressives and moderates compete to run for their party to win the presidency. In addition, there is a smaller group of conservative Democrats who can hold power in certain political contexts, as we will see.

Liberals or progressives

Liberals/progressives are the more left wing or liberal of the main Democrat factions. They are seen as most determined in their desire to fight for social justice. This means that progressives have a stronger desire to regulate the economy, protect socio-economically disadvantaged groups and fight for equality for minorities. In particular, progressives are associated with the protection of workers' rights and the provision of a strong role for government in the form of policies such as free healthcare and education.

Many progressives join the Congressional Progressive Caucus (CPC) (see Figure 7.1), which includes chair Pramila Jayapal as well as Senator Bernie Sanders. Some progressives have chosen to join this formal caucus and some have opted to operate outside it, suggesting that the names progressive, moderate and conservative can also represent loose ideological movements within the party as much as an organised group.

Source: Jemal Countess / Stringer via Getty Images

Photo 7.3: Progressive Caucus Chair Pramila Jayapal

Membership in Congress in 2023
Seats in the House: 100
Seats in the Senate: 1

Figure 7.1 The Congressional Progressive Caucus (CPC)

In economic policy, progressives have been particularly vocal in their opposition to the Trans-Pacific Partnership (TPP), a trade agreement involving the United States and eleven other countries including Japan and Australia. Progressives in the party, such as Senator Elizabeth Warren, attacked the position of President Obama, a keen advocate of TPP, because international free trade can harm the job prospects of lower paid US workers. Progressives are closely aligned with America's largest trade union, the AFL-CIO (American Federation of Labor and Congress of Industrial Organizations), who oppose the trade deal.

In welfare policy, progressives push for a greater government role in the provision of health and education benefits such as the cancellation of student debt. In 2023 CPC Chair Pramila Jayapal strongly supported the Biden executive order to cancel $10,000 of all student's debt but wanted this forgiveness figure to be much higher. Progressives are also associated with a policy called single-payer healthcare. This policy would pay for health insurance for everyone with general taxation. Senator Sanders ran on a 2016 and 2020 platform that pushed for single-payer healthcare as well as free college tuition for all. This is a move that many Democrats do not support, typically stating excessive taxpayer cost.

✓ Liberals/progressives are a significant force as the largest ideological caucus in the Democratic Party. With high numbers, they have a strong voice within Congress and a higher impact when voting. The CPC under the leadership of Jayapal has continuously pushed the Biden administration to adopt or protect progressive policies. Jayapal has had regular meetings with senior White House staff, particularly regarding the passage of major bills and scored successes with Biden's policy of cancelling student debt in 2023.

✓ The progressive faction of the Democrats is experiencing an increase in its profile and power. Some of this stems from the failure of moderate Democrat Hillary Clinton to win the presidency in 2016. This gave greater authority to progressives who could claim that their brand of Democrat policy was more popular amongst core voters. Progressives are ensuring that their policy positions are a central part of the debate within the party with greater acceptance of calls for a $15 minimum wage and a single-payer healthcare policy. Progressive Congresswoman Alexandria Ocasio Cortez hailed Biden's first 100 days as exceeding progressive expectations.

✓ Progressives are rising to more prominent positions within the party and in the eyes of the public. This is helping to push moderate candidates further to the left to maintain support. The rise of Senator Bernie Sanders as a close rival to Hillary Clinton in the 2016 Democrat primaries is likely to be a reason why she eventually opposed the Keystone Pipeline during the primary campaign. Progressives such as Sanders opposed the pipeline, which would carry oil from Canada to both Illinois and Texas, for environmental reasons.

✗ Progressive Democrats in Congress are outnumbered by moderate and conservative Democrats. As such, few of their main policy ideals have passed Congress with single-payer healthcare and the $15 minimum wage increase failing to gain sufficient support to have it placed into US law. Nancy Pelosi, the long-serving House Speaker, is clearly on the progressive side of the party but as a pragmatist has led the party to compromises with moderate Democrats and Republicans. On the retirement of Pelosi, House Democrats were then led by Hakeem Jeffries. Whilst he is a former member of the CPC, he is seen as pragmatic and in the centre of his party.

✗ Progressives have not been successful in winning Democratic primaries or other key positions. Clinton and Biden as moderate Democrats won the primaries in 2016 and 2020 and the two most recent Democrat presidents are best described as moderate. Moderate Chuck Schumer has been the Democrat majority leader of the Senate since 2021 and has resisted many progressive measures.

✗ Progressives are hampered by their ideological position on one end of the ideological spectrum of the United States. Moderate and conservative Democrats' positions are more likely to pass Congress with moderate Republican support. This is a particular problem when Democrats have a slim majority and either need all Democrats to unite around a policy or to gain Republican support.

Moderates

Moderate Democrats are less critical of the unregulated economy and levels of inequality than progressives. They do not call for such a strong role for government in trying to overcome inequalities. Whilst they might support Obama's Affordable Care Act and oppose Republican efforts to repeal it, they do not necessarily support more radical health proposals such as Sanders's Medicare for All Act or calls for free college tuition.

In economic policy they are more likely to accept Republican Party arguments for lower taxes and lower federal expenditure or be more cautious about tax rises. They are more likely to support free trade agreements or defend stronger security policy than their progressive counterparts.

The moderate position is associated with senior Democrats such as Senator Chuck Schumer, Senate majority leader in 2024, and Hillary Clinton. The most notable moderate caucus in Congress is the New Democrat Coalition, which describe themselves as 'a solutions oriented coalition seeking to bridge the gap between left and right by challenging outmoded partisan approaches to governing. New Democrats believe the challenges ahead are too great for Members of Congress to refuse to cooperate purely out of partisanship' (https://newdemocratcoalition.house.gov/about-us). The New Democrat Coalition (see Figure 7.2) lists ninety-six members in the House in 2023. Annie Kuster, chair of the caucus, opposes free college tuition and criticised Sanders' Medicare for All Act as being too expensive.

Figure 7.2 **New Democrat Coalition**

✓ Moderates in the House grew in numbers as a result of the swing towards Democrats in the 2018 mid-term elections, in which Democrats won many marginal House districts. Many are keen to maintain centrist positions or even compromise with Republicans to maintain popularity for upcoming elections. Whilst they supported Biden's successful Infrastructure Investment and Jobs Act, moderates were largely happy to accept reductions on the overall spending plan.

✓ Moderates have been successful in holding critical positions within the Democratic Party, with Hillary Clinton, Obama and Biden all being closely associated with moderate Democrats. Senator Chuck Schumer has also played a key role as the leader of Senate Democrats in recent years. This has helped policy successes reflect a moderate Democrat agenda that progressives have often criticised as being excessively right wing. Progressives such as Ocasio Cortez have frequently criticised the policy and approach of other senior Democrats such as Biden and Schumer for being too willing to compromise with Republicans or for not being sufficiently radical in policy proposals.

✓ Moderates have an advantageous ideological position because they can argue that more progressive policies will not receive the much-needed votes from conservative Democrats or moderate Republicans to pass through Congress. In short, their position is the only one with a chance to gain sufficient congressional support. They held a more important role after Republicans took control of the House in the mid-term elections of 2022, as they can compromise with moderate Republicans to achieve policy success. This faction is aided by the Problem Solvers Caucus, a bipartisan group of moderate Democrats and Republicans which seeks to overcome gridlock in Congress by finding cross-party agreements. Their website lists sixty-three members in 2023, allowing them to hold the balance of power within the lower chamber.

✗ Moderates are engaged in an ongoing struggle with progressive Democrats to determine the policy direction of the party. The limits to moderates' power and evidence of their failure can be seen in the outline of the success and power of progressive Democrats, which we have already explored.

Conservative Democrats

Historically, the Democratic Party held very conservative attitudes, supporting the continuation of slavery and separate facilities based on race. The party therefore remained popular in the South until southern Democrats became a declining force as the party transformed, especially in the 1960s, starting to lead the way on racial minority rights. A conservative wing remains today and whilst it certainly no longer supports segregation, this group is conservative on moral and social issues and sometimes economic ones. This faction tends to oppose the dominant view of their party by supporting gun rights and being less supportive of gay rights or abortion. Conservative Democrats opposed Obama's Affordable Care Act (with thirty-nine Democrats voting against in total), many citing its abortion provisions as a major reason for this.

The main conservative faction is represented by the Blue Dog Coalition. Its Co-Chair, Jared Golden, opposed Biden's student debt forgiveness programme and many members of the Blue Dog Coalition also voted against Biden's plan to protect clean water in the United States. There are other conservative Democrats in Congress who are not part of the Blue Dog Coalition, which is based in the House of Representatives only. Senator Joe Manchin is a pro-life, pro-gun politician who has been endorsed by the National Rifle Association, who is not part of the Blue Dog Coalition. Manchin represented a Republican State (West Virginia) between 2010 and 2024. Biden only achieved 29% of the vote in this state in 2020. Only a conservative Democrat has a realistic chance of electoral success there.

Source: Paul Morigi / Stringer via Getty Images

Photo 7.5 **Jared Golden, one of the co-chairs of the Blue Dog Coalition**

Figure 7.3 **The Blue Dog Coalition**

✓ Conservatives, whilst a relatively small group, often hold the balance of power during a Democrat presidency. Without the support of conservative Democrats, a Democrat president may not be able to pass their policy proposals. Conservative Democrats played a key role in slowing down and opposing certain aspects of President Obama's Affordable Care Act, eventually forcing Obama to drop a major part of his bill, the public option, which would have created a federal health insurance company to compete with private insurers.

✓ Under the Biden presidency, conservative Democrat Senator Joe Manchin was instrumental in undermining some of Biden's agenda, especially those policies pushed by progressive Democrats. This came about because the Democrats had such a slim majority in the Senate (after both the 2020 and 2022 elections) and usually needed all Democrat votes to pass a measure through the upper chamber. Whilst the vast majority of Democrats support a rise in the federal minimum wage to $15, the policy foundered as a result of opposition from Manchin alone.

✗ Conservative Democrats may be successful in blocking or moderating some policies proposed by moderate and progressive Democrats but find it difficult to achieve policy goals of their own. This means they are successful where they support the status quo but have not been able to bring about a reduction in gun regulations or greater restrictions on abortion, for example.

✗ At other times they cannot even block a policy they dislike. In 2023 Manchin was one of four Democrats in the Senate (alongside some Blue Dog Democrats in the House) who voted to oppose a Biden administration regulation aimed to promote and protect clean water. Manchin voted with

Republicans arguing it provided too much regulation restricting the farming industry alongside other corporations. This pushed Biden into issuing the second veto of his presidency in 2023, blocking the goal of conservative Democrats as well as Republicans.

✖ Conservative Democrats are very small in number and have declined a great deal since the 1960s; their overall influence in the party is dwindling. At times when Democrats have a sizeable majority, the faction becomes less significant. They declined even further as a result of the mid-term elections of 2022 leaving them with just eight members.

Key Topic Debate Summary: Are each of the main factions in the Democratic Party powerful?

FOR	KEY CRITERIA	AGAINST
✓ High numbers give a strong voice within Congress and a higher impact when voting. ✓ The progressive faction of the Democrats is experiencing an increase in power. Progressives are ensuring that their policy positions are a central part of the debate within the party. ✓ Progressives are rising to more prominent positions within the party and in the eyes of the public.	Are **liberal / progressives** a powerful force?	✖ Progressive Democrats in Congress are outnumbered by moderate and conservative Democrats. As such they have been unsuccessful in achieving their policy goals. ✖ Progressives have not been successful in winning Democratic primaries or other key positions. ✖ Progressives are hampered by their ideological position on one end of the ideological spectrum of the United States with moderate and conservative Democrats' positions more likely to pass Congress with moderate Republican support.
✓ Moderates in the House grew in numbers as a result of the swing towards Democrats in the 2018 mid-term election. Many are keen to maintain centrist positions or even compromise with Republicans to maintain popularity and get re-elected. ✓ Moderates have been successful in holding the critical positions within the Democratic Party with Hillary Clinton, Obama and Biden all being closely associated with moderate Democrats. ✓ Moderates can argue that more progressive policies will not receive enough votes from conservative Democrats or moderate conservatives to pass through Congress	Are **moderates** a powerful force?	✖ Moderates are engaged in a battle with progressives. The progressives are emerging as the more dominant force in the Democratic Party. ✖ Progressives are gaining more prominent positions in the Democratic Party in the House, undermining the power of moderates.

continued

✓ Conservatives often hold the balance of power during a Democrat presidency. ✓ They become more powerful if Democrats have a small majority in Congress or can help Republicans achieve their goals. Without support of conservative Democrats, a Democrat president may not be able to pass their policy proposals.	Are **conservatives** a powerful force?	✗ As a very small group, conservative Democrats find it difficult to achieve policy goals of their own. This means they are successful where they support the status quo but have not been able to bring about a reduction in gun regulations or greater restrictions on abortion. ✗ Conservative Democrats have declined a great deal since the 1960s. As such their overall influence in the party is dwindling.

Exam Tip: Improving AO2 Analysis and AO3 Evaluation

It is important for you to arrive at a well-supported judgement about which faction is the most powerful. Additionally, you can add to your analysis and evaluation by examining the impact of the changing political context. Election results can affect the relative power of factions. Progressives are most likely to achieve their policy goals when there is a Democrat not a Republican heading the White House. Conservatives will be influential when Democrats hold a small majority in Congress but can see their power vanish if Democrats have a commanding lead in congressional election results.

KEY TOPIC DEBATE: ARE EACH OF THE MAIN FACTIONS WITHIN THE REPUBLICAN PARTY POWERFUL?

Arguably, the Republican Party is more factionalised than the Democrats with a greater number of ideological subgroups. Having said that, it is commonly argued that Republicans are generally more united around a conservative fiscal and moral agenda. They pushed to the right from the 1990s onwards in response to the Bill Clinton and Obama presidencies. In addition, the aggressive leadership of the Trump presidency made Republicans fear speaking out against the president, further uniting the party. Despite being part of different factions, there is arguably a limited difference between the two major groups of moderate and conservative Republicans.

Moderates

Moderate Republicans are closest to the centre ground within the Republican Party. It is these Republicans who are most likely to find common ground with Democrats. Whilst they might be fiscally conservative they would not seek tax cuts or federal expenditure cuts to the level pushed for by fiscally conservative Republicans. The moderate nature of these Republicans is seen in their approach to economic policy, social and moral policy or both. They might be more willing to accept federal involvement in the economy or welfare provision or be likely to raise concerns about a lack of civil rights protections.

There are several different organisations, inside and beyond Congress, that represent moderate Republicans. Some Congressional politicians are members of more than one group at the same time. The Republican Governance Group had forty-two Republican House members in 2023 but the largest moderate group is the Main Street Caucus (see Figure 7.4). Whilst they are more moderate than other factions in the Republican Party, it can be argued that they hold policy positions which are relatively close to the more right-wing factions in the party.

Whilst moderates make up a sizeable faction in the Republican Party, there is only a very small number of particularly moderate politicians who tend to resist the more conservative agenda of the party as a whole. Very few Republicans voted against the agenda of President Trump and Republican congressional leaders. The two notable figures in the Republican Party are Senators Lisa Murkowski (Alaska) and Susan Collins (Maine). Under the Biden presidency, the divisions are more apparent, with moderate Republicans being more likely to accept Biden and Democrat positions. This suggests that Democrats are more united than Republicans, with Democrat President Biden able to get some support for his measures, as well as nominations to the executive and legislature from more moderate Republicans.

Source: Tom Williams / Contributor via Getty Images

Photo 7.6 **Chair of Main Street Caucus Dusty Johnson**

Membership in Congress: 2023
Seats in the House: 67
Seats in the Senate: 5

Figure 7.4 **The Main Street Caucus**

✓ Moderate Republicans have the ideological advantage of being able to compromise with Democrats. They can be especially influential when there is a small Democrat majority in Congress. They can seek to water down the more progressive elements of Democrat policy in return for moderate Republican support to pass moderate Democrat bills.

✓ Moderates were also successful during the Trump presidency as a result of the Republicans' small majority in the Senate. A very small number of moderate Republican senators blocked some of the Republican Party's more conservative policies. Senator Susan Collins, for example, had a major impact in effectively blocking the repeal of the Affordable Care Act.

✗ The Republican Party has shifted to the right since the 1990s with the decline of moderate forces within the Republican Party. Fiscal conservatism has come to dominate the party.

✗ The Trump presidency marked a further decline in the power of moderates within the party. President Trump, with his aggressive leadership style and activist following, generated high levels of loyalty to his policy positions. This meant that socially conservative policies dominated party thinking, for example on immigration and transgender rights.

Fiscal conservatives

Fiscal conservatives are arguably the dominant group within the Republican Party. They focus on reducing the role of government in economic and welfare policy. In other words, they want to reduce welfare expenditure and lower taxation and government expenditure in general. This group began its ascendancy in the 1990s under the leadership of Republican House speaker Newt Gingrich, who aggressively pushed the idea of balanced budget politics. A balanced budget requires the government to spend less than their income for a specific year and is something that almost never happens in the modern United States.

Fiscal conservatives have pushed for major reductions in government expenditure as well as the lowering of taxation such as corporate tax and income tax for high earners. Fiscal conservatives have also sought to deregulate the economy, allowing corporations greater freedom. This group is also associated with a determination to reduce federal welfare provisions. They are less likely to accept compromise with Democrats on key issues, with many fiscal conservatives taking a highly partisan approach, refusing any attempts at negotiation with Democrats.

The main caucus promoting fiscal conservativism is the Republican Study Committee (RSC) in the House of Representatives (see Figure 7.5). Its main focus is to achieve major cuts in non-defence spending and deregulation of the economy, but it has also advocated conservative legislation in areas such as abortion and guns.

Photo 7.7 **Republican Study Committee Chair, Kevin Hern**

Source: Bill Clark / Contributor via Getty Images

Figure 7.5 **The Republican Study Committee**

In addition, there is an ultra-conservative group called the Freedom Caucus. Whilst it has smaller numbers (thirty-three in the House in 2023) its votes are often needed for the Republicans to get over the 50% plus line when the House votes. These ultra conservatives take even more right-wing economic positions but are also quite aggressive in their tactics and unwillingness to compromise. In this sense it is hard to ignore this caucus. In 2023 many members of the Freedom Caucus would not vote for Kevin McCarthy to become the head of the Republicans in the House, declining to support his bid to become House speaker. They pushed McCarthy into a series of compromises over the organisation of the party and caused McCarthy to have to go through fifteen ballots of Republican House members, the longest House speaker battle since 1859, before he gained sufficient support across the Republican Party. MCarthy was forced to resign after less than a year in post as a result of opposition from just eight hard right members of the House Freedom Caucus members. They initiated a motion to vacate and force him out, with these eight and all Democrats then voting to remove McCarthy. Their success can be seen in his eventual replacement, Mike Johnson who is even more conservative than MCarthy.

✓ Fiscal conservatism has become the dominant force in the Republican Party in recent years. Even more moderate Republicans are pressurised into accepting fiscally conservative positions. This can be seen in the success of fiscal conservatives in reducing taxes from 39% to 21%, including corporation tax, under the Trump presidency. The deregulation of the economy under President Trump was a huge victory for fiscal conservatives with a major reduction in environmental regulations, for example. Almost 80% of House Republicans were members of the Republican Study Committee in 2023, showing the dominance of this group.

✓ Fiscal conservatives have the advantage of wanting to block new proposals for federal expenditure and welfare. It is much easier to block legislation in Congress than to successfully execute new policy initiatives. The determination of fiscal conservatives has contributed to legislative gridlock and federal shutdown as they have refused to compromise on reductions in federal expenditure.

✖ Fiscal conservatives are less likely to be influential overall during Democrat presidencies if the Democrats also have a majority in both chambers of Congress. Whilst all Republicans opposed Biden's Inflation Reduction Act, fiscal conservatives would be particularly dismayed at the major increases in expenditure and taxation on the wealthy. They may dominate the thinking of the Republican Party but may be unable to achieve any of their policy aims when the Democrats dominate the presidency and/or Congress.

✖ The COVID-19 pandemic and global warming have both challenged fiscal conservative values because they require major government intervention in the economy and welfare. Both Republican President Donald Trump and Democrat President Joe Biden successfully proposed major financial stimulus packages to combat the impact of COVID-19. Fiscally conservative Republicans have been unhappy with the level of regulation of businesses as well as the amount of welfare provided for individuals.

✖ For further limits or failures see the discussion on the successes of moderate Republicans.

Social conservatives

Social conservatives tend to focus their attentions on moral policy, typically applying conservative Christian values to their decision-making. Socially conservative Republicans are part of the **religious right**, typically evangelical Christians who see it as their duty to protect their religious moral vision. Social conservatives will typically address policy areas such as abortion, gay and transgender rights, and immigration. Whilst this group has no organised congressional caucus, it has become a significant group within the Republican Party, influencing Republican thinking on moral issues. Whilst social conservatives focus on this specific policy area many are also associated with fiscal conservative values.

Spec key term

Religious right: A movement of conservative Christians who campaign on social issues such as abortion, gay rights and immigration.

✔ Social Conservatives have grown in importance since the 1980s with an increase in evangelical activism in politics and growth in the number of senior Republicans in Congress who are evangelicals. Senator Ted Cruz and Vice President Mike Pence have exerted considerable influence in recent years. They achieved many policy victories under the Trump presidency, including a ban on transgender individuals serving in the military and a much more aggressive immigration policy. The selection of Mike Johnson to be the Republican Speaker of the House is a major boost to social conservatives. Johnson has strongly opposed gay and transgender rights and in 2023 likened abortion in the United States to 'a holocaust'.

✔ Social conservatives are highly influential within the Republican Party because they represent a major part of the Republican support base. Exit polls from the 2020 election show that 28% of voters identified as evangelicals. President Trump received over 75% of their votes. In short, Republican candidates at a national level often rely on evangelical support for electoral success, pressurising Republican presidential primary races to adopt popular evangelical candidates.

✖ Social conservatives can be limited by moderates in the party. They are weaker when the Republican Party has a small majority in Congress, relying on moderate support to pass bills. See the success of moderate Republicans for further evidence of the failure of evangelicals.

✖ Social conservatives do not have a formal caucus within Congress, suggesting that Republicans want to focus on social and economic policy reform more than moral issues.

Key Topic Debate Summary: Are each of the main factions within the Republican Party powerful?

FOR	KEY CRITERIA	AGAINST
✓ Moderates have the ideological advantage as they are able to compromise with Democrats. They can be especially influential when there is a small Democrat majority. ✓ Moderates were successful during the Trump presidency as a result of the Republicans' small majority in the Senate, effectively blocking the repeal of the Affordable Care Act, for example.	Are **moderates** a powerful force?	✗ The Republican Party has shifted to the right since the 1990s with a major decline in moderate forces within the party. Fiscal conservatism has come to dominate the party. ✗ Socially conservative policies, for example on immigration and transgender rights, have dominated party thinking.
✓ Fiscal conservatism has become the dominant force in the Republican Party in recent years. Even more moderate Republicans are pressurised into accepting fiscally conservative positions. ✓ Fiscal conservatives have the advantage of attempting to block new proposals for federal expenditure and welfare. It is much easier to block legislation in Congress than to successfully execute new policy initiatives.	Are **fiscal conservatives** a powerful force?	✗ Fiscal conservatives are less likely to be influential overall during Democrat presidencies if the Democrats also have a majority in both chambers of Congress. ✗ Social and economic crises have challenged fiscal conservative values. This has required major government intervention in the economy and welfare.
✓ Social conservatives have dominated Republican Party thinking in recent years with a growing number in the party and significant policy wins during the Trump presidency. ✓ Evangelicals make up a large number of voters, especially amongst Republican Party supporters, influencing the policy of individual politicians who seek (re)-election.	Are **social conservatives** a powerful force?	✗ Social conservatives can lack power as a result of moderate Republican opposition to their policies. ✗ They are less likely to achieve policy goals with a small Republican congressional majority or during times of divided government in which Democrats will not compromise with them.

Exam Tip: Improving AO2 analysis and AO3 evaluation

The power of a faction within a party can be measured by the extent to which they achieve policy goals. Focus your analysis on the extent to which factions are able to put their policy aims into practice. You should do this by showing policy details and what passed or failed to be adopted by the party or Congress as a whole. There is also a useful distinction between factions bringing about change by introducing new policies and being successful in blocking the proposals of others. Arguably the former shows a higher degree of success.

Evaluative View

Of the three main factions, fiscal conservatives are clearly the dominant force within the Republican Party. This can be seen in the size of the fiscal conservatives faction, which is by far the biggest group within the party. In addition, this faction has controlled the policy direction of the party, achieving many of their main economic policy goals. The party as a whole has moved right, causing polarisation with the Democrats since the 1990s. It is true that social conservatives have made some gains in achieving their policy goals in recent years and that moderates have blocked some changes proposed by fiscal conservatives. These achievements, however, are not as significant as the policy achievements of fiscal conservatives in shifting the focus of the whole of US politics further to the right.

Consider the key topic debate and debate summary as well as any new evidence you can find. Do you agree or disagree with this evaluative view?

COALITION OF SUPPORTERS

Specific social groups can show particular voting patterns, especially in terms of consistent support for one political party. The two main parties often rely on key voting groups with a particular demographic generally loyal in their support. In this section we will explore the extent to which certain groups of voters show a strong preference for one party over the other. This is summarised in statistics from the *New York Times* exit polls seen in Figure 7.6.

GENDER

Men and women vote in roughly equal numbers for the Democratic or Republican Party, although there is a long-standing pattern in which more men typically vote Republican and more women typically vote Democrat. For example, 57% of female voters selected Biden rather than Trump in the 2020

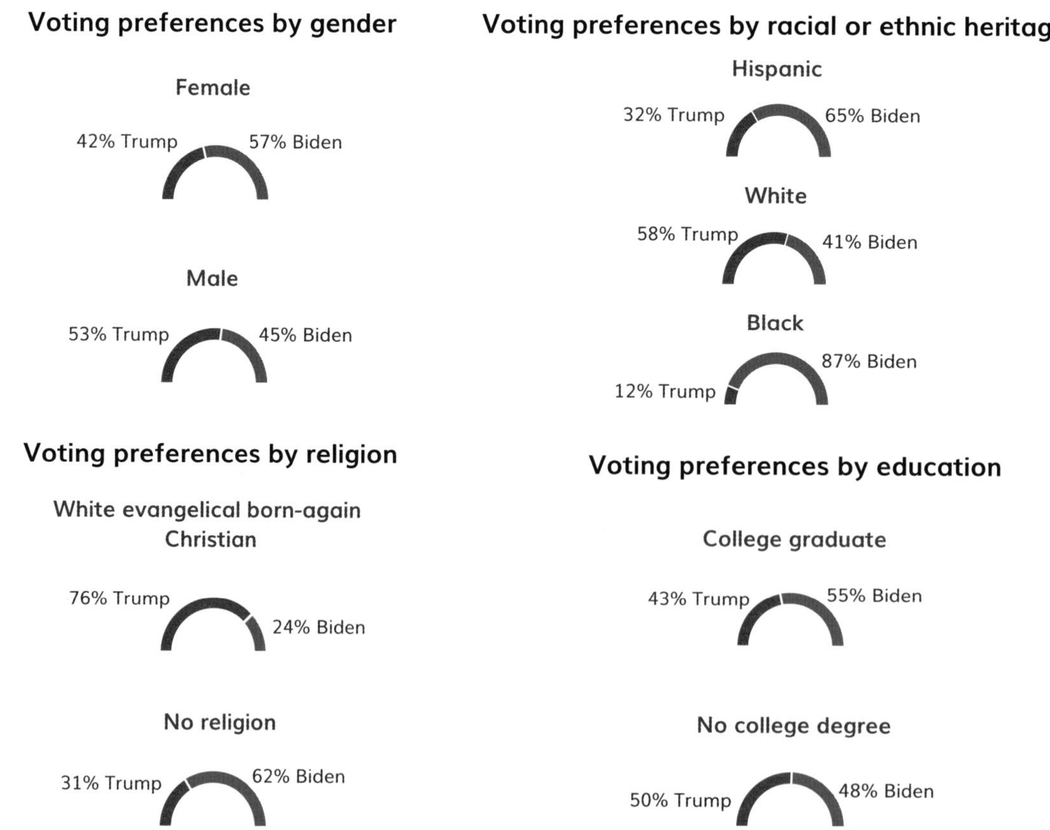

Figure 7.6 **Voting preference by different social groups in the 2020 presidential election**

election. Women may have a marginal preference for Democrats as the party that has campaigned heavily for women's rights. It was the Democratic Party that initiated the Violence Against Women Act, funding the investigation and prosecution of violent crimes against women, whereas Republicans have been reluctant to renew this act in recent years, for example.

✓ There is a clear trend of women showing a stronger preference for the Democratic Party, as seen in the 2020 election with 57% of women voting for Biden.

✓ This is consistent with other recent elections; in 2012, 55% of women voted for the Democrat candidate and in 2016 this figure was 54%.

✗ There is no major difference between the vote preference of men and women, with a relatively small percentage point difference in support of men between the Democratic and Republican parties. Whilst the gap has been wider in recent years, in 2020 men split 45% to 53% for Biden and Trump.

✗ Other social groups are far more significant in determining voting behaviour. If we combine gender with racial groups, we can see a much bigger division in support between the Democratic and Republican parties. As Table 7.1 shows, 87% of Black men and 95% of Black women supported Biden in the 2020 election. This data suggests that race is far more important than gender in influencing voting patterns.

Table 7.1 **Voter preference by gender and race in the 2020 election**

	Biden	Trump
Black men	87%	12%
Black women	95%	5%
Hispanic men	57%	40%
Hispanic women	61%	37%
White men	40%	57%
White women	46%	53%

Source: Pew Research Center.

RACE

Given the racist history of the United States and the ongoing concerns surrounding race today, it is unsurprising that there are major divisions amongst different racial groups in their support for a particular party. It is this social group that shows some of the biggest indicators of voter preference. There is a huge difference in Black support for the Democrats and Republicans, whilst this difference is lower amongst Hispanic voters it is still extremely significant. This racial difference has been apparent since the 1960s as the Democratic Party has increasingly supported measures to promote racial equality.

✓ Racial minority groups show overwhelming support for the Democratic Party. This can be seen in the 87% of Black voters who opted for Biden in the 2020 election, as well as the 65% of Hispanic voters who chose the Democrats. Although it could be argued that socio-economics is a contributing factor, when over 90% of Black voters support the Democrat candidate in many elections, it is clear that race is the driving factor here.

✓ Other racial minority groups show a strong preference for the Democratic Party. Native American voters typically support the Democratic Party while there is a clear majority support amongst white voters for the Republicans. The Republican candidate gained around 58% of the white vote in the 2012, 2016 and 2020 presidential elections.

✗ Hispanic voters have been more volatile, with Republicans managing to secure significant Hispanic support. The high point for the Republicans came in 2004 when George W. Bush managed to secure 44% of the Hispanic vote. Also, party support amongst white voters is not as predictable as it is for other racial groups, with a lower percentage point difference in how this group splits for Democrats and Republicans.

RELIGION

There is also a correlation between a person's religion and their voting preference. Unsurprisingly, the clearest evidence of this relates to white evangelical voters who typically support the Republican Party. There are many evangelicals within the Republican caucus in Congress, such as Senator Ted Cruz, a strong opponent of gay and transgender rights and opponent of liberal border policies. Immigration in the United States is seen by many white evangelicals as a threat to traditional conservative Christian values. There is also a clear division amongst Jewish voters, who strongly support the Democratic Party. American Jews tend to strongly identify with liberal values supporting the redistribution of wealth.

✓ There is very strong support amongst white evangelical born-again Christians for the Republican Party, with 76% in this group voting for Trump in the 2020 election. There is a consistent pattern in recent years of white evangelicals strongly opting for the Republican Party.

✓ Other religious groupings such as Jewish people and those without religion also provide a strong indicator of voter preference.

✗ The difference amongst Christians in general in their support for the Democrats or Republicans is not so clear, with Catholics typically favouring the Democratic Party over the Republican Party, albeit by a very small margin. The difference only becomes strongly apparent when we factor in the conservative values of *white evangelical* Christians.

EDUCATION

The higher the level of education, the more likely it is that a person will support the Democratic Party. This is perhaps surprising given that education also correlates with wealth. Whilst higher income groups have historically tended to support the Republican Party, education is now emerging as a more important factor. President Trump's populist agenda and his anti-elitism and nationalism attracted support from those in lower education groups. There is a connection between education and ideology with the prevalence of liberal values amongst the more highly educated.

✓ The higher the level of education, the more liberal that person is likely to be. This can be seen in the 55% of college-educated voters who supported Biden in the 2020 election with this figure rising to 67% for those who completed postgraduate education.

✗ Education is only emerging as an important factor in more recent elections. In fact, there was a smaller gap in support for the Democrats versus Republicans amongst college-educated voters in 2020 compared to 2016 and 2012.

✗ Again, other social groupings particularly race and income and age may have a bigger bearing on voter choice than levels of education.

Learning Review

1. What are the three main factions of the Democratic Party? What are the arguments for and against each of these groups being influential within the party?
2. What are the main caucus groups within the Democratic Party and who are the key figures in each group?
3. What are the three main factions of the Republican Party? What are the arguments for and against each of these groups being influential within the party?
4. What are the main caucus groups within the Republican Party and who are the key figures in each group?
5. Which social groups tend to support the Democratic Party and which tend to support the Republican Party? What does the evidence from 2020 tell us?

Comparative Learning Review

1. How unified are the main parties in the United States compared to the United Kingdom?

THE SIGNIFICANCE OF INTEREST GROUPS

The term 'interest group' refers to any group that is not elected but attempts to influence those in power. Many interest groups attempt to promote a specific cause that they feel strongly about, such as the environment, civil liberties or the removal of nuclear weapons. Others might be more self-interested, attempting to promote the specific interest of their members such as trade unions or racial minority groups. Corporations also act as interest groups given their strong interest and influence in relation to government policy. Figure 7.7 gives details of four important interest groups in the United States today.

The American Association of Retired Persons (AARP)

AARP promotes issues relating to those over the age of 50. It is hugely influential because it is the largest interest group in the United States with over 38 million members. Given that older people are far more politically active, this group has major political clout, in particular, it has successfully protected or expanded Medicare expenditure. The members' magazines are the two largest-circulation publications in the United States. It regularly calls on its members to contact their senator or congressman over bills introduced in Congress.

The American Federation of Labor and Congress of Industrial Organizations (AFL-CIO)

The AFL-CIO is the largest trade union organisation in the United States and has over 12 million members. It has strong links with the Democratic Party, making major donations to them and using its huge membership to canvass for higher voter turnout at elections. It is opposed to free trade agreements (which threaten US workers) and has pushed for better working conditions, including an increase in the federal minimum wage.

American Israel Public Affairs Committee (AIPAC)

AIPAC is a pro-Israel lobby in the United States calling for more US support for the Israeli state. Whilst it only has a small membership it has enormous influence over politicians of both parties. It is common for its conferences to be attended by the vast majority of congressional politicians from both parties. Joe Biden (as vice president), then-senator Kamala Harris and Donald Trump (as a 2016 presidential candidate) have given addresses to their conventions.

League of Conservation Voters (LCV)

LCV is a pro-environment group that aims to exert influence mainly through influencing electoral outcomes. It monitors the voting record of each politician, as well as their links to organisations such as energy companies. It campaigns in favour of pro-environment candidates but is most well known for its Dirty Dozen Campaign. At each election, the LCV targets twelve politicians with the worst environmental voting record mainly through negative TV adverts.

Figure 7.7 **Selected interest groups in the United States**

Interest groups can be categorised into three main strands: policy groups, professional groups and single-interest groups.

RESOURCES

Interest groups can utilise their resources to exert considerable influence in the US political system. Some interest groups have hugely significant resources:

- Membership – An active membership might lobby members of Congress to support or oppose legislative proposals. In addition, interest groups with a large membership can have significant voting power in general elections. As such, they may be very persuasive over politicians in Congress.
- Money – Many groups have major financial resources drawn from donations or membership subscriptions. This money can be used for effective publicity campaigns, to hire professional lobbyists or to donate money to political parties. Corporations typically have huge finances.

Spec key term

Policy group: Any group that attempts to influence whole policy areas.

Professional group: A group based on a specific profession which represent the interests of their members.

Single-interest group: A groups that focus on a limited or specific issue such as the National Rifle Association.

Definition

Revolving door: A process in which politicians and their advisers move on to work for corporations and vice versa. This establishes a policy network of close connections between business and politicians.

- *Expertise* – As a result of their specialism, these groups can be highly influential when lobbying politicians and their advisers. Many interest groups use legal expertise to fight cases in the court system.
- *Networking* – Interest groups will seek to maximise political connections, often by employing former politicians or their advisers. There are a huge number of professional lobbyist companies based in Washington who specialise in establishing political connections through the **revolving door**. You can see details of a professional lobbyist, Akin Gump, and its work in Table 7.2

Table 7.2 Akin Gump Strauss, a professional lobbyist

Akin Gump Strauss	
Annual turnover	$1 billion
Employs	69 lobbyists 1,000+ lawyers
Revolving door staff	73.9%
Clients include	AT&T, Exxon Mobil, Healthcare Leadership Council, American Airlines, the Japanese Government
Interest groups, especially corporations, employ the services of professional lobbyists to give them greater access to the political world. This is an enormous business in the United States. Akin Gump Strauss is typically the biggest professional lobbyist company in the United States and has major connections with the White House and Capitol Hill. It employs three former members of Congress, a former adviser to President Bill Clinton and many former advisers to members of Congress. It carefully monitors policy statements and bills on behalf of its clients and uses its connections to lobby members of Congress to change bills so that they favour the interests of their clients.	

TACTICS

The tactics of pressure groups are the main methods they use to achieve their policy goals:

- *Lobbying* – This involves interest groups contacting and persuading those in power. This can be done directly by interest group leaders or professional lobbyists employed by the interest group. Alternatively, many interest groups use their websites and social media to urge their members to contact politicians.
- *Direct action and demonstrations* – Interest groups often organise demonstrations, typically as a high-profile way of showing strong feelings. Sometimes direct action is used to disrupt politicians or a particular activity that the interest group is campaigning against.
- *Legal methods* – Interest groups can litigate by taking a case to court, often to protect an individual or to overturn a government policy. Interest groups are also able to issue amicus briefs in which they provide written information to justices ahead of a court case.
- *Electioneering* – Groups utilise the frequent and expensive elections, gaining influence through publicity, donations or canvassing potential voters. It is common for interest groups to produce scorecards for members of Congress, showing voters how well their elected politicians have performed.

CASE STUDY 7.1: BLACK LIVES MATTER AND THE MURDER OF GEORGE FLOYD 2020

Source: Helen H. Richardson/MediaNews Group/The Denver Post via Getty Images / Contributor via Getty Images

Photo 7.8 Black Lives Matter George Floyd protest, Denver, 2020

Overview

In May 2020 Floyd, a Black American man died after Derek Chauvin, a white police officer, pressed his knee on Floyd's neck for nearly eight minutes. Floyd was handcuffed and lying on the floor with two other police officers restraining him. During this interval, Floyd became unconscious, but the officer did not remove his knee. There were several sets of video footage, some from eyewitnesses. His death led to global protests with major demonstrations taking place in cities and towns across the United States. Black Lives Matter (BLM) were active in organising demonstrations and calling for police reform.

Congress

Black Lives Matter pushed for police regulations and had support from the Democratic majority in the House. The George Floyd Justice in Policing Act provided greater regulation of the police, including greater powers for the Federal Government to investigate incidents or patterns of racism within a police force. It also required police to wear and use bodycams and removed some of the immunity that police officers receive from prosecution. The Senate proposed their own, less stringent proposal. The House and Senate could not agree on a version of the bill meaning that this police reform failed, demonstrating their role as equally powerful chambers.

Parties

Democrats have typically strongly expressed support for BLM with Senate Majority Leader Chuck Schumer making a number of statements alongside BLM leaders. Democrats unanimously voted for the House bill on policing reform and Republicans unanimously voted against it. This partisan vote is a common occurrence. Republicans saw some of the measures as excessively strong and proposed their own version. There are clear ideological divisions with Democrats taking the more liberal approach of protecting the individual from government/police power and racial discrimination and Republicans emphasising strong police power to prevent crime.

Interest groups

The killing led to a series of protests across America. This show of strength can influence powerful bodies such as legislators. Whilst raising huge amounts of awareness, the event and subsequent protests have brought about limited changes in federal and state law, however. There has been success in influencing corporations who have shown greater support for campaigns to end discrimination. Apple, Amazon and Microsoft are just a few of the many corporations to donate to Black Lives Matter. Arguably BLM has lacked influence, failing to achieve the major legal changes it has called for. President Biden called for Congress to send him legislation on these issues in the form of the George Floyd Justice in Policing Act but there was insufficient support across Congress to get a new law passed. BLM may have held more influence in raising awareness and changing public attitudes on issues of race, racism and policing.

Race and civil rights

The death of George Floyd was the latest in a series of deaths of Black people by white police officers where there were significant concerns about the force used. It connects with wider concerns about racial profiling, arrests and prosecutions of racial minorities and is evidence for a lack of equality in the United Sates. The reaction to the killing, including the success of attempts to pass laws/reforms can be used to evaluate the extent to which inequality has been overcome. There has been increased recognition of issues of race and racism. Some companies have taken action by declaring support, giving donations or changing their practices. On the other hand, there continues to be major concerns about racial discrimination even after the hugely publicised case of George Floyd. The Mapping police Violence Database showed that in 2022, Black people were three times more likely than white people to be killed by a police officer, although they were 1.3 times more likely to be unarmed.

Elections 2020

The death of George Floyd and the political reaction led to race and policing becoming a more central part of the election campaign. Trump used the issue of race to try to maximise support from a loyal white conservative base using highly divisive language and images. He re-tweeted a video of someone shouting 'white power', whilst he claimed that he did not hear the comment and deleted the tweet, he did not apologise for doing so. Trump also had police clear a peaceful George Floyd demonstration from Lafayette Square, near the White House, so that he could walk to St John's Church. The walk was a photo opportunity to show that the president was in control, push a tough on crime agenda, aiming to please conservative Christians (even though Trump did not enter the church). All of this was intended to maintain control of key voter groups in the election. A *New York Times* poll found that 9 in 10 voters saw the Black Lives Matter protests as a major issue affecting their voting. Among those who cited the protests as a factor, 53% voted for Mr Biden, and 46% for Mr Trump.

President

President Trump threatened to veto the Justice in Policing Act, but the bill never reached his desk. President Biden supported the Act, but Congress was unable to pass this through the Senate with its ultra-slim Democrat majority. Black Lives Matter leaders regularly asked for meetings with Biden and were frustrated at the lack of dialogue between them. Eventually BLM had meetings with White House officials but not Biden or Vice President Harris. Black Lives Matter strongly welcomed Biden's May 2022 Equity Plan requiring agencies and government departments to review policy and procedure to reduce inequality. At the same time, they do not feel that the Biden administration is doing enough to stop over-policing and unfairness in the criminal justice system.

INTEREST GROUPS AND DEMOCRACY

Interest groups have a positive impact on democracy by providing representation for different views, restricting the government and facilitating public participation in the political process. On the other hand, there are democratic concerns. Wealthy, well-connected interest groups may serve to concentrate power in the hands of the few, for example.

KEY TOPIC DEBATE: DO INTEREST GROUPS IMPROVE THE LEVEL OF DEMOCRACY IN THE UNITED STATES?

Representation

✓ Interest groups promote pluralist democracy, with virtually all groups in society being represented by a diverse set of interest groups.

✓ Interest groups are effective at representing smaller groups that may be overlooked or even deliberately marginalised by politicians, either because of their size or because of the prevailing ideology of those in power.

✓ Interest groups can add a great deal of democratic value because of the limited representation provided by first-past-the-post voting and the existence of only two political parties for voters to choose from.

» In 2023 the American Civil Liberties Union (ACLU) used their legal expertise to file a lawsuit on behalf of Zooey Zephyr against the state legislature of Montana. They claim that her First Amendment rights to free speech are being restricted. Zooey, an elected representative of the state legislature, was accused by Republicans of disruptive and dangerous activity during a debate on transgender rights. The state legislature passed laws limiting transgender rights that Zephyr was speaking against. She said that, 'this effort by House leadership to silence me and my constituents is a disturbing and terrifying affront to democracy itself ... House leadership explicitly and directly targeted me and my district because I dared to give voice to the values and needs of transgender people like myself.'

» LGBTQ+ groups and others such as the ACLU are attempting to ensure that the interests of transgender individuals are promoted. In 2022 Human Rights Campaign, an LGBTQ+ rights group, said that more than 250 anti-LGBTQ+ bills were introduced in states legislatures.

✖ Instead of providing pluralist representation wealthy and well-connected groups concentrate the power of a small section of society. This **elitism** undermines democracy by creating high levels of political inequality.

✖ Corporations have high financial resources that they use to hire professional lobbyists or make major donations to parties' or politicians' campaigns at election time. As such they are over-represented.

✖ Interest groups may not always have a negative impact on democracy but do little to add democratic value either. The constitutional system already has high levels of democracy with frequent elections and strong rights protection.

» President Biden's Build Back Better bill failed in the Senate in 2021 because of the opposition of just one Democrat, Senator Joe Manchin. Manchin received over $400,000 in donations from the oil and gas industry during the Build Back Better negotiation period alone and has received millions of dollars from the industry during his political career. Build Back Better would have provided universal pre-kindergarten places, expanded healthcare access and supplied generous tax incentives for green energy whilst further regulating global warming. Powerful corporate interest groups contributed to the rejection of the wishes of the larger population, represented by the AFL-CIO and its 12 million members.

Definition

Elitism: A process in which power or resources are held by a small group (the elite) with the vast majority having very limited power or resources.

Checks on government

✔ Interest groups are effective at identifying and challenging government corruption or self-interest. They act as a kind of democratic police force, ensuring that politicians work in the interests of the people, not in the interests of themselves or their own party.

✔ Interest groups can also help to ensure that politicians and parties carry out the policies that they promised at election time, protecting mandate theory and enhancing representative democracy.

» In 2020 the League of Conservation Voters used their Dirty Dozen list to campaign against politicians who have the worst environmental voting records. They defeated six of their twelve in the 2020 elections and ten of twelve in 2018. By creating digital adverts and direct mail, spending $14 million on a media programme attacking President Trump's environmental record in the battleground states such as Arizona, Florida and Michigan, they helped to empower voters and influence the presidential election result. The adverts targeted Trump's denial of global warming and sought to expose his business connections, highlighting his positioning of corporate energy business owners in key positions within his own organisation.

✖ The checks that interest groups place on elected politicians might undermine democracy by preventing elected politicians from carrying out their policy promises. It is politicians who are given the mandate to govern, not unelected and often self-interested interest groups.

✖ The US political and constitutional system already creates high levels of checks. As such, American voters are already well protected from abuse of power, with interest groups contributing little to democracy.

» After the Sandy Hook Elementary School shootings in 2012, President Obama was prevented from successfully passing new gun laws as a result of the National Rifle Association (NRA), who targeted marginal and moderate Democrats in the Senate. Opinion polls consistently showed high levels of support for further regulation. Many Democrats in the Senate refused to support these regulations, fearing the activism of the NRA in the upcoming elections.

Participation

✔ Interest groups enhance democracy by allowing people to become actively involved in the political process. They facilitate demonstrations and encourage a greater connection between voters and elected politicians, using websites and social media to alert the public.

✔ Interest groups can add a great deal of democratic value given the low levels of participation in elections. Many people gain their political influence as a result of participating via pressure groups rather than voting.
Black Lives Matter has facilitated participation and political influence by organising and encouraging demonstrations to challenge ongoing racial discrimination in the United States. The movement has the

ability to mobilise large numbers of people using #BlackLivesMatter on social media. In 2020 following the murder of George Floyd by police officer Dennis Chauvin, it was estimated that between 15 million and 26 million people participated in demonstrations. The group demand criminal justice reform, with the BLM website issuing critical statements following President Biden's 2022 budget as a result of a lack of police reform.

✖ Interest group participation sometimes involves violence or other lawbreaking activities to gain influence. This challenges laws that have been passed through the representative democratic process.

✖ Violent or illegal activity can be a major threat to democracy because it can restrict the individual rights of others. Rather than increasing the power of the people, interest groups can undermine essential freedoms and undermine the liberal democratic status of the United States.

» Environmental groups such as Extinction Rebellion have organised disruptive protests especially in cities. In 2019 more than twenty people were arrested by police in New York after protesters organised a 'die in' blocking traffic on Wall Street. They poured fake blood over the famous charging bull statue, a symbol of American capitalism, the economic system that Extinction Rebellion argue is a major cause of environmental disaster. Extinction Rebellion were preventing people from pursuing the freedom of their daily life as well as potentially breaking the law. In 2023 it announced it would continue to demonstrate but would temporarily avoid disruptive activity.

Source: Erik McGregor / Contributor via Getty Images

Photo 7.9 Extinction Rebellion organise a 'die in' on Wall Street

Key Topic Debate Summary: Do interest groups improve the level of democracy in the United States?

FOR	KEY CRITERIA	AGAINST
✓ Interest groups promote pluralist democracy, representing specific groups or interests in society. This includes smaller groups that may be otherwise overlooked. ✓ Interest groups can add democratic value because of the limited representation provided by first-past-the-post voting and the limited range of parties.	Do interest groups increase levels of **representation**?	✗ Interest groups are responsible for the over-representation of some interests in society, creating elitism. ✗ Corporations have high financial resources and significant contacts, leading to political inequality. ✗ Interest groups can add little democratic value given that there are already so many elections and therefore high levels of representation in the United States.
✓ Interest groups identify and challenge government corruption as well as the self-interested actions of politicians. ✓ Interest groups can also help to ensure that politicians and parties carry out the policies that they promised at election time.	Do interest groups promote positive **checks** on politicians?	✗ Checks might undermine democracy by preventing elected politicians from carrying out policy promises. ✗ Interest groups may have little democratic value because of the high level of checks and balances already in existence.
✓ Interest groups allow more people to become actively involved in the political process, for example via demonstrations or raising awareness, using their websites and social media to alert the public. ✓ Interest groups can add a great deal of democratic value given the low levels of participation in US elections.	Do interest groups create democratic **participation**?	✗ Interest group participation sometimes involves violence or other lawbreaking activities to gain influence. ✗ Violent or illegal activity can be a major threat to democracy because it can restrict the individual rights of others.

Exam Tip: Improving AO2 analysis and AO3 evaluation

This is not a theoretical debate only – you can improve your analysis and evaluation by having a clear sense of how democratic the structure of the United States is in general. The United States provides for representative democracy, for example through frequent elections to several different political offices. You might view the United States more critically, supporting the view that FPTP voting and the dominance of two similar parties does not provide sufficient representation. You can evaluate the extent to which interest groups either enhance or undermine *the level of democracy already in place*.

INFLUENCE ON THE THREE BRANCHES OF GOVERNMENT

We are now in a position to evaluate the extent to which interest groups have an impact over the Federal Government by examining their influence on the three main branches of government. Drawing on their considerable resources, interest groups can use a range of tactics to achieve their policy goals.

Spec key term

Political action committee (PAC): A federally-registered organisation that is legally responsible for conforming to campaign finance laws when donating money to parties or politicians. Any group that wants to donate money to a candidate or party must set up their own PAC.

Super PAC: A group created to take donations and spend money to influence election outcomes without the money going directly to a party or candidate, thereby escaping the most significant legal restrictions on donations.

THE ROLE OF SUPER PACs

One of the main ways in which interest groups can influence politicians is by donating money to political campaigns. Interest groups might do this to ensure that their chosen candidate or party wins the election. There are several laws that seek to regulate the role and influence of money, however. Interest groups are required by law to set up their own **political action committee (PAC)** if they wish to donate to a campaign. Campaign finance regulations (which were explored in detail in Chapter 6, pages 186–189) limit how much money these PACs can donate.

There are, however, ways of donating or spending money whilst avoiding these regulations. This is known as soft money. One way of avoiding almost any regulations whatsoever is to fund party campaigns via **super PACs**, which are not directly connected to a specific candidate in an organisational sense. Instead, these super PACs raise money, pledging to spend that money to help a specific party or candidate to win. The super PAC typically spends almost all of its money on publicity. The super PAC itself, not the candidate or party, decides how best to spend that money. As long as a candidate or party do not work directly with a super PAC there are no campaign finance regulations placed on that super PAC. Their advantage is that donors can give unlimited money and the super PAC has no limits placed on how much it spends.

» In 2020 $1.6 billion was spent on the Biden campaign alone. Approximately $1 billion was donated to and spent by the Biden team itself. The rest came in the form of money donated to and spent by super PACS, totalling around $600 million.

Super PACS are a great way of circumventing campaign finance regulations, allowing wealthy donors or corporations to attempt to influence election outcomes or candidate policy. The concern is that politicians, who need to raise considerable funds to compete in elections, feel the need to please these major donors by creating new policies and laws that serve their interests to keep the money flowing.

» The leading pro-Biden super PAC, Unite the Country, spent $38 million campaigning for Biden in 2020 with no restrictions on money donated to the group or on how much the group could spend. In reality, the super PAC has close connections to Biden as it was created by Larry Rasky, who worked with Biden to raise money in his previous attempts to become president. Unite the Country attracts major donors because it is created by those close to the Biden and Obama campaign teams.

As well as favouring specific presidential candidates, super PACs can be created with other electoral goals in mind. The Senate Majority PAC was created to ensure a Democrat majority by funding candidates in tight House and Senate races. Other super PACs are issue based, for example campaigning for the environment (LCV Victory Fund) or for stronger female representation in Congress (Women Vote!). Table 7.3 provides a list of the leading super PACs in the 2020 election cycle.

Table 7.3 **Highest spending super PACS in 2020**

Group	Independent Expenditures	View	Supports	Total Raised
Senate Leadership fund	$293,731,548	C		$475,353,506
Senate Majority PAC	$230,406,668	L		$372,293,746
Congressional Leadership fund	$142,783,829	C		$165,741,326
America First Action	$133,819,980	C	supports Trump	$150,128,473
Preserve America PAC	$102,983,479	C	supports Trump	$105,322,042
American Crossroads	$79,476,030	C		$81,809,711
Club for Growth Action	$65,481,764	C		$71,990,841
American Bridge 21st Century	$59,719,576	L	supports Biden	$85,463,766
Independence USA PAC	$56,530,420	L	supports Biden	$67,713,620
The Lincoln Project	$49,633,016	L		$87,404,907
Americans for Prosperity Action	$47,732,979	C		$60,382,094
LCV Victory Fund	$42,266,596	L		$61,134,693
Unite the Country	$38,923,591	L	supports Biden	$49,938,340
Peachtree PAC	$37,845,498	C		$38,000,000
Women Vote!	$36,769,678	L		$46,750,932
Black PAC	$31,989,594	L		$44,044,053

Note: C = Generally supports conservative candidates; L = Generally supports liberal candidates.
Source: OpenSecrets.

KEY TOPIC DEBATE: DO INTEREST GROUPS HAVE A HIGH LEVEL OF INFLUENCE OVER THE THREE MAIN BRANCHES OF GOVERNMENT?

We could evaluate interest groups' level of influence by examining their impact on each of the three branches of government in turn. An equally effective approach, however, is to explore three main reasons why interest group influence in the United States appears to be high.

Access points

✓ The separation of powers and the high levels of checks and balances between the main branches means that interest groups have four powerful institutions to choose from when trying to achieve their policy goals. By choosing between the president, the House of Representatives, the Senate and the Supreme Court, an interest group can choose the most receptive institution, usually the one that is ideologically in tune with the views of that group.

✓ It is common to have divided governments, in which more than one party controls the federal institutions at the same time. If an interest group is unable to gain influence in an unsympathetic White House, they might be able to turn to the House, the Senate or the Supreme Court for assistance, for example.

✓ Party leaders in Congress have limited influence over congressional politicians, leaving scope for interest groups to exert influence.

» During the last two years of the Trump presidency, the Democrats held a majority of seats in the House of Representatives. Liberal, left-leaning groups were unable to influence the president's agenda but were able to push their policy goals through a receptive House of Representatives. Racial minority groups and immigration rights campaigners were able to maintain pressure on Democrats to prevent Trump's agenda of building a wall across the US–Mexico border and also successfully lobbied to undermine the more excessive aspects of his immigration policy.

✗ Some interest groups may have limited access or influence during periods when one party dominates federal institutions and there is a lack of ideological compatibility between these groups and the party majority.

✗ A consensus between the two parties that control the Federal Government may not be in line with the aims of an interest group, leaving them relatively powerless in the long term. This is especially true if we accept the view that both Democrats and Republicans promote wealthy and corporate interests.

» During the re-emergence of violent conflict between Hamas and the Israeli government in 2021, President Biden was quick to show his support for the Israeli State, in line with the vast majority of members in Congress. It was reported that Biden spoke six times to Israel's prime minister, Benjamin Netanyahu, by phone with no such direct conversations with progressive Democrats or pro-Palestinian groups. In 2023 Biden met with both Muslim and Jewish American leaders after the Hamas attack on Israel, suggesting that interest groups can have a more pluralist influence. Many progressive Democrats, however, have criticised Biden for not listening to all voices and failing to attempt to prevent the death of Palestinians when he refused to call for a ceasefire.

Number and frequency of elections

✓ Interest groups can exploit the high number and frequency of elections, for example by using publicity to campaign for and against a candidate. The relatively weak levels of party unity and separate elections and mandates for the House, Senate and president means that the individual voting records of members of Congress can play a key role in their re-election chances.

✓ US elections are incredibly expensive, with congressional and presidential candidates relying on funding from interest groups. Interest groups can use this as an opportunity to financially support their favoured candidates or party by donating money via PACS or super PACs.

» In 2020, a new super PAC, Future Forward USA, raised and spent nearly $100 million backing Biden and attacking President Trump. It ran a series of slick pro-Biden or anti-Trump adverts in key swing states including Pennsylvania, Michigan and Florida. Future Forward is created and funded by several Silicon Valley billionaires such as Dustin Moskovitz, the co-founder of Facebook, who donated $22 million. All tech companies are aware that the Biden administration has to deal with this developing industry in relation to regulations or maintaining competitiveness with China.

✗ In any election there are winners and losers. Interest groups may fail to get their favoured candidates or parties elected and thus lose policy advantage.

✗ There is no guarantee that winning candidates will propose laws that are favourable to a donor. Once in office, politicians are subject to a number of competing pressures, including public opinion, and may have priorities beyond those of a specific interest group.

» In 2020 Sheldon Adelson, casino owner, donated over $218 million of his own fortune to Republican candidates, giving nothing to Democrats, only to see the Democratic Party seal victories for the White House, House of Representatives and the Senate. Adelson essentially achieved nothing from his huge expenditure.

Rights protection

✓ The United States has a high level of rights protection guaranteed by an entrenched Bill of Rights and a sovereign constitution. Interest groups in general can use this to promote freedom of expression and the right to protest.

✓ Other interest groups have their main policy goals enshrined in the US Constitution. Groups such as the National Rifle Association (Second Amendment right to bear arms) and the NAACP (Fourteenth Amendment protections against racial discrimination) can use a powerful Supreme Court to secure their aims.

» In *NAACP v Trump* (2020) the historically named National Association for the Advancement of Colored People successfully litigated, forcing President Trump to reintroduce the liberal immigration laws created by the Obama presidency. This allowed children who arrived in the United States as illegal immigrants to have the right to remain.

✗ As with any court case there are winners and losers with interest groups on one side of the debate destined to fail to achieve policy success.

✗ In recent years a conservative majority on the court has arguably failed to provide sufficient rights protections. This has meant significant losses for groups such as the American Civil Liberties Union (ACLU), racial rights groups, and gay and transgender rights groups.

» In 2022 *Dobbs v Jackson* overturned *Roe v Wade*, removing the guarantee of the constitutional right to abortion. During the case seventy-three women's rights groups including the National Women's Law Center, plus other groups such as the ACLU, wrote amicus briefs for the Supreme Court, arguing that abortion should continue to be constitutionally protected. Regardless of the dispute over rights, these groups clearly lacked influence in this case.

Key Topic Debate Summary: Do interest groups have a high level of influence over the three main branches of government?

FOR	KEY CRITERIA	AGAINST
✓ The separation of powers and the high levels of checks and balances means that interest groups have several powerful institutions to choose from when trying to achieve their policy goals. ✓ If an interest group is unable to gain influence in an unsympathetic White House they might be able to turn to the House, Senate or Supreme Court for assistance. ✓ Interest groups are assisted by weak parties leaving scope for interest groups to exert influence.	Can interest groups successfully use the variety of **access points** to gain influence?	✗ Some interest groups may have limited access or influence during periods when one party dominates federal institutions. ✗ Some interest groups find themselves permanently sidelined if both Democrats and Republicans oppose their cause.
✓ Interest groups can exploit the high number and frequency of elections, campaigning for and against a candidate. Negative campaigns can be particularly effective. ✓ US elections are incredibly expensive with congressional and presidential candidates relying on funding from interest groups via PACs or super PACs creating an expectation of policy favours in return.	Can interest groups successfully exploit the **high number and frequency of elections**?	✗ Interest groups may fail to get their favoured candidates/parties elected and lose the ability to gain policy advantages. ✗ There is no guarantee that winning candidates will push through laws that are favourable to a donor.

✓ Interest groups in general can use constitutional rights to promote the freedom of expression and the right to protest. ✓ Some interest groups such as the NRA and NAACP have their main policy goals enshrined in the Constitution.	Does the **high level of rights protection** ensure that interest groups are highly influential?	✗ As with any court case there are winners and losers, with interest groups on one side of the debate destined to fail to achieve policy success. ✗ A conservative majority on the court has failed to provide rights protection on the grounds of the First and Fourteenth Amendments, undermining interest group power.

Exam Tip: Improving AO2 analysis and AO3 evaluation

The political context in which interest groups are operating is dynamic. Election results, changes in campaign finance laws and key Supreme Court rulings can all affect interest group power. Whilst your evaluation will require you to judge the extent of power overall, you can use this changing context to add further sophistication to your answer.

Learning Review

1. What are the main resources of interest groups?
2. What are the main tactics of interest groups?
3. How do interest groups promote democracy in the United States?
4. How do they undermine democracy?
5. What are super PACs and why are they influential?
6. What features of the US political system allows interest groups to have high levels of influence?
7. How are interest groups limited in each of these feature areas?

Comparative Learning Review

1. What are the similarities and differences in the methods of US and UK interest groups?
2. In what ways might US interest groups be more powerful than those in the United Kingdom?

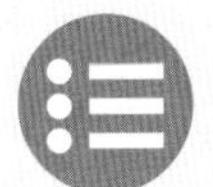

Chapter Summary

- ✓ The United States has two main parties, the Democratic and Republican parties, who have conflicting policies and values in the area of social and moral policy, the economy and welfare. There are also overlaps and similarities between the parties.
- ✓ Each party is internally divided, and each contains key factions.
- ✓ Specific social groups based on gender, race, education or age are likely to show strong levels of support for one party more than another.
- ✓ Interest groups have a major impact on those who live in the United States as a result of policy-making impact and their contribution to democracy. They focus their influence on the president, Congress and the Supreme Court.
- ✓ PACs and super PACs help interest groups to gain influence, using campaign finance to achieve their goals. Super PACs can evade the most significant campaign finance restrictions.
- ✓ Interest groups influence the main branches of government, but the extent of their impact can be limited.

Exam Style Questions

- **Evaluate the view that the Democratic and Republican parties share similar views and policies. (30 marks)**
- **Evaluate the view that the Republican Party lacks internal unity. (30 marks)**
- **Evaluate the view that moderate Democrats have more in common with Republican politicians than with progressive Democrats. (30 marks)**
- **Evaluate the view that interest groups make a positive contribution to US democracy. (30 marks)**
- **Evaluate the view that interest groups find it easy to influence all three branches of government. (30 marks)**

Further Resources

Campbell, J. (2018) *Polarized: Making Sense of a Divided America* (Princeton, NJ and Oxford: Princeton University Press).

Drucker, D. (2021) *In Trump's Shadow: The Battle for 2024 and the Future of the GOP* (New York: Twelve).

Stevens, S. (2021) *It Was All a Lie: How the Republican Party Became Donald Trump* (New York: Penguin/Random House).

Evers-Hillstrom, K. (2020) 'More Money, Less Transparency: A Decade under Citizens United', OpenSecrets, 14 January 2020, available at https://www.opensecrets.org/news/reports/a-decade-under-citizens-united (accessed 29 July 2023).

'America's Political Scientists Are Worried about "Lethal Partisanship"' (2022), *The Economist*, 7 October 2022, available at https://www.economist.com/united-states/2021/10/07/americas-political-scientists-are-worried-about-lethal-partisanship (accessed 29 July 2023).

Visit https://bloomsbury.pub/colclough-essentials-us to access additional materials to support teaching and learning.

8 COMPARATIVE US AND UK POLITICS

Chapter Preview

This chapter will allow you to improve your understanding of the US and UK political systems by comparing them. It will also help you to tackle the comparative questions on your component 3 exam paper. Once you have covered all the US and UK topics, this comparative chapter will provide a revision of some of the content of previous chapters. You should note that the specification does not require you to compare *all* parts of a topic you have studied; it sets out specific areas in each topic for you to compare. This chapter will give you the opportunity to become familiar with all these comparative areas.

Throughout this chapter you will develop the essential skill of *comparing and contrasting* different political systems and can find more information on answering comparative questions in Chapter 9, 'Exam Focus'. One important addition is that you will be introduced to comparative theories in this chapter. These are three different perspectives (rational, cultural and structural) that you will learn to *apply* to explain key similarities and differences between the two countries.

Key Questions and Debates

- What are the main theoretical approaches and how can they be used to compare the United States and United Kingdom?
- How different are the US and UK constitutions, especially in relation to the extent to which power is shared and the extent to which regions are powerful?
- To what extent are Parliament and Congress powerful bodies?
- What are the main similarities and differences in the role and power of the prime minister and the president?
- How powerful are the US and UK supreme courts and to what extent are they independent bodies?
- How well are rights protected in each country and what is the role of pressure groups in protecting such rights?
- How similar are party policies in the United States to those in the United Kingdom?
- How effectively is campaign finance regulated in each country?
- What are the roles, methods and powers of pressure groups in each country?

Specification Checklist

6.1 Theoretical approaches

- **Understanding rational, cultural and structural approaches and the how they explain similarities and differences between the USA and UK.**

6.2 Similarities and differences in the USA and UK

6.2.1 Comparative constitutions

- **Their nature (codified/uncodified) and their sources, provisions and principles.**
- **The similarities and differences between US federalism and UK devolution.**

6.2.3 Comparative legislatures

- **Powers, strengths and weaknesses of each of the Houses.**
- **The extent to which each of the Houses are equal.**

6.2.5 Comparative executives

- **The role and powers of the US President and the UK Prime Minister and their impact on politics and government.**
- **Extent of accountability to the US and UK legislature.**

6.2.7 Comparative Supreme Court and Civil rights

- **Basis for and relative extent of powers of Supreme Court in US and UK.**
- **Relative independence of the Supreme Court in the US and UK.**
- **Effectiveness of the protection of rights in each country.**
- **Effectiveness of interest groups in the protection of civil rights in the USA and the UK.**

6.2.9 Comparative democracy and participation

- **The party systems (two-party and multiparty).**
- **Degree of internal unity within parties.**
- **The policy profiles of the two main parties in each country.**
- **Debates around campaign finance and party funding.**
- **The relative power, methods and influence of pressure groups.**

6.2.2; 6.2.4; 6.2.6; 6.2.8. The extent to which rational, cultural and structural theoretical approaches can be used to account for similarities and differences in the USA and UK

Source: belterz via Getty Images

THEORETICAL APPROACHES

This section examines the following theoretical approaches as a way of examining key similarities and differences between the two countries: rational, cultural and structural. These theories are always *applied* to explain a similarity or difference. There is one question on the exam paper in which you are required to apply these theories. You can find more details on this in Chapter 9, 'Exam Focus'.

Definition

Rational approach: An approach that suggests that individuals will act rationally, choosing to act in a particular way because it will give them a beneficial outcome.

RATIONAL

The **rational approach** focuses on individuals such as single politicians in Parliament or Congress, the president, the prime minister or a single voter. This perspective suggests that these individuals will act rationally to pursue their own interests or goals. This might include achieving their own ideological aims or maintaining power. It explores the way in which individuals within the political system are often free from the constraint of external structures such as a constitution or the power of others.

The rational theory could be *applied* to understand *a similarity* between a US president and a UK prime minister. They can both use their power to appoint people to the executive branch to push their political agenda regardless of what others in the executive want to achieve.

The rational theory could also be *applied* to demonstrate *a difference* between US senators and UK peers. Non-elected members of the House of Lords are not accountable to the public and therefore far more able to vote according to their own personal ideology compared to senators who have to seek re-election. Senators act rationally by responding to constituents to get re-elected, whereas peers act rationally by using their own personal judgement.

Definition

Cultural approach: An approach suggesting that individuals will act in line with a group that they are a member of, conforming to the norms or culture of that group.

CULTURAL

The **cultural approach** focuses on the importance of groups such as pressure groups, political parties, factions and identifiable groups of voters. This theory tells us that individuals behave the way they do because they are part of a specific group. The group has shared values and goals; in other words, a group culture. By being part of a group the individual may adopt the norms of that group with everyone acting in a similar political manner.

Cultural theory could be *applied* to show *similarities* between the two countries in which the approach to policy of both presidents and prime ministers is informed by pressure from other members of that party such as core voter groups or elected party politicians. Presidents and prime ministers might modify their policies if they are out of step with the dominant culture of the party they belong to.

We can also *apply* cultural theory to see *a difference* between political parties in the United States and United Kingdom. Arguably elected members of a political party in the United Kingdom show higher levels of party unity than those in the United States. There is a stronger group culture within UK political parties with MPs within a party showing much greater ideological cohesion than can be seen within the Democratic or Republican parties in Congress. Greater ideological diversity within parties in the United States tells us that there is not such a strong shared culture within a political party.

Definition

Structural approach: An approach that demonstrates the way in which individual politicians and political institutions act as a result of being limited by external political forces.

STRUCTURAL

The **structural approach** is focused on the way political structures restrict individuals and groups in the political process. These political structures are usually the main institutions of a political system such as the Constitution, the courts, heads of governments and legislative bodies. The structural approach can be used to show how structures such as the US and UK constitutions influence or determine political behaviour.

The structural approach can be *applied* to shine a light on *similarities* regarding civil liberties in the two countries. Constitutional structures in both countries provides a list of legally protected rights that empowers individuals to challenge any public body which limits any of these rights. Individuals have legal protection in both countries.

The structural approach could also be *applied* to demonstrate *differences* between the supreme courts of the two countries. In the United Kingdom, the Supreme Court is far more constrained than the court in the United States. This is because the UK Constitution awards sovereignty to Parliament, which can ultimately overturn Supreme Court decisions. On the other hand, the sovereignty of the US Constitution gives the Supreme Court enormous power to regulate the laws produced by Congress.

CONSTITUTIONS

Constitutions provide the rules for the game of politics. They set out the roles, powers and limits of political institutions as well as defining the power relationship between people and politicians. Constitutions are a useful place to begin exploration of comparisons between the United States and United Kingdom because they shape so much of politics in each country, influencing the way in which the main political processes and institutions operate.

NATURE AND SOURCES

One major difference is that the US Constitution is codified whereas the UK Constitution is uncodified. This means that the US Constitution is a written constitution placed in a single document. As such it has one main **source**: the Constitution itself, with its seven original articles established in 1789 alongside the twenty-seven amendments passed since then. The United Kingdom's uncodified constitution has several sources. The rules cannot be found in one single document but instead are spread across statute law, common rulings of courts and conventions.

In theory this should mean that the nature of the US Constitution allows for the meaning to be clearer than the UK Constitution. The United Kingdom has no single, written authoritative text that can be examined if there is a constitutional dispute. Having said that, the US Constitution, however, is a very short document that contains many ambiguities; it is not always a clear guide to the rules of politics.

Definition

Source: The location where constitutional rules can be found.

PROVISIONS AND PRINCIPLES

The **provisions** of a constitution are the main contents that explain *how* the political system should operate. These include, for example, the extent of separation of powers between branches of government, the amendment process and the nature of elections. The principles of a constitution refer to the values of the Constitution; what is it that the authors of the Constitution are trying to achieve? This could include the idea of limited government, having an effective, powerful government or maximising democracy. The **principles** or values held by the authors of a constitution typically lead to their choice of provisions. This puts the theory into practice.

One fundamental similarity between the provisions of the US and UK constitutions is the creation of three branches of government. However, the way in which they are created and the power given to each branch is very different. Having an awareness of the arrangement of the three main branches of government provides an overview of a great deal of comparative politics and is summarised in Table 8.1.

The two countries are considered to be liberal democracies and have a constitutional system that requires power to be shared. Having said this, there are considerable differences between the provisions of the two constitutions, which means that political practice operates very differently in the United Kingdom and the United States. These key differences are outlined in Table 8.2.

Definition

Provisions: The main contents that determine the way in which a political system will work.

Principles: The key theoretical values that a constitution is trying out in practice.

Exam Tip – The concept of the separation of powers is a much-misunderstood phrase. Given its central place in US politics you should ensure that you are clear about its meaning *and* implications. In the United States each branch has its own powers or roles. At the same time, the separation of powers also allows powers or roles of branches to be shared or to overlap. For example, the process of appointing Supreme Court justices is shared by the president and Congress. The president can appoint member of the Supreme Court, but the Senate has to ratify these appointments. The separation of powers is a simple idea that says the personnel of government are separated into three branches – it is not possible for people in one branch to also be in another.

Table 8.1 The branches of government in the United States and United Kingdom

Branch	Role	United States	United Kingdom
Executive	• To provide leadership and representation for the whole country. • To initiate policy ideas. • To put those ideas into practice using government departments and bureaucracies.	• President. • Vice president. • Cabinet. • Government departments.	• Prime minister. • Cabinet. • Government departments, including the Civil Service.
Legislature	• To legislate (make laws). • To represent the public usually on a constituency basis. • To check the executive branch.	• Congress, which has two chambers – the House of Representatives and the Senate.	• Parliament, which has two chambers – the House of Commons and the House of Lords.
Judiciary	• To uphold laws by interpreting them. • To uphold constitutional laws/rules. • To provide a check on the other two branches.	• The Supreme Court.	• The Supreme Court.

Table 8.2 Main differences in the constitutional provisions of the US and UK constitutions

	United States	United Kingdom	Implications
Separation of powers/fusion of powers	• Clear separation of powers between the executive, legislature and judiciary. • This refers to a separation of personnel between these three branches. It is not possible to be a member of more than one branch at the same time. • For example, the president and their cabinet cannot also be members of Congress. • There are separate elections for the president and Congress.	• Members of the executive (the prime minister and cabinet) are also members of the legislature (Parliament). • Members of the cabinet, including the prime minister, are required to be members of Parliament. • There is only one election, which is for Parliament. There are no separate elections for government or prime minister.	In the United Kingdom the executive (or government) tends to dominate Parliament. The president, on the other hand is relatively weak, often lacking the powers to force Congress to accept their policy agenda.

Continued

Table 8.2 **Continued**

	United States	United Kingdom	Implications
Checks and balances	• High levels of checks and balances between the three branches of government. • The president can propose and veto legislation, but Congress can propose, amend and pass legislation as well as overturn a presidential veto with a two-thirds vote. • The Supreme Court can overturn actions or laws made by the president and Congress if they break the Constitution. The president can appoint justices to the court, subject to Senate ratification and Congress and the states play a role in amending constitutional rules, which the Supreme Court rules on.	• Much lower levels of checks and balances. The government, with its in-built majority in Parliament, can usually dominate the legislative process. • Using this majority, and a powerful patronage system, the prime minster has a great deal of power. • The Supreme Court is given a much lower level of power. The UK Supreme Court is not given the power to overturn acts of Parliament.	Power is concentrated much more in the United Kingdom than it is in the United States. The UK prime minister has much greater power over the policy direction of their own country than a president typically has. The sharing of power in the United States means that the system is slower to produce new policies or laws. The United Kingdom could be argued to have a more effective system of government in which the executive branch can achieve their goals, achieve them more quickly and achieve them with less need for compromise.
Location of sovereignty	• The Constitution is sovereign. This means that the Constitution is above all politicians and political institutions. It is the Supreme Court that enforces the Constitution by interpreting it and deciding whether it has been broken. • To protect the sovereignty of the Constitution, it is entrenched; amendments require super-majorities in the House, Senate and states.	• Parliament, not the Constitution, is sovereign. • Parliament can make or remove any law it wishes to. The Supreme Court of the United Kingdom cannot overturn decisions made by Parliament.	The UK Supreme Court is significantly weaker than its US counterpart. Any judicial interpretation can be overturned by a new act of Parliament in the United Kingdom. If the government dislikes a court ruling, it could easily change it. In the United States, the courts use the power of judicial review to overturn the actions of any institution, including Congress. The entrenched nature of the US Constitution means that court decisions are unlikely ever to be overturned by politicians.

Continued

Table 8.2 **Continued**

	United States	United Kingdom	Implications
Amendment process	• The US Constitution is entrenched, requiring support from two-thirds of the House of Representatives, two-thirds of the Senate and three-quarters of the states in state legislatures.	• The UK Constitution is amended with a bill passing Parliament. With the Commons having supremacy over the Lords, this ultimately only requires a 50% plus vote in the Commons.	It is much easier to amend the Constitution in the United Kingdom than the United States. This might mean that the US Constitution becomes outdated. Features such as the Electoral College can be seen as highly undemocratic yet are nearly impossible to remove. The UK Constitution is more readily updated with many radical reforms since the New Labour government in 1997, such as devolution and the Human Rights Act. On the other hand, the amendment process in the United Kingdom may be more open to abuse. A government with an absolute majority in Parliament can easily change constitutional rules in the self-interest of the party in government.

REGIONAL POWER: DEVOLUTION AND FEDERALISM

The way in which power is shared between regional and central governments is strongly influenced by the different constitutional principles in the two countries. The United States is a federal system whereas the United Kingdom has devolution.

DIFFERENCES

To properly compare the political systems of the United States and United Kingdom, you will need to understand how regional power differs in both countries. There are several key differences between the use of federalism in the United States compared to devolution in the United Kingdom. In the United States power is divided between the central government located in Washington DC (known as the Federal Government including the president and Congress) and regional government (known as states). In the United Kingdom, power is divided between the central government, located in London, and regions with devolved areas such as Wales, Scotland and Northern Ireland as well as English Metro areas such as Greater Manchester.

Constitutional protection

The US system of federalism provides constitutionally protected powers for the regions. The Federal Government cannot change the Constitution to reduce or remove the power of the states. Any such changes would require a constitutional amendment, which requires the support of over three-quarters of the states. In contrast, in the United Kingdom, the principle of parliamentary sovereignty means that there are no such constitutional protections for regional power. The UK Parliament can pass any law, including new rules to reduce or remove the power of regions.

Equality of power

In devolved systems such as the United Kingdom it is common to award different levels of power to different regions, often referred to as asymmetrical power. Some regions have much higher levels of policymaking power than others within the United Kingdom. For example, whilst Wales can vary the rate of income tax based on bands created by the UK government, Scotland can create its own tax bands altogether. Some areas of the United Kingdom have no power at all; there is no devolved parliament for England and many areas of England have not been given regional devolution. Under the principles of federalism, all regions are given the same level of power. Each state has the same ability to make laws in specific policy areas and all are limited in the same way, having to comply with the federal Constitution, regardless of the size of that state. Large population states such as Texas and California have the same policymaking power as small states such as Wyoming and Rhode Island.

Level of power

In practice there are higher levels of regional power in the United States than the United Kingdom, with states having more power to determine policy than regions in the United Kingdom. In the United States the Constitution was created in 1787 for separate colonies with strong regional identities, who would only agree to form the United States as long as there were considerable protections for their power. The growth of Scottish and Welsh nationalism has taken place more recently, being first recognised by the Labour government of 1997. Since then, regional power has increased hugely but still not to the level of the US states. You should be aware that there is nothing in the principles of devolution or federalism that means this has to be the case; it is *possible* to give regions more power under devolution than under federalism, but it is not the case here.

SIMILARITIES

Despite the different constitutional arrangements relating to regional power, the practices of devolution and federalism have a number of comparable features as they operate in practice in the two countries.

Division of power

In both the United States and the United Kingdom power is divided between central and regional governments. US states and the devolved regions of the United Kingdom both have considerable ability to determine policy, having a great deal of control in areas such as health and welfare, transport, the environment and some economic affairs. This means that there is a policy diversity *within* each country.

Protection of power

In practice, regions in the United States and the United Kingdom can both expect to be able to *maintain* high levels of policy control. US states have that power protected in the entrenched Constitution. UK regions do not, but nevertheless, there is now a strong expectation among citizens, especially of Wales and Scotland, that they will continue to enjoy the benefits of devolved power. Whilst there are no legal guarantees, high public support for devolution means that a government with a desire to get re-elected is highly unlikely to attempt to reduce regional power.

Level of power

It is also worth pointing out that this picture is evolving and arguably both countries provide for similar levels of regional power in practice. In the United States, the power of states has been eroded especially since the 1930s with an increase in federal mandates (that provide national legal standards which states have to follow) and a succession of Supreme Court rulings that have typically favoured Federal Government power. Devolved regions of the United Kingdom have seen major gains in their power after the Labour government initially created devolution. The threat of Scottish independence pushed the Conservative government to award more powers to Scotland especially after the independence referendum of 2014. Wales have experienced considerable increases in control moving from an assembly to a parliament, with much greater legislative power especially in areas such as taxation.

Exam Tip – Devolution and federalism are one of the key areas of comparison between the key provisions of the two constitutions. The Pearson Edexcel A-Level Politics specification lists comparative devolution and federalism separately from the idea of constitutional provisions and principles. As such, it would be wise to be prepared to produce a full comparative answer on this area.

THEORETICAL APPROACHES TO COMPARING CONSTITUTIONS

As with all comparative areas, one way to develop your knowledge and understanding is to take each of the similarities and differences above and determine whether you think this is explained by rational, cultural or structural approaches. Table 8.3 outlines some ways in which the three different approaches could be applied to constitutional similarities and differences.

Table 8.3 Theoretical approaches and comparative constitutions

	Similarities	Differences
Rational	The rational approach reveals the way in which individuals in both countries are able to seek protection from government through the legal protection of rights. In both the United States and United Kingdom, individuals can access the Supreme Court to challenge the actions of any public body that limits constitutional rights. People in the United States can make use of the Bill of Rights and the Fourteenth Amendment and those in the United Kingdom can use the Human Rights Act to benefit themselves when faced with restrictions of rights.	The rational approach can be applied to show how justices in the United States have much greater ability to act according to their own ideological goals than those in the United Kingdom. In the United States, the vague Constitution gives much discretion to justices and allows self-interested justices to apply their own interpretations to it. This is backed up by the power awarded by the constitutions of each country, which means that US justices have far greater ability to put their own values into practice because they enforce a sovereign, entrenched Constitution.
Cultural	The cultural approach can be applied to argue that the two countries have similarities in the area of regional identity. In both the United States and United Kingdom, people within a regional group (such as Wales or Wyoming) have a strong affiliation with their region and the shared values of people within it. As such these group cultures exert a great deal of political pressure to protect and promote regional power and interest.	The cultural approach reveals that attitudes to regional power vary greatly between the two countries. There is a much greater division between the two main parties in the United States than there is in the United Kingdom. In the United Kingdom, each of the main parties, as well as the majority of Scottish and Welsh citizens, are in strong agreement in their support of devolution. The cultural approach suggests that is the accepted value system held by these groups. In the United States, the ideological cultures of the Democrats and Republicans are at odds over the desirability of regional power. Republicans often seek protection of state power and Democrats attempt to regulate states to achieve ideological goals such as gun regulation, gay and transgender rights or immigration reform.
Structural	The constitutional structures of the two countries can explain considerable similarities in the role and power of the legislative branch. Both are empowered to legislate and can restrict the executive branch. The constitutions of both countries provide mechanisms by which the legislative branch can remove the head of government. In the United States, Congress has the power to impeach and remove a president, and in the United Kingdom, Parliament can use a vote of no confidence to remove the whole government, including the prime minister.	The structural approach clearly highlights a major difference in the extent to which power is shared between the executive and legislature of the two countries. In the United States there is a much higher level of separation of powers and checks and balances than in the United Kingdom. The UK Constitution, therefore, allows for greater levels of executive domination compared to the US Constitution. The US Constitution restricts the power of the head of government to a greater extent than in the United Kingdom.

LEGISLATURES

Congress and Parliament are both hugely influential institutions within their respective political systems. This comes from their main role of legislating as well as the many other ways in which they can provide checks on the executive branch.

Source: iStock.com/mr-fox

Source: iStock.com/JavenLin

Photo 8.1 **US Congress (*left*) and UK Parliament (*right*)**

The main focus of this section is comparing the House of Representatives with the House of Commons (lower chambers) and the Senate with the House of Lords (upper chambers). It is useful to remember some overall constitutional differences between Congress and Parliament. These are covered throughout the comparative constitution section above, and are summarised here:

- **In relation to the executive branch**, Congress is far more powerful than Parliament. The separation of powers and checks and balances means that the US Congress is more powerful than the UK Parliament. In the United Kingdom, the Constitution typically allows the executive to dominate Parliament.
- **In relation to the judicial branch**, Parliament is more powerful than Congress. Parliamentary sovereignty means that courts cannot overturn acts of Parliament. Parliament is also easily able to pass new laws that overturn Supreme Court decisions. In contrast, the US Supreme Court can use its power of judicial review to invalidate an act of Congress. The entrenched Constitution means that Congress will find it extremely difficult to successfully overturn a judicial ruling.

Powers and limits of the House of Commons and the House of Representatives

The two lower chambers have a number of key differences in their powers and limitations.

Differences

Electoral mandate

In the United States there are separate mandates for the president and Congress via separate elections for each branch. In the United Kingdom, the prime minister and MPs are elected in the same general election. Voters have a single vote that determines both the make-up of the House of Commons and who becomes prime minister and therefore controls the executive branch. This gives significantly more power to the House of Representatives than the House of Commons. In the United Kingdom, the prime minister claims the mandate with backbench MPs having to follow the nationally determined manifesto. This is in contrast to the United States where representatives can claim an equal mandate to the president with members of the president's own party often pursuing an alternative agenda to the president.

Legislative power

The House of Representatives arguably has much greater control over bills than the House of Commons. Executive domination over the UK Parliament tends to make MPs more accepting of the legislative goals of the government than their US counterparts. To gain promotions in government, backbenchers will often follow the party line. In the House of Representatives, on the other hand, politicians from the president's own party will often be far more proactive in proposing their own legislation or rejecting and demanding the president's agenda. It is far more common for the House of Representatives to reject executive legislation than is the case with the House of Commons in the United Kingdom.

Executive checks

The House of Representatives will typically be far more effective at restricting the executive branch compared to the House of Commons. The underlying difference between the separation of powers (in the United States) and the **fusion of powers** (in the United Kingdom) creates different power relationships between the executives and legislatures in each country. The House of Representatives is highly independent from the president and willing to challenge the political agenda particularly when the president lacks a majority in the House. By definition, the UK government will always have some kind of majority in the House of Commons making the lower chamber less likely to challenge government policy and action. The power to remove the executive branch (and force an election) is held exclusively by the House of Commons, which can remove the government through a vote of no confidence. In the United States, the president can only be removed from office if they have committed a high crime or misdemeanour but the ability to remove the president, via the impeachment process, is shared by the House and the Senate.

Definition

Fusion of powers: An overlap in the personnel between two of the three main branches of government. In the United Kingdom this means that the legislative and executive is fused with all members of the cabinet also having seats in Parliament.

Similarities

Electoral mandate

Both the House of Representatives and the House of Commons are directly elected by the public. In each country the lower chamber can claim sufficient democratic legitimacy to have the right to have a major voice on political issues. Politicians from both chambers can and often do promote the interests of their constituents within the lower chamber even when this conflicts with the wishes or interests of their own political party. Representatives and MPs will raise local issues, propose legislative amendments or even oppose whole bills which damage the interests of their constituents.

Legislative power

A basic similarity can be seen in the ability of the House of Commons and the House of Representatives to play a significant role in the legislative process. Both chambers can initiate legislation through the use of private members bills in the United Kingdom and via individual members of Congress or congressional leaders in the United States. In addition, politicians in both the House of Representatives and the House of Commons can vote to amend or reject legislative proposals initiated by the executive branch.

Executive checks

The lower chambers in both countries have several mechanisms that allow them to provide executive scrutiny. As well as being able to vote on executive bills, they both have committees that specialise in the investigation of the executive branch. Departmental select committees in the United Kingdom and policy-based standing committees in the United States regularly investigate executive departments by requesting departmental documents and holding committee hearings that require members of the executive branch to attend.

Powers and limitations of the House of Lords and the Senate

The two upper chambers have a number of key differences in their powers and limitations.

Differences

Electoral mandate

There is a significant difference between the power of the unelected Lords and the elected Senate. The Senate has much greater legitimacy than the Lords. As a result, it is considered unacceptable for the second chamber in the United Kingdom to hold power over the elected government or House of Commons. The Salisbury Convention states that the Lords will not use their power to delay any policy proposals which featured in the government's party manifesto. No such convention applies to the Senate, which can, and often does, seek to block or amend policies that the president presented at election time.

Legislative power

The Senate also has considerably more legislative power than the Lords. The Senate can reject or amend legislative proposals from the president or the House of Representatives. The Lords, on the other hand, are constrained by the supremacy of the House of Commons. Any amendments from the Lords can ultimately be rejected by the lower chamber.

Executive checks

The US Constitution awards the Senate considerably more exclusive powers to check the president compared to the UK House of Lords. The Senate is given the ability to ratify treaties negotiated by the president allowing them to reject a key part of a president's foreign policy. In addition, the Senate can reject presidential appointments to senior positions in the executive branch as well as to the Supreme Court. Neither of these ratification powers is held by the House of Lords. As a result, the Senate plays a far more prominent role in checking presidential power than the House of Lords in attempting to restrict the executive branch in the United Kingdom.

Similarities

Electoral mandate

Despite the different provision for elections to the Senate and the House of Lords, this may not make a great difference to their overall *willingness* to challenge the lower chamber or the executive. The unelected Lords are arguably appointed for their expertise. This level of authority alongside their independence from party labels and party leaders means that they can be very forceful in challenging the executive branch. In the same way that members of the Senate are not limited by presidential patronage power, members of the Lords will not be passive in relation to the government.

Legislative power

Ultimately whilst there is a major difference between the legislative power of the two chambers, both the Senate and the Lords can exert influence over legislation. Both can use their ability to amend bills. In addition, The Senate can block legislation and the Lords have successfully achieved the same thing by using their power to delay government bills until the following parliamentary year, which has sometimes resulted in the government giving up on a legislative priority.

Executive checks

Although the Senate has considerably more power in restricting the executive, both upper chambers have mechanisms that allow them to limit prime ministers and presidents. The Lords can challenge executive policy or action using their individual expertise. The most significant overlap between the two institutions can be found in their ability to limit executive bills.

The strengths and weaknesses of the legislative chambers

As well as examining the similarities and differences between the houses in Congress and Parliament in terms of power, we can also look at this in terms of the desirability of each chamber to carry out its key roles. A summary of the main strengths and weaknesses of each chamber, in terms of the abilities of each body, is laid out in Tables 8.4 and 8.5.

Table 8.4 Strengths and weaknesses of the House of Commons and the House of Representatives

Strengths and weakness of the House of Commons	Role of lower chambers	Strengths and weakness of the House of Representatives
✓ Has the ability to propose, amend and reject legislation. ✓ Uses public bill committees to carefully scrutinise bills. ✗ Public bill committees are all temporary with MPs lacking expertise on a particular bill. ✗ Government domination of Parliament restricts the ability of the Commons to successfully amend or block bills.	Do both chambers provide a positive **legislative** role?	✓ Has the ability to propose, amend and reject legislation. ✓ Separation of powers means that it does not passively accept presidential bills, but it is an active legislative chamber. ✗ Can provide excessive resistance to presidential bills as a result of extreme partisanship. ✗ This can lead to ineffective government and federal shutdown during periods of divided government.
✓ Can use prime minister's Question Time and select committees to scrutinise and challenge the prime minister and their government. ✓ Vote of no confidence can be used to remove the government from office. ✗ The Commons are dominated by the government as a result of the government majority, the whip system and prime ministerial patronage power. ✗ Votes of no confidence are ineffective unless the government lacks an absolute majority of seats.	Can the lower chambers provide effective **checks** on the executive branch?	✓ Separation of powers makes the House of Representatives an active check on the executive branch. ✓ Congressional committees investigate presidential action and policy. ✗ Checks can become partisan. If the president has a majority in the House this may lead to a lack of scrutiny. ✗ The president may evade restrictions from the House of Representatives, for example, by using executive orders to bypass the usual need to legislate through Congress.
✓ Free and fair elections at least every five years. ✓ Single-member constituencies ensure a strong link between MP and voters. ✗ First-past-the-post voting is unfair, leading to safe seats and disproportionality between votes and seats. ✗ There is a lack of social representation, with women and racial minority groups lacking presence in the Commons compared to the population as a whole.	Are lower chambers sufficiently **representative**?	✓ Members of the House of Representatives are extremely sensitive to public opinion as a result of their very short two-year term. ✓ Uses single-member constituencies like the United Kingdom. ✗ First-past-the-post voting can produce unfair results and many safe seats that are not competitive. ✗ There is also a lack of social representation in the House of Representatives.

Table 8.5 **Strengths and weaknesses of the House of Lords and the Senate**

Strengths and weakness of the House of Lords	Role of upper chamber	Strengths and weakness of the Senate
✓ Experts in the Lords can provide input that improves the quality of legislation. ✓ The Lords can affect legislation without placing excessive limits on the government's agenda, promoting both democracy and effective government. ✗ The Lords have very limited power, allowing the government to dominate the legislative process. ✗ Many Lords lack expertise and are often appointed because of their connections to a political party.	Do both chambers provide a positive **legislative** role?	✓ Senators have a high level of power to check executive legislation. ✓ Individual senators sit on many congressional committees developing their policy expertise. ✗ The Senate can provide excessive restrictions preventing presidents from achieving their policy promises. ✗ The filibuster in the Senate is undesirable allowing just one politician to block legislation.
✓ The Lords has a willingness to challenge the government because of their independence from the government and from party labels. ✓ Their expertise may give them greater weight when challenging government policy or action. ✗ The Lords are ultimately limited in their ability to check. ✗ Arguably the checks that the Lords do provide are excessive due to their unelected nature.	Can the two chambers provide effective **checks** on the executive branch?	✓ The Senate acts as a powerful challenge to the executive as a result of the separation of powers. ✓ The Constitution awards specific checking powers such as the ability to ratify presidential appointments and presidential treaties. ✗ The Senate can act excessively in providing checks on the executive leading to legislative gridlock. ✗ The president might bypass treaty restrictions using executive agreements.
✓ Lords provides complementary representation to the House of Commons given their unelected nature. ✓ The Commons responds to the wishes of the people, whereas the Lords attempt to use their own judgement to promote the interests of the people. ✗ The unelected Lords is extremely unrepresentative and therefore undemocratic. ✗ There are still too many Lords drawn from an elitist background with a lack of representation from lower socio-economic groups.	Are both chambers sufficiently **representative**?	✓ Senators are elected to serve a six-year term. ✓ The separation of powers allows senators to respond to the wishes of their constituents. ✗ The Senate is an unrepresentative institution because there are two senators for every state, regardless of population. ✗ The use of first-past-the-post, winner-takes-all voting means that the Senate as a whole often fails to reflect voting patterns in the United States.

THEORETICAL APPROACHES TO COMPARATIVE LEGISLATURES

As with comparative constitutions, you can review the similarities and differences above and assess which of the three approaches can be applied in each case. Table 8.5 provides additional information on the way in which the three approaches can give an insight into similarities and differences between Congress and Parliament.

Table 8.6 **Theoretical approaches and comparative legislatures**

	Similarities	Differences
Rational	The rational approach can be used to show how members of both the House of Commons and the House of Representatives pursue their own ideological goals by proposing amendments to legislation, voting against bills or even proposing legislation of their own. In both countries members of the lower chamber have resisted pressure from their party or executive leader in voting for what they personally believe in.	The rational approach highlights a key difference between members of the Senate and members of the Lords. Peers are free from pressure from the public, making them far more able to pursue their own ideological goals than senators. For senators, acting rationally, for their own benefit often involves responding to public opinion to maximise chances of re-election.
Cultural	A major similarity between Congress and Parliament lies in the strong levels of partisanship within the political parties in each country. Both Congress and Parliament are dominated by two parties with high levels of party unity. This means that the two legislatures operate in a similar manner when the president has a majority in Congress. In this scenario members of a party often work together and can be passive in challenging the executive branch.	Cultural theory can be used to demonstrate a contrast between the Senate and the House of Lords. There is a much lower level of shared values amongst members of one party in the Lords plus the addition of many independents; party unity is low. Senators from one party are more likely to work together for collective values. This can allow the Lords to be more aggressive in challenging the executive branch compared to senators, especially if the president has a majority in the Senate.
Structural	The constitutions of both countries are structures that give both Congress and Parliament the power to legislate. The House and the Senate in the United States can influence legislation through their power to amend or reject bills. The Commons in the United Kingdom has similar legislative influence to Congress.	The structural approach reveals a major difference between Congress and Parliament with the former having much greater power over the executive branch. The high levels of checks and balances created by the separation of powers means that Congress heavily restricts the president. In the United Kingdom, Parliament is often passive being dominated by the executive, which has the government majority and patronage power over the back benches in the House of Commons.

EXECUTIVES

The US and UK executive branches contain the most powerful figure in each country, namely the president and prime minister. This section will examine their relative roles and powers.

ROLES OF THE PRESIDENT AND PRIME MINISTER

Presidents and prime ministers have some significant similarities and differences in their roles.

Head of State

This role of head of state is held by the president in the United States whereas it is held by the monarch in the United Kingdom. This gives the president a far more important symbolic role in leading and uniting the nation compared to a prime minister. The presidency combines a larger set of roles and responsibilities than the position of prime minister.

Source: Leon Neal / Staff via Getty Images

Photo 8.2 **UK Prime Minister Rishi Sunak and US President Joe Biden at an AUKUS national security meeting in March 2023**

Chief diplomat and war powers

The president and prime minister are the main negotiators with other countries, representing their country abroad and negotiating with other nation states. As such they have significant control in determining the relationship between their country and the rest of the world.

This role is limited in both countries by the power of Congress and Parliament. The Senate can reject treaties negotiated by the president. In contrast, the prime minister has prerogative powers giving them (and not Parliament) absolute control over treaties. In practice, it has become a somewhat accepted convention that Parliament holds power to reject treaties with prime ministers usually seeking a vote.

In addition, the prime minister has prerogative powers to declare war without restriction from Parliament. Again, in practice there is a great deal of political pressure on prime ministers to seek a vote in Parliament before taking military action. The president's influence over military matters is based on their constitutional role as Commander in Chief of the Armed Services. This appears to give the president complete control over military matters. The US Constitution, however, gives Congress the power to declare war. As with the United Kingdom, there is a degree of constitutional ambiguity here.

Chief legislator

In the United States and United Kingdom political leaders have arguably assumed the leading role in the legislative process. In the United Kingdom the prime minister is the head of the party with a majority (usually absolute) of seats in Parliament and the ability to use patronage and a whip system to control that majority. In addition, there is an increased media focus on the prime minister, which gives them a personal mandate to govern. In the United States, the modern presidency has been able to use the national mandate and superior resources to become known as the chief legislator. On the other hand, a US president faces considerably greater opposition to their political agenda from the legislature than a UK prime minister.

POWER OF THE PRESIDENT AND PRIME MINISTER

The exact power level of a prime minister or a president will also be affected by the political context in which they are operating. Whilst they have fixed constitutional roles and powers, other factors such as the extent of their majority in Parliament or Congress can have a major impact on their level of power. Other factors include their level of public support and divisions within their party. Table 8.7 provides a summary of the powers, roles and limits of prime ministers and presidents.

ACCOUNTABILITY TO LEGISLATURES

The extent to which prime ministers and presidents are restricted by the legislative branch in their own country is strongly affected by the nature of the constitutions, which was covered in the comparative constitution section. The power of the legislatures over the executive is reviewed in the comparative legislatures section. Table 8.8 summarises the ways in which Congress and Parliament can and cannot hold the president and prime minister to account.

Table 8.7 Powers, roles and limits of UK prime ministers and US presidents

US President	UK Prime Minister
Has a direct mandate from the public that is separate from the mandate given to Congress. There is a complete separation of personnel between the president and the rest of their executive team, on the one hand, and Congress, on the other.	Elected as an MP and chosen by the party to be party leader. Power is fused as the PM sits in government and Parliament.
Has power of patronage over the executive branch. No ongoing system of patronage over members of Congress.	Has power of patronage over members of the executive and backbenchers in Parliament.
Has complete authority within the executive branch.	The cabinet contains rivals for the prime minister's position with an expectation of collective cabinet decision-making.
Uses their national mandate and control of the executive branch to develop and propose a policy agenda.	Uses their position as head of government and head of party to develop and propose a policy agenda.
Typically acts as the driving force for legislation based on their nationally elected position. They use the State of the Union Address and proposal of the annual budget to help set a political agenda. They can veto legislation passed by Congress. They are often limited by Congress due to the separation of powers and checks and balances.	Finds it relatively easy to push the government's legislative agenda through Parliament given the government majority and whip system. The House of Lords can offer limited resistance to the government's legislative agenda.
Commander in Chief of the Armed Services but Congress given the power to declare war. Senate must ratify treaties.	Has royal prerogative powers giving control over treaties and military power but increasingly expected to consult Parliament.

Table 8.8 The accountability of the president and prime minister to legislative bodies

US President	UK Prime minister
Separation of powers, separate mandate and checks and balances promote high levels of checks from Congress. Possibility of divided government.	Parliamentary system, government majority and patronage make Parliament relatively passive in restricting the prime minister.
Appointments to senior executive positions and the judiciary must be ratified by the Senate.	Appointments to the executive branch are not ratified by Parliament. The PM does not appoint members of the judiciary.
Not subject to questions in Congress.	Directly accountable to the Commons at prime minister's Question Time.
Subject to impeachment and removal by the House and Senate if there is evidence that the president has committed a high crime or misdemeanour.	Subject to a vote of no confidence alongside the rest of government. This can remove the prime minister from office.

THEORETICAL APPROACHES TO COMPARING EXECUTIVES

In reviewing the similarities and differences above you can now consider how the three theoretical approaches can help explain a specific similarity or difference. Table 8.9 demonstrates the three approaches in relation to the president and prime minister.

Table 8.9 **Theoretical approaches and comparative executives**

	Similarities	Differences
Rational	Both presidents and prime ministers can use their considerable power to pursue their policy goals. Both can use their power within the executive to benefit themselves by surrounding themselves with supportive cabinet members or by removing those who resist their political agenda.	The rational approach highlights a significant difference with presidents being given a role to appoint members of the judiciary. Presidents can use this to gain greater support for their ideological position within the US Supreme Court. Presidents make appointments on an ideological basis to benefit themselves in a way that prime ministers are unable to.
Cultural	Both presidents and prime ministers are sometimes influenced by their party or core voter groups when determining their political agenda. Respecting the cultural values of the group means that they may alter their own ideas in the face of the response from their party or add in policies which they feel will be respected by those within their group.	The cultural theory reveals that prime ministers work more closely with their own party in Parliament compared to the extent to which presidents work with party members in Congress. As such it is harder for prime ministers to ignore the dominant values of the party. A president is more distant from their party, working separately in the White House to secure support from any groups in Congress that will secure their legislative goals.
Structural	Both presidents and prime ministers are restricted by the legislature in their own country. Both Parliament and Congress can block their legislative proposals and even remove them from office.	Presidents faces much stronger structural limitations than prime ministers. Presidents may lack a majority in Congress, facing a hostile majority, whereas prime ministers will typically have an absolute majority of seats in the Commons.

SUPREME COURTS AND CIVIL RIGHTS

This section examines the relative power of the supreme courts in the United States and United Kingdom. It also focuses on the extent to which rights are protected in general, including the role played by interest groups in protecting rights.

BASIS FOR AND RELATIVE EXTENT OF POWERS

The role of the supreme courts of the two countries is to uphold constitutional law by interpreting its meaning in cases brought to the court. The US and UK supreme courts both can overturn the action of public bodies if they break constitutional rules. The prime minister, for example, can be limited by court rulings as Boris Johnson was in 2019 when he prorogued Parliament. The court declared that his suspension of Parliament, closing down the chamber for a break during Brexit negotiations, was unconstitutional.

Despite this similarity, the two courts have very different levels of power:

Source: iStock.com/lucky-photographer

Source: iStock.com/bpperry

Photo 8.3 **US Supreme Court (*left*) and UK Supreme Court (*right*)**

Relationship with Congress and Parliament

The US Supreme Court has considerably more power because it rules on the sovereign, codified Constitution. The principle of constitutional sovereignty allows the court to overturn any institution in the United States, including invalidating acts of Congress. In the United Kingdom, the principle of parliamentary sovereignty means that the Supreme Court is more limited as it cannot overturn acts of Parliament. In the United States the courts are effectively above Congress whereas in the United Kingdom the courts are subordinate to Parliament.

The constitutional amendment process

The concept of parliamentary sovereignty also limits the court because it means that Parliament can easily overturn a ruling of the Supreme Court if it strongly opposes the outcome. The entrenched constitution in the United States makes this almost impossible; if the president or Congress lose a case then they are unlikely to be able to alter the Constitution to overcome the ruling of the court.

Level of authority

The Constitution has enormous authority amongst US citizens and politicians. Having a codified document, which has high levels of respect, increases the authority of the Supreme Court as the guardians of the Constitution. In the United Kingdom, there is no single document for people to identify with and support. This lack of awareness of key constitutional rules gives the Supreme Court lower levels of recognition and authority in the United Kingdom as they are not upholding a revered document as justices do in the United States.

RELATIVE INDEPENDENCE

The independence of the courts requires freedom from external pressure, especially powerful institutions such as governments. This independence is essential if justices are to give rulings based on a neutral interpretation of the Constitution and can rule against politicians if they break constitutional rules. The following areas affect the level of independence:

Security of tenure

Justices in both countries have high levels of independence because they cannot be removed from office unless they themselves break the law. The executive branch cannot sack justices in either country, allowing them to exercise their power without fear of political repercussions. In both countries justices can and do give rulings that undermine the executive in terms of their power or policy priorities.

Appointment process

Arguably the appointment process in the United States threatens the independence of the Supreme Court, as justices are selected by the president and ratified by the Senate. Justices in the United Kingdom are appointed by an independent body, the Judicial Appointments Committee, and not the prime minister. This factor affects neutrality much more than it affects independence because the president makes an ideological choice. Once in office, however, a justice is not at all accountable to the president who appointed them. Many presidents find that their own appointees give rulings against them.

External pressure

In both countries, the controversial nature and huge importance of constitutional cases means that there is often external pressure on justices. In both countries the public and senior politicians have put pressure on individual justices. Arguably, justices in the United States experience much greater external pressure, in part because the major constitutional issues the court deals with – such as guns, abortion and gay rights – are contested issues on which US society is deeply divided.

EFFECTIVENESS OF THE PROTECTION OF RIGHTS

The supreme courts of the United States and the United Kingdom play a critical role in the protection of rights. They do this by upholding the civil rights outlined in the Constitution of each country. In the United Kingdom the main legal protections for individuals are contained in the Human Rights Act 1998, whereas in the United States constitutional rights are outlined in the Bill of Rights and the Fourteenth Amendment to the US Constitution.

The differences in constitutional arrangements suggest that the courts in the United States are likely to provide much greater protection of rights compared to the United Kingdom. The two main differences are:

- Parliamentary versus constitutional sovereignty, which means that US courts possess greater power to protect rights.
- The entrenched versus un-entrenched nature of the constitutions means that UK court rulings protecting rights could be overturned by a new act of Parliament.

There are reasons, however, why this might not be the case. These reasons might be used to suggest that in practice there are *similar* levels of rights protection in each country or even that rights are better protected in the United Kingdom:

- In practice, the UK Supreme Court has issued many declarations of incompatibility using the Human Rights Act to suggest that Parliament may have limited rights. Parliament has responded in virtually every case by amending or passing law that overcome the rights restriction.
- The level of rights protection depends on the interpretation and possible bias of justices in each country. The current US Supreme Court has a strong conservative bias, which means that it is less likely to protect rights compared to a liberal majority court. Having said that, the UK Supreme Court has given rulings in favour of the government, allowing limits on the rights of the individual.
- Arguably there is a stronger culture of rights protection in the United Kingdom than the United States. The United States is increasingly a divided society with strongly conflicting values on rights-based issues. There is considerable conflict over the issues of abortion, guns, gay and transgender rights, and race in the United States whereas in the United Kingdom there is a much greater consensus. This suggests that within the United Kingdom there are fewer challenges to individual rights from society itself.

EFFECTIVENESS OF INTEREST GROUPS IN THE PROTECTION OF CIVIL RIGHTS

Both the United States and United Kingdom have a significant range of interest groups that seek to protect civil liberties. In the United States, groups such as the ACLU have campaigned on the full range of constitutional rights, whereas some interest groups such as the NAACP have sought to protect the rights of racial minorities. In the United Kingdom, Liberty has campaigned to protect many different rights whereas groups such as the LGBT Foundation campaign for gay and transgender rights specifically. As we have seen throughout this section, a major similarity between the United States and United Kingdom is that interest groups can make use of the legal system to challenge individual rights abuses in the courts.

There are three reasons why US interest groups might be more successful in protecting rights than their UK counterparts:

1. ***Constitutional status of rights*** – The entrenched sovereign Constitution of the United States is likely to allow US interest groups to be more successful in protecting civil rights than those in the United Kingdom.

2 **Access points** – The US political system provides a greater number of *powerful* institutions (the president, House of Representatives, Senate and Supreme Court) that interest groups can choose from when trying to gain access to politicians. It is generally easier for civil rights groups to find a like-minded majority in one of the main political institutions. In the United Kingdom, with its concentration of power in the hands of the executive, interest groups may find it more difficult to exert political influence if the government is not receptive to their views.

3 **Weak parties** – Low levels of party unity in the United States can present an opportunity for civil rights groups to successfully persuade individual politicians. In the United Kingdom, the higher tendency to vote as a group, whipped by party leaders, may prevent civil rights groups from gaining support from individual politicians.

Whilst the political and constitutional system of the United States appears to allow interest groups to be more successful in protecting civil liberties than those in the United Kingdom, this may not always be the case in practice. The ideology of the government of the day, or the ideology of the majority on the court, can affect the extent to which civil liberties can be protected.

THEORETICAL APPROACHES AND COMPARATIVE COURTS AND RIGHTS

As with the other sections, theoretical approaches can be used to explain a specific similarity or difference covered so far in this section. Table 8.10 shows how each of the three comparative approaches can be applied to demonstrate similarities and differences between the US and UK supreme courts as well as the protection of civil rights.

Table 8.10 Theoretical approaches and comparative courts and rights

	Similarities	Differences
Rational	The rational approach can be used to show that individuals in the United States and United Kingdom both seek to protect their individual liberties. They attempt to protect their own self-interest, or that of the group they represent, by challenging the political institutions in court. Individuals will attempt to promote their own civil liberties using the Human Rights Act in the United Kingdom and the Bill of Rights and the Fourteenth Amendment in the United States. The liberal value system of both countries shows respect for individual rights and encourages people to pursue their personal freedoms.	Arguably there are differences in the value systems of the two countries. In the United States, individuals are more likely to press for freedoms from the government. The foundation of the United States is based on a rejection of excessive government power, which created a rights-based value system. In the United Kingdom, individualism and concerns about excessive government power are less prominent. Arguably Britons are more accepting of government power and social responsibility for others. Whilst there is a danger of generalising too much, this suggests that individuals in the United States are more likely to pursue individual rights claims.
Cultural	In both the United States and United Kingdom, the cultural approach can show how individuals can develop group identities and values to pursue their collective rights. At specific points in US and UK history, members of social groups have campaigned for group rights. The Black Lives Matter movement in each country is an example of individuals that have worked together to promote common values of the group, for example through direct action and demonstrations.	The cultural approach can account for a significant difference in the appointment process of justices to the US and UK supreme courts. In the United States, the president and Senate nominate and ratify justices, respectively. They tend to make ideological appointments that will please politicians and voters, and presidents are expected to operate according to the values of their party group. Such cultural considerations are not possible in the UK system, where justices are appointed by an independent committee. The United Kingdom as a whole has a stronger culture of maintaining an independent and neutral judiciary compared to the United States.

Continued

Table 8.10 **Continued**

	Similarities	Differences
Structural	In both countries the legal system empowers justices on the Supreme Court to protect civil rights. The courts have the power to overturn infringements of civil liberties when presented with cases from individuals. Justices in each country are equally limited because they cannot initiate cases but must wait for a constitutional claim to be taken to their courts.	In the United States, the entrenched sovereign Constitution provides a powerful structure that gives much greater power to US justices. UK justices do not have recourse to a codified constitution making their power and authority more limited than their US counterparts.

DEMOCRACY AND PARTICIPATION

This section will explore differences and similarities between the United States and United Kingdom in relation to parties, the party system and pressure groups as well as campaign finance regulations.

Source: The Washington Post / Contributor via Getty Images

Source: WPA Pool / Pool via Getty Images

Photo 8.4 **Donald Trump (Republican) and Joe Biden (Democrat) represent the only two parties in a 2020 presidential TV debate (left), and representatives of the seven largest parties in the UK Parliament attend a 2019 election debate (*right*)**

THE NATURE OF THE PARTY SYSTEMS

A party system refers to the number of parties that have significant political power. It is typically measured over an extended period of time such as three or four electoral cycles. Parties can gain significant political power mainly via electoral success in executive, legislative and regional elections. Whilst, arguably, two parties dominate in each system, it is possible to discern several differences between the party systems of the United States and the United Kingdom.

Two-party versus multiparty

The United States clearly has a very strong two-party system. In any given year the two main parties hold 100% of seats in Congress. Third parties have been extremely unsuccessful in competing for the presidency, with the third-placed party in the 2020 election, Libertarian Party candidate Jo Jorgenson, receiving only 1.18% of the national vote. The United Kingdom is closer to a multiparty system with six different parties, alongside parties from Northern Ireland, successfully winning seats in Parliament in 2019. The Liberal Democrats held considerable power between 2010 and 2015 when they formed a coalition with the Conservative Party.

Regional variations

Whilst the two main parties of the United States dominate in every state, in the United Kingdom there are much greater regional variations in the *total number* of parties that have control as well as variations in *which parties* are dominant. The Scottish Nationalist Party has emerged as the dominant power in the Scottish Parliament forming all governments in Scotland since 2007. The use of proportional representation voting systems has typically led to multiparty systems for devolved legislatures. In 2016, Plaid Cymru (20.0%) and UKIP (11.7%) held a significant number of seats in the Welsh Parliament and could exert significant influence with the winning party, Labour, only having a simple majority in the Parliament.

Time variations

In the United Kingdom the Labour and Conservative parties have dominated the formation of government. At any point in time, one party usually possesses virtually all the power with the absolute majority of seats in Parliament. Over time the make-up of government will change with a new party winning the election; two parties will share power. This is in contrast to the United States where it is common for two parties to be in control of significant political offices at the same time. Separate elections for the presidency, the House and the Senate often result in divided government in which both Democrats and Republicans have power *at the same time*.

THE DEGREE OF INTERNAL UNITY WITHIN PARTIES

Whilst maintaining a degree of ideological cohesion and party unity, the main parties in each country are characterised by internal divisions. These divisions are sometimes formalised into factions that attempt to steer the party in a specific ideological direction. These factions can be seen in Table 8.11.

The nature of the two constitutional political systems of the United States and the United Kingdom typically leads to much higher levels of party unity within parties in the United Kingdom compared to the United States. Nevertheless, the issue of the European Union, culminating in the United Kingdom European Union membership referendum 2016, led to major divisions within the Labour and Conservative parties. After Britain's exit from the EU these divisions have become less prominent. In more recent years there has been a major increase in levels of partisanship in the United States in which Democrats are typically united in their opposition to Republicans and vice versa.

Despite these changes in each country, persistent rebellion by individual politicians is more common in the United States than the United Kingdom. Large-scale rebellions, for example against the president from the same party, are also more noticeable in the United States. It is rare for a large number of MPs to rebel from their own party on legislative matters. There are three major reasons for this difference in party unity:

Table 8.11 Factions in US and UK parties

UK	**Labour**	**Conservative**
	• Labour to Win – a moderate faction created after Keir Starmer's victory in the Labour leadership contest. Moderates are referred to as New Labour. • Momentum/Old Labour.	• European Research Group (strong Eurosceptics). • Northern Research Group (over fifty MPs representing constituencies in Northern England and also Wales and Scotland).
US	**Democrats**	**Republicans**
	• The New Democrat Coalition (moderate). • Progressive Caucus (progressive/liberal wing). • Blue Dogs (conservative).	• The Maine Street Partnership (moderate). • The Republican Study Committee (fiscal conservatives). • Social conservatives (no organised factions in Congress but many Republican members of Congress and core Republican voters support conservative evangelical moderate policies).

The separation and fusion of powers

Separate elections and the separation of powers in the United States makes it much harder for the president to control congressional members of their own party. Members of Congress are accountable to their constituents and may vote against the president's position if it is unpopular in their state or district. The fusion of power in the United Kingdom, on the other hand, means that the prime minister works closely with their own parliamentary party and has significant patronage power over backbenchers, promoting party unity. Voters in the United Kingdom are less concerned with the individual voting record of their MP. They are given one vote at election time and are strongly influenced by national parties and leaders.

Selection of legislative candidates

To compete for a seat in the UK Parliament running under a party label, candidates have to seek approval from the national party. This can help to achieve a degree of ideological coherence. In contrast, in the United States, party leaders do not choose congressional candidates for their own party. This decision is made by the public in congressional primaries with anyone able to stand. This encourages much greater policy diversity within US political parties.

Regional power

The United States use of federalism establishes a much stronger system of regional power compared to the United Kingdom. As well as the national parties, it has been said that there are an additional fifty state Democratic parties and fifty state Republican parties. Republican politicians running for state office in Texas or New York are unlikely to share exactly the same policy goals as senior Republicans at the federal level. Whilst devolution exists in the United Kingdom, there are only a small number of regions with significant political power. Whilst there is a Scottish Conservative Party and Scottish Labour Party for example, there is much less regional diversity within a party, across the United Kingdom.

THE POLICY PROFILES OF THE TWO MAIN PARTIES IN EACH COUNTRY

A comparison can be drawn between the UK Labour Party and the US Democratic Party as the more left wing of the two main parties in each country. As such they may have a similar policy profile attempting to realise similar ideological goals. Similar comparisons could be made between the UK Conservative Party and the US Republican Party, who represent the right wing of politics in their countries.

We must recognise, however, that the centre of US politics is further to the right than in the United Kingdom. In terms of welfare and economic policy, for example, the United Kingdom is more in line with Western Europe in having a stronger socialist tradition; this can be exemplified by considering healthcare policy. The (right wing in UK terms) Conservative Party largely support the principle of the National Health Service (NHS), advocating free access to hospitals, paid out of general taxation. Republicans, on the other hand, would not accept this and do not even support much lower levels of government involvement in healthcare. They rejected Obamacare which maintained private hospitals but required everyone to have health insurance. Even most Democrats do not support the idea of an NHS-style health system for the United States.

It remains the case that the Democratic and Labour parties have reasonably similar ideological instincts and policies as do Republicans and Conservatives. These similarities can be seen in Table 8.12.

Table 8.12 Policy similarities between the main two parties in the United States and United Kingdom

Democrat and Labour	Republican and Conservative
The economy	
• Support an active role for government in the economy to overcome socio-economic disadvantage. • Favour higher government expenditure especially in health, welfare and education. • Support greater regulation of the economy to tackle climate change.	• Aim to reduce the role of government in the economy and emphasise personal freedom from regulation. • Favour low levels of government expenditure in health, welfare and education. • Have resisted many measures to tackle climate change.
Health and welfare	
• See a positive role for the state in providing health and welfare. • See social inequality is unfair, and it is the responsibility of the government to address it. • Typically favour welfare interventions such as the creation of the NHS by the Labour Party and the introduction of the Affordable Care Act by the Democrats under President Obama. Some Democrats call for a single-payer healthcare policy similar to the NHS system in the United Kingdom.	• Often critical of government intervention in health and welfare, emphasising the need for personal responsibility. • More likely to view social inequality as natural and inevitable based on individual efforts and talents. • Typically seek to reduce health and welfare interventions by the government.
Social and moral policy	
• Acted as a liberal force in developing civil rights in their country. • Typically called for greater protections for gay and transgender rights. • It was the Labour Party that created the Human Rights Act in 1998 leading to major increases in legal protection for rights. The Democratic Party initiated the For the People Act 2022, to prevent racial discrimination in US elections.	• Typically resisted the extension of civil rights or sought to reduce rights protection often favouring greater power for the government in this area, for example in security and policing policy. • The Conservative Party opposed the creation of the Human Rights Act and announced a review of the Act in 2021 whilst the Republicans voted to defeat the For the People Act in Congress. • The Conservative and Republican parties have opposed transgender rights (such as President Trump's ban on transgender individuals in the military and the Conservative Party refusing to ban transgender conversion therapy after internal party divisions).

DEBATES AROUND CAMPAIGN FINANCE AND PARTY FUNDING

The role of money in US and UK politics has raised serious concerns, mainly centred around the threat that money poses to the democratic system. These concerns include:

- The influence of major donors on politicians and parties.
- The inequality of finances between parties leading to unequal campaign competition.
- The legal regulations on campaign finance and the extent to which they have been effective.

To combat these concerns both countries have created campaign finance legislation that seeks to regulate the use of money for electoral purposes. The nature of regulations in each country can be seen in Table 8.13.

Table 8.13 Campaign finance regulations in the United States and United Kingdom

United States	United Kingdom	Comparison
Legal and constitutional provisions		
• The Federal Election Campaign Finance Act (FECA) 1974 introduced the Federal Election Commission to oversee finance regulations and introduced public funding of elections and maximum expenditure limits. • The Bipartisan Campaign Finance Reform Act (BCRA) aimed to tighten up on money spent by pressure groups and wealthy individuals in advertising at election time without donating to parties. • *Citizens United v FEC* (2010) undermined the BCRA and led to the creation of super PACs – groups that take unlimited amounts of money in donations and spend this on election adverts without donating to parties directly.	• The Political Parties Elections and Referendums Act 2000 created a legal framework for campaign expenditure and requires all parties to register with the Electoral Commission.	• In both countries there is an extensive legal framework regulating the use of money in elections. Both countries have a body that will police the use of campaign finance and ensure that individuals, parties and the interest groups conform to legal regulations.
Public funding of parties		
• Public funding was established by FECA (1974) on a matching funds basis. For every dollar raised the candidate receives a dollar up to a maximum expenditure limit. • This system is redundant as no presidential candidate now takes federal funding. George W. Bush was the first to refuse federal funding in 2000. The 2012 election was the first in which neither party accepted federal funding.	• There is no provision of public funding of parties for UK elections.	• Despite the existence of public funding laws in the US, in practice, both countries are in the same position: parties and candidates do not have their election campaigns funded by the government. As such, in both countries, it is harder for third parties to compete with larger parties.
Expenditure limits		
• Expenditure limits technically exist but US law requires that these can only be imposed on parties if they accept federal funding. George W. Bush and future candidates calculated they could raise more than the maximum expenditure limit and therefore refused federal funding. Bush went on to massively outspend Gore in the 2000 presidential election.	• In 2019 parties could spend a maximum of £30,000 campaigning in each constituency giving a maximum expenditure of £19.5 million for any party with candidates running in all 650 constituencies.	• Expenditure limits are far more important in the UK and total expenditure is much lower than in the US. This suggests that money plays a less important role in the UK. There is greater equality of expenditure between the main Labour and Conservative parties at elections, whereas in the US there is often a huge gap between spending by the Democrat and Republican presidential candidates. Arguably money could swing an election result more in the US.

Continued

Table 8.13 **Continued**

United States	United Kingdom	Comparison
Donation limits		
• Whilst donation limits exist there are a significant number of loopholes allowing groups and wealthy individuals to make major donations. • The use of campaign finance that is not restricted by the law is known as soft money. • There has been a major growth in soft money in US elections. The rise of super PACs since the Citizens United case in 2010 has led to a major increase in groups and individuals donating unregulated money to super PACs, who campaign for a candidate without directly donating to their campaign.	• There is no maximum donation limit. Any donation above £7,500 has to be publicly declared.	• In the US there are many loopholes and court rulings which means that donations cannot be strongly limited. As a result, in practice, in both countries, there are very few limits on the ability of pressure groups to donate as much as they want to. This could lead to the excessive influence of pressure groups on parties and party policy in both countries. Overall US elections are far more expensive, making donations more critical for US politicians. This, and the rise of SuperPACs, means that rich individuals and corporations are donating much higher figures in the US and arguably gaining an even higher level of influence over politicians than in the UK.

THE RELATIVE POWER, METHODS AND INFLUENCE OF PRESSURE GROUPS

The methods used by pressure groups in each country are broadly similar although they might be used with different levels of success. These methods include:

- **Lobbying** – Pressure groups contact and persuade politicians to push for desired changes to policy in the law and often to attempt to block policy proposals that conflict with the group's interests.
- **Direct action and demonstrations** – Many pressure groups organise a demonstration, often held near political institutions in Washington DC or London, as a show of strength. A large demonstration sends a message to the government that many people feel strongly about a particular issue. Direct action is sometimes used to physically intervene often to prevent a policy from being carried out. It has been commonly used in both the United States and the United Kingdom by environmental groups who have sought disruptive tactics to bring about climate action.
- **Electioneering** – Pressure groups often intensify their activity at election time to raise awareness of key issues or to change electoral outcomes. Some pressure groups rely on publicity often using negative campaigns against individual politicians or candidates. Others make use of donations. This method is more prevalent in the United States given the high number and frequency of elections and the huge cost of a campaign.
- **Litigation** – Pressure groups can launch a legal challenge to achieve their policy goals. This is particularly common amongst groups seeking to promote civil rights in both the United States and the United Kingdom.

THE POWER AND INFLUENCE OF PRESSURE GROUPS

The power and influence of pressure groups can vary within a country as a result of factors such as the resources of the group, the level of public support or the extent of ideological compatibility between the group and those in power. Overall, it could be argued that US groups have more power and influence than UK pressure groups.

Access points

The separation of powers and federalism creates a high number of access points for pressure groups in the United States, giving them a great deal of potential to exert influence. Pressure groups can choose the most receptive institution to help their cause. Failure to have influence with one political institution does not have to limit the power of this group with the White House, House of Representatives and Senate often being controlled by different parties. These access points do not exist in the same way in the United Kingdom with the government dominating the Commons and Lords and the Supreme Court having a lower level of power in the United Kingdom than the United States.

Number and frequency of elections

There are significantly more elected officers in the United States as well as more frequent elections with congressional elections taking place every two years. This provides an opportunity for pressure groups to exploit these elections through publicity and donations. US politicians rely heavily on campaign finance donations from pressure groups. This has led to claims that politicians are forced to respond to the policy demands of these groups to maintain a flow of funding. In the United Kingdom fewer elections means the pressure groups have less opportunity to influence politicians. In addition, UK elections are far less expensive and maximum expenditure limits are well established. This means that UK politicians are less in need of campaign finance contributions compared with politicians in the United States.

THEORETICAL APPROACHES AND COMPARATIVE DEMOCRACY

The three comparative approaches can be used to explain the variety of differences and similarities outlined in this section. Table 8.14 shows how the different approaches can be applied when comparing parties, party systems, pressure groups and campaign finance in the United States and the United Kingdom.

Table 8.14 **Theoretical approaches to comparing democracies**

	Similarities	Differences
Rational	The rational approach can be used to show that individual politicians may act rationally and reject the views of the majority within their own party. In both the United States and the United Kingdom individual politicians have responded to public opinion in their constituency to maintain popularity and power at the next election. Members of Congress often rebel from their party if the party view conflicts with their constituency interests. Individual MPs in the Labour and Conservative parties have often responded to constituency views on Brexit more than the position of their party or party leaders.	Arguably, in the United States members of the public have a greater opportunity to act rationally as a result of the higher number and frequency of elections and the greater influence of pressure groups. Individuals in the United States are more able to use these processes to promote their own interests compared to individuals in the United Kingdom where elections are less frequent and pressure groups exert lower levels of influence.
Cultural	In both the United States and the United Kingdom the cultural approach can show the extent to which parties are united in their shared values. In both countries each political party has a degree of ideological cohesion and there is also a sense that politicians are influenced by partisan drives in which they align themselves with the position of their own party often to defeat the opposing party.	The cultural approach highlights how the United States has a stronger history of individualism than the United Kingdom. In the United Kingdom there are stronger shared values within political parties and individual politicians are more likely to conform to the norms of their party. In the United States individual politicians are more likely to rebel against the dominance of their party.
Structural	Structural theory shows how in both the United States and the United Kingdom pressure groups and wealthy donors can be limited in their electoral influence. Campaign finance regulations in both countries restricts expenditure, with a particular similarity in the requirement that parties disclose the source of donations.	Structural theory can be used to explain the difference in the power levels of pressure groups in the United States and United Kingdom. In the United States the separation of powers and federalism provide structures that can help to empower pressure groups. In the United Kingdom pressure groups may exert lower levels of influence because of executive domination within the system. This means that groups that are ideologically incompatible with the government can find themselves left as outsiders, lacking influence.

Chapter Summary

- ✓ There are three main theoretical approaches – rational, cultural and structural – that can be used to compare and contrast the politics of the United States and United Kingdom.
- ✓ The constitutions of the two countries have several significant differences, such as the separation/ fusion of powers and federalism/devolution, that have a major impact on the way in which power is shared or concentrated in the United States and United Kingdom.
- ✓ The Senate and Lords have some similar roles and powers, but the Senate is a more powerful second chamber. Overall, Congress is more powerful than Parliament as it is less dominated by the executive branch.
- ✓ The president and prime minister have a number of overlapping roles and powers as they are both the head of government, the chief diplomat and often the driving force for legislative change.
- ✓ The US Supreme Court is in a more powerful constitutional position than the court in the United Kingdom as a result of the difference in the location of sovereignty.
- ✓ There are strong mechanisms in place to protect rights in both countries with pressure groups playing an active role in attempting to protect civil rights.
- ✓ The Democrats and Labour have similar policy visions as do the Republicans and Conservatives, although the political culture of the United States is further to the right overall.
- ✓ The failure of regulations in the United States means that money plays a much greater role in US elections than in UK elections.
- ✓ Pressure groups use similar methods in each country, but in a given country pressure groups may rely on some methods more than others. US pressure groups are arguably more influential than those in the United Kingdom.

Exam Style Questions

Section A questions

- **Examine the ways in which the Senate has more power than the House of Lords. (12 marks)**
- **Examine the differences between devolution in the United Kingdom and federalism in the United States. (12 marks)**
- **Examine the way in which rights are well protected in both the United States and the United Kingdom. (12 marks)**

Section B questions

These questions require you to apply at least one comparative approach to explain similarities or differences:

- **Analyse the differences between the power of the prime minister and the president. (12 marks)**
- **Analyse the similarities in the influence of pressure groups in the United States and United Kingdom. (12 marks)**
- **Analyse the independence of the US and UK supreme courts. (12 marks)**

Further Resources

McCormick, J., Hague R. and Harrop, M. (2022) *Comparative Government and Politics: An Introduction* (London: Bloomsbury).

McRague, T. (2020) 'Why America Radicalizes Brits', *The Atlantic*, 26 February 2020, available at https://www.theatlantic.com/international/archive/2020/02/america-britain-boris-johnson-europe-pittsburgh/607054/ (accessed 30 July 2023).

Osborne, P. (2023) *The Assault on Truth: Boris Johnson, Donald Trump and the Emergence of a New Moral Barbarism* (London: Simon & Schuster).

'The Supreme Court of the United States and the Supreme Court of the United Kingdom: A Comparative Learning Tool', *The Supreme Court*, available at https://www.supremecourt.uk/docs/the-supreme-court-of-the-united-states-and-the-supreme-court-of-the-united-kingdom-a-comparative-learning-tool.pdf (accessed 30 July 2023).

Visit https://bloomsbury.pub/colclough-essentials-us to access additional materials to support teaching and learning.

9 EXAM FOCUS

Introduction

The aim of this chapter is to help you to understand the way in which A-Level examiners will assess your work and what makes a successful answer. We will work through the three different types of question for *Paper 3: Comparative Politics – USA*. This will involve careful consideration of how examiners assess your responses using three Assessment Objectives (AOs). These Assessment Objectives are types of academic and writing skills. This chapter will help you to understand what the Assessment Objectives mean and, most crucially, how to incorporate them into your answers to both essay and comparative questions. The Pearson Edexcel exam board do not state a single format for writing answers. In addition they do not require a specific number of points be covered for any of the question types on this paper. This chapter gives guidance on how you can successfully format answers and how many points to cover in order to gain reward in the Assessment Objectives as set out by the exam board.

You will be led, step by step, through all the elements that make up the skills and knowledge needed to do well and see how you can structure your answers. You will be furnished with specific techniques as well as be shown how they have been put into practice with extracts from students' work. You will be able to sharpen your understanding by reading stronger and weaker student extracts, with a commentary explaining their strengths and weaknesses.

EXAM OVERVIEW

Paper 3: Comparative Politics – USA is split into three sections as follows:

Section	Question types	Choice?	Marks	Suggested timings (minutes)
A	Comparative questions	Complete 1 response from a choice of 2.	1 × 12	15
B	Comparative theory question	Complete 1 response with no choice. This is a compulsory question.	1 × 12	15
C	United States essays	Complete 2 responses from a choice of 3.	2 × 30	2 × 45
		Total	**84**	**120**

THE TYPES OF QUESTION – AN OVERVIEW

The three different types of question are outlined below, giving you an overview of the whole paper. There are more details on the specific requirements of each question and how to approach them later in the chapter.

Section A comparative questions

These questions require you to *compare* the United States and United Kingdom in your answer. They will always start with the command 'Examine'. This is asking you to compare by considering similarities or differences between the United States and United Kingdom in a specific area. The wording of the question might mean that you can consider similarities as well as differences. Here are some sample questions:

Sample Section A questions

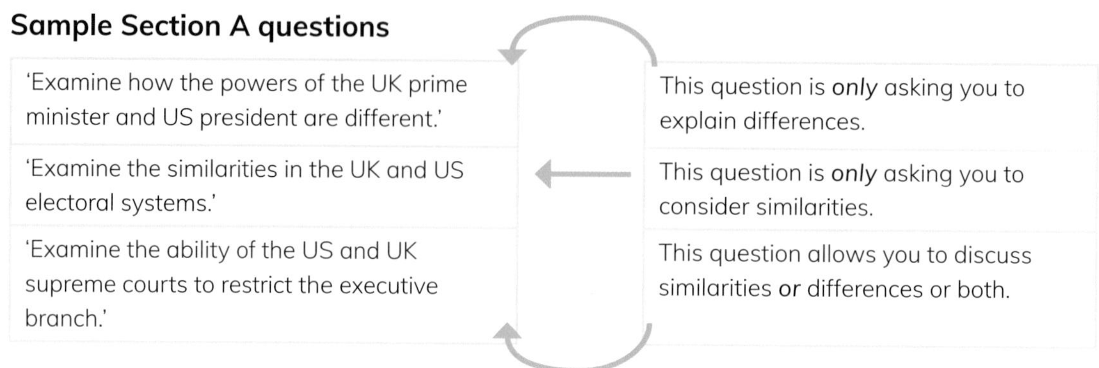

Section B comparative theory questions

These questions also require you to compare the United States and United Kingdom. As with Section A questions, they may refer to similarities or differences or both. The command word used for these questions is 'Analyse'. This refers to the need for you to apply comparative theory in your response. Section B questions also require you to apply at least one comparative theory to show similarities or differences. These three comparative theories are:

Rational theory	This focuses on how individuals behave, especially in meeting their own self-interest.
Cultural theory	This focuses on how groups may determine the behaviour of those in the groups.
Structural theory	This focuses on how political structures such as constitutional rules determine the political behaviour of individuals and institutions.

These are explored in more detail later in the chapter.

Sample Section B questions

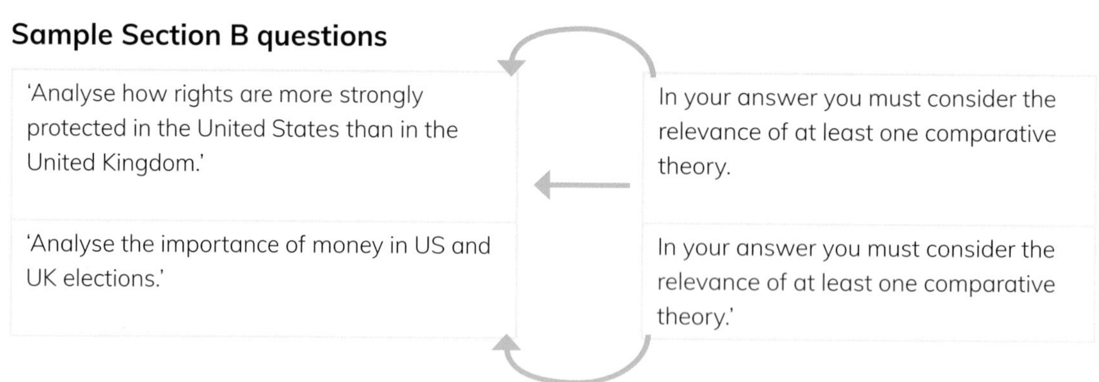

Section C US questions

These questions will focus on specific aspects of US politics and cover the majority of marks for this paper. Each essay is allocated more marks and require longer responses than the comparative questions. All Section C questions will use the command 'Evaluate'. This requires you to consider different perspectives or viewpoints *and* make a judgement about which perspective or viewpoint is more valid. UK essays and source responses in Paper 1 and Paper 2 have the same evaluative requirement. This is explored fully later in the chapter.

Sample Section C questions

'Evaluate the view that Supreme Court justices have too much power.'	You must consider this vie alternative to this view in way.
'Evaluate the extent to which presidential primaries and caucuses can be described as representative.'	You must consider this v alternative to this view i way.

Exam Preparation:

A major aspect of exam preparation is revision. It is essential to revise early and often as repetition helps you to remember things. The most important exam preparation tip is to be absolutely sure you have the best revision technique for you. Reading through notes is usually not a good way to revise. Active revision, in which you are processing the information, is usually more helpful. This might involve making more concise notes or testing yourself. How do you know whether you can remember the information? A successful revision technique involves recall in which you try to remember your notes. This means setting out prompts or questions that you have to respond to either verbally or in writing.

ASSESSMENT OBJECTIVES

The A-Level specification sets out three Assessment Objectives (AOs). These are three specific skills you will demonstrate in your response to questions. Examiners will assess answers based on the ability you demonstrate in these three assessment areas. The table below shows which AOs apply to which question types. You should consider all AOs (which apply to that question) as being equally important in your answer.

Section	Question types	Question Command	Which AOs apply (how many marks are available)?
A	Comparative questions	Examine	AO1 (6) AO2 (6)
B	Comparative theory question	Analyse	AO1 (6) AO2 (6)
C	United States essays	Evaluate	AO1 (10) AO2 (10) AO3 (10)

AO1

'Demonstrate knowledge and understanding of political institutions, processes, concepts, theories and issues.'

AO1 is often summarised as 'knowledge and understanding'. This relates to your awareness of relevant facts and your understanding of the relevant political processes. This includes good knowledge of relevant contemporary evidence.

What does this mean in practice?

Example Section C question: 'Evaluate the view that Congress is not representative.'

The knowledge and understanding (AO1) requirement for this question will cover your appreciation of the different reasons why Congress is and is not representative as well as relevant evidence on either side of the debate. You will show that you understand relevant processes in relation to Congress and its ability to represent the US population, as well as examples of these processes.

AO2

'Analyse aspects of politics and political information, including in relation to parallels, connections, similarities and differences.'

AO2 is often referred to as 'analysis'. This requires a more detailed examination of a relevant aspect of your answer. In simple terms you can think of analysis as developing an idea. It involves explaining something so that you *apply* your knowledge and understanding of US politics to the specific words of the question. AO2 therefore requires you to have the knowledge and understanding required by AO1, and to build on this by developing the ideas further.

What does this mean in practice?

Example Section C question: 'Evaluate the view that Congress is not representative.'

The analysis (AO2) requirement for this question will involve you explaining an argument in detail. For example, if you have suggested that the use of first-past-the-post voting restricts the extent to which Congress is representative, you will demonstrate a good awareness of *why and how* FPTP causes problems for representation. You can connect to other relevant political concepts to help show insight such as the role of safe seats or the way in which FPTP limits choice to effectively vote for third parties.

AO3

'Evaluate aspects of politics and political information, including to construct arguments, make substantiated judgements and draw conclusions.'

AO3 is often summarised as 'evaluation'. This requires you to make a judgement based on an awareness of different perspectives or competing arguments. You will decide which side of a debate is stronger *and* justify your answer.

What does this mean in practice?

Example Section C question: 'Evaluate the view that Congress is not representative.'

The evaluation (AO3) requirement for this question will involve looking at competing claims which suggest that Congress is and is not representative, deciding which claim is stronger and explaining why you have come to that judgement. You might explore the ideas that Congress is representative because it is elected, compared to the idea that the first-past-the-post voting system used is not very representative. You might evaluate by deciding that, overall, Congress is quite representative because the concerns over FPTP are not particularly significant and FPTP provides good representation, explaining why you are making this judgement. This explanation of your judgement is crucial to AO3.

The above provides a basic introduction to the AOs. Later in the chapter we will be exploring ways to incorporate them into answers and will be looking at good (and not so good!) practice.

SYNOPTICITY AND BREADTH

Synopticity involves making connections across topics or across papers and demonstrating your awareness of these connections in your answer. In this way you will show accumulated knowledge and understanding from across the whole A-Level. There is an obvious synoptic requirement on *Paper 3: Comparative Politics – USA*, where you will write Section A and Section B answers that compare the United States with the United Kingdom using material you covered in papers 1 and 2.

Section A and B

These comparative questions will naturally have cross-topic connections because they require you to compare the United States and United Kingdom. You should be aware that the comparative questions are not drawn from any part of the UK or US topics. The Pearson specification gives a specific list of areas that need to be addressed. Comparative questions will only be drawn from these areas, and you should ensure that you are familiar with this.

Exam Preparation:

To prepare for A-Level exams, you should certainly look at ALL past paper questions and write plans for them. This will develop the skills you need to tackle unfamiliar questions. In addition, you could make up your own questions by combining topics or subsections of topics or ask a teacher for a set of A-Level questions. You can start by collating the questions in this chapter and writing plans for them.

Section C

There is no specific requirement to demonstrate synopticity in the mark scheme for these questions. Having said that, you should not be surprised to find questions that connect or cover two or more US topics. Exam papers are designed to assess students' ability to *apply* their knowledge, perhaps to specific questions they have not encountered before. For example:

- 'Evaluate the extent to which the Supreme Court has successfully regulated presidential power.'
- 'Evaluate the view that pressure groups and parties play a negative role in US elections.'
- 'Evaluate the view that Congress has played a greater role in protecting civil rights than the Supreme Court.'

Level-based mark scheme

Level-Based Mark Scheme (LBMS) are used by Pearson and other boards to assess student answers. Examiners will use the descriptors that explain what standard is required to be awarded a certain level. For 30-mark essays the levels go from 1 (lowest) to 5 (highest), and for comparative questions, from 1 to 4. The AOs are equally weighted for both comparative questions (AO1 and AO2 only) and 30-mark essays (AO1, 2 and 3). Examiners will judge which level you have reached for each Assessment Objective. They will then determine a 'best fit' deciding which level you have reached overall and where you are in this level. You will then be awarded a mark based on this level. To do well, it is therefore essential to do well across all three AOs. You can use Pearson's A-Level Politics mark schemes for full details of how to apply level based marking but here is a guide which explains what is required to reach each level:

Level-based mark scheme for 12-mark comparative questions

	12-Mark Comparative Descriptor Summaries AO1
Level 1	Superficial knowledge and understanding, limiting the ability to underpin analysis and evaluation.
Level 2	Some accurate knowledge and understanding, some of which is selected appropriately.
Level 3	Mostly accurate knowledge and understanding, much of which is selected appropriately.
Level 4	Accurate knowledge and understanding, which is carefully selected.

12-Mark Comparative Descriptor Summaries AO2	
Level 1	Limited comparative analysis with partial logical reasoning, making simplistic connections.
Level 2	Some emerging comparative analysis with some focused logical reasoning, making some relevant connections.
Level 3	Mostly focused comparative analysis with focused logical reasoning, making mostly relevant connections.
Level 4	Consistent comparative analysis with coherent logical reasoning, making relevant connections.

Level based mark scheme for 30-mark essays

30-Mark US Essays & Sources Descriptor Summaries AO1	
Level 1	Superficial knowledge and understanding, limiting the ability to underpin analysis and evaluation.
Level 2	Some accurate knowledge and understanding, some of which is selected appropriately.
Level 3	Mostly accurate knowledge and understanding, much of which is selected appropriately.
Level 4	Accurate knowledge and understanding, which is carefully selected.
Level 5	Thorough and in-depth knowledge and understanding, which is selected effectively.

30-Mark US Essays & Sources Descriptor Summaries AO2	
Level 1	Limited comparative analysis with partial logical reasoning, making simplistic connections.
Level 2	Some emerging comparative analysis with some focused logical reasoning, making some relevant connections.
Level 3	Mostly focused comparative analysis with focused logical reasoning, making mostly relevant connections.
Level 4	Consistent comparative analysis with coherent logical reasoning, making relevant connections.
Level 5	Perceptive comparative analysis, with sustained, logical reasoning making cohesive and convincing connections.

30-Mark US Essays & Sources Descriptor Summaries AO3	
Level 1	Superficial evaluation, constructing simple judgements, many which are descriptive and lead to unsubstantiated conclusions.
Level 2	Some relevant evaluation, constructing occasionally effective judgements, some are partially substantiated and lead to generic conclusions.
Level 3	Generally relevant evaluation, constructing generally effective judgements, many of which are substantiated and lead to some focused conclusions that are sometimes justified.
Level 4	Mostly relevant evaluation, constructing mostly effective judgements, which are mostly substantiated and lead to mostly focused, justified conclusions.
Level 5	Fully relevant evaluation, constructing fully effective substantiated judgements, which are consistently substantiated and lead to fully focused and justified conclusions.

These level descriptors will give you an indication of what is expected for higher standards in your answers. They are used by examiners who receive extensive training to make sure they get the standards right. Do not expect the levels to be too easy to understand on their own. There is a lot more guidance on what makes strong standards for each Assessment Objective below, which you are likely to find more helpful. You can use the student extracts and the commentary on these, to help you make sense of the AOs. In addition, there is detailed guidance for essays starting on page 268 and detailed guidance for comparative questions in the section which follows.

HOW TO TACKLE SECTION A COMPARATIVE QUESTIONS

These questions require you to compare the United States and United Kingdom. Remember that there are no marks awarded for AO3 evaluation for these questions. You are not trying to come up with an overall judgement. Instead, you are trying to show your knowledge and understanding of the two political systems (AO1) as well as your ability to analyse similarities or differences (AO2).

Each question is out of a possible 12 marks with a suggested time of 15 minutes in the examination to complete.

Exam Preparation:

Before the examination you should spend lots of time on each question type trying to improve your approach by practising answers. At first you should take your time when writing answers. You will need to think about what you are doing and how to construct your answer successfully. It is not advised that you start by completing timed work but by taking the time to think and finesse your answers. You will need to learn to walk before you try to run.

There are no hard rules about what is required but the following guidelines should help you to maximise your marks.

Plan your answer

This is a two-stage process:

1. Consider what, exactly, the question is asking. Is it about similarities, differences or both? What are the keyword(s) you need to focus on? It is often helpful to think what the question is NOT asking.
2. Draw up a two- or three-point plan. If you can learn to write three short sections this will give you a greater chance to show off your knowledge and understanding, applying your analysis to a wider set of points than just one or two comparisons. You have limited time in the examination; this plan should be as brief as it possibly can be whilst also clarifying what your two or three main points will cover. Most importantly, your plan should be based on the similarities or differences between the two countries. In other words, your plans should allow you to write sections that compare the United States and United Kingdom directly in each section (or paragraph) of your answer.

Putting it into practice – plan your answer

'Examine how US pressure groups can have a greater impact on policy than UK pressure groups.' (12 marks)

1. What is the question asking? 'Examine how US pressure groups can have a greater impact on policy than UK pressure groups.'	This question is only asking about differences as we can see by the use of the word 'greater'. It assumes that US pressure groups do have greater impact. Your response should only show how US pressure groups have more impact. Any material suggesting that they are the same or that UK pressure groups have more impact **cannot be rewarded**. The topic area is pressure groups but the keywords in this case are 'impact on policy'. The answer can analyse by demonstrating good connections between pressure groups and their impact on policy. It is not generally asking about the power of pressure groups but is more focused than this.
2. The plan a. *Weak parties* b. *Access points* c. *Number/frequency of elections*	This is a good approach to planning because ... 1. It helps you to know what each of the three main sections your answer will cover. 2. It is focused on key differences between the United States and United Kingdom. This will allow you to compare directly throughout. The plan uses three reasons why US pressure groups are generally more powerful than those in the United Kingdom. You can read details of comparative US and UK pressure groups in the comparative democracy section page 250. 3. It is brief. This allows you to start writing quickly in an examination.

Writing sections

Once armed with a three-point plan, you are ready to start writing. You are aiming to write three sections (or paragraphs). In each section you should compare the United Kingdom and United States directly. Always start a section with a direct answer to the question being asked. This means that your starting point is focused on the keyword(s) of the question itself. You should then develop this by comparing directly throughout. This means writing about the United States and United Kingdom in the same sentence or consecutive sentences.

The simplest way of dealing with sections is to write half a paragraph about each country, comparing in the middle. So after writing about say the United Kingdom you might say 'In contrast in the United States' or 'Similarly in the United States'. The danger with this approach is that it only gives one opportunity to compare in a paragraph. We will see how you can compare effectively below.

Remember to use examples to illustrate your point. Your examples should be applied to the question. Do not just state what happened when using examples but explain how this can be related to the question.

Familiarise yourself with comparative words and useful phrases to help you. Some of these are listed in the table below.

Useful words and phrases to help you compare

Similarities	Differences	
Similar to	More than	Unlike
In both	Less than	In contrast
Similarly	Greater than	Whereas
Likewise	Easier	On the other hand
Shared feature of	Harder	Whilst
Identical	Better	Compared to
Corresponding	Worse	Although
The same as		

STUDENT EXTRACT – 'Examine the differences between the US and UK constitutions.' (12 marks)

The US and UK constitutions are different because the UK Constitution is much easier to amend than the US Constitution. The US Constitution is entrenched and requires super-majorities to alter whereas the UK Constitution only requires a 50% plus vote in Parliament. In addition, the US Constitution requires three bodies to agree unlike the UK Constitution which only requires support from the House of Commons. This means that the US arguably has many outdated constitutional procedures such as the electoral college. The UK Constitution has been modernised removing outdated processes and institutions such as hereditary peers. There are a very few amendments to the constitution in the US (27) but the UK has more frequent changes with many more laws changing the constitution since 2000 such as new Devolution Acts, the EU Withdrawal Act and the Fixed Term Parliament Act. In contrast, the US Constitution failed to be amended on numerous occasions such as the attempts to have equal rights or flag protection amendments added.

1. The first sentence directly answers the question. It compares and uses the keyword of the question.

2. It then develops the main point. It does this by explaining the difference in more detail. Note how the two countries are closely compared throughout.

3. It then uses examples to illustrate the point being made. In this case the examples are used to show the differences in the constitutions of the two countries.

Putting it into practice – writing a section

Here you will see a student response to one section or paragraph of an answer. Each section could follow the same approach. You might write three of these sections for a complete answer.

Now let us look at the same section again and identify how it makes use of useful comparative language.

STUDENT EXTRACT – 'Examine the differences between the US and UK constitutions.' (12 marks)

*The US and UK constitutions are **different** because the UK Constitution is much **easier** to amend **than** the US Constitution. The US Constitution is entrenched and requires supermajorities to alter **whereas** the UK Constitution only requires a 50% plus vote in Parliament. In addition, the US Constitution requires three bodies to agree **unlike** the UK Constitution which only requires support from the House of Commons. This means that the US arguably has many outdated constitutional procedures such as the Electoral College. The UK Constitution has been modernised removing outdated processes and institutions such as hereditary peers. There are a very few amendments to the constitution in the US (27) **but** the UK has **more** frequent changes with many **more** laws changing the constitution since 2000 such as new Devolution Acts, the EU Withdrawal Act and the Fixed Term Parliament Act. **In contrast**, the US Constitution failed to be amended on numerous occasions such as the attempts to have equal rights or flag protection amendments added.*

The comparative words and phrases are highlighted in red. Note just how often this answer is able to compare throughout. This is partly because of the three-point approach in which it gives a direct answer, develops and compares using theory and then finally compares again using evidence. This student has learnt how to structure a section and use comparative words and phrases.

Achieving the Assessment Objectives

The approach to Section A comparative answers outlined above is designed to help you to address the two Assessment Objectives for this question.

Students will perform well in AO1 knowledge and understanding by showing a good factual awareness of relevant US and UK political institutions or processes and of relevant contemporary examples. In the section above, the response shows knowledge and understanding by identifying and explaining the amendment processes of each country as well as giving examples of changes or lack of changes to the US and UK constitutions.

AO2 analysis will then develop those facts. This can be achieved by:

1. Explaining the implication or significance of a difference or similarity.
2. Making relevant assessments about the extent of a similarity or difference.
3. Applying evidence. Rather than reporting what happened the answer explains what this tells us about the question.

STUDENT EXTRACT – 'Examine the effectiveness of the US and UK Supreme Courts' ability to protect rights.' (12 marks)

Rights are more effectively protected in the United States than the United Kingdom due to the different locations of sovereignty. In the US it is the constitution which is sovereign in contrast with parliamentary sovereignty in the UK. As a result, the US Supreme Court is in a much stronger position than the UK equivalent, to protect rights. If political bodies including Congress restrict rights, then the Court has the power to overturn this using its power of judicial review. UK courts, on the other hand, do not have the power to overturn an act of Parliament. They can issue a statement of incompatibility if they feel that Parliament has undermined the Human Rights Act. This means that if the legislatures of each country restrict rights then the US courts are more able to prevent this than the UK courts. It might also provide a stronger deterrent effect in the United States. Rights are better protected because Congress, unlike Parliament, knows it could be blocked by the court. In Texas v Johnson the US Supreme Court overturned Congress' Flag Protection Act which made it a criminal offence to deface the US flag. In doing so they upheld First Amendment free speech rights having the final say over Congress in a way that the UK Supreme Court cannot do over Parliament. In 2022 the government introduced new laws in Parliament which would water down the Human Rights Act showing that in the UK Parliament is free to reduce the level of rights protection in a way that Congress is not.

AO1 – The response shows an awareness of the different locations of sovereignty and accurately names the location of sovereignty in each country.

AO2 – This develops the idea to show how the difference affects the level of rights protection in the two countries. Notice also the use of the extent word 'much' to add to the analysis. These words show 'how much' or 'how little', adding more complexity to your analysis.

AO1 – This is much more focused on AO1 again, giving key facts about the United Kingdom.

AO2 – This explains the implication of the different locations of sovereignty to demonstrate in more detail how and why rights are better protected in the United States.

AO1 – This shows relevant knowledge of a court case (*Texas v Johnson*) without any application to the question.

AO2 – The First Amendment example is now carefully applied to the question by showing how the example can be used to demonstrate greater rights protection in the United States. Note how this sentence directly compares the United States and United Kingdom.

AO1 – The first part of the sentence is fact based.

AO2 – The second part of the sentence starts to connect this with the question in more detail.

Putting it into practice – achieving the Assessment Objectives

Here you will see a student response to one section of an answer. It uses the same approaches as those outlined above. This time we will consider where the answers is achieving marks in AO1 and in AO2 and why.

Introductions and conclusions for comparative questions

Given the short amount of time to write an answer, it is difficult to find time for these. Introductions and conclusions are not expected. There is a danger that you waste time on an introduction when you could be tackling the first main section of your response. Where students have written introductions in exams, they could often be removed without reducing their overall mark (even by one) especially when they cover key facts that are simply repeated in the answer.

Conclusions are important for US essays (as we will see) but this requirement **does not** exist for 12-mark comparative answers. If you do have a conclusion, you should ask yourself whether it provides extra analysis. There is little point repeating your main points, but you could gain more marks by adding something new to your analysis. You could, for example, say which of your two or three points are most significant in showing a similarity or difference or give an overall sense of the extent of a difference or similarity you have explored.

The table below summarises the advice we have given so far for Section A comparative answers.

Tips for Section A comparative questions

DO . . .	DON'T . . .
write a very brief plan covering two or three comparative points. Three is helpful.	write all you know without thinking of how to structure the points.
get straight into your first point when writing – be direct and answer the question.	write introductions. Conclusions are not essential – think: can I add anything to my analysis that I have not already said?
compare the two countries directly in each section or paragraph of your answer.	write half an answer on the United States and then half on the United Kingdom (or vice versa).
use comparative language – having both countries covered in one sentence is good practice.	write about the United States and United Kingdom separately without comparing.
use brief examples to illustrate your point.	forget examples.

Exam Preparation:

Practising question interpretation, planning and writing are all essential parts of exam preparation. Now it is your turn! Write a plan for a comparative question. Then write you answer. Once you have finished, use the DO and DON'T checklist to assess your answer. Stuck for a question? Try this – **'Examine the differences between federalism in the United States and devolution in the United Kingdom.'**

HOW TO TACKLE SECTION B COMPARATIVE QUESTIONS

Section B comparative questions have the same requirements as those for Section A. You will be comparing the United States and United Kingdom with marks awarded based on AO1 and AO2. As such, you can use the same approaches as those outlined above to maximise your marks. The one additional element is the requirement to apply comparative theories to your answer. This means that you will explain how a theory reveals similarities or differences between the United States and United Kingdom.

What are comparative theories?

In examining a difference or similarity you will show an awareness of how this can be explained by at least one of the following comparative theories:

- Rational theory
- Cultural theory
- Structural theory.

Three comparative theories

	Rational	Cultural	Structural
Focuses on	The individual	The group	Political and constitutional structures
Details	The individual has control over how they act. The individual is acting according to their own wishes and interests. They are not controlled by an external force such as a group or structure.	There is group conformity. People in a group all act in a similar way because they are in that group. Common views or values create a shared culture. The individual wants to conform or is subject to social pressure.	There are external forces that determine political behaviour. Political processes are determined by the Constitution or the power of others. People or institutions are influenced or forced to act in a specific way because of these external forces.
In the United Kingdom or United States this refers to . . .	Individual politicians such as an MP, member of Congress, prime minister or president, or individual voter.	Any group such as a political party, pressure group, faction or congressional caucus.	Constitutional frameworks or powerful people such as prime minister or president forcing political behaviour.
Example language you might be using	• The individual • Is free to • Can act in a self-interested manner • Is not constrained by	• Conform to the group • Shared values • Norms • Common values • Peer pressure	• External forces that • Is forced to • Is/are compelled by • The constitution ensures that

How do I apply them?

The theories are used to explain a similarity or difference. You can approach a question in the same way as Section A questions by working out what the question requires and then writing a plan. This plan will be based on similarities and/or differences between the two countries. Once you have the plan, decide which of the three theories best explains each similarity or difference. In the opening part of each section you will still directly answer the question. In addition, you can add a phrase to show which theory explains that similarity or difference. You will then analyse by explaining HOW this theory reveals the similarity or difference as you write each section.

Putting it into practice – applying comparative theories

You could begin all comparative questions by working out what the question is asking you to focus on. You can then write your plan. After that, decide which theory best explains the similarity or difference. The specification requires you to apply *at least one* comparative theory. This means that you could choose different theories for each section or decide that one theory best explains your comparison in all sections of your answer.

STUDENT EXTRACT – 'Analyse the differences in party unity in Congress and Parliament.' (12 marks)

UK parties less divided/US more because ...

1. *UK MPs influenced by PM patronage. US president has limited patronage – structural theory (power of president versus power of PM in forcing party unity)*
2. *Membership of Congressional caucus can be strong in US/factions weaker in UK – cultural theory (congressional members feel pressurised or want to conform to norms of the caucus group)*
3. *Greater public pressure on members of Congress than MPs so members of Congress may prefer to vote with constituents not party – rational theory (both act in a self-interested manner to further their career. US members of Congress decide to vote against the party to get re-elected. UK politicians vote with their party to gain promotion via the PM).*

These are the key points in the plan.

The theories chosen to explain the comparison are shown in blue.

This explains why that theory was chosen in each case. This is for illustrative purposes here. It is something you would cover in your full response but you should not spend valuable time writing this out in the plan during an examination.

Exam Preparation:

Practise interpreting and planning for these types of questions. Once you have a plan decide which theory or theories you will use for each point in your plan. Stuck for a question? Try this: 'Analyse the differences in the ability of Congress and Parliament to hold the executive branch to account.'

In the following extract, we can see how the theory is applied in practice. The writer has chosen to use the rational theory to begin one of their sections. They would then go on to develop their answer by exploring a similarity or difference.

STUDENT EXTRACT – 'Analyse the differences in the power of US and UK Supreme Court justices.'

The rational theory shows how justices in the US have much greater ability to act according to their own ideological goals than those in the UK. The vague Constitution gives much discretion to justices in the US and allows self-interested justices to apply their own interpretations to it.

The section begins with an application of the theory – it shows which theory explains the difference in power.

It then starts to develop by explaining how the difference can be explained by rational theory using some of the keyword(s) associated with this theory such as 'discretion' and 'self-interest' to show that the individual is in control.

What might this look like in a whole section? The following is one part of an answer to a Section B comparative question.

STUDENT EXTRACT – 'Analyse the ways in which the US and UK party systems appear to have the same characteristics.'

One similar characteristic is that the US and UK have strong two-party systems. This similarity can be explained by the structural theory as it is the use of first past the post (FPTP) which allows the two parties to dominate and excludes third parties. FPTP used for both Congress, president and Parliament discourages voters from selecting third parties because it is likely to lead to wasted votes. The structure of FPTP elections strongly influences voting behaviour. In the US third parties gain virtually no votes with the third placed candidate Jo Jorgensen of the Libertarian Party in 2020 gaining only 1.18% of the vote in the presidential election. Furthermore, even when third parties do gain votes, the structure of the voting system can

The section begins with a direct answer to the question AND an application of comparative theory. It shows which theory explains the difference in power.

It then develops by explaining how this similarity has occurred. It does this by detailing how a structure (in this case FPTP) has created this similarity.

This gives a relevant example and achieves some reward for AO1, but it neither makes connections with the question nor makes comparisons with the United Kingdom.

prevent third parties from gaining seats and power. In 2019, the Liberal Democrats achieved 11.9% of the vote but only 1.7% of the seats. Third parties in the US are also restricted by the structure of FPTP. In Maine state Rep. Norman Higgins won 30.9% of the vote in 2020 but lost his bid for re-election.

It now goes back to theory and the differences between the United States and United Kingdom, achieving reward in AO2 by showing a second way in which FPTP restricts third parties, also making direct connections with structural theory.

This is a better use of evidence as it makes comparisons between the two countries and relates back to comparative theory.

Capping statement

The specification places a cap (or upper limit) on the number of marks you can receive if you do not show a knowledge of comparative theory in comparative Section B responses. The A-Level marks schemes state that if you do not apply any comparative theory then you can only achieve a maximum of 9 marks out of 12.

Tips for Section B comparative questions

DO . . .	DON'T . . .
follow the same guidance for Section A comparative answers.	assume that comparative Section B answers require a totally different approach compared to Section A answers.
determine which comparative theory best applies to each point in your plan, to explain a difference or similarity.	judge the extent to which a theory is relevant. You are not trying to argue that one theory applies *better than* another.
apply the theory to show how it explains a similarity or difference. Two or three direct references to comparative theory in each section is plenty.	feel that you have to cover all three theories in one answer.

SECTION C US ESSAYS

Section C will require you to respond to essay questions solely focused on US politics. You will complete two essays from a choice of three. All three Assessment Objectives play an important part in the assessment of your answer. You might see questions based on a single topic or questions that cover two or more US topics.

GENERAL GUIDANCE

We will begin with some general guidance on essays, before looking in more detail at Assessment Objectives. Finally, we will consider an approach or formula for producing paragraphs/sections of an answer that are designed to help you to achieve those Assessment Objectives.

What does balance mean?

The command word for all US 30-mark essays is 'evaluate'. After each question you will see the following words, '*You must consider this view and the alternative to this view in a balanced way.*'

This has been misinterpreted by some students who think they must cover both sides of an argument but remain balanced by not favouring one side of the debate. This is not what is required! The balance statement and the need for evaluation work together. They require you to show an awareness of different perspectives or both sides of a debate and to come down on one side of the debate. It is essential that you evaluate by making a judgement. You will do this by showing the reader which side of the debate you think is stronger and why. You should **not** spend most of your response explaining only one viewpoint. It is useful to aim for around a 50/50 split, but you should avoid straying from anything that goes beyond a 60/40 split of coverage in outlining each side of the debate. For example, if the question asks you to evaluate the extent to which the Democrat and Republican parties have similar views and values, then you should use approximately half of your answer covering material which shows similarities and the other half on differences.

How many points should I use in my answer?

There are no hard rules here. There is always a trade-off between depth and breadth. If you cover, say, seven arguments and counters for each, then each point will be very brief. This will undermine your AO2 analysis and AO3 evaluation. Using two points could work but you risk having a narrow answer that only explores a limited number of arguments and shows a limited range of AO1 knowledge and understanding. For this reason, most students attempt three main sections of an answer in which each explores an argument and counter argument. The majority of top answers use this approach.

How can I plan and structure an answer?

It is essential that you identify exactly what the question is asking and write a short plan in an examination. A common and useful approach is to identify the three main areas you would like to evaluate. In each area you will discuss the arguments and evidence from different perspectives to create balance. You could think of these as three mini debates. If you are writing your essay in two halves, firstly covering one side of the debate and then the other, you will find it hard to gain credit for AO3 evaluation. Essays requires you to evaluate *throughout* your answer. This will be further explored shortly.

How do I make sure I am answering the question?

It is a common complaint of A-Level examiners that a student's response did not fully focus on the keyword(s) of the question but wrote more generally on the topic. This is a key skill to master. It requires practice and preferably lots of feedback on your response. There are a number of activities you can complete that will improve your ability to focus on the question. One of these involves breaking the question down into three component parts:

1. **The command or stem** – this is telling you what to do with the information and for essays it will always be 'evaluate'.
2. **Topic/subtopic** – this is the content that you are likely to have studied such as primaries and caucuses, the Electoral College, the president, imperial presidency, the Roberts Court, etc. It will include your knowledge of contemporary evidence – what has been happening in US politics in recent years.
3. **The keyword(s)** – this is what you need to focus on. By identifying and highlighting these you can think carefully what they mean *and* apply your topic.

Let's consider two US essay questions and how we might be focused on the question. The topic or subtopic is in blue and the keyword(s) are in red.

How important is evidence?

One of the main aims of the Pearson A-Level Politics specification is that it wants to 'develop an interest in, and engagement with, contemporary politics'. The use of relevant evidence is essential to producing a strong answer. This refers to your awareness of what has been happening in US politics in recent years. Evidence brings the theory of US politics to life and helps to give it meaning. From an assessment perspective, examiners are always impressed by a response that shows a wealth of relevant knowledge of US political developments. This can improve your answer in all three Assessment Objectives.

Evidence and AO1 – Most obviously, contemporary evidence can show good knowledge and understanding. Top-level answers will typically include a good range of relevant, contemporary evidence. This goes beyond generalised examples and give *specific* details. For example:

Question	Weaker approach	Stronger approach
'Evaluate the view that the US Constitution is not fit for purpose.'	The response uses a list of advantages and disadvantages of the Constitution learnt in class and recorded in notes. This is used to decide how desirable the Constitution is.	The response shows an awareness of the *purpose* of a constitution. This could be the roles or requirements of a constitution. This is used to generate three mini debates. Each looks at the extent to which the US Constitution meets this *purpose*.
'Evaluate the view that interest groups are able to achieve their policy goals.'	The answer outlines the methods used by interest groups and also why they might not work. It names examples of interest groups and generally says whether they have been successful.	The response is focused on the keywords achieve policy goals. It shows a detailed awareness of examples with specific evidence and detail on policies they have and have not achieved. This is likely to relate to a very specific policy or campaign the interest group pursued.

STUDENT EXTRACT – 'Evaluate the view that civil rights pressure groups have been successful in promoting equality.'

The NAACP has run lots of campaigns aimed at promoting equality. This includes demonstrations and initiating Supreme Court cases. Many of these have been unsuccessful in recent years with a lack of rights protection and inequality and continued racism in states. The NAACP has failed to achieve their policy goals with little success in achieving racial equality.

A weaker approach to evidence
This response does get some reward for AO1, but it is very basic. It has generic knowledge of the NAACP but does not show any awareness of specific campaigns or policy failures.

The NAACP have experienced significant failure in many of their attempts to achieve greater equality in the courts. Despite massive lobbying efforts, targeting moderate Democrat and Republican members of Congress, they were unable to persuade enough politicians to vote for the For the People Act pushed by Biden in 2021 to stop voter restrictions such as photo ID laws passed by states. They also issued an amicus brief in Shelby v Holder which ended in policy failure for the group. The court overturned a central provision of racial equality in the US by repealing key sections of the Voting Rights Act. Despite their Moral Monday direct action protests at state legislatures such as North Carolina there is still huge discrimination on the voter process.

A stronger approach to evidence
This response gets a high reward in AO1 because, firstly, it shows detail of a specific policy goal and provides details of their lack of ability to achieve it. The response is also boosted by the use of two examples. This is not essential but does gain reward as they are combined to add weight to the idea that pressure groups have not been successful in promoting equality.

Evidence and AO2 – Whilst this may seem less obvious, an awareness of contemporary evidence can be very important in improving your analysis. A good understanding of contemporary evidence can help you to speak the language of politics more fluently. It can help you to develop your ideas further, especially when evidence is carefully *applied* to the question.

Evidence and AO3 – Finally, evidence can play a central role in strong evaluation. Winning an argument involves having the evidence to back up your points. Often it is more effective to have evidence that shows weaknesses in the opposition's argument, or to use evidence to contradict an opponent's points.

What do I write in my introduction and conclusion? Are they important?

Introductions for 30-mark questions

Introductions are an important part of an essay, and you are encouraged to write one. The introduction is the first thing an examiner will see, and you should use this to make a positive impression. You can do this by reassuring the examiner that you understand what the question requires. Do not write generally about the topic or give unnecessary background information. Instead, you should use the keyword(s) you have identified to show:

1. How you will structure you answer.
2. What your overall judgement will be – you can start to pick up evaluation marks straight away!

Here are three extracts that show complete introductions with a commentary on their strengths and weaknesses.

STUDENT EXTRACT – 'Evaluate the view that Congress lacks political significance.'

Command	Evaluate
Topic	Congress
Keyword(s)	political significance

Congress is a bicameral legislature consisting of the House and the Senate. There are arguments for and against the political significance of Congress which will be evaluated. Congress is increasingly problematic because of partisanship and gridlock. Congress has been criticised as a do nothing Congress.

A weaker approach to introductions

This is a weak introduction, mainly because it does not answer the question and does not show that it understands what the question is asking. This will make the reader concerned that the student is not going to focus on the question in their essay.

There is no need to explain what Congress is or does. Definitions are not necessary for most introductions. This first sentence does nothing to answer the question set.

It is obvious that there will be arguments for and against and there is no need to write this for a 30-mark evaluate essay. The extract has still not shown any relevant knowledge or insight.

The final sentence shows two problems, but these are not connected to the question in this extract and seem like randomly made points.

The political significance of Congress can be judged by the way in which it fulfils its three main roles of legislating, representing and checking the executive. This can mainly be done by looking at the extent to which it has a major or minor impact in fulfilling these three functions. In addition, its significance could be positive or negative, improving or causing problems for the US system.
This essay will argue that Congress has huge political significance but that this is sometimes negative.

A stronger approach to introductions

This is a strong introduction. It gets straight to the keyword of the question in the opening line, quickly showing that the student understands exactly what is required. Useful approaches:

1. The keyword significance is explained because it is the key to answering this question.
2. It also provides an outline of what the essay will cover. The reader knows which areas will be explored.
3. It also tells the reader what the overall judgement is going to be. This is a very powerful way of maximising evaluation. This student knows what they are going to argue and makes this clear in the introduction. They can now set about justifying their view whilst showing an awareness of other perspectives.

STUDENT EXTRACT: Evaluate view that the Supreme Court can heavily restrict the president and Congress.

Command	Evaluate
Topic	Supreme Court, president and Congress
Keyword(s)	heavily restrict

The Supreme Court is able to restrict both the president and Congress through their main powers of judicial review and interpretation supported by a sovereign, entrenched constitution as well as their independence from other institutions. On the other hand, the court is limited in its ability to restrict the president and Congress as it can only check them in constitutional areas and may face external pressure. Overall, it is more convincing to argue that the Supreme Court can indeed place heavy restrictions on the president and Congress

A stronger approach to introductions

Again, this introduction is strong because it answers the question. It immediately takes the keyword of the question (restrict) and uses it to outline the key areas that will be covered. It shows both sides of the debate and does so briefly. The introduction should not be any longer than this. It also gives the evaluative judgement again so we know the judgement that the student will attempt to justify throughout their answer.

Notice that no definitions were necessary in this introduction other than explaining the keyword in the context of the question. Also notice that the student avoids using 'I' but says 'overall it is more convincing to argue' to demonstrate their view.

Conclusions for 30-mark questions

Conclusions are essential! You need them to finalise your overall evaluation. As such you should always set aside some time to write a conclusion even if it is very short. Your conclusion needs to be quite definite in answering the question. Do not state that there are ideas on each side or that it is difficult to decide. You should also make sure that your conclusion is not a surprise to the reader. It should back up and summarise the judgements you have already made.

Exam Preparation:

A very useful exercise is to write introductions and conclusions for every essay question you can find. This will enable you to practise your essay-writing skills, but it will also help you to think about your evaluations and revise at the same time.

Here are two conclusions. They are the conclusions from one of the introductions above and you should see consistency in the evaluation between the introduction and conclusion.

STUDENT EXTRACT – 'Evaluate the view that Congress lacks political significance.'

There are many different reasons why Congress is and is not significant. Congress' main problem is that it is not representative as a result of its social composition and the use of FPTP as well as the issue of two senators for each state. On the other hand, Congress can have an impact by legislating and checking the president. It did this with Trump when it stopped him building his border wall.

A weaker approach to conclusions

This is a weak conclusion mainly because it does not answer the question. The first sentence is generic and does not answer the question. It does not deliver an evaluation. It then appears to have lost sight of the question and is focusing on why Congress is undesirable without a clear link to political significance. It then rehearses an outline of the debate rather than giving the evaluation. Giving a single example here does not evaluate. You should also avoid giving new information in your conclusion – it is a bringing together of what you have already covered.

It is clear that Congress is a hugely significant body. Whilst there are some limits to its power and impact, it plays a major role in representing and checking the president. Its most significant political role, as we have seen, is its legislative function. This is because this can and does have a massive impact on the daily lives of millions of people in the US. Whilst it has less impact today as a result of partisanship and gridlock it still passes new and major laws on an annual basis which change the direction of the country. At times it can play a negative role which is still unfortunately significant. This is especially the case with its representative function where Congress often misrepresents the US public. Overall, then, Congress is highly significant in all three roles but is sometimes significant in a negative manner.

A stronger approach to conclusions

This is a strong approach to conclusions, stating an overall judgement and summarising the main reasons for this conclusion. Note that it does not need to use 'I' to show what the student view is, stating that 'it is clear' instead. It gets straight to the keyword of the question in the opening line and gives the students' judgement using an extent word (hugely). It also acknowledges the other viewpoint whilst explaining why it is, essentially, wrong. The conclusion contains lots of judgements. It says which of the areas it has discussed is the most important and justifies this. It also makes a useful evaluative distinction between positive and negative significance. There is then a final summary statement with a clear judgement in answering the question.

How do I deal with all of this in timed, exam conditions?

Students commonly ask how much they should write. It may be frustrating to find out that there is no official rule. Ultimately, the more relevant material you write the higher your standards are likely to be in each AO. This is particularly apparent for AO1, where coverage of more processes and examples can only help boost your level.

It is in your interest to improve your timed writing skills. This comes through a huge amount of practice. You may spend hundreds of hours studying A-Level Politics, but timed typing or writing will influence your grade. You will have already been advised to practise, and this is very good advice indeed. Perhaps a more useful way to think of this is by comparing it to going to the gym. We all know that the more you visit the gym and get on that running machine, the more you will improve your heart, lungs and muscles to allow you to run further and further. It is the same with timed writing. Most students can improve both the quantity and quality of their timed work enormously but only with continued practice. There are timing guidelines in the table earlier in this chapter.

Exam Preparation:

You should set an alarm for the required amount of time and then attempt a question. Stop when the alarm goes off – there is no point teaching yourself to have longer time. Instead, you can start to internalise what 15 minutes (for comparative answers) or 45 minutes (for US essays) feels like. One excellent exercise is to break it down. For essays, you will have just under 15 minutes for a section, if you cover three sections. You can set an alarm for 13 minutes and write individual sections. I know many students who have had great success with this *if* they completed several of these exercises every week over several months.

The actual examination can be a time of stress. Students often feel that they have gone blank as the exam starts or cannot do a question at first sight. Taking a few deep breaths and giving yourself time to think about the question and what it is asking tends to clear your mind and allow you to get started. You should remember that examiners are fully aware that A-Level students are young adults, not well-experienced academics or writers. They are also aware that you are only given a short amount of time to show what you know and to apply this with analytical and evaluative skill. You should always try to get better and try to maximise your marks in exams, but examiners are aware that there are limits to what can be achieved.

ASSESSMENT OBJECTIVES AND 30-MARK ESSAYS

How to use AO1 effectively

Here we take a closer look at the use of knowledge and understanding for 30-mark essays and what makes for a successful approach for this AO.

- **Use a range of points/processes.** Having a plan based on three sets of arguments and counterarguments will encourage you to show more knowledge and understanding of relevant processes and institutions. By exploring these six arguments you should then be able to demonstrate a good knowledge of US political institutions and processes. Your answer can make use of technical (i.e. politics specific) words. The Pearson specification contains a list of specification key terms that are also covered in the margins of this book. One very useful exercise is to write a list of key concepts for each topic you have studied.
- **Use a range of specific and relevant evidence.** Demonstrating an awareness of relevant examples is a very useful way of improving your standards in AO1.
- **Don't overdo it.** Take care not to write long descriptive sections to your answer. The danger is that you start writing all you know without focusing on the question. Whilst you should show AO1 knowledge and understanding, you will always need to apply that to the question to answer it. This application of knowledge is a requirement for AO2 and AO3. This is not as scary as it might sound! We will put all the assessment advice together for you in 'Approach to writing a section'.

STUDENT EXTRACT – 'Evaluate the view that Congress is not representative.'

Congress is made up of two chambers the House of Representatives and the Senate. It is not representative as a result of the use of first past the post for US elections. This means that votes are disproportional to seats and voters do not get what they have voted for. This is totally unacceptable in a modern democracy in which voters are misrepresented. It is not fair and reasonable for voters to be treated this way. Democrats have been underrepresented in Congress as a result of the unfairness of the system. Congress is an unrepresentative body which could be improved by the use of proportional representation.

A weaker approach to AO1

This response does get some reward for AO1 with a knowledge that congressional elections use first past the post but it is very limited. The extract could make use of more technical, political concepts, for example replacing 'fair' and 'reasonable' with political terms. The first sentence does not give any fact that can be used for this question. Students should avoid simply stating facts but try to apply their AO1 knowledge to the question. Disproportionality between votes and seats is not necessarily the main problem with representation in the United States and perhaps this student is relying on their UK knowledge rather than what actually happens in the United States. There is a very generalised use of evidence about the Democratic Party that gains some reward but is not the kind of evidence required for higher level answers.

Congress is not representative as a result of FPTP elections. This undermines the extent of representation hugely because it can and does produce results in which the party with the most votes in Congress does not get the most seats. This completely rejects a basic principle of representation, with the most popular party not being given the mandate and power they deserve. This is made much worse in the Senate because the population size of each state constituency is so different, but each state has two senators. This is a massive problem as all voters are not treated equally which incidentally also overrepresents the Republican Party. In the 2018 mid-terms, Democrats

A stronger approach to AO1

This response gets high reward in AO1 because it covers a wealth of different relevant key concepts including processes and institutions.

It also makes very good use of contemporary evidence with specific examples. The knowledge of a specific election year, overall results for one chamber and knowledge of results in specific states, demonstrates excellent knowledge and understanding that can be highly rewarded in AO1.

led Republicans by more than 12 million votes in Senate races, and yet still suffered losses on the night and failed to win a majority of seats in the chamber. This clear misrepresentation of the public can be further seen in individual states. Democrat Chuck Schumer won his seat with 5.2 million votes whereas Republican Lisa Murkowski was able to gain a seat with just 138,000 votes in Alaska. Republicans such as Murkowski are overrewarded because they tend to win in smaller rural states. In addition, FPTP reduces voter choice by discouraging voters from choosing a third party which they might support. The use of winner-takes-all single member constituencies prevents third parties from winning seats.

Note also, the breaking down of Congress into two parts. This response shows an understanding of why representation is a specific concern in the Senate and not just Congress as a whole.

How to use AO2 effectively

We referred to AO2 in simplistic terms as developing relevant ideas. More specifically, it requires the *application* of AO1 knowledge and understanding to answer the specific question set. Using the Pearson mark schemes we could break this down into two aspects or approaches:

- To examine and explore AO1 in more detail, or as the Level Based Mark Scheme puts it, to make 'logical chains of reasoning'.
- To make 'comparative analysis' by 'drawing on similarities and differences'. Comparative analysis can also be shown by examining changes over time.

The first aspect of AO2 requires you to develop AO1 points you make by exploring them further in relation to the question asked. It is not simply giving more factual detail but explaining *how* these facts help us to understand an argument related to the question. It often involves *applying* your initial argument or fact by answering these sorts of questions:

- How?
- In what way?
- Why?
- To what extent?

The following phrases can be useful in leading you to analyse, as they indicate to the person reading your answer that analysis is probably about to take place:

- this suggests
- as a consequence
- this means that
- therefore
- this leads to
- this is because
- this shows that
- . . . indicates that.

The second aspect of AO2 occurs when students show awareness of comparisons and contrasts. This involves examination of two different features and then comparing or contrasting them to see where there might be similarities and/or differences. This is used to sharpen analysis and give a clearer picture of political reality. Rather than shining a broad light on a whole subject it is more like shining two focused lights or lasers on specific parts, allowing us to see and compare specific details of the subject. It can also make use of comparison over time, for example comparing the power of the president today with their power in the past, perhaps to show a trend or to examine how the extent of power changes over time. In your answer you would be comparing two points in time to show different power levels. In the extract above ('Evaluate the view that Congress is not representative') the student specifically explores the Senate. Comparative analysis could bring the House and Senate together, for example to show how one is *more representative* than the other or how they both *misrepresent the public in different ways.*

A very useful way to enhance comparative analysis is by using comparative language. This will enable you to draw comparisons and contrasts between different arguments. Some simple ways to incorporate comparative analysis is by using some of the following words:

- whereas
- despite
- however
- similarly
- although
- not only
- but also
- in contrast
- both
- as well as
- instead
- no longer
- still.

STUDENT EXTRACT – 'Evaluate the view that the constitutional amendment process is highly undesirable.'

The amendment process is highly undesirable because it is undemocratic. To change the US Constitution, a two-thirds super-majority is required in each chamber of Congress, allowing just over one-third to block an amendment. In addition, three-quarters of states need to agree to the amendment making it even harder to change. States are diverse and are unlikely to have enough ideological overlap to allow a change to take place. For example the Equal Rights Amendment failed to pass, giving equal rights for women in the Constitution. The Founding Fathers deliberately made it difficult to change which is why there have only been 27 amendments which does not reflect the needs of modern society.

A weaker approach to analysis

There is very little AO2 analysis to reward in this extract. There is a very useful first sentence that makes a connection; it gives a reason why the amendment process in undesirable by stating that it is undemocratic. After that, the response gets a little lost and does not answer the question. It explains the amendment process in detail (AO1) which it should not do – this does not answer the question. It should be explaining how, why and to what extent the amendment process is undemocratic. It gives an example but does not show what this is an example of; it does not say how or why this shows a lack of democracy. The final part of the last sentence relates back to a criticism but there is no clear link or application with the initial idea of democracy, and therefore there is no development in AO2.

The amendment process is undesirable because it is highly undemocratic. The two-thirds requirement in Congress means that an amendment can have huge support from elected politicians but still not pass. This is undemocratic because a key aspect of representative democracy is ignored when even a strong majority cannot get what they want. This is worse in the states where there is a higher threshold of 75%, giving excessive power to the minority making the process seem more elitist than democratic. The ERA aimed to give women equal constitutional rights and had huge popular support with over two-thirds of Congress agreeing to it. It was blocked by mainly southern states meaning that the clear will of the people was denied in this case leading to an undemocratic outcome.

A stronger approach to analysis

This response gets high reward in AO2 because it explains how and why the amendment process is undemocratic in some detail. It has the same starting sentence but goes on to apply knowledge directly to the question. This explains how or why the amendment process is undemocratic. Notice the use of two phrases which lead on to analysis; 'because' and 'meaning that'. The concept of representative democracy and not just democracy is well used here. There is also comparative analysis here which is used to give greater insight into the extent of the democratic problem. It achieves this by directly comparing US states with Congress. This is simple but effective.

How to use AO3 effectively

A03 evaluation requires you to make a reasoned judgement about competing viewpoints. It requires you to specify an opinion or argument and justify this. Students often misunderstand this Assessment Objective, or find it hardest to put into practice, but this can easily be overcome with some guidelines, practice and feedback. Putting in thought and time to get this right can make a major difference to your writing overall. Here are some key things to bear in mind:

- Evaluation is much easier to achieve when trying to weigh up or judge competing viewpoints. By bringing in two conflicting arguments or ideas you can evaluate which is stronger AND why.
- Do not mistake *describing* an argument with evaluating. Stating that Congress is unrepresentative because of the use of first past the post is, in itself, not evaluative. Evaluation comes when you explain that Congress is *representative* due to frequent and fair elections, it is *not representative* due to the use of FPTP but *overall* it is not very representative, giving your reasons for making this judgement.
- You cannot be indecisive. There is no point in saying there are strong arguments on both sides or that it is difficult to decide. Instead, you need to pick a side and try to justify it throughout your answer. This can take confidence but go for it! It is better to try, as this will improve your AO3 level.
- The stronger AO3 answers are those in which the student knows what their view is before they start writing. This means completing the work before an examination to make sure you are more confident in knowing what you think about different aspects of the US political system. You should also be confident in making judgements for questions you may not have seen before.
- Evaluation is something that should happen *throughout* your answer. The earlier you make a judgement the stronger your evaluation levels are likely to be. Many students state what they will argue in their introduction and then use the essay to justify their view. We will look at how you can achieve this below. Some student answers *describe* several arguments and counterarguments and then give a judgement at the very end in their conclusion. This will lead to a low level being achieved for this AO because there is little chance to explain and justify the evaluation. At worst, it can suggest to the examiner that a student has tossed a coin at the end and decided to come down on one side with little or no justification.

STUDENT EXTRACT – 'Evaluate the view that the Constitution is effective in restricting presidential power.'

Presidents are not restricted by the Constitution because of their ability to use executive orders. Presidents can bypass Congress and avoid the need to pass legislation through Congress as intended by the Founding Fathers. As such they are clearly unrestricted. President Obama failed to pass his DREAM Act through Congress but overcame such constitutional restrictions by issuing DAPA and DACA executive orders to allow a wide range of illegal immigrants to have the right to remain in the US as his Act had intended.

A weaker approach to AO3 evaluation

There is very little to reward here by way of AO3. This might look like the student is arguing and they are probably offering their viewpoint, but it is hard to see a justified judgement without the consideration of an alternative viewpoint. This takes us back to the wording at the end of each question on an exam paper asking students to respond in a balanced manner. This means covering different perspectives whilst also making a judgement about which is stronger. This is not present in this extract.

It could be argued that the president is restricted by the need to pass legislation through Congress to achieve their policy goals. Congress has the ability to amend or even reject presidential proposals. President Trump was limited because of his inability to get new laws through Congress to repeal Obamacare, even though he had a majority in both chambers of Congress. President Biden has also been frustrated by Congress, passing his COVID-19 relief bill but having to compromise on key measure stopping him from achieving an increase in the federal minimum wage for example. On the other hand, the president is not restricted by the Constitution, however, because of the use of executive orders. These allow the president to bypass Congress and achieve their policy goals when they should be legislating through the House and Senate which could block them. President Obama failed to pass his DREAM Act through Congress but overcame such constitutional restrictions by issuing DAPA and DACA executive orders to allow a wide range of illegal immigrants to have the right to remain in the US as his Act had intended.

A weaker approach to AO3 evaluation

This answer is getting closer to good AO3 evaluation compared to the extract above because it presents two viewpoints or competing arguments. It is still limited in its AO3 evaluation, however. This is because it describes two competing views, which gains reward in AO2 analysis. It does not make a judgement by giving an overview of which side of the debate is stronger or the extent to which a president is restricted overall. It leaves some questions open: Can presidents simply bypass Congress whenever they want to? Are they usually restricted but sometimes not?

This sentence indicates a change of viewpoint using the phrases 'on the other hand' and 'however'. It does not help to show what the overall judgement is but appears to be describing another view.

The phrase 'it could be argued' suggests that the student does not support this viewpoint. Phrases such as these are called signposts and are very important for AO3. They let the reader know whether the student agrees with/supports this view or not. The difficulty an examiner would have in reading this is that it is not clear whether the writer really disagrees with this view. The student could make better use of signpost language to make this clear. There are suggestions for useful signposting phrases in the table below.

The most accurate view here is that the president is heavily restricted by the Constitution when trying to put policy into practice. The alternative view to this is that the president is not restricted by the Constitution, however, because of the use of executive orders. Supporters of this view might argue that these orders allow the president to bypass Congress and achieve their policy goals when they should be legislating through the House and Senate which could block them. Possible evidence which could be used to support this is Obama's DREAM Act, which he failed to pass through Congress but overcame constitutional restrictions by issuing DAPA and DACA executive orders to allow a wide range of illegal immigrants to have the right to remain in the US as his Act had intended. This argument is very limited, however, as in reality the president is often restricted by Congress and cannot usually use executive orders, especially for major policy goals.

The opening sentence starts with an evaluation. It makes it clear that this is the view of the writer, which now has to be justified. It does this by using the phrase 'the most accurate view is'.

The next sentence turns to a view the student disagrees with. This is made apparent to the reader by the signposting of 'the alternative view' and the student clarifies their position with the phrase 'supporters of this view', which distances the writer from this argument.

A stronger approach to evaluation

This is a very strong AO3 evaluation response. It shows two sides but what the writer thinks is always clear, and it is evident when the student is presenting a view they disagree with. Importantly, they show why they have come to that judgement and support their argument well. Notice that this is not hugely different from extract B. By changing the order and the signposting language, the evaluation become more apparent. Finally, it uses another evaluative technique by giving an overview, summarising the main judgement overall.

In reality, it is clear that the president is restricted by the need to pass legislation through Congress to achieve their policy goals. Congress has the ability to amend or even reject presidential proposals. President Trump was limited because of his inability to get new laws through Congress to repeal Obamacare, even though he had a majority in both chambers of Congress. President Biden has also been frustrated by Congress, passing his COVID-19 relief bill but having to compromise on key measure stopping him from achieving an increase in the federal minimum wage for example. On the whole presidents can sometimes use executive orders but are still often limited by the constitutional requirement to pass laws through Congress.

The argument returns to the view of the reader and again signposts this clearly. It does this by directly attacking the argument above, which is a useful technique. It is much like having an argument in real life in which one person speaks and then another person challenges them. It also reinforces the signposting when it says 'in reality it is clear that ... '. The phrase 'in reality' shows that this is what the writer thinks.

Finally, it uses another evaluative technique by giving an overview, summarising the main judgement overall.

Useful signposting phrases for AO3

Writing about my view	Writing about the view I disagree with
To defend your view: • It is clear that • The most accurate view • The strongest view • In reality • Overall • A more valid interpretation. To attack the other view: • This argument is limited • This view is flawed • The evidence does not support this view.	• Opponents of this view may argue • Some might argue • Supporters of this view might say • A weaker argument is • A limited argument states that. Note that phrases such as 'it could be argued' or 'or one view is' could be used to signpost that this is not the view of the reader. Their effectiveness in signposting depends on when and how they are used in the context of the answer. They are not as explicit in saying 'this is not my view' than the phrases above. Note that we do not use 'I' or 'I think' in academic writing.

PUTTING IT ALL TOGETHER – AN APPROACH TO WRITING SECTIONS/PARAGRAPHS FOR ESSAYS

We have already considered the benefits of having three main sections in your answer, using each section to explore different views or arguments and making an evaluative judgement. In very basic terms you should ensure that each section:

- Directly answers the question set by focusing your analysis and evaluation on the keyword(s).
- Has a clear evaluation, making your view clear and justifying this.
- Shows an awareness of different perspectives.
- Provides evidence on both sides of the debate and also applies this to the question.

You should ensure that you adopt the points above. There are different ways of applying these successfully to reach high standards, and one approach is laid out below. It is a more detailed eight-point guide or formula designed to allow you to develop your answer and to maximise your attainment in all three AOs.

STUDENT EXTRACT – 'Evaluate the view that the Democratic and Republican parties share similar views and values.'

Although the Democratic and Republican parties have sometimes shared similar approaches to economic policy, it is clear that there is still a strong ideological divide between the two. Those emphasising similarities between the two might focus on the moderate policies of the Democrats and how they have come to abandon progressive values. The two parties could be seen to share similar pro-business policies. The Democrats have moved towards the right wing of the political spectrum sharing economic values with Republicans. This is shown with Obama and Congressional Democrats' left the market unchecked, protecting the interests of big business. Compared to Western European tax rates neither party wants high corporation tax or tax on high income earners suggesting shared values. This view is limited, however, and ignores the strong disputes between the two parties on economic policy. It is much more accurate to argue that the two parties have conflicting policies and values. Democrats are far more likely to value progressive economic policies with higher Federal Government to provide greater support for those who are less well off. Republicans are far more likely to favour free market economics cutting regulations on business or taxes on the wealthy. There is consistent evidence to support this, showing a clear divide between the parties. The unanimous opposition of Democrats to the Trump administration's Tax Cuts and Jobs Act 2017, covering $1.3 billion in tax cuts mainly for the wealthy and a reduction for tax benefits for low-income people, shows a strong divide. The unanimous opposition of Republicans to the Biden administration's Coronavirus Relief Bill, the American Rescue Plan Act further supports this view as Republicans opposed plans to support those on lower incomes and increase environmental regulations on businesses. Overall, therefore, there is significant ideological and policy difference between the two parties in the economy.

1. A single sentence that tells the reader the view being held.

2. Followed by the alternative perspective that is well signposted; the reader knows it is not the view of the writer. See underlined phrases for useful signposting language.

3. This alternative perspective is then explored.

4. An example/evidence is given to support this. It provides specific detail of something that happened.

5. The writer now goes back to their original view and again signposts that it is their view. They do this by attacking the view they disagree with. See underlined phrases for signposting.

6. And develops this by explaining the argument/idea.

7. It then presents evidence that is related to the question.

8. There is a summary sentence that states a clear view which has been argued for in this section.

Now let's do it all again, but this time looking at the section from the perspective of Assessment Objectives. Here is a virtually identical extract but this time with a commentary on the right-hand side that explains how the extract covers the Assessment Objectives.

STUDENT EXTRACT – 'Evaluate the view that the Democratic and Republican parties share similar views and values.'

Although the Democratic and Republican parties have sometimes shared similar approaches to economic policy, it is clear that there is still a strong ideological divide between the two. Those emphasising similarities between the two might focus on the moderate policies of the Democrats and how they have come to abandon progressive values. The two parties could be seen to share similar pro-business policies. The Democrats have moved towards the right wing of the political spectrum sharing economic values with Republicans. This is shown with Obama and congressional Democrats' limited regulations in response to 2009 Banking Crisis which demonstrates how, like Republicans, the Democrats left the market unchecked protecting the interest of big businesses. Compared to Western European tax rates neither party wants high corporation tax or tax on high-income earners suggesting shared values. This view is limited, however, and ignores the strong disputes between the two parties on economic policy. It is much more accurate to argue that the two parties clearly have conflicting policies and values. Democrats are far more likely to value progressive economic policies with higher Federal Government involvement to provide greater support for those who are less well off. Republicans are far more likely to favour free market economics cutting regulations on business or taxes on the wealthy. There is consistent evidence to support this, showing a clear divide between the parties. The unanimous opposition of Democrats to the Trump administration's Tax Cuts and Jobs Act 2017, covering $1.3 billion in tax cuts mainly for the wealthy and a reduction for tax benefits for low-income people, shows a strong divide. The unanimous opposition of Republicans to the Biden administration's Coronavirus Relief Bill, the American Rescue Plan Act further supports this view as Republicans consistently opposed Democrat plans to support those on lower incomes and increase environmental regulations on businesses. Overall, therefore, there is significant ideological and policy difference between the two parties in the economy.

AO3 – It starts with an AO3 sentence. There is no support given yet, but it tells the reader what judgement is being made.

AO2 – This develops the idea of similarity. It uses key political concepts to explain how and why they are similar. It also shows some AO1 knowledge of parties and values when it uses the phrase 'progressive values'.

AO1 – Here we have a factual example of banking regulations and tax rates compared to Europe.

AO2 – The second part of this sentence analyses – it is applied to show what this tells us about similarities using the phrase 'which demonstrates'.

AO3 – we now go back to evaluation as the extract returns to the student's view. This directly attacks the argument above, signposting this with 'much more accurate to argue' and 'clearly'.

AO2 and AO3 – This section is closely connected with AO2 analysis, developing an idea. It is also clearly designed to support a judgement already made and therefore strengthens AO3.

AO3 – The extract states that their argument is strong and backed up by evidence.

AO1 – The example shows new factual information by giving the 2017 example. The student uses this factual example, which is applied to the question, demonstrating AO2.

AO3 – The student presents a summary, rounding up the section to further support the student's view.

FINAL WORDS

The information in this chapter will hopefully help you to understand how to respond in the examination and give you plenty of ideas for what you can work on to prepare. No one can expect this to be easy and it takes plenty of practice. Practising your writing and getting feedback on it will help you to move to the next stage.

The advice given in this chapter may not be exactly the same as the advice of your teachers. This is totally understandable, as there is more than one way of doing well. Your teachers should know your strengths and the areas you need to work on – they are in a good position to know what is helpful for you. If you feel that you are receiving advice that is contradictory to this chapter, rather than different, then I hope you can talk to your teacher about this.

This chapter is designed to help you with specifics of Pearson's A-Level Politics course, and it focuses in particular on what strong answers look like. There are many more skills you will use when studying for A-Levels. Some skills are more closely related to academic matters, such as how to revise effectively. Many students do not have effective revision techniques, and some find it difficult to revise, so it is important that you consult with teachers on this if you are unsure. Other important factors are time and stress management. Studying for A-Level Politics should be an interesting, exciting and enjoyable experience, but for many people these exams can bring stresses and strains. Considering advice on how to be healthy and manage stress can be a big help.

Finally, I would like to thank you for making use of this book! I hope that both the content and skills advice will help you to love the study of politics as well as aiding your success in the A-Level examinations.

GOOD LUCK!

Further Resources

Cottrell, S. (2012) *The Exam Skills Handbook* (London: Bloomsbury).
Cottrell, S. (2018) *Mindfulness for Students* (London: Bloomsbury).
Cottrell, S. (2019) *The Study Skills Handbook* (London: Bloomsbury).

The Pearson A-Level Politics website has a huge array of resources including past paper questions, mark scheme and examiner reports. It has marked exemplars of student work with examiners' comments. You can find these in the teaching and learning materials section under the heading 'exemplars', visit https://qualifications.pearson.com/en/qualifications/edexcel-a-levels/politics-2017.html

Index

Page references for in margin 'Spec key term' and 'Definition' are in **bold**.